# *Rick Steves*®

# BELGIUM:
## BRUGES, BRUSSELS, ANTWERP & GHENT

Rick Steves & Gene Openshaw

# CONTENTS

# Welcome to Rick Steves' Europe

Travel is intensified living—maximum thrills per minute and one of the last great sources of legal adventure. Travel is freedom. It's recess, and we need it.

I discovered a passion for European travel as a teen and have been sharing it ever since—through my bus tours, public television and radio shows, and travel guidebooks. Over the years, I've taught millions of travelers how to best enjoy Europe's blockbuster sights—and experience "Back Door" discoveries that most tourists miss.

Written with my talented co-author, Gene Openshaw, this book offers a balanced mix of Belgium's lively cities and cozy towns, from medieval Bruges to slick, fashion-forward Antwerp. It's selective: Rather than listing dozens of Flemish art museums, we recommend only the best ones. And it's

in-depth: Our self-guided museum tours and city walks provide insight into the country's vibrant history and today's living, breathing culture.

We advocate traveling simply and smartly. Take advantage of our money- and time-saving tips on sight-seeing, transportation, and more. Try local, characteristic alternatives to expensive hotels and restaurants. In many ways, spending more money only builds a thicker wall between you and what you traveled so far to see.

We visit Belgium to experience it—to become temporary locals. Thoughtful travel engages us with the world, as we learn to appreciate other cultures and new ways to measure quality of life.

Judging by the positive feedback we receive from readers, this book will help you enjoy a fun, affordable, and rewarding vacation—whether it's your first trip or your tenth.

Have a *prachtig* trip! Happy travels!

*Rick Steves*

# BELGIUM

Belgium falls through the cracks. Wedged between Germany, France, and the Netherlands, and famous for waffles, Smurfs, and a statue of a little boy peeing, it's no wonder it can get lost in the mix.

But Belgium rewards with richer sights than you might expect—and fewer tourist crowds. Five hundred years ago, a trade boom left it with dazzling art and architecture. And today it has re-emerged as a trade capital of Europe.

For travelers, Belgium is a breeze—it's well organized, there's almost no language barrier, and the people are wonderful. Everything's close together: My favorite Belgian cities—Bruges, Antwerp, Ghent, and Brussels—are within 90-minute train rides of one another.

Bruges is the Belgium of the past—a wonderfully preserved medieval gem that at one time was one of the largest cities in the world and a powerhouse in commerce and arts. Once mighty, now mighty cute, it comes with fancy beers in fancy glasses, lilting carillons, and filigreed Gothic souvenirs of a long-gone greatness.

The thriving towns of Antwerp and Ghent—also former medieval bigwigs—demonstrate how the country has rebounded to again be a global trendsetter. Design-forward Antwerp offers interesting contrasts, from its high-fashion couture scene to its racy red light district. In the university town of Ghent, you'll find a richly detailed Renaissance altarpiece amid a vibrant urban landscape.

And finally, there's Brussels: the unofficial capital of the European Union, with a low-rise Parisian ambience that exudes joie de vivre. With the finest town square in the country (if not the Continent), a chocolate shop on every corner, a French taste for class and cuisine, and a smattering of intriguing museums (including the Royal Museums of Fine Art, where you can view Flemish and Belgian masterpieces by Van der Weyden, Bruegel, Bosch, Rubens, and Magritte), it's equally ideal for a quick stopover as it is for a multiday visit.

Belgium's town squares bristle with soaring spires and warm-brick gables. Its museums house lush paintings celebrating the glories of everyday life. And away from the quaint-but-touristy central squares, the back streets host a Belgium that's lived-in, a bit funky, and authentic.

A bit smaller than the state of Maryland and with nearly 950 people per square mile, Belgium is one of the most densely populated countries in Europe. Despite its small size, it's divided—linguistically, culturally, and politically—between French-speaking Wallonia in the south and Dutch-speaking Flanders in the north, with the bilingual capital city Brussels

*Baroque portrait by Peter Paul Rubens; gabled architecture in Brussels' Grand Place*

## Belgian Taste Treats

A waiter in Belgium once told me, "Belgians eat as hearty as the Germans and as fine as the French." But Belgian fare has its own flair. For example, Belgians have perfected the art of cooking with their own unique beers, imbuing the cuisine with a hoppy sweetness.

If a dish is cooked Flemish-style *(à la flamande)*, that usually means it's either made with beer or smothered in a sauce of butter, chopped parsley, and a crumbled hard-boiled egg. Look for *lapin à la flamande (konijn met pruimen* in Dutch)—marinated rabbit braised in onions and prunes; meatballs *(balletjes/boulets* in Dutch/French) served Liège-style—with a dark syrup of apples, pears, and dates; and the warm Liège salad (green beans, potatoes, tomatoes, and bacon). Stews abound: Ghent's creamy *waterzooi* (made with chicken, eel, or fish), *stoofvlees/ carbonnade* (beef stew with onions, mustard, and beer)...and of course *biersoep/soupe à la bière*—beer soup.

Mussels are perhaps the most famous of Belgium's signature dishes. The classic preparation is *à la marinière:* cooked in white wine, onions, celery, parsley, and butter (though some cooks use light Belgian beer for the stock). For a high-calorie version, *moules à la crème* is thickened with heavy cream. You'll also find mussels served plain, with white wine, or in a tomato sauce *(provençale).* From about mid-July through April, you'll get the big Dutch mussels (most are from the coastal Zeeland area to the north). Locals take a break from mussels in May and June, when only the puny Danish kind are available.

*Belgium is known for its delicious cuisine, with German and French influences: Beer, meatballs, and mussels are specialties.*

The mussels come with another Belgian specialty on the side, *frieten—* what we call "french fries" and the ▶▶▶

▶▶▶ Dutch call "Flemish fries." In Belgium, fries are an art form. The fries are extra-delicious because they're deep-fried twice—once to cook them and once to brown them. The best fries are cooked to a crisp in flavorful ox fat.

Flemish fries are generously topped with sauces like mayonnaise (the most traditional), tartar sauce, curry ketchup, or *currysaus* (without the ketchup). Ketchup is sometimes available for the Yankees, but I encourage you to skip it and go on a sauce adventure. When I see a sauce that's scary sounding—maybe *joppiesaus* (sweet yellow curry and onion) or "samurai sauce" (mayo with spicy chili flavor and a hit of tomato)—I go for it.

Belgium is justifiably famous for its exquisite chocolates. But make sure to save room for another sweet Belgian specialty—waffles. You'll see little windows, shops, and trucks selling them either plain (for Belgians and purists) or topped with fruit, jam, chocolate sauce, ice cream, or whipped cream (for tourists). Belgians recognize two general types of waffles. The common take-out version is the dense, sugar-crusted, and very sweet Liège-style waffle, usually served warm. Brussels-style waffles are lighter and fluffier, dusted with powdered sugar, and sometimes topped with marmalade. Though Americans think of waffles as a breakfast food, Belgians generally have them as a late-afternoon snack.

Of course, if you need something sudsy to wash down your meal, there's beer aplenty: Belgium has hundreds of options (see the Practicalities chapter for guidance). *Smakelijjk!* Enjoy! ■

*Save some calories for Belgium's famous fries, chocolates, and waffles.*

in between and a small population of German-speakers in the east. (The Dutch spoken in Belgium is also called "Flemish.") And, because of Brussels' international business and political connections, English is frequently spoken as a common language there.

In contrast to its own divisions, Belgium flies the unifying flag of Europe more vigorously than any other place on the Continent. There's a feeling of being at the center of global events. The "Benelux" economic union (joining Belgium, the Netherlands, and Luxembourg) was established in Brussels in 1944, planting the seed that today has sprouted into the European Union.

Belgium is at the crossroads of Western Europe, where Romance languages meet the German world, and where the Protestant north meets the Catholic south. It was born as a merchant entity in medieval times (c. 1300-1500), when energetic traders made it one of Europe's richest, most cosmopolitan, and most sophisticated countries. On the other hand—located as it is in the crossfire between larger powers—Belgium has also been Europe's battlefield. From Charlemagne to Napoleon, from the Habsburgs to Germany in two world wars, this country has paid a heavy price.

But even with a thousand years of history behind it, the country seems determined to write a new chapter in its long and illustrious tale. Tiny Belgium has survived by producing savvy businesspeople and excellent linguists, and by welcoming new trends. I recently asked a local, "What is a Belgian?" He

said, "We are a melting pot. We're a mix culturally: one-third English for our sense of humor, one-third French for our love of culture and good living, and one-third German for our work ethic."

Belgians have a directness that some find refreshing (and others find brusque). They revel in their wry, sardonic sense of humor—it can be hard sometimes to tell whether they're putting you on. The art of the comic

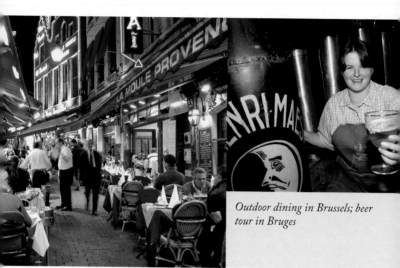

*Outdoor dining in Brussels; beer tour in Bruges*

strip is deeply respected: The Smurfs and Tintin were created by Belgians.

Belgians are said to be born with a "brick in their stomach"—meaning they feel a deep-seated need to own a house, decorate it just so (hence the abundance of furniture and antique shops), and invite their friends for dinner. Belgians are social, meeting up at sidewalk cafés or cozy pubs after work. On a beautiful spring day, it might seem like nobody here has a job—they're all outside drinking beer.

Belgians take their beers as seriously as the French do their wines, even pairing beer with food. When it comes to variety, Belgium has more than any other country—with hundreds of breweries and local brews, including a heavily fermented type brewed by Trappist monks. Belgium is also home to some of Europe's finest cuisine, including the creamiest chocolates and tastiest french fries.

Go ahead...indulge in Belgium's many delights. Digging into a dish of mussels while seated on a sunny square beneath the outline of a lacy medieval spire...you're in Belgium.

# Belgium's Top Destinations

It's a small country, but there's plenty to see in Belgium. This book presents the best of its four great cities: fine food, rich history, and sensuous art, as well as the modern scene that makes Belgium the face of Europe today.

To help you decide where and how to spend your valuable time, I've ranked Belgium's top places and suggested a minimum number of days to allow for each.

### ▲▲▲Bruges (allow 2 days)

A perfectly pickled Gothic city of charming cobbles and cozy squares, Bruges has fanciful gilded architecture, serene Flemish masterpieces, and, according to locals, the best beer in the world. Here you can bike along a dreamy canal, savor heavenly chocolate, and see Flemish Primitives and a Michelangelo—all within earshot of a bell tower with a hyperactive carillon. Sights include a top collection of Flemish paintings at the Groeninge Museum, Hans Memling's glowing Primitive masterpieces displayed in a medieval hospital, the mansion of a 15th-century wealthy Bruges merchant, and two fun brewery tours.

### ▲▲Brussels (2 days)

The urbane capital of Belgium, the European Union, and NATO, Brussels boasts one of Europe's grandest squares, colorful urban zones, and a beloved statue of a little boy peeing. There's lots to see, including the European Parliament and a wide array of museums (Old Masters, turn-of-the-century art, and the Magritte's surrealism; musical instruments; Belgian history; fashion and lace; comic strips; and more).

### ▲▲Antwerp (1 day)

This gentrified port city offers Belgium's best fashion and an engaging mix of urban grittiness and youthful trendiness. Among its top sights are a cathedral with paintings by Peter Paul Rubens, an Industrial Age train station, and interesting museums covering printing, emigration, aristocratic home life, and more.

### ▲Ghent (1 day)

A pleasant, lively university city, Ghent has a fine historic quarter and several worthwhile museums (fine art, design, and history). The vast St. Bavo's Cathedral hosts the city's top sight: the breathtaking Van Eyck altarpiece.

### Flanders Fields (1 day)

An easy day trip from Bruges by bus tour or car, the infamous WWI battlefields near Ypres are filled with artillery craters, memorials, and cemeteries, set amid pastoral pastures and fine museums.

*Colorful Market Square in Bruges; cheeky Manneken-Pis in Brussels; somber Flanders Fields; detail of Van Eyck's altarpiece in Ghent*

# Planning Your Trip

To plan your trip, you'll need to design your itinerary—choosing where and when to go, how you'll travel, and how many days to spend at each destination. For my best general advice on sightseeing, accommodations, restaurants, and more, see the Practicalities chapter.

## DESIGNING AN ITINERARY

As you read this book and learn your options…

### Choose your top destinations.

My recommended itinerary (see the sidebar on page 17) gives you an idea of how much you can reasonably see in a week, but you can adapt it to fit your own interests and time frame.

### Decide when to go.

For tourist hot spots like Bruges, peak season is summer, especially June and early July. Business towns like Brussels, Antwerp, and Ghent tend to be more crowded in spring and fall. With long days, lively festivals, and sunny weather, summer is a great time to visit despite the crowds in places like Bruges. It's rarely too hot for comfort. Plus, Brussels' fancy business-class hotels are discounted in the summer.

Late spring and fall are also pleasant, with generally mild weather and lighter tourist crowds (except during holiday weekends—see "Holidays and Festivals" in the appendix).

Travel from late October through mid-March is cold and wet, as coastal winds whip through the low, flat country. It's fine for city visits, but smaller towns and countryside sights feel dreary. Some sights and tourist information offices (TIs) keep shorter hours, and many outdoor activities vanish altogether.

For weather specifics, see the climate chart in the appendix.

## Connect the dots.

Link your destinations into a logical route. Decide if you'll travel by car or public transportation. With Belgium's short distances and excellent rail system, trains make it easy to connect Antwerp, Ghent, Bruges, and Brussels. Flanders Fields is easiest to reach by car or with a bus tour, but you can also get there from Bruges or Ghent via train.

Begin your search for transatlantic flights at Kayak.com. For a multicountry trip, decide which cities you'll fly into and out of.

To determine approximate travel times between destinations, visit Bahn.com for train schedules or, if driving, check Google Maps.

Note that Brussels can splice neatly into a wider-ranging trip, with direct train connections to Amsterdam, Cologne, Paris, and London. Compare any long train ride with the cost of a budget flight; check Skyscanner.com for intra-European flights.

*It's easy to reach most destinations within Belgium by train; connections are fast and frequent.*

## Write out a day-by-day itinerary.

Figure out how many destinations you can comfortably fit in your time frame. Don't overdo it—few travelers wish they'd hurried more. Allow enough days per stop (see estimates in "Belgium's Top Destinations," earlier).

To minimize one-night stands, consider taking a late-afternoon train ride or drive to settle into your next destination for two consecutive nights—and gain a full, uninterrupted day for sightseeing. Staying in a home base (like Bruges) and making day trips can be more time-efficient than changing locations and hotels.

Take sight closures into account. Avoid visiting a town on the one day a week its must-see sights are closed. Check if any holidays or festivals fall during your trip—these attract crowds and can close sights (for the latest, visit www.visitflanders. com). Note experiences where advance reservations are smart.

Give yourself some slack. Every trip, and every traveler, needs downtime for doing laundry, picnic shopping, people-watching, and so on. Pace yourself. Assume you will return.

## Belgium's Best One-Week Trip by Train

| Day | Plan | Sleep |
|-----|------|-------|
| 1 | Arrive in Brussels, train to Bruges | Bruges |
| 2 | Bruges | Bruges |
| 3 | Bruges | Bruges |
| 4 | Day-trip to Ghent or Flanders Fields, late train to Antwerp | Antwerp |
| 5 | Antwerp | Antwerp |
| 6 | To Brussels | Brussels |
| 7 | Brussels | Brussels |
| 8 | Link to your next European destination, or fly home | |

**Notes:** Trains travel several times hourly between Belgium's major cities, with most connections under 1.5 hours. While I've outlined a loop trip, you could instead stay in a single home base (I prefer Bruges) and day-trip by train to Ghent (30 minutes), Brussels (1 hour), or Antwerp (1.5 hours). With less time, skip Flanders Fields. You're never more than two hours by train from the main airport in Brussels.

*Chocolate confections in Antwerp;
Brussels' Atomium exterior
(right) and interior (bottom);
cozy Bruges hotel room*

## Trip Costs Per Person

Run a reality check on your dream trip. You'll have major transportation costs in addition to daily expenses.

**Flight:** A round-trip flight from the US to Brussels costs about $900-1,500, depending on where you fly from and when.

**Transportation:** For a one-week trip, allow about $55 per person for public transportation (train tickets).

**Car Rental:** Allow roughly $350-500 per week (booked well in advance), not including tolls, gas, parking, and insurance.

AVERAGE DAILY EXPENSES PER PERSON

**$160**
Applies to cities, figure on less for towns

**Lodging**
Based on two people splitting the cost of a $140 double room (includes breakfast).
$70

**Meals**
$20 for lunch and $30 for dinner
$50

**City Transit**
Buses and taxis/Uber
$15

**Sights and Entertainment**
This daily average works for most people.
$25

## Budget Tips

To cut your daily expenses, take advantage of the deals you'll find throughout Belgium and mentioned in this book.

Avid sightseers buy combo-tickets that cover multiple sights. If a town doesn't offer deals, visit only the sights you most want to see, and seek out free sights and experiences (people-watching counts).

Some businesses—especially hotels and walking-tour companies—offer discounts to my readers (look for the RS% symbol in the listings in this book).

Reserve your rooms directly with the hotel. Some hotels offer a discount if you pay in cash and/or stay three or more ▶▶▶

## Rick Steves Belgium

▶▶▶ nights (check online or ask). Rooms can cost less in spring and fall (May, June, Sept, and Oct). And even seniors can sleep cheaply in hostels (most have private rooms) for about $30 per person. Or check Airbnb-type sites for deals.

It's no hardship to eat inexpensively in Belgium. You can get tasty, affordable meals at chain restaurants, cafés, take-away spots, and street vendors. Cultivate the art of picnicking in atmospheric settings.

When you splurge, choose an experience you'll always remember, such as a concert or special art exhibit. Minimize souvenir shopping; focus instead on collecting wonderful memories. ◼

*Belgian experiences: fine dining; Belgian waffles; a visit to Brussels' Royal Army and Military History Museum*

## BEFORE YOU GO

You'll have a smoother trip if you tackle a few things ahead of time. For more details on these topics, see the Practicalities chapter and RickSteves.com, which has helpful travel-tip articles and videos.

**Make sure your travel documents are valid.** If your passport is due to expire within six months of your ticketed date of return, you need to renew it. Allow six weeks or more to renew or get a passport (www.travel.state.gov). Check for current Covid entry requirements, such as proof of vaccination or a negative Covid-19 test result.

**Arrange your transportation.** Book your international flights. Overall, Kayak.com is the best place to start searching for flights. Figure out your transportation options: It's worth thinking about renting a car, buying train tickets online in advance, getting a rail pass, or booking cheap European flights. (You can wing it once you're there, but it may cost more.)

**Book rooms well in advance,** especially if your trip falls during peak season or any major holidays or festivals.

**Hire local guides in advance.** Reserve ahead by phone or email; popular guides can get booked up.

**Reserve ahead for key sights.** While most of Belgium's sights do not require advance reservations, it can be smart to prebook online to view the Ghent Altarpiece on weekends or from July through August.

**Consider travel insurance.** Compare the cost of insurance to the cost of your potential loss. Check whether your existing insurance (health, homeowners, or renters) covers you and your possessions overseas.

**Call your bank.** Alert your bank that you'll be using your debit and credit cards in Europe. Ask about transaction fees, and, if you don't already have one, get a "contactless" credit card (request your card PIN too). You don't need to bring euros; you can withdraw euros from cash machines in Europe.

**Use your smartphone smartly.** Sign up for an international service plan to reduce your costs, or rely on Wi-Fi in Europe instead. Download any apps you'll want on the road, such as maps, translators, transit schedules, and Rick Steves Audio Europe (see sidebar).

**Pack light.** You'll walk with your luggage more than you think. I travel for weeks with a single carry-on bag and a day pack. Use the packing checklist in the appendix as a guide.

## Rick's Free Video Clips and Audio Tours

Travel smarter with these free, fun resources:

**Rick Steves Classroom Europe,** a powerful tool for teachers, is also useful for travelers. This video library contains about 500 short clips excerpted from my public television series. Enjoy these videos as you sort through options for your trip and  to better understand what you'll see in Europe. Check it out at Classroom.RickSteves.com (just enter a topic to find everything I've filmed on a subject).

The **Rick Steves Audio Europe** app makes it easy to download audio content to enhance your trip. Use the app to listen to audio tours of Europe's top sights, plus interviews (organized by country) from my public radio show with experts from Europe and around the globe. Find it in your app store or at RickSteves.com/AudioEurope.

# Travel Smart

If you have a positive attitude, equip yourself with good information (this book), and expect to travel smart, you will.

**Read—and reread—this book.** To have an "A" trip, be an "A" student. Note opening hours of sights, closed days, crowd-beating tips, and whether reservations are required or advisable. Check the latest at RickSteves.com/update.

**Be your own tour guide.** As you travel, get up-to-date info on sights, reserve tickets and tours, reconfirm hotels and travel arrangements, and check transit connections. Visit local TIs. Upon arrival in a new town, lay the groundwork for a smooth departure; confirm the train, bus, or road you'll take when you leave.

**Outsmart thieves.** Pickpockets abound in crowded places where tourists congregate. Treat commotions as smokescreens for theft. Keep your cash, credit cards, and passport secure in a money belt tucked under your clothes; carry only a day's spending money in your front pocket or wallet. Don't set valuable items down on counters or café tabletops, where they can be quickly stolen or easily forgotten.

**Minimize potential loss.** Keep expensive gear to a minimum. Bring copies or take photos of important documents (passport and cards) to aid in replacement if they're lost or stolen. Back up photos and files frequently.

**Guard your time and energy.** Taking a taxi (or Uber) can be a good value if it saves you a long wait for a cheap bus or an exhausting walk across town. To avoid long lines, follow my crowd-beating tips, such as sightseeing early or late.

**Be flexible.** Even if you have a well-planned itinerary,

expect changes, strikes, closures, sore feet, bad weather, and so on. Your Plan B could turn out to be even better.

**Attempt the language.** Most Belgians—especially in the tourist trade and in cities—speak English, but if you learn some French or Dutch, even just a few pleasantries, you'll get more smiles and make more friends. Apps such as Google Translate work for on-the-go translation help, but you can get a head start by practicing the survival phrases near the end of this book.

**Connect with the culture.** Interacting with locals carbonates your experience. Enjoy the friendliness of the Belgian people. Ask questions; most locals are happy to point you in their idea of the right direction. Set up your own quest for the best local beer, tastiest fries, or most picturesque square. When an opportunity pops up, make it a habit to say "yes."

Belgium...here you come!

# BRUGES

# ORIENTATION TO BRUGES

*Brugge • Bruges*

With pointy gilded architecture, stay-a-while cafés, vivid time-tunnel art, and dreamy canals dotted with swans, Bruges is a heavyweight sightseeing destination. It's also a joy: Where else can you ride a bike along a canal, munch mussels and wash them down with the world's best beer, savor heavenly chocolate, and see Flemish Primitives and a Michelangelo, all within 300 yards of a bell tower that jingles every 15 minutes? *And* do it all without worrying about a language barrier?

The town is Brugge (BROO-ghah) in Dutch, and Bruges (broozh) in French and English. Its name comes from the Viking word for "wharf." Right from the start, Bruges was a trading center.

In the 11th century, the city grew wealthy on the cloth trade. As the middleman in the sea trade between northern and southern Europe, Bruges was an economic powerhouse and became one of the biggest cities in the world (as large as London, for a time). By the 14th century, it was the most important cloth market in northern Europe.

In the 15th century, while England and France were slugging it out in the Hundred Years' War, Bruges was the favored residence of the powerful Dukes of Burgundy—and at peace. Commerce and the arts boomed. The artists Jan van Eyck and Hans Memling had studios here.

But by the 16th century, the harbor had silted up and the economy had collapsed. The Burgundian court left, Belgium became a minor Habsburg possession, and Bruges' golden age abruptly ended.

For generations, Bruges was a backwater. In the 19th century, a new port, Zeebrugge, brought renewed vitality to the area. And in the 20th century, tourists discovered the town. These days, some 8 million people visit each year.

Today, Bruges prospers because of tourism, but even with the crowds, it's the kind of place where you don't mind being a tourist. Just an hour west of Brussels by train, this uniquely well-preserved Gothic city is a handy gateway to Europe.

## PLANNING YOUR TIME

Bruges needs at least two nights and a full, well-organized day. With one day—other than a Monday, when the Groeninge Museum and Sint-Janshospitaal Memling Collection are closed—a speedy visitor could try this ambitious Bruges blitz (which is outlined in my Bruges City Walk):

9:30 Climb the bell tower on the Markt (Market Square).

10:00 Tour the sights on Burg Square.

11:30 Tour the Groeninge Museum or the Gruuthuse Museum.

13:00 Eat lunch and buy chocolates.

14:00 Take a short canal cruise.

14:30 Visit the Church of Our Lady and see Michelangelo's *Madonna and Child*.

15:00 If planned renovations have finished, tour the Memling Collection inside Sint-Janshospitaal (St. John's Hospital).

16:00 Catch the De Halve Maan Brewery tour (can reserve in advance) or relax in the Begijnhof courtyard.

17:00 Ride a bike around the quiet back streets of town.

20:00 Enjoy the low light of magic hour on the Markt, then lose the tourists and find dinner elsewhere. Finish the evening with a unique Belgian beer in a local pub.

If this schedule seems too ambitious, skip the bell tower and the brewery—or stay another day.

# Overview

The tourist's Bruges is less than one square mile, contained within a canal (the former moat). Nearly everything of interest and importance is within a convenient cobbled swath between the train station and the Markt (Market Square; a 20-minute walk). Most tourists are concentrated in the triangle formed by the Markt, Burg Square, and the Church of Our Lady; outside of that tight zone, the townscape is sleepy and relatively uncrowded. Many of my charming recommended accommodations lie just beyond this zone.

## TOURIST INFORMATION

You'll find branches of the TI at the **train station** (Mon-Sat 10:00-17:00, Sun until 14:00) and in the Historium building on the **Markt** (daily 10:00-17:00). Pick up the free city map and museum

# Bruges

200 Meters

200 Yards

🚤 CANAL BOAT TOURS

🐴 HORSE-AND-BUGGY TOURS

<u>Chocolate Shops</u>

❶ Dumon Chocolate (3)
❷ The Chocolate Line
❸ BbyB Chocolate
❹ Confiserie De Clerck

<u>Accommodations</u>

❺ Waterside B&B
❻ To Vegan B&B AM/PM
❼ Snuffel Backpacker Hostel

brochure with the latest hours, and get your questions answered. Both TIs also sell a substantial booklet outlining four city walks. The In&Uit ("In and Out") TI in the big red concert hall on the square called **'t Zand** is helpful for performing arts tickets (Mon-Sat 10:00-17:00, Sun until 14:00; 't Zand 34). All three TIs share the same phone number and website, which lists events and concerts (+32 50 444 646, www.visitbruges.be).

## ARRIVAL IN BRUGES

**By Train:** Bruges' train station is in a clean, parklike setting, where travelers step out the door and see a taxi stand and a roundabout with center-bound buses circling through every few minutes. Coming in by train, you'll see the bell tower that marks the main square (Markt, the center of town). The station has a TI, ATMs, handy bike rental, and lockers.

The easiest way to get to the town center is by **free shuttle bus.** These leave from the station's "kiss-and-ride" area, straight ahead from the station doors (no ticket required, daily 7:30-17:00, runs every 20 minutes to the Markt and other city-center stops, www.bruges.be/shuttlebus).

You can also get to the center via a regular **city bus** (for details, see "Getting Around Bruges," later). A **taxi** from the train station to most hotels is about €10-15.

It's a 20-minute **walk** from the station to the center. To reach the Markt, head for the tall brick bell tower. Cross the busy street in front of the station and veer left on a pleasant path through the park. Emerging at the square called t'Zand, turn right on Zuidzandstraat, which leads directly to Markt.

You can rent a **bike** at the train station for the duration of your stay, but other bike-rental shops are closer to the center (see "Helpful Hints," later).

**By Car:** Driving in town is complicated because of the one-way system. The best plan for drivers: Park at the train station, visit the TI there, and take a bus or taxi into town. A handy two-story garage is just behind the train station (€5.50 for 24 hours). The parking fee includes a round-trip same-day bus ticket into town for up to four people in your car (get your free bus ticket by showing your parking ticket to staff at Lijnwinkel ticket office just outside the station).

There are pricier underground parking garages at the square

called 't Zand and around town (€14.40/day, all well marked), but why bother when you have the great train station garage option?

## HELPFUL HINTS

**Sightseeing Tips:** The Musea Brugge Card **sightseeing pass** is a good deal (available at www.museabrugge.be, the TI, and covered museums; see the next chapter for details). If you're in Bruges on a **Monday,** when several museums are closed, consider the following activities or attractions: bell-tower climb on the Markt, Begijnhof, De Halve Maan Brewery tour, Basilica of the Holy Blood, City Hall's Gothic Room, Bruges Beer Experience, chocolate shops and museum, and Church of Our Lady. You can also join a boat, bus, or walking tour, or rent a bike and pedal into the countryside.

**Market Days:** Bruges hosts markets on Wednesday morning (on the Markt) and Saturday morning ('t Zand). On good-weather Saturdays, Sundays, and public holidays, a flea market hops along Dijver in front of the Groeninge Museum (March-Oct). The fish market *(vismarkt)* sells souvenirs daily and seafood Wednesday through Saturday mornings until 13:00.

**Bookstore:** A good travel bookstore (**De Reyghere,** which carries my guidebooks) is at #12 on the Markt.

**Laundry:** Bruges has several self-service launderettes. Ask your hotelier for the nearest, but one of the most central is **The Laundrette** (daily 10:00-21:00, next to Hotel Marcel at Niklaas Desparsstraat 5—see the "Bruges" map for location, +32 50 335 502, www.thelaundrette.be).

**Bike Rental:** Rates are generally the same around town (about €4-5/hour, €13-15/day, more for specialty bikes). For locations see the "Bruges" map.

    **Bruges Bike Rental** is central and cheap, with friendly service and long hours (show this book to get student rate—€11/day, daily 10:00-20:00, free child seats, behind the far-out iron facade at Niklaas Desparsstraat 17, +32 50 616 108, www.brugesbikerental.be).

    **Koffieboontje Bike Rental** is just under the bell tower on the Markt (tandem bikes available, daily 9:30-22:00, free child seats, Hallestraat 4, +32 50 338 027, www.adventure-bike-renting.be).

    **De Ketting** is less central, but cheaper than most (Mon-Sat 10:00-17:00, closed Sun, Gentpoortstraat 23, +32 50 344 196, www.deketting.be).

    **Fietspunt Brugge** is a big outfit at the train station (€10/10 hours, Mon-Fri 7:00-19:00, Sat-Sun 9:00-17:00, just outside the station and to the right as you exit in the huge bicycle parking garage, +32 50 396 826).

**Best Town View:** The bell tower overlooking the Markt rewards those who climb it with the ultimate Bruges view.

**Jogging:** Locals love the five-mile run, walk, or bike ride that follows a path along the inside of the circular canal, tracing the old city wall and passing four medieval gates.

**Christmas Markets:** Bruges is a popular holiday destination. It hosts Christmas markets at three locations throughout December, with ice skating, a winter bar, and a 30-minute illuminated walk through the city.

## GETTING AROUND BRUGES

Because the city is easily walkable, most visitors won't need a bus or taxi except for traveling between the train station and the city center at the Markt.

**By Bus:** The free shuttle bus from the train station to the town center (see "Arrival in Bruges," earlier) may be all you need. Nearly all regular city buses go directly from the train station to the city center and fan out from there. Any bus marked *Centrum* will get you to the center in a few minutes. Buses #4, #13, and #14 drop you right on Markt square; #4 and #14 continue to the northeast part of town (to the windmills and recommended accommodations on and near Carmersstraat, stop: Gouden Handstraat). Buses #1, #6, #11, #12, and #16 stop on Dijver street, a block south of the Markt. At night, buses can be infrequent; the Google maps app can alert you to the next available bus—or just take a taxi.

To return from the city center to the train station, catch any bus labeled *Station*. The handiest stop is Stadsschouwburg, two blocks north of the Markt on Vlamingstraat, right across from the City Theater—buses stopping here all go to the station (every five minutes). It's always smart to confirm with the driver as you board.

A bus **ticket** is €2.50 and good for an hour. At the train station, you can buy tickets at the Lijnwinkel shop that's curbside, just outside the station (credit card; buy as many tickets as you need in advance). While you cannot buy tickets on the bus, you can simply tap your credit card to pay for the ride. If you're going to Antwerp or Ghent and plan to use public transportation there as well, consider the **10-ride ticket** for €17. You can use it in all three cities (and anywhere else in Flanders), and you can share the ticket with others. Though various day passes are available, there's probably no need to buy one for your visit. Bus info: www.delijn.be.

**By Taxi:** You'll find taxi stands at the station and on the Markt (€8/first 1.5 kilometers; to get a cab in the center, call +32 50 36 36 49). Uber has yet to arrive in Bruges.

# Tours in Bruges

### Boat Tours

The most relaxing and scenic (though not informative) way to see this city of canals is by boat, with the captain narrating. All com-panies offer essentially the same thing: a 30-minute route (roughly 4/hour, daily 10:00-17:00), a price of €12, and narra-tion in three or four languages on the same tour. Qualitative differences are due to individual guides, not compa-nies. Let them know you speak English to ensure you'll understand the spiel. Two companies give a RS% group-rate discount to individuals with this book: **Boten Stael** (just over the canal from Sint-Janshospitaal at Katelijnestraat 4, +32 50 332 771) and **Gruuthuse** (Nieu-wstraat 11, opposite Groeninge Muse-um, +32 50 333 393).

### Bike Tour

**QuasiMundo Bike Tours** leads daily five-mile bike tours around the city (€28, RS%, 2.5 hours, departs March-Oct at 10:00, in Nov only with good weather, no tours Dec-Feb). For more details and contact info, see the listing under "Near Bruges," later in this sec-tion.

### City Minibus Tour

**City Tour Bruges** gives an overview of the town in an 18-seat, two-skylight minibus with dial-a-language headsets and videos (€20, 50 minutes, pay driver). The tour leaves every 30 minutes from the Markt (10:00-19:00, until 18:00 in fall, fewer in winter, +32 50 355 024, www.citytour.be). The narration is slow-moving, but the tour is a lazy way to roll past virtually every sight in Bruges.

### Walking Tour

The **TI** arranges two-hour "Bruges from the Heart" walks through the core of town (€12.50, almost daily in busy season, Sat year-round, limited to 16 people, depart from TI on 't Zand Square at 14:30, schedule at www.visitbruges.be). To propel you beyond the pretty gables and canal swans of Bruges, they're good medicine.

### Local Guides

**Sylvie Brems** gives three-hour walks (€170) and full-day tours (€345) and can join you in your car for a guided tours of Ypres and the WWI battlefields (+32 478 822 978, sylvie.brems@gmail.com).

**Patrick Verleye** is also good—especially considering his rates (€25/2-hour private tour). Patrick's food tours provide eight tastings—cheese, shrimp, waffles, chocolate, beer, and more (€65, 3 hours, generally leave at 10:30; +32 497 4684 33, www.tourinbruges.com, info@tourinbruges.com).

You can also hire a guide through the **TI**'s VisitBruges.be website (typically €80 for a two-hour tour, reserve at least one week in advance).

### Horse-and-Buggy Tour

The buggies around town can take you on a clip-clop tour (€60, 35 minutes; price is per carriage, not per person; seats five; buggies gather in the Markt).

## NEAR BRUGES

Popular tour destinations from Bruges are Flanders Fields (famous WWI sites about 40 miles to the southwest; see that chapter for more information) and the picturesque town of Damme (four easy-to-bike miles to the northeast).

### Quasimodo Countryside Tours

This company offers an entertaining, all-day bus tour to WWI battlefields, trenches, memorials, and poppy-splattered fields (Tue-Sun 9:15, no tours Mon or in Jan, 8 hours, visit to In Flanders Fields Museum not included). Be ready for lots of walking.

Tours cost €79 (cash preferred, make required reservation online, at TI, or by calling +32 50 370 470, www.quasimodo.be).

### Bike Tours

For do-it-yourself bike tours, see my bike ride to the historic town of Damme (page 52). My self-guided walk from the Markt to the moat is also good fun on a bike (page 41). For bike rental shops in Bruges, see "Helpful Hints," earlier.

**QuasiMundo Bike Tours** offers a daily "Border by Bike" tour through the nearby countryside to Damme (€38, €25 if you already have a bike, RS%, reservations required, March-Oct, departs at 13:00, 15 miles, 4 hours, +32 50 330 775, www.quasimundo.com). Meet at QuasiMundo's office at Predikherenstraat 28 (be there 10 minutes before departure). Jos, who leads most departures, is a high-energy and entertaining guide.

**Pink Bear Bike Tours,** run by charming Mieke, takes small groups on an easy and delightful 3.5-hour guided pedal along a canal to Damme and back, finishing with a brief tour of Bruges.

English tours go daily through peak season and nearly daily the rest of the year (€28, €22 if you already have a bike, RS%, meet at 10:25 under bell tower on the Markt, +32 476 744 525, www. pinkbear.be).

# SIGHTS & EXPERIENCES IN BRUGES

While Bruges has several worthwhile museums and churches, the ultimate sight here is the town itself. After seeing the essential sights, I enjoy slowing down and savoring the city, whether it's getting lost on the back streets away from the lace shops and waffle stands, taking a bike ride along a quiet canal, learning about beer from passionate locals, or sampling chocolate at one of Bruges' fine chocolatiers. This chapter covers both the top sights and best experiences Bruges has to offer.

**Sightseeing Pass:** The **Musea Brugge Card** covers admission at 13 museums (€32, valid for 3 days, purchase at www.museabrugge.be, at the TI, and at included museums). Because the Groeninge Museum and Sint-Janshospitaal Memling Collection cost €26 combined, you'll likely save money with this pass if you plan to see at least one other covered sight. Note, though, that the Sint-Janshospitaal Memling Collection is closed for renovations in 2023.

## Sights in Bruges

These sights are listed by neighborhood, covering the area around the Markt (Market Square) and Burg Square; the cluster of sights south of the Markt; and the less touristy area northeast of the core. Note that many city-run sights (including the Groeninge Museum, Church of Our Lady, Sint-Janshospitaal Memling Collection, City Hall, Folklore Museum, St. Janshuys Windmill, and Gruuthuse Museum) have the same hours (Tue-Sun 9:30-17:00, closed Mon).

### ON OR NEAR THE MARKT
These sights are described in greater detail in the Bruges City Walk chapter—including details on visiting the interiors of the

# Bruges at a Glance

▲▲**Bell Tower** Overlooking the Markt with 366 steps to a fine view and carillon close-up. **Hours:** Daily 9:00-20:00, Nov and Jan-Feb until 18:00. See page 38.

▲▲**Burg Square** Sight-filled historic square with impressive architecture. See page 38.

▲▲**Church of Our Lady** Tombs and church art, including Michelangelo's *Madonna and Child.* **Hours:** Mon-Sat 9:30-17:00, Sun from 13:30. See page 39.

▲▲**Gruuthuse Museum** A mansion providing a peek at old Bruges elegance and city history. **Hours:** Tue-Sun 9:30-17:00, closed Mon. See page 40.

▲▲**Groeninge Museum** Top-notch collection of mainly Flemish art. **Hours:** Tue-Sun 9:30-17:00, closed Mon. See page 40.

▲▲**Sint-Janshospitaal Memling Collection** Art by the greatest of the Flemish Primitives, displayed in a medieval hospital. May be closed for renovation in 2023. **Hours:** When open, likely Tue-Sun 9:30-17:00, closed Mon. See page 40.

▲▲**Begijnhof** Peaceful medieval courtyard. **Hours:** Daily 6:30-18:30; vespers service at 16:30. See page 41.

▲**Markt** (Market Square) The modern heart of the city. See page 38.

▲**Basilica of the Holy Blood** Romanesque/Gothic church housing a relic of the blood of Christ. **Hours:** Daily 10:00-17:00. See page 39.

▲**City Hall** Beautifully restored Gothic Room from 1400, plus the Renaissance Hall. **Hours:** Daily 9:30-17:00. See page 39.

▲**Folklore Museum** Well-presented exhibits of life in Bruges' industrious golden age. **Hours:** Tue-Sun 9:30-17:00, closed Mon. See page 46.

▲**De Halve Maan Brewery Tour** Fun beer tour. **Hours:** Tours on the hour Sun-Fri 11:00-16:00, Sat until 17:00. See page 47.

▲**Bourgogne des Flandres Brewery Tour** Entertaining and informative brewery tour. **Hours:** Tue-Sun 10:30-18:00, closed Mon. See page 48.

Basilica of the Holy Blood, the City Hall's Gothic Room, and Renaissance Hall.

### ▲Markt (Market Square)

The crossroads of Bruges is one of the most enjoyable town squares in Belgium—and in this country, that's really saying something. In Bruges' heyday as a trading center, a canal came right up to this square. And today it's still the heart of the modern city. The square is ringed by the frilly former post office, enticing restaurant terraces, great old gabled buildings, and the iconic bell tower. Under the bell tower are two stands selling classic Belgian (not French) fries. The streets spoking off this square are lined with tempting eateries and shops.

### ▲▲Bell Tower (Belfort)

Most of this bell tower has presided over the Markt since 1300, serenading passersby with cheery carillon music. The octagonal lantern was added in 1486, making it 290 feet high—that's 366 steps. The view is worth the climb...and probably even the pricey admission. Some mornings and summer evenings, you can sit in the courtyard or out on the square to enjoy a carillon concert (for details, see page 59).

**Cost and Hours:** €14—advance online booking recommended during peak times; open daily 9:00-20:00, Nov and Jan-Feb until 18:00, last entry one hour before closing; pay WC in courtyard, +32 50 448 767.

### Historium

This much-hyped "sight" is little more than a commercial venture with as many actual historic artifacts as a Disney ride. For a steep price you'll don headphones and follow a 35-minute story through a handful of rooms taking you back to Bruges in the 1430s. You finish what I consider a waste of time and money with a nice view over the Markt.

**Cost and Hours:** €17, €21 with VR option; daily 11:00-18:00, Sat until 22:00, last entry one hour before closing; Markt 1, +32 50 270 311, www.historium.be.

### ▲▲Burg Square

This opulent, prickly-spired square is Bruges' civic center, the historic birthplace of Bruges, and the site of the ninth-century castle of the first count of Flanders. It's home to the Basilica of the Holy Blood and City Hall (both described next). Today, it's an atmospheric place to take in an outdoor concert while surrounded by six centuries of architecture.

### ▲Basilica of the Holy Blood (Heilig-Bloedbasiliek)

Originally the Chapel of Saint Basil, this church is famous for its relic of the blood of Christ, which, according to tradition, was

brought to Bruges in 1150 after the Second Crusade. The lower chapel is dark and solid—a fine example of Romanesque style. The upper chapel (separate entrance, climb the stairs) is decorated Gothic. An interesting treasury museum is next to the upper chapel.

**Cost and Hours:** Church-free, treasury-€5, daily 10:00-17:00, Burg Square, +32 50 336 792, www.holyblood.com.

### ▲City Hall (Stadhuis)

This complex houses several interesting sights, including a room full of old town maps and paintings, and the highlight—the grand, beautifully restored **Gothic Room** from 1400, starring a painted and carved wooden ceiling adorned with hanging arches. Your ticket also covers the less impressive **Renaissance Hall** (Brugse Vrije) next door, basically just one ornate room with a Renaissance chimney (separate entrance—in corner of square at Burg 11a).

**Cost and Hours:** €7, daily 9:30-17:00, +32 50 448 743, www. museabrugge.be.

## SOUTH OF THE MARKT

📖 Most of the following sights are covered in more detail in either the Bruges City Walk chapter or individual tour chapters.

### ▲▲Church of Our Lady (Onze-Lieve-Vrouwekerk)

This imposing church brims with reminders of the wealth of medieval Bruges. Its prized possession is a delicate *Madonna and Child*

sculpture, the only Michelangelo statue to leave Italy in his lifetime (a Belgian cloth merchant with connections in Italy shipped the statue home in 1506).

**Cost and Hours:** Entry to the rear of the church is free. Access to the main section costs €7, while a €16 comboticket includes the Gruuthuse Museum (church open Mon-Sat 9:30-17:00, Sun from 13:30; Mariastraat, +32 50 448 711, www.museabrugge.be).

📖 For more on the church, see the Bruges City Walk chapter.

### ▲▲Gruuthuse Museum

The fine 15th-century mansion of the powerful Gruuthuse family stands next to the Church of Our Lady, its 17 rooms filled with artifacts. You'll see antique maps, paintings, tapestries, lace, and the noble family's private oratory overlooking the church's chancel, allowing them to "go to Mass" in private. Exhibits, explained in English, track and explain the growth of Bruges through the ages.

**Cost and Hours:** €14, includes audioguide, €16 combo-ticket with adjacent Church of our Lady; Tue-Sun 9:30-17:00, closed Mon; Dijver 17, +32 50 448 711, www.museabrugge.be.

### ▲▲Groeninge Museum

This museum houses a world-class collection of mostly Flemish art, from Memling to Magritte. While there's plenty of worthwhile modern art, the highlights are the vivid and pristine Flemish Primitives. (In Flanders, "Primitive" simply means "before the Renaissance.") Flemish art is shaped by its love of detail, the egos of its merchant patrons, and the power of the Church. Lose yourself in the halls of Groeninge: Gaze across 15th-century canals, into the eyes of reassuring Marys, and through town squares littered with leotards, lace, and lopped-off heads.

**Cost and Hours:** €14; Tue-Sun 9:30-17:00, closed Mon; Dijver 12, +32 50 448 743, www.museabrugge.be.

📖 See the Groeninge Museum Tour chapter.

### Arentshuis Museum

This small museum features the art of Frank Brangwyn (1867-1956), who was born in Bruges and built an international career in several fields. Brangwyn's style is accessible and varied. You may see his brooding self-portrait. His specialty was dark engravings of grimy Industrial Age workers and homeless people. You may catch glimpses of Bruges (like the Begijnhof). He also did a series of the *Stations of the Cross,* some large, colorful Art Nouveau canvases, and even designed some furniture. He made Bruges proud.

**Cost and Hours:** Free; Tue-Sun 9:30-17:00, closed Mon; Dijver 16, +32 50 448 743, www.museabrugge.be.

### ▲▲Sint-Janshospitaal Memling Collection
### (St. John's Hospital)

This former monastery is one of the oldest hospital buildings in Europe, and may be closed for renovation in 2023. Besides preserving medieval wards where monks and nuns cared for the sick, its museum has a fine collection of artworks from the monastery chapel. Hans Memling, the greatest of the Flemish Primitives, created his *St. John Altarpiece* triptych for the hospital, along with a miniature, gilded-oak shrine to St. Ursula.

**Cost and Hours:** €12; Tue-Sun 9:30-17:00, closed Mon; across the street from the Church of Our Lady, Mariastraat 38, +32 50 448 743, www.museabrugge.be.

📖 See the Sint-Janshospitaal Memling Collection Tour chapter.

### ▲▲Begijnhof

The courtyard called the Begijnhof was once enclosed by buildings inhabited by members of a lay sisterhood, the Beguines. Though the original buildings are no longer there, the atmosphere may still make you want to don a habit and fold your hands as you walk under its wispy trees and whisper past modest little homes. Only a few sisters still live and pray here.

**Cost and Hours:** Courtyard-free, daily 6:30-18:30. The public is welcome at a daily vespers service in the chapel at 16:30.

**Nearby:** Just south of the Begijn-hof is the waterway called **Minnewater,** an idyllic world of flower boxes, canals, and swans.

📖 For more on the Begijnhof and Minnewater, see the Bruges City Walk chapter.

## NORTHEAST OF THE MARKT

The less touristy streets north and east of the Markt are worth a wander—they don't suffer from the intense crowd congestion of the main Markt-Burg-Church of Our Lady thoroughfare.

### ▲Markt to the Moat Stroll

This tranquil walk takes you along postcard canals and through sleepy residential areas to the moat, where you can climb up inside a working windmill. The walk takes about 30 minutes (longer if you enter the sights). It's also great on a bike and can be extended with a longer ride to the town of Damme (described later).

➡ **Self-Guided Walk:** From the Markt, head up Vlaming-straat (with the bell tower at your back, exit straight ahead up the top-right corner of the square).

**Vlamingstraat:** Two short blocks up this street, on the left, you'll spot the stately, Neo-Renaissance-style **City Theater** (Stadsschouwburg). Notice how atypically broad this street is for claustrophobic Bruges. That's because several old buildings were torn down to build this theater in 1869. This was a time of Flemish cultural revival—when Dutch-speaking people began to take pride in what differentiated them from the dominant French-speaking Belgians—and Dutch-language theater was an important symbol of Flemish pride. (Flemish is to Dutch essentially what American is to English—the same language spoken by people in two different countries.)

Notice the large plaza in front of the main entrance, dating from a time when classy horse carriages would drop off well-heeled theatergoers. The fine gabled facades that surround you are generally just that: facades fronting otherwise plain buildings, added to boost the egos of the merchants who lived there.

• *A few steps past the theater, on the left, notice the* **Friet Museum**, *dedicated to the esteemed fry (described later in the chapter). A bit farther up and also on the left, look for the angled building set slightly back from the street, with yellow bricks and narrow windows. This marks a small square known as...*

**Oude Beursplein** (Old Stock Exchange): While Amsterdam likes to lay claim to inventing the stock market, Bruges' predates it. (See the old sign reading *Huis Ter Beurze—House of the Stock Market.*) In the mid-13th century, the Van der Beurse family built an inn here and offered beers to passing merchants on their way between the tollhouse (which we'll see soon) and the Markt. Gradually these hangouts began to host more formalized trading of goods and services. Much of this business took place out in this square; traders would scurry under awnings in case of bad weather. To kick off these meetings amid this chaos, they'd ring a bell, which is still used today to start and end stock trading sessions. And to this day, in most European languages, some variation of the word "Beurse" (*Börse, borsa,* etc.) means "stock market." (Conveniently, the family name also means "purse.")

Just after the old stock market, turn right up Academiestraat. If you have a sweet tooth, don't miss **Confiserie De Clerck,** an old-school chocolate shop with some of the best deals in town (about €1.80/100 grams—about six pieces). For more about this shop, see the listing under "Experiences in Bruges," later.

The big building near the end of the street on your right is the **Burghers' Lodge** (Poortersloge)—a meeting place for local businessmen, similar to today's Rotary clubs. Pause at the building's ornate doorway, just before the square. Just above, notice the sign with golden Latin words declaring "This building rises like a phoenix from the ashes"; if you add them up, the seemingly random capital letters represent the year of the building's reconstruction after a devastating fire (VIXXCIVVIVMDVIVI—1655).

• *You'll pop out into a square called...*

**Jan van Eyckplein:** A large **statue** honors the painter in the middle of this charming waterfront square. He's identified twice:

the Dutch *Jan van Eyck* on the side facing you, and the French *Jean van Eyck* on the side facing the canal.

In 1830 Belgium won its independence and began a campaign to celebrate its distinctive heritage by erecting statues to leading cultural figures. Back then the French were the wealthy Belgians and the Flemish were the poor ones. Notice here the 13th-century buildings with their gabled facades—many were rebuilt in the 19th century.

On the left side of the square, you can't miss the building with the big, fire-engine red doors. Sure enough, this was once the firehouse. But before that, it was the **tollhouse** *(tolhuis).* This canal once went all the way to the Markt (water still runs under this square); entering vessels paused here to pay duties.

The extremely skinny facade just left of the tollhouse (with the four carved figures over the red door) is the **Dockworkers' House** (Pijndershuisje). Above the door, the detailed carvings show hardworking stevedores hunched beneath heavy loads. Bruges was a member of the medieval Hanseatic League, a powerful society of trading cities stretching all the way to Norway and the Baltic Sea. As the entry point for trade into the city, this neighborhood, lined with busy warehouses, was an eclectic zone of sailors from around the world. Many international dockworkers lived in little enclaves near here. Looking at a map, you'll see street names that echo this past: Spanjaardstraat ("Spaniard Street"), Biskajerplein ("Basque Square"), and Engelsestraat ("English Street").

Bruges is rich with legends. Here's a nice story: Facing the canal, find the brick house on the left corner. On the upper story, a **statue of Mary** stands in a niche, next to an old lamp. In the 18th century, when Bruges was in decline and in need of beautification, local authorities made landowners a deal: If they added a statue of Mary to their house, the city would install a gas light to illuminate it (benefiting the homeowner with more light and security). Many burghers took them up on the offer, and more than 350 statues of Mary continue to decorate the city (many still with a lamp nearby). Once you start looking for them, you'll see them everywhere.

• *From here, enjoy a stroll through a...*

**Residential Canal Zone:** From the square, head straight along the canal (left side), simply enjoying the serene scenery. When you hit the wide cross-canal, jog left, cross the bridge, and continue straight up Carmersstraat. At the fifth street on the right—tiny Korte Speelmansstraat—you're a short block from the **Folklore Museum,** the **Lace Center,** and the **Adornes Domein** (all described later). If you detour there, backtrack to Carmersstraat after your visit and carry on straight until you pop out at the dike that separates Bruges from the old moat that surrounds it.

• *Sitting on top of the dike is the...*

**St. Janshuys Windmill:** In its heyday, bustling Bruges had 28 windmills, mostly used to grind grain. Built in 1770, this one was funded by several local bakers. Notice how its narrow base allows it to swivel to catch the prevailing wind. Windmill keepers were as skilled at rig-

SIGHTS & EXPERIENCES IN BRUGES

# Lace

Beginning in the 1500s and especially throughout the 1600s, lace collars, sleeves, headdresses, and veils became fashion-

able with members of royalty, the aristocracy, and the Catholic Church. All this fine lace was made by hand—and was expensive. For a time, lacemaking was a significant part of several European economies. Even so, it was primarily a cottage industry, with women working from their homes, using patterns and threads supplied to them by lace dealers. The lacemakers made little money for their effort, but the industry helped many peasant families support themselves (the lace dealers, however, became wealthy from the trade).

Men stopped wearing lace with the French Revolution of 1789, when suddenly lace for men seemed undemocratic and unmanly. Around 1800, machines replaced human hands, and except for ornamental pieces, the demand for lace died out.

These days, handmade lace is usually also homemade—produced by dedicated, sharp-eyed hobbyists who love their work. Lacemakers create their own patterns or trace tried-and-true designs. It requires total concentration to follow the intricate patterns. Producing a piece of lace by hand is time-consuming—which is why a handmade tablecloth can easily sell for €250 and up.

There are two basic kinds of lace: bobbin lace (a specialty in Bruges) and needle lace. To make bobbin lace, the lacemaker juggles many different strands tied to bobbins, "weaving" a design by overlapping the threads. Needle lace is more like sewing. The lacemaker uses a threaded needle to make loops and knots on top of a pattern in a fancy design. To see lace being made, drop by a demonstration at the Lace Center.

ging as sailors—ready to cover the blades with canvas when the conditions were right. If you're curious about how this remarkable old technology operated, you can climb up the steep ladder-like stairs to enter the windmill (€4; generally May-Aug Tue-Sun 9:30-12:30 & 13:30-17:00, closed Mon and off-season; +32 50 448 743). In the top section, you'll see the mighty gears and appreciate how wind power not only spun the giant millstones, but also harnessed pulleys to hoist up heavy sacks of grain from the ground below. The grain steadily trickled into the ever-spinning millstones, which ground it and poured it down the spout, in the lower area of the windmill. There it was bagged and hoisted down to send off to the awaiting baker.

• *If you're on foot, you can keep strolling and explore the moat and other nearby windmills.*

*If you're on a bike, you can turn left and head up along the moat—past three more windmills—before you angle off to the right and head for the town of Damme (see directions later, under "Bike Ride to Damme").*

## ▲Folklore Museum (Volkskundemuseum)

While "folklore" usually indicates farming lifestyles and colorful costumes, urbane Bruges dedicates its Folklore Museum to the occupations that kept the city humming through its industrious golden age. It's a well-presented little slice of Bruggian life, with exhibits filling a row of eight charming, interconnected 17th-century almshouses.

**Cost and Hours:** €7, €11 combo-ticket with Lace Center; Tue-Sun 9:30-17:00, closed Mon; Balstraat 43, +32 50 448 764, www.museabrugge.be. To find it, ask for the Jerusalem Church.

**Visiting the Museum:** As you enter, borrow the English descriptions (or use the QR code to read on your device) to bring each room to life. You'll see a schoolhouse; workshops for a cobbler, clogmaker, and barrelmaker; a grocery; and exhibits featuring devotional objects and pipes.

In the garden courtyard, you can play a traditional folk game, then head back up to the main building to see the rest of the collection: the late-19th-century inn/pub (In de Zwarte Kat—look for the resident black cat), a typical living room, candy shop, pharmacy, hatmaker, tailor, costume collection, and more.

## Lace Center (Kant Centrum)

Across the street from the Folklore Museum, this lace museum and school lets you learn about lacemaking and see lace being made.

**Cost and Hours:** €6, €11 combo-ticket with Folklore Museum; Mon-Sat 9:30-17:00, closed Sun, come when demonstrations are scheduled (usually 14:00-17:00); +32 50 330 072, Balstraat 16, www.kantcentrum.eu.

**Visiting the Lace Center:** Your tour starts with a brief movie about the history of lace (and why it was regarded as women's work). Next are exhibits explaining the different ways to make lace. A computer lets you try different techniques for making lace yourself.

The payoff is upstairs in the demonstration room, where ladies chat merrily while making lace, usually using the bobbin technique perfected in Bruges. Observe as the artisans toss bobbins madly

SIGHTS & EXPERIENCES IN BRUGES

while their eyes go bad. They follow mazelike patterns with a forest of pins to help guide their work.

Lace handiwork is on sale in the gift shop, along with materials for making lace on your own.

**Nearby:** Just down the street from the Lace Center is a lace shop with a good reputation, 't **Apostelientje** (generally Tue-Sat 13:00-17:00, closed Sun-Mon, Balstraat 11, +32 495 562 420).

### Adornes Domein

This 15th-century noble estate is still maintained by the family that has owned it for 17 generations. Today they are committed to preserving its character and sharing it with the public. While the exhibit has a fine chapel from 1429 and a special charm, it's otherwise pretty humble (€8, Mon-Sat 10:00-17:00, closed Sun, Peperstraat 3, +32 50 338 883, www.adornes.org).

# Experiences in Bruges

Bruges has some top-notch museums, but many of its charms are experiential: beer drinking, chocolate tasting, and bike riding.

## BEER

Much as wine flows through all aspects of French or Italian cuisine, Belgians prize beer above all else. Bruges offers a wide variety of places to sample brews, a couple of enjoyable brewery tours, and an interesting beer museum. For more on Belgian beers, see the "Eating" section of the Practicalities chapter. For recommendations on shops where you can buy bottles, see page 105.

### Pubs and Beer Halls

Hoisting a glass of beer is a quintessential ▲▲▲ Bruges experience. Here, pubs are not just pubs, they're destinations. Places in the old center—which you'd think would be overrun by tourists—are the proud domain of locals who are happy to educate you on the (sometimes) hundreds of choices. I've listed some of my favorite spots to sample Bruges beer starting on page 345.

### ▲De Halve Maan Brewery Tour

Belgians are Europe's beer connoisseurs, and this handy tour is a great way to pay your respects. The only working family brewery in Bruges, De Halve Maan produces two beers: Brugse Zot ("Fool from Bruges") and Straffe Hendrik ("Strong Henry"). They also give entertaining and informative 45-minute tours. Avoid crowds by visiting early or late.

Their bistro, where you'll drink your included beer, serves quick, hearty lunch plates daily (and dinner Thu-Sat). You can eat indoors with the smell of hops, or outdoors with the smell of hops. This is a good place to wait for your tour or to linger afterward.

**Cost and Hours:** €15 tour includes a beer, RS%—ask for a €2 discount; tours run on the hour Sun-Fri 11:00-16:00, Sat until 17:00; smart to book online or call for a reservation, lots of steep steps but a great rooftop panorama; Walplein 26, +32 50 444 222, www.halvemaan.be.

### ▲Bourgogne des Flandres Brewery Tour

Set idyllically on a canal, this brewery offers a fun walk through a historic brewery accompanied by an audioguide. The visit includes a glass of their famously "impossible to describe" beer on a scenic canalside terrace. To savor the terrace and included beer while enjoying a quick and cheap lunch, consider splitting the hearty €13 meat board (€14 tour includes audioguide and a beer; Tue-Sun 10:30-18:00, closed Mon, last tour at 17:00; Kartuizerinnenstraat 6, +32 50 335 426, www.bourgognedesflandres.be).

### Bruges Beer Experience

With a red-carpet entrance just off the Markt, this homage to beer's frothy history overlooks the square from the top of the former post office.

**Cost and Hours:** €12, €18 ticket includes three tastings, daily 10:00-18:00, last entry one hour before closing, Breidelstraat 3, +32 50 699 229, www.mybeerexperience.com.

**Visiting the Museum:** Head up three flights of steep stairs (lined with fun and historic local beer ads) to the museum's entrance, where you'll get an iPad and headphones to tour the exhibit and learn about the history of beermaking. The most interesting section is on the top floor, where you can run your hands through raw hops, yeast, and barley while getting a step-by-step guide to modern brewing.

When you've had your historical fill, saunter down to the bar and trade the iPad for three tokens good for your choice of tasting-size beers from a rotating list of 16 local drafts. The bar offers Markt views and is open to the public (ticket not required).

## CHOCOLATE

Bruggians are connoisseurs of fine chocolate. You'll be tempted by chocolate-filled display windows all over town. While Godiva is the best big-factory/high-price/high-quality brand, there are plenty of smaller family-run places in Bruges that offer exquisite handmade chocolates. All of the following chocolatiers are proud of their creative varieties and welcome you to assemble a 100-gram assortment of five or six chocolates.

A rule of thumb when buying chocolate: Bruges' informal "chocolate mafia" keeps the price for midrange pralines quite standard, at about €28 per kilogram (or €2.80 for 100 grams). Swankier and "gastronomical" places (like The Chocolate Line or BbyB) charge significantly more but only aficionados may be able to tell the difference. On the other hand, if a place is priced well *below* this range, be suspicious: Quality may suffer.

By the way, if you're looking for value, don't forget to check the supermarket shelves. Since the country is the largest producer of raw chocolate, Belgium's stores always have a wall of quality chocolate. Try Côte d'Or's Noir de Noir for a simple bar of pure dark chocolate that won't flatten in your luggage.

### ▲Chocolate Shops

Katelijnestraat, which runs south from the Church of Our Lady, is "Chocolate Row," with a half-dozen shops within a few steps. Locals rarely buy chocolate along here (as the prices are marked up for tourists), but this is a convenient place to shop. For locations, see the map on page 28.

**Dumon:** Some of Bruges' smoothest, creamiest chocolates are at Dumon (a selection of five or six chocolates are a deal at €3.40/100 grams). Try a small mix-and-match box to sample a few out-of-this-world flavors. Chantal is enthusiastic about her pralines—but warns that the Tonka variety is such strong chocolate that it's banned in the US (daily 10:00-18:00, +32 50 333 360, past the Church  of Our Lady near the Halve Maan Brewery at Walstraat 6). Additional locations are north of the Markt at Eiermarkt 6 and between the Church of Our Lady and the Markt at Simon Stevinplein 11.

**The Chocolate Line:** Locals and tourists alike flock here to taste the *gastronomique* varieties (pricey at about €7.60/100 grams) concocted by Dominique Persoone—the mad scientist of chocolate—and his son Julius. Their unique creations mix chocolate with various, mostly savory, flavors. Even those that sound gross can be surprisingly good: Havana cigar (marinated in rum, cognac, and Cuban tobacco leaves), Saké (bitter ganache and Japanese rice wine), and the green-hued Brasil (cilantro, chili, Cachaça rum, and lime). The kitchen—busy whipping up 80 varieties—is on view in the back. Enjoy the window display, refreshed monthly (Tue-Sat 9:30-18:30, Sun-Mon from 10:30, between the Church of Our Lady and the Markt at Simon Stevinplein 19, +32 50 341 090).

**BbyB:** This chichi, top-end chocolate gallery (whose name stands for "Babelutte by Bartholomeus," for the Michelin-starred restaurateur who owns it) lines up its pralines in a minimalist display case like priceless jewels, each type identified by number. If you don't mind the pretense, the chocolates are top-notch (about €6 for a 5-flavor sleeve, €12 for a sleek 10-flavor sampler box; generally Tue-Sat 10:00-18:30, closed Sun-Mon; between the Markt and Muntplein at Sint-Amandsstraat 39, +32 50 705 760, www.bbyb.be).

**Confiserie De Clerck:** Third-generation chocolatier Jan sells his handmade chocolates for about €1.80/100 grams (about six pieces), making this a bargain. Some locals claim his chocolate's just as good as at pricier places, while others insist that any chocolate this cheap must be subpar—taste it and decide for yourself. The time-warp candy shop (hardly changed in 90 years) is so delightfully old-school, you'll want to visit one way or the other (Mon and Wed-Sat 10:00-18:00, closed Sun and Tue, near the Old Stock Exchange at Academiestraat 19, +32 50 345 338). While Jan is generous with samples, Inge (his wife) runs the beer shop next door—and she isn't.

### Choco-Story: The Chocolate Museum

This kid-friendly museum with lots of artifacts fills you in on the history and production of chocolate.

**Cost and Hours:** €11, includes audioguide and samples; various combo-tickets include the Lamp Museum, Friet Museum, and Diamond Museum; daily 10:00-17:00, last entry one hour before closing; where Wijnzakstraat meets Sint Jansstraat at Sint Jansplein, three-minute walk from the Markt; +32 50 612 237, www.choco-story-brugge.be.

**Visiting the Museum:** Head up the stairs by the gigantic chocolate egg to follow the chronological exhibit tracing 4,000 years of chocolate history. You'll discover why, in the ancient Mexican world of the Maya and Aztec, chocolate was considered the drink of the gods, and cocoa beans were used as a means of payment.

Higher up, you'll learn how chocolates are made and how Belgian pioneers perfected the process. And on the top floor, you'll view a delicious little video and learn more about the big-name

# A Brief History of Chocolate

While Belgium's chocolatiers rake in the euros today, their customers are just the latest in a long line of chocoholics.

Ancient Central American indigenous groups—from the Aztecs to the Mayans to the Olmecs—indulged in cocoa products for centuries; the earliest evidence of cocoa consumption dates to around 2000 BC. Cocoa was so prized that some societies used it as currency.

In 1519, the Aztec emperor Montezuma served Spanish conquistador Hernán Cortés a cup of hot cocoa (xocoatl) made from cocoa beans, which were native to the New World. It ignited a food fad in Europe—by 1700, elegant "chocolate houses" in Europe's capitals served hot chocolate (with milk and sugar added) to wealthy aristocrats. By the 1850s, the process of making chocolate candies was developed, and Belgium, with a long tradition of quality handmade luxuries, was at the forefront.

Cocoa comes from a big orange fruit that grows primarily in the tropical climates of Central and South America. The fruit's gooey pulp and beans are scooped out and left to ferment, then sun-dried for two weeks. The beans are roasted, creating "nibs"—the essence of cocoa.

Chocolate straight from the bean is very bitter, so nibs are processed into cocoa paste or cocoa butter, and the byproduct is ground again to make cocoa powder. Cocoa butter and cocoa paste are mixed together and sweetened with sugar to make chocolates. (Dark chocolate has a higher concentration of cocoa paste, while milk chocolate has more cocoa butter as well as milk powder.)

Europeans created the first chocolate bar in 1847. In 1876, a Swiss man named Henry Nestlé added concentrated milk, creating milk chocolate. And in 1912, Swiss confectioner Jean Neuhaus invented the Belgian praline in Brussels. Later innovators perfected the process, among them the Greek American chocolatier Leonidas Kestekides, who started his internationally renowned company in Belgium.

Belgians divide their confections into two categories: **Truffles** have soft, crumbly chocolate shells filled with buttercream, while **pralines** are made of a hard chocolate shell with a wide range of fillings—totally different from the sugar-and-nuts French praline.

Belgians take chocolate seriously, and rightly so: It's an essential—and delicious—part of the economy.

Belgian chocolatiers (including some less-than-subtle product placement for Belcolade, which sponsors this museum). The finale is downstairs, with all-you-can-eat sample bins and a 10-minute cooking demo.

## Nearby Sights

The owners of the Chocolate Museum operate two similarly quirky museums that are open the same hours.

The museum owner's wife got tired of her husband's ancient lamp collection...so he opened the **Lamp Museum** (Lumina Domestica) next door. While its appeal is limited, this collection of lamps through the ages is jam-packed and well-described (€16 combo-ticket with Choco-Story—no individual ticket for Lamp Museum).

The same folks also run the fun-loving and kid-friendly **Friet Museum**, a few blocks away (€8, includes audioguide, Vlamingstraat 33, www.frietmuseum.be). While it tries hard to elevate the story of the potato, this is—for most—one museum too many. Still, it's the only place in the world that enthusiastically tells the story of Belgian fries.

## BIKING

The Dutch word for bike is *fiets* (pronounced "feets"). And though Bruges' sights are close enough for easy walking, the town is a treat for cyclists. A bike quickly gets you into dreamy back lanes without a hint of tourism. Take a peaceful evening ride through the town's nooks and crannies and around the outer canal. Consider keeping a bike for the duration of your stay—it's the way the locals get around. You can try one of the following rides, or ask at the rental shop for maps and ideas (see "Bike Rental" on page 31).

### ▲Markt to the Moat Ride

My self-guided walk from the Markt to the Moat (earlier in this chapter) is equally fun on a bike. As this area is less touristy, it's less congested and easy to navigate on a bike. When you reach the end of the described route, you can continue riding, following the routes described next.

### ▲Bike Around Bruges

The medieval city is defined by its circular canal, which traces the old medieval wall and passes four surviving medieval gates. Today a delightful five-mile path along the canal is ideal for bikers (and walkers), offering any visitor a wonderfully scenic and peaceful circle tour.

### ▲▲Bike Ride to Damme

For the best short bike trip out of Bruges, pedal four miles each way to the nearby town of Damme. You'll enjoy a whiff of the countryside and see a working windmill while riding along a canal to a charming (if well-discovered) small market town. While Damme is cute, it's sleepy, with little to see—take this ride mostly as an excuse to pedal through the countryside, between canals and farm fields. Allow about two hours for the leisurely round-trip bike ride and a brief stop in Damme. The Belgium/Netherlands border is a 40-minute pedal (along the same canal) beyond Damme.

• *Head east from Bruges' Markt through Burg Square and out to the canal. (Or, for a more entertaining route, follow the directions under my "Markt to the Moat Stroll," earlier.) At the canal, circle to the left, riding along the former town wall and passing four windmills (including the St. Janshuys Windmill, described earlier). After the last windmill, at Dampoort, turn right across the second of two bridges (at the locks), then continue straight along the north/left bank of the Damme Canal (via Noorweegse Kaai/Damse Vaart-West).*

**The Damme Canal** (Damse Vaart): From Dampoort you'll pedal straight and level along the canal directly to Damme. Start on the left bank because there's no opportunity to cross the canal until you reach the town. The farmland to your left is a polder—long ago a salt marsh that flooded each spring, until it was reclaimed by industrious local farmers. The Damme Canal, also

called the Napoleon Canal, was built in 1811 by Napoleon (actually by his Spanish prisoners) in a failed attempt to reinvigorate Bruges as a port. Today locals fish this canal for eels. Before climate change, skaters eagerly awaited the first winter freeze. Old-timers have fond memories of skating to Holland on this canal—but nowadays such a hard freeze is a rare event (ask locals about the winter of 2008-2009).

**Schelle Windmill** (Schellemolen): Just before arriving in Damme, you'll come upon a working windmill that dates from 1867. This one is ingeniously designed so just the wood cap—rather than the entire building—turns to face the wind. If it's open, climb up through the creaking, spinning, wind-powered gears to the top floor (free, may be closed for renovation—check locally; otherwise open Sat-Sun 9:30-12:30 & 13:00-18:00, closed Mon-Fri and Oct-March).

In its day (13th-15th century), Bruges was one of the top five European ports...and little Damme was important as well. But its once-bustling harbors silted up and the sea retreated. Pause atop the bridge just beyond the windmill, with the windmill on your right and the spire of Bruges' Church of Our Lady poking up in the distance. It's easy to imagine how, at Napoleon's instructions, the canal was designed to mimic a grand Parisian boulevard—leading to the towering church back in Bruges.

• *From here, the canal continues straight to Holland. (If tempted...you're a third of the way to the border.) Instead, cross the bridge and follow Kerkstraat, which cuts through the center of town, to Damme's main square and City Hall.*

**Damme:** Damme was once the place where big oceangoing ships offloaded cargo onto smaller boats to float farther inland to Bruges. Its economy was fishing, shipping, and warehousing. Today's Damme is a tourist center—a tiny version of Bruges. It has a smaller but similar City Hall, a St. John's Hospital, and a big brick Church of Our Lady. Five hundred years ago, Damme must have been rolling in money—its City Hall is made of expensive imported French limestone rather than more typical Belgian brick. Originally the ground floor was a market and fish warehouse, with government offices upstairs.

• *Continue on Kerkstraat as it leads two blocks farther to the Church of Our Lady. Along the way, you could side-trip to the left, down Pottenbakkersstraat, to a quaint little square called Haringmarkt (the Herring Market that made Damme rich in the 15th century). The trees you see from here mark the lines of the town's long-gone 17th-century ramparts.*

*Returning to Kerkstraat, continue on to the big church.*

**The Church of Our Lady:** This church, which rose and fell with the fortunes of Damme, dates from the 13th century. Inside are two Virgin Marys: To the right of the altar is a 1630 wooden statue of Mary, and to the left is Our Lady of the Fishermen (c. 1650, in a glass case). Over the nave stands Belgium's oldest wooden statue, St. Andrew, with his X-shaped cross.

Outside, behind the 13th-century church tower, is a three-faced, modern fiberglass sculpture by the Belgian artist Charles Delporte. Called *View of Light,* it evokes three lights: morning (grace), midday (kindness), and evening (gentleness). If you like his work, there's more at a nearby gallery.

• *To return to Bruges, continue past the church on Kerkstraat. Just before crossing the next bridge, follow a scenic dirt lane to the right that leads you back to the Damme Canal (and Damse Vaart-Zuid). Take this road back to Bruges. If you want a change of pace from the canal, about halfway back turn off to the left (at the white bridge and brick house), then immediately turn right on Polderstraat and follow the smaller canal back to the outskirts of Bruges.*

# BRUGES CITY WALK

Bruges is made for walking. In just a couple of hours, you can get the lay of the land, pop in to a few sights, and mentally bookmark others to come back to later. On this walk, we'll get a sampling of what makes Bruges, Bruges. It's a city with a thousand years of history, and its citizens preserve their buildings and carry on their traditions with pride.

We'll start on the vast square with a towering bell tower that shows off the golden age of the 1400s, when Bruges was one of the richest cities on earth. We'll see art by Memling and Michelangelo, oak pilings from Bruges' foundations, the pious home of cloistered women, and maybe even a few drops of Christ's blood. Along the way you can sample local beer, watch swans glide beneath willow trees, and enjoy postcard views of a tranquil city reflected in a quiet canal.

## Orientation

**Length of This Walk:** Allow two hours for the walk, plus more time for touring sight interiors.

**Sightseeing Tip:** If you're planning to visit all the sights listed on this walk, consider buying the **Musea Brugge Card** sightseeing card sold at City Hall and the Renaissance Hall, near the start of the walk (see page 36).

**Bell Tower:** €14—advance online booking recommended during peak times; open daily 9:00-20:00, Nov and Jan-Feb until 18:00, last entry one hour before closing.

**Basilica of the Holy Blood:** Church-free, treasury-€5, daily 10:00-17:00.

**City Hall and Renaissance Hall:** €7; daily 9:30-17:00.

**Church of Our Lady:** Free to glance down the nave, €7 to see art-filled apse and choir; Mon-Sat 9:30-17:00, Sun from 13:30.

**Sint-Janshospitaal Memling Collection:** May be closed for renovation in 2023; when open likely €12, Tue-Sun 9:30-17:00, closed Mon.

**De Halve Maan Brewery Tour:** €15, tours run on the hour Sun-Fri 11:00-16:00, Sat until 17:00 (smart to book ahead).

**Begijnhof:** Courtyard free to enter, daily 6:30-18:30, vespers service at 16:30.

# The Walk Begins

### ❶ Markt (Market Square)

Ringed by the frilly-spired county hall post office, lots of restaurant terraces, great old gabled buildings, and the massive bell tower, this is the modern heart of the city.

The square is adorned with **flags:** There's the lion flag of Bruges (red, white, and blue) and the lion flag of Flanders (yellow and black)—Bruges is the capital of the region of West Flanders. There's also the flag of Belgium (black, yellow, and red) and the flag of the European Union (blue with yellow stars). Visitors from all over Europe and the world roam the square, in peak season often including large groups of cruise passengers (from the port 10 miles away) following the numbered ping-pong paddles of their guides.

Imagine this square back in the 1300s, during Bruges' glory days as a trading city. Back then (before the geography changed), Bruges itself was a major seaport, with a harbor that connected it to the open sea. Here on the Markt, a canal came right up to the square. Boats once moored next to where the Historium and TI stand today.

Cranes (powered by humans in hamster wheels) loaded and unloaded the boats. Right next to the dock, there was a vast warehouse where businessmen from all nations stored and traded goods. Most of the old buildings are gone, but on the opposite side of the square, locate the rectangular-shaped house with the modern gold ball on top—this is **Bruges' oldest house** (15th century). In former times, farmers shipped their cotton, wool, flax, and hemp to the port at Bruges. The industrious locals would spin, weave, and dye it into a finished product, then load it onto boats to ship throughout the known world.

# Bruges City Walk

CANAL BOAT TOURS
HORSE-AND-BUGGY TOURS

1 Markt
2 Bell Tower
3 Burg Square
4 Basilica of the Holy Blood
5 City Hall
6 Renaissance Hall
7 Ruins in Crowne Plaza Hotel
8 Blinde-Ezelstraat
9 Fish Market
10 Huidevettersplein
11 Postcard Canal View & Canalside Walk
12 Picturesque Bridge & Gruuthuse Palace
13 Church of Our Lady
14 Sint-Janshospitaal Memling Collection
15 Walplein
16 Begijnhof
17 Minnewater

By 1400, Bruggians were trading more refined goods such as trendy clothes, tapestries, chairs, jewelry, and cotton-rag paper—a relatively new innovation (replacing parchment) made in Flanders. One of the Continent's first bookmakers worked here in Bruges.

The **statue** depicts two friends, Jan Breydel and Pieter de Coninck, who helped put this city on the world map. It's the year 1302, and clutching sword and shield, they look toward France, preparing to lead the citizens of Bruges against their French oppressors. The rebels identified potential French spies by demanding they repeat two words—*schild en vriend* (shield and friend)—only Flemish locals (or foreigners with phlegm) could pronounce them. As you can see in the reliefs, the French knights, thinking that fighting these Flemish peasants would be a cakewalk, wore their dress uniforms into battle. But the Flemish cleverly used hooks to pull the knights from their horses, scoring the medieval world's first victory of foot soldiers over cavalry, and of common people over nobility. The peasants had a field day afterward scavenging all the golden spurs from the fallen soldiers. And with that, Flanders won its freedom in what came to be called the Battle of the Golden Spurs.

Want a coffee? Consider the **Café-Brasserie Craenenburg** on the Markt (at #16). The building has been here since the 15th century, and it's been a café since 1905. Most of the square's "typical" old buildings were actually rebuilt in the 19th century. As Bruges recovered from centuries of decline, the city fathers wanted to return it to its former medieval glory. They built in an exaggerated medieval style called Neo-Gothic, full of spiky spires, fanciful towers, lacy stonework, and leering gargoyles. The result is a medieval-era town that actually looks medieval—or "more Gothic than Gothic," as Bruges is often described.

• *Turn your attention to the...*

### ❼ Bell Tower (Belfort)

This bell tower has stood over the Markt since 1300. The octagonal lantern was added in 1486, making it 290 feet high. The tower

displays many architectural elements: medieval crenellations, pointed Gothic arches, round Roman arches, flamboyant spires, and even a few small flying buttresses (two-thirds of the way up).

At the base of the tower is another compelling feature—**Belgian fries.** While locals are fiercely loyal to one stand or the other, you can stay out of the fray and just try some from either of the takeout stands. While the fries come with an array of exotic sauces, traditionally Belgians dip in mayonnaise—not ketchup!

Enter the courtyard. The public sits on benches here to enjoy free **carillon concerts** (several times a week—see the posted schedule and photos under the arch where you entered). A pay WC is in the courtyard.

The tower has 47 bells that chime periodically. Every 15 minutes, the carillon plays a little ditty. This is done mechanically, through the action of a giant barrel and movable tabs (like a barrel organ or player-piano roll). At other times, there's a human carillonneur who plays concerts, using a keyboard and foot pedal (like an organist). In fact, playing the carillon is so strenuous that the musician needs to use fists and feet, rather than fingers.

You can **climb the tower** (though the entry fee is steeper than its 366 steps). Just before you reach the top, peek into the carillon room to see the mechanisms. Be there on the quarter hour, when things ring (the bell experience is best at the top of the hour). Atop the tower, survey Bruges. On the horizon, you can see the towns along the North Sea coast.

• *Back out on the square, get oriented. Steenstraat, the people-packed main shopping street, stretches from in front of the belfry to the big 't Zand Square and eventually all the way to the train station. Geldmuntstraat, a block northwest of the square, has fun shops and eateries you might check out later.*

*Now, facing the bell tower, turn left (east) onto Breidelstraat, and thread yourself through the lace and waffles to...*

## ❸ Burg Square

For over a thousand years, this opulent square has been Bruges' historical birthplace, political center, and religious heart. Today it's still the place where the citizens of Bruges carry on timeless traditions in local festivals and parades.

Pan the square counterclockwise to see six centuries of architecture. You'll go from Romanesque (the interior of the fancy, gray-and-gold Basilica of the Holy Blood, in the corner), to the pointed Gothic arches and prickly steeples of the white sandstone City Hall, to the well-proportioned windows of the Renaissance Hall (next door, under the gilded statues). Continue spinning, past the park, until you reach the elaborate 17th-century Baroque Provost's House (at the head of Breidelstraat).

## Bruges History

**Beginnings:** The city is founded in the 800s as a safe haven from Viking raiders.

**1100s Piety:** The relic of the Holy Blood makes Bruges a major pilgrimage destination.

**1200s Growth:** With its harbor on an inlet, Bruges begins trading with oceangoing ships as far as England (for raw wool) and the Mediterranean.

**1300s Independence:** Flanders wins its independence from France.

**1400s Golden Age:** This is Bruges' glory time, when trade, textile manufacture, pioneering painters, and a population of 150,000 make it one of Europe's greatest cities.

**1500s Changes:** Bruges and Flanders become part of the vast Habsburg empire—both augmenting the city and diminishing its independence.

**1600s Decline:** The harbor silts up, and trade routes shift, beginning two centuries of decline.

**1800s Inertia:** Bruges is a poor, rundown village adrift in an Industrial Age world. But its very backwardness inspires an idea...

**1900s Revival:** The citizens revamp the medieval (and medieval-looking) city, attracting visitors from around the world.

Now backtrack to the modern Crowne Plaza Hotel, which sits atop thousand-year-old ruins (we'll visit shortly).

Dominating the square is **City Hall,** a symbol of Bruges' proud independence. The facade's 49 statues feature several key figures in Bruges' history. Baldwin I (bottom row, fourth statue from left) built a fort here in the 9th century, founding Bruges. Thierry of Alsace (in the upper-right tower) grabs his sword, hoping to secure the holy relic that would put Bruges on the pilgrimage map.

• *Let's go see the relic. Approach the gray building decorated with gold statues in the corner of Burg Square.*

## ❹ Basilica of the Holy Blood

The gleaming knights and ladies on the church's facade remind us that this church was built (c. 1150) by a brave Crusader to house the drops of Christ's blood he'd brought back from Jerusalem. The relic is still here today, and it still connects the people of Bruges to their roots.

**Visiting the Basilica:** Start by entering the ground-level lower chapel through the door labeled *St.-Basiliuskapel.*

**Lower Chapel:** The stark and dim decor reeks of the medieval piety that drove crusading Christian Europeans to try to free the

## The Legend of the Holy Blood

Several drops of Christ's blood, washed from his lifeless body by Joseph of Arimathea, were preserved in a rock-crystal vial in Jerusalem. In 1150, the patriarch of Jerusalem gave the blood to a Flemish soldier, Thierry of Alsace, as thanks for rescuing his city from the Muslims during the Second Crusade. Thierry returned home and donated it to the city. The old, dried blood suddenly turned to liquid, a miracle repeated every Friday for the next two centuries, and verified by thousands of pilgrims from around Europe who flocked here to adore it. The blood dried up for good in 1325.

Every year on Ascension Day (the 40th day after Easter), Bruges' bankers, housewives, and waffle vendors put on old-time costumes for the parading of the vial through the city. The slow-mo parade involves 1,700 locals and 50 floats: Crusader knights re-enact the bringing of the relic, Joseph of Arimathea washes Christ's body, and ladies in medieval costume with hair tied up in horn-like hairnets come out to wave flags. It takes 1.5 hours to watch the entire processional trudge past from beginning to end. Most of the remaining Bruges citizens just take the day off.

Holy Land from Muslim rule. With heavy columns and round arches, the style is pure Romanesque. Step into the annex to see somber statues of Christ being tortured and entombed, plus a 12th-century relief panel over a doorway—it shows St. Basil (a fourth-century scholar-monk) being baptized by a double-jointed priest, and a man-size dove of the Holy Spirit. Now let's visit the place where the holy relic is kept.

• *To reach the upper chapel, go back outside and up the staircase.*

**Upper Chapel:** This chapel is as bright and cheery as the lower one was dim. After being gutted by secular-humanist French revolutionaries in 1799, the upper chapel's original Romanesque decor was redone by 19th-century Romantics in a Neo-Gothic style. The nave is colorful, with a curved wooden ceiling, painted walls, a round pulpit carved from a single massive oak, and stained-glass windows of the dukes who ruled Flanders, along with their duchesses.

The **big painting** stretching behind the main altar tells the story of how the Holy Blood got here. Find Thierry of Alsace, count of Flanders (kneeling at lower left), the Crusader knight who brought the relic here. Having helped defend Bethlehem *(Bethlema)* and Jerusalem *(Hierosolyma)* from Muslim incursions, he kneels before the grateful Christian patriarch of Jerusalem, who rewards him with the relic. Thierry returns home (right) and kneels before Bruges' bishop to give him the vial of blood. This church was built to display the relic for the hordes of believers who flocked to see it and feel its miraculous powers.

The **relic** itself—some red stuff preserved inside a clear, six-inch tube of rock crystal—is kept in the adjoining room (through the three arches). It's in the tall, silver tabernacle on the altar. (The tabernacle's doors are typically open daily from noon to 16:00 so you can actually see the vial of blood.) On holy days, the relic is shifted across the room and displayed on the throne under the canopy.

• *For more on the relic, step into the adjoining treasury (requires a ticket).*

**Treasury:** Here you can see the impressive gold and silver, gem-studded, hexagonal **reliquary** (c. 1600, left wall) that the vial of blood is paraded around in on feast days. The vial is placed in the "casket" at the bottom of the three-foot-tall structure. Flanking the shrine are paintings of the Brotherhood of the Holy Blood. For centuries, this 31-member fraternity has tended the shrine and organized the pageantry. The Brotherhood is still in action today, and it's their job to carry the reliquary on their shoulders, parading it through the city streets on special occasions.

Elsewhere in the room are the Brotherhood's **ceremonial objects:** necklaces, chalices, and so on. A centuries-old hunting horn is used to sound the alarm every year on the anniversary of the murder of a Flemish nobleman 100 yards from here, back in 1127 (which coincidentally allowed Thierry to take power). You may also see a fine tapestry, a remnant of Bruges' glory days of textile manufacture.

Finally, find the **small lead box** holding a broken glass tube. This is a replica of the precious rock-crystal vial that holds the blood of Christ. The lead box once protected the vial of blood from Protestant extremists (1578) and French revolutionaries (1799) bent on destroying what, to them, was a glaring symbol of Catholic mumbo jumbo.

• *Go back out into the square.*

# ❺ City Hall (Stadhuis)

Built in about 1400, when Bruges was a thriving bastion of capital-ism with a population of 35,000, this building served as a model

for Town Halls elsewhere, including Brussels. The white sandstone facade is studded with statues of knights, nobles, and saints with prickly Gothic steeples over their heads. A colorful double band of coats of arms represent the towns of Flanders. The building is still the City Hall, so it's not unusual to see couples arriving here to get married.

**Visiting City Hall:** The ground-level lobby leads you to a **picture gallery** (free, closed Mon) with scenes and portraits from Belgium's history, from the Spanish king to the arrival of Napoleon, shown meeting the mayor here at the City Hall in 1803. Don't miss the two paintings (behind glass) that show the Markt and Burg Square in the 1600s. The mayor's office is at the end of the hallway.

• *You can pay to climb the stairs for a look at the...*

**Gothic Room:** Some of modern democracy's roots lie in this ornate room, where, for centuries, the city council has met to dis-

cuss the town's affairs (as it still does monthly). In 1464, one of Europe's first parliaments, the Estates General of the Low Countries, convened here. The fireplace at the far end is inscribed with a 1305 proclamation: "All the ar-tisans, laborers...and citizens of Bruges are free—all of them."

The elaborately carved and paint-ed wooden ceiling (a Neo-Gothic re-construction from the 19th century) features tracery in gold, red, and black. Five dangling arches ("pendentives") hang down the center, now adorned with modern floodlights.

The late-19th-century Ro-mantic **wall murals** depict epi-sodes in the city's history. (Info sheets tell the stories scene by scene.) For a few highlights, start with the largest painting along the left wall, and work clockwise.

In the **big painting on the left wall,** everyone cheers, flags wave, trumpets blare, and dogs bark as Bruges' knights, dressed in gold with black Flemish lions, return triumphant after driving out French oppressors and winning Flanders' independence. The Battle of the Golden Spurs (1302) is remembered every July 11.

Next, the **painting on the fireplace wall** shows cardinals in red flocking to this elaborate ceremony. In what may have been Bruges' high-water mark, Philip the Good of Burgundy (seated, in black) assembled his court here in Bruges and solemnly founded the knightly Order of the Golden Fleece (1429).

Next, the Crusader knight, Thierry of Alsace, returns from the Holy Land and kneels at the entrance of St. Basil's Chapel to present the relic of Christ's Holy Blood (c. 1150).

On the **back wall,** it's a typical market day at the Halls (the courtyard behind the bell tower). Arabs mingle with Germans in fur-lined coats and beards in a market where they sell everything from armor to lemons.

And finally, a bishop blesses a new canal (1404) as ships sail right by the city. This was Bruges in its heyday, before the silting of the harbor. At the far right, the two bearded men with moustaches are the brothers who painted these murals.

**Adjoining Room:** Old paintings and maps show how little the city has changed through the centuries. Find a copy of one well-known **map** (in pale white, aqua, and gold at the end of the left wall). It shows in fascinating detail the city as it looked in 1562. Find the bell tower, the Church of Our Lady, and Burg Square, which back then was bounded on the north by a cathedral. Notice the canal (on the west)  leading from the North Sea right to the Markt. A moat encircled the city with its gates, unfinished wall, and 28 windmills (four of which survive today). The mills pumped water to the town's fountains, ground grain, made paper, and functioned as the motor of the Middle Ages. Many locals own a copy of this map that shows how their neighborhood looked 400 years ago.

• *Leaving City Hall, turn right and go to the corner of the square to enter...*

## ❻ Renaissance Hall (Brugse Vrije)

This elaborately adorned mansion has served Bruges as a governing palace, a courthouse, and (today) as the city archives. The white facade with gold and red trim dates from the 1720s. Notice the crowned heads, each with its unique personality.

**Visiting the Hall:** Go inside to find the elaborately decorated Renaissance Hall. If you're into heraldry, it's fascinating. If not, you'll wonder where the rest of the museum is.

This ornate room was where the town's burghers met. They'd sit on the green benches around the perimeter, under a lavish wood-beamed ceiling and surrounded by tapestry-covered walls. The big green table at one end is where they played medieval snooker. (Actually, it was the dais for the presiding bigwigs.)

The highlight of the room is the grand **fireplace mantelpiece** carved from oak by Bruges' Renaissance Man, Lancelot Blondeel,

in 1531. In the center of it stands the most powerful man in Europe—Holy Roman Emperor Charles V. His crown, sword, and orb symbolize his power—as does his bulging codpiece.

Charles had recently freed Bruges (yet again) from French rule, making the city part of his pan-European Habsburg empire, so the city fathers honored him here. They also included their hometown duke (to the left), who was related to Charles.

The duke's crown, orb, and codpiece mirror those of Charles, indicating the family jewels were well-guarded. By making the connection to the Holy Roman Emperor clear, this carved family tree helped substantiate the power of Bruges' nobility. You'll also see the double-eagle emblem (above Charles and elsewhere in the room), the Habsburg family symbol. The other coats of arms belong to the many European nobles under Charles' powerful reign. Check out the expressive little cherubs.

Notice the **painting** that stands nearby. It depicts this very same hall you're standing in: There's the fireplace, the same paneled walls, and the raised green table where justices sat in judgment. The painting shows the room in action in 1659, as the lace-collared judges hear the pleas of a repentant man before deciding his punishment. One of the judges is about to pull that long chain to ring a bell and seal his fate.

• *Leaving the building, walk straight ahead and hook around the cream-colored building to your right.*

## ❼ Ruins in the Crowne Plaza Hotel

One of the old town's newest buildings (1992) sits atop the ruins of the town's oldest structures—the original fort that established Bruges. In the late 9th century, when Viking ships regularly docked here to rape and pillage, Baldwin I (also known as Iron Arm) built a fort *(castrum)* to protect his Flemish people. In 950, the fort was converted into St. Donatian's Church, which became one of the city's largest. That church was destroyed in the 1800s during Napoleon's invasion (leaving nothing but a park bordering Burg Square). In the 20th century, the Crowne Plaza rose over the ruins, but only on the condition that visitors be allowed to see them.

**Visiting the Ruins:** Ask at the hotel's reception desk to see the archaeological site (ruins of the fort and the church). If there's no conference in progress, they'll let you walk down the stairs and have a peek.

In the basement, the modern conference rooms are lined with old stone walls and display cases of objects found in the ruins of earlier structures. Trace the history.

See thousand-year-old oak pilings, carved to a point, once driven into this former peat bog to support the original fort and

shore up its moat. Next, see paintings that show the church that replaced it. The curved stone walls you walk among are from the foundations of the ambulatory around the church altar.

A document (*Vente de Materiaux*, posted back where you entered) announces the "sale of material" when Napoleon destroyed the church in the early 1800s and auctioned off the bricks. A local builder bought them, and now pieces of the old cathedral are embedded in other buildings throughout Bruges.

Display cases around the room show what modern archaeologists found around here—the refuse of a thousand years of habitation: pottery, animal skulls, rosary beads, dice, coins, keys, thimbles, pipes, spoons, and Delftware. There's also a 14th-century sarcophagus painted with the Crucifixion on the west end and a Virgin and Child on the east.

• *Back on Burg Square, find the passageway by Renaissance Hall. This alley is called...*

## ❽ Blinde-Ezelstraat

At the alley's entrance—on the corner of City Hall—is a **statue of the Virgin Mary** known to locals as Our Lady of the Inkpot. In past times, locals nodded to the statue as they passed, and she is still the protector of the town council.

Head down the alley. Midway down on the left side (thigh

level), see an original **iron hinge** from the city's south gate, back when the city was ringed by a moat and closed nightly at 22:00. On the right wall, at eye level, a square black patch shows you just how grimy the city had become before a 1960s cleaning. Despite the clean-ing and a few fanciful reconstructions, the city today looks much as it did in centuries past.

The name "Blinde-Ezelstraat" means "Blind Donkey Street." Perhaps in medieval times, the donkeys, carrying fish from the North Sea on their backs, were stopped here so that their owners could put blinders on them. Otherwise, the donkeys wouldn't cross the water between the old city and the fish market.

From the end of the alleyway, look back and up for a nice pho-to-op of the Goldfinger family standing atop the alley's sky bridge.
• *Step onto the bridge over one of Bruges' many canals. This particular canal was the 13th-century city moat around the old town. Crossing the bridge, ahead on your left you can see are the arcades of the...*

## ❾ Fish Market (Vismarkt)

The North Sea is just about 10 miles away and until a generation ago, this was a thriving fish market. Its fine ar-cades were built in the 17th century with Tuscan pillars. Locals loved the shrimp—cooked on the boat before arriving at the market. Today, one stall still sells fish, the rest sell mostly crafts and souvenirs...and tourists are the big catch.
• *Take an immediate right (west), entering a courtyard called...*

## ❿ Huidevettersplein

This tiny, picturesque, restau-rant-filled square was origi-nally the headquarters of the town's skinners and tanners. The lions atop the square's lone column hold the tanners' logo. On the facade of the Hotel

Duc de Bourgogne, four old relief panels above the windows show scenes from the leather trade—once a leading Bruges industry. First, tan the hide in a bath of acid; then, with tongs, pull it out to dry; then beat it to make it soft; and, finally, scrape and clean it to make it ready for sale.

• *Continue a few steps to Rozenhoedkaai street, where you can look back to your right and get a great...*

## ⓫ Postcard Canal View and Canalside Walk

The bell tower reflected in a quiet canal lined with old houses—this view is the essence of Bruges. (When I told a local friend "It looks just like Amsterdam," she said, "No, Amsterdam looks just like Bruges.") Seeing buildings rising straight from the water makes you understand why this has also been called the Venice of the North. Can you see the bell tower's tilt? It leans about four feet. The tilt has been carefully monitored since 1740, but no change has been detected.

The tourist boat landing below originally served salt merchants and fishermen with goods for the market. All of these canals were a practical necessity as the city was built upon a swamp with a high water table. And through the centuries, shipping was actually cheaper and safer by boat than over land.

As you face the view, to your left (west) down the Dijver canal (past a weekend flea market) looms the huge spire of the Church of Our Lady, the tallest brick spire in the Low Countries. Between you and the church is Europa College, a prestigious post-graduate institution that has produced many well-known "Eurocrats"—diplomats, lawyers, and economists who run the European Union.

Walk ahead, toward the steeple of Our Lady. Beer lovers can detour over the first bridge: The first door on the right leads to the 2Be bar with its **"beerwall"** (described on page 105); the first left lane leads to the **Bourgogne des Flandres Brewery** (described on page 48).

Back on Dijver, about 100 yards ahead on the left, is the copper-colored sign that points the way to the **Groeninge Museum.** This sumptuous collection of paintings highlights Bruges' own Flemish Primitives, with all their glorious detail (□ see the Groeninge Museum Tour chapter).

Continue another half-block past the Groeninge Museum. At

Dijver 16, turn left into a quiet courtyard. You'll pass by the entrance to the little **Arentshuis Museum,** featuring the art of Frank Brangwyn (described on page 40).

• *Continue through the courtyard to the far right corner, where you'll find a...*

## ⑫ Picturesque Bridge and Gruuthuse Palace

Standing atop this tiny stone bridge over a little canal, take in the scene and savor its beauty. Start with the back end of the church, admiring Our Lady's big buttresses and round apse. Panning clockwise, find a teenytiny window at the corner of a building—a tollkeeper's lookout. Below that, at canal level, you could snap a photo of your travel partner at the iron bars. Continue panning until you find the old relief panel of a boat (directly behind you) celebrat-

ing the work of the fishermen's guild. Next comes the old wooden house along the canal. The city was once made of wood like this. Fires were a big problem, so brick rather than wood became the norm—both safer and a symbol of wealth.

Cross the bridge and veer to the right down a narrow path to the courtyard (on the right) of the **Gruuthuse palace.** Above the door, find a carving of the first great Gruuthuse on a horse from 1415—with his motto below, which roughly translates to "Don't underestimate yourself." Tickets to the fine Gruuthuse Museum and the Church of Our Lady are sold at the modern ticket booth in this courtyard (for museum details, see page 40).

• *Exiting the courtyard, walk along around the side of the church to find the entry to the...*

## ⑬ Church of Our Lady (Onze-Lieve-Vrouwekerk)

This towering brick church stands as a memorial to the power and wealth of Bruges in its heyday. Step inside. While you can stand in the back and marvel at its interior for free, to get a close-up look at its historic tombs and art—including a Michelangelo sculpture—you'll need to pay for a ticket.

**Visiting the Church:** Enter and stand in the back to admire the

Church of Our Lady—whitewashed walls below, gray stone mid-way up, and a red-brick ceiling above. Its 14th- and 15th-century stained glass was destroyed by iconoclasts, so the church is lit more brightly today than originally. Like most churches in Belgium, this one is Catholic. The medieval-style screen (topped with the organ) once divided the clergy from the commoners who gathered here in the nave. Worshippers are still attended by 12 Gothic-era statues of apostles, each with his symbol, and by a grandiose Baroque wooden pulpit, with a roof that seems to float in midair. It was from this fancy perch that the priest would interpret the word of God.

If you have a ticket for the complete visit, there is plenty of interest to see. Here are the highlights:

**Tombs at the High Altar:** The altar features the Passion Triptych from 1534 with five dramatic scenes culminating in the crucifixion. Two statues lying atop coffins mark the tombs of the last local rulers of Bruges: Mary of Burgundy and her father, Charles the Bold. The dog and lion at their feet are symbols of fidelity and courage. Underneath the tombs are the actual excavated gravesites with mirrors to help you see the well-lit, centuries-old tomb paintings.

These tombs represent the point in time when the city began its slow, four-century decline. Charles the Bold died prematurely, in war, in 1477. And in 1482, 25-year-old Mary tumbled from her horse and died. She left behind a toddler son and a husband who was heir to the Holy Roman Empire. The twin deaths meant Bruges now belonged to Austria and would soon be swallowed up by the empire and ruled from Vienna by Habsburgs—who didn't understand or care about its problems. Meanwhile, Bruges' North Sea port silted up, and trade routes shifted to nearby Antwerp and Amsterdam. The city was eventually mothballed—until this sleeping beauty of Flemish towns was rediscovered by modern-day tourists. The first tourists were Americans and Canadians who came in the wake of World War I to visit the graves of loved ones in nearby cemeteries.

To the left of the altar is a wooden balcony on the wall. It's part of the Gruuthuse mansion next door (now a museum), and once provided that noble family with prime seats for Mass.

To the right of the altar is a side chapel with fascinating 14th-century tombs found during excavations. Some are painted with images of Mary as Queen of Heaven (on a throne, carrying a crown and scepter) and Mother of God (with the Baby Jesus on her lap). Since Mary is in charge of advocating with Jesus for your salvation, she's a good person to have painted on the wall of your tomb. The tombs also show lots of angels—generally patron saints of the dead person—swinging incense burners.

*Madonna and Child* by Michelangelo: This small marble Michelangelo statue is an artistic highlight in this city of art. It's the only Michelangelo statue to leave Italy in the artist's lifetime, bought in Tuscany by a wealthy Bruges businessman, who's buried in the same chapel (to the right).

As Michelangelo chipped away at the masterpiece of his youth, *David*, he took breaks by carving this one in 1504. Mary, slightly smaller than life-size, sits while young Jesus stands in front of her. Their expressions are mirror images—serene, but a bit melancholy, with downcast eyes, as though pondering the young child's dangerous future. Though they're lost in thought, their hands instinctively link, tenderly. The white Carrara marble is highly polished, something Michelangelo only did when he was certain he'd gotten it right.

• *Near the church on Mariastraat is the entrance to perhaps the city's most visit-worthy museum—though note that it may be closed for renovation during your visit.*

## ⓮ Sint-Janshospitaal (St. John's Hospital)

When open, the former wards and church of Sint-Janshospitaal are home to a museum with two delightful elements: a look at the one-time hospital's main hall, filled with displays on medieval medicine; and a collection of masterpieces by Hans Memling, the German painter who made his artistic mark in Bruges.

☐ See the Sint-Janshospitaal Memling Collection Tour chapter.

• *Leaving the museum, turn right and go about 30 paces to enjoy a fine canal view. Before you is one of many canal tour boat companies. The canal here was once part of the city moat. Standing here in the 15th century, you would have just left town through the Maria Gate.*

*Continue 50 yards down Katelijnestraat, then turn right and go down a tiny lane, Stoofstraat. This was "Stove Street"—where the neighborhood's public bathhouse stood—which in times past served (like ancient Roman baths) as a place to bathe, work out, and socialize. Stoofstraat leads into the pleasant square called...*

## ⓯ Walplein

Leafy Walplein square was the original brewing center of Bruges. Ahead on the right, De Halve Maan Brewery is one of two breweries in town still giving tours. On busy days, tours can fill up, so you may want to reserve a spot online or call in advance (see page 47).

A half-block to your left down Walstraat at #6 is the recommended **Dumon** chocolate shop.

• *Leaving the leafy square at the far end, turn right on Wijngaartstraat. You'll reach a **horse-head fountain**, where the horse-and-buggy horses stop to drink. From the fountain, turn right and pause in the center of a picturesque pedestrian bridge. Before you, above the gate, a sign reads* Sauve Garde—*you are entering the protection of the sisters and leaving the jurisdiction of the city. The relief above shows St. Elizabeth taking care of the handicapped. Walk through the gate (open until 18:30) and, as the lacy charm of Bruges crescendos, enter the...*

### ⑯ Begijnhof

Begijnhofs (buh-*H*INE-hof) were built to house women of the lay order, called Beguines. Though obedient to a mother superior, they did not have to take the vows of a nun. They spent their days deep in prayer, spinning wool, making lace, teaching, and caring for the sick. The Beguines' ranks swelled during the golden age, when so many women were widowed or unwed due to the hazards of war and overseas trade. The order of Beguines offered such women a dignified place to live and work. When the order died out, many begijnhofs were taken over by towns for subsidized housing. Today, single religious women live

in the small homes. A few Benedictine nuns still live in a building on the far side.

In the **church,** enjoy the peaceful interior, with its carved pulpit and tombstones on the floor. The altar has corkscrew columns and a painting of the Beguines' patron, St. Elizabeth of Hungary. On the right wall is an 800-year-old gilded statue of Mary. The rope that dangles from the ceiling is yanked by a nun to announce a sung vespers service. The Benedictine nuns gather at 16:30 daily for this worship service, which includes the sisters singing and chanting a cappella in the choir of the church. The public is welcome.

• *Exiting the church, turn left, and leave the Begijnhof courtyard. Take your first left, through the gate, to a view of the lake known as...*

## ⓱ Minnewater

Just south of the Begijnhof is Minnewater ("Lake of Love"), a peaceful, lake-filled park with canals, weeping willows, and swans. This was once far from quaint—it was a busy harbor where small boats shuttled cargo not from seagoing vessels but from shipping on the inland canal system (mostly from Ghent) onto smaller barges. From this point, the cargo was transferred to flat-bottomed boats that went through the town's canals to their respective warehouses and to the Markt. Today, Minnewater is actually a reservoir designed to regulate the water level of Bruges' canals and control flooding.

When locals see swans gliding on the water here, they recall the 15th-century mayor—famous for his long neck—who collaborated with the Austrians. The towns-folk beheaded him as a traitor. The Austrians warned them that similarly long-necked swans would inhabit the place to forever remind them of this murder. And they do. With this sweet little murder story, we end our tour of perhaps the cutest town in Europe.

• *You're a 5-minute walk from the train station or a 15-minute walk from the Markt. If you walk back to the town center, consider a detour along Nieuwe Gentweg to visit one of about 20* **almshouses** *in the city. At #8, go through the door marked* Godshuis de Meulenaere 1613 *into the peaceful courtyard (free). This was a medieval form of housing for the poor. The rich would pay for someone's tiny room here in return for lots of prayers.*

# GROENINGE MUSEUM TOUR

*Groeningemuseum*

In the 1400s, Bruges was northern Europe's richest, most cosmopolitan, and most cultured city. New ideas, fads, and painting techniques were imported and exported with each shipload. Beautiful paintings were soon an affordable luxury, like fancy clothes or furniture. Internationally known artists set up studios in Bruges, producing portraits and altarpieces for wealthy merchants from all over Europe.

Understandably, the Groeninge Museum has one of the world's best collections of the art produced in the city and surrounding area.

Early Flemish art is less appreciated and understood today than the Italian Renaissance art of the same era. This chapter highlights several masterpieces to give you an introduction to this subtle, technically advanced, and beautiful style. Hey, if you can master the museum's name (HROON-ih-guh), you can certainly handle the art.

As you wander, notice that many artists, having lived and worked in Bruges, included scenes of the picturesque city in their pieces, proving that it looks today much as it did way back when. Enjoy the many painted scenes of old Bruges as a slice-of-life peek into the city and its people back in its glory days.

# Orientation

**Cost:** €14.

**Hours:** Tue-Sun 9:30-17:00, closed Mon.

**Information:** +32 50 448 743, www.museabrugge.be.

**Getting There:** The museum is at Dijver 12, near the Church of Our Lady.

**Tours:** Use the museum's QR code to download a free audioguide.

**Length of This Tour:** Allow one hour.

**Starring:** The meticulous details and limpid atmosphere of Flemish Primitive art; Jan van Eyck's *Canon Joris* and *Portrait of Margareta van Eyck;* and Rogier van der Weyden's *Duke Philip the Good.*

# The Tour Begins

The collection fills 10 rooms on one easy floor, arranged chronologically from the 15th to the 20th century. As the collection is far bigger than the actual gallery, some paintings featured here may be rotated out or in a different location. English information cards are available in each room.

## GOLDEN AGE MASTERS

In Rooms 1-3, look for the following paintings—the core of the collection.

### Jan van Eyck, *Madonna with Canon Joris van der Paele,* 1436

Jan van Eyck (c. 1390-1441) was the world's first and greatest oil painter, and this is his masterpiece—three debatable but defensible assertions.

Mary, in a magnificent red gown, sits playing with her little baby, Jesus. Jesus glances up as St. George, the dragon-slaying knight, enters the room, tips his cap, and says, "I'd like to introduce my namesake, George (Joris)." Mary glances down at the kneeling Joris, a church official dressed in white. Joris takes off his glasses and looks up from his prayer book to see a bishop in blue, St. Donatian, patron of the church he hopes to be buried in.

Canon Joris, who hired Van Eyck, is not a pretty sight. He's old and wrinkled, with a double chin, weird earlobes, and blood-

## Flemish Primitives

Despite the "Primitive" label, the Low Countries of the 1400s (along with Venice and Florence) produced the most refined art in Europe. Here are some common features of Flemish Primitive art.

**Primitive 3-D Perspective:** Expect unnaturally cramped-looking rooms; oddly slanted tables; and flat, cardboard-cutout people with stiff postures. Yes, these works are more primitive (hence the label) than those using later Italian Renaissance perspective.

**Realism:** Everyday bankers and clothmakers in their Sunday best are painted with clinical, warts-and-all precision. Even saints and heavenly visions are brought down to earth.

**Details:** Like meticulous Bruges craftsmen, painters used fine-point brushes to capture almost microscopic details—flower petals, wrinkled foreheads, intricately patterned clothes, the sparkle in a ruby. The closer you get to a painting, the better it looks.

**Oil Painted on Wood:** They were the pioneers of newfangled oil-based paint (while Italy still used egg-yolk tempera), working on wood before canvas became popular.

**Portraits and Altarpieces:** Wealthy merchants and clergymen paid to have themselves painted either alone or mingling with saints.

**Symbolism:** In earlier times, everyone understood that a dog symbolized fidelity, a lily meant chastity, and a rose was love.

**Materialism:** Rich Flanders celebrated the beauty of luxury goods—the latest Italian dresses, jewels, carpets, oak tables—and the ordinary beauty that radiates from flesh-and-blood people.

GROENINGE MUSEUM

shot eyes. But the portrait isn't unflattering; it just shows unvarnished reality with crystal clarity.

Van Eyck brings Mary and the saints down from heaven and into a typical (rich) Bruges home. He strips off their haloes, banishes all angels, and pulls the plug on heavenly radiance. If this is a religious painting, then where's God?

God's in the details. From the bishop's damask robe and Mary's wispy hair to the folds in Jesus' baby fat and the oriental carpet to "Adonai" (Lord) written on St. George's breastplate, the painting is as complex and beautiful as God's creation. The color scheme—red Mary, white canon, and blue-and-gold saints—are Bruges' city colors, from its coat of arms.

Mary, crowned with a jeweled "halo" and surrounded by beautiful things, makes an appearance in 1400s Bruges, where she can be adored in all her human beauty by Canon Joris...and by us, reflected in the mirror-like shield on St. George's back.

### Jan van Eyck, *Portrait of Margareta van Eyck,* 1439

At 35, shortly after moving to Bruges, Jan van Eyck married 20-year-old Margareta. They had two kids, and after Jan died, Margareta took charge of his studio of assistants and kept it running until her death. This portrait (age 33), when paired with a matching self-portrait of Jan, was one of Europe's first husband-and-wife companion sets.

She sits half-turned, looking out of the frame. (Jan might have seen this "where-have-you-been?" expression in the window late one night.) She's dressed in a red, fur-lined coat, and we catch a glimpse of her wedding ring. Her hair is invisible—very fashionable at the time—pulled back tightly, bunched into horn-like hairnets, and draped with a headdress. Stray hairs along the perimeter were plucked to achieve the high forehead look.

This simple portrait is revolutionary—one of history's first individual portraits that wasn't of a saint, a king, a duke, or a pope, and wasn't part of a religious work. It signals the advent of humanism, celebrating the glory of ordinary people. Van Eyck proudly signed the work on the original frame, with his motto saying he painted it *"als ik kan" (ALC IXH KAN)...*"as good as I can."

### Rogier van der Weyden, *St. Luke Drawing the Madonna,* c. 1500

Rogier van der Weyden (c. 1399-1464), the other giant among the Flemish Primitives, added the human touch to Van Eyck's rather detached precision. He is thought to have created the original of this composition for the chapel of St. Luke's Guild in Brussels.

As Mary prepares to nurse her child, Baby Jesus can't contain his glee, wiggling his fingers and toes, anticipating lunch. Mary, dressed in everyday clothes, doesn't try to hide her love as she tilts her head down with a proud smile. Meanwhile, St. Luke (the patron saint of painters, who was said to have experienced this vision) looks on intently with a sketch pad in his hand, trying to catch the scene. These small gestures, movements, and facial expressions add an element of human emotion that later artists would amplify.

The painting is neatly divided by a spacious view out the window, showing a river stretching off to a spacious horizon. Van der Weyden experimented with 3-D effects like this one (though ultimately it's just window-dressing).

### Rogier van der Weyden, *Duke Philip the Good,* c. 1450

Tall, lean, and elegant, this charismatic duke transformed Bruges from a commercial powerhouse to a cultural one. In 1425, Philip moved his court to Bruges, making it the de facto capital of a Burgundian empire stretching from Amsterdam to Switzerland.

Philip wears a big hat to hide his hair, a fashion trend he himself began. He's also wearing the gold-chain necklace of the Order of the Golden Fleece, a distinguished knightly honor he gave himself. He inaugurated the Golden Fleece in a lavish ceremony at the Bruges City Hall, complete with parades, jousting, and festive pies that contained live people hiding inside to surprise his guests.

As a lover of painting, hunting, fine clothes, and many mistresses, Philip was a role model for Italian princes, such as Lorenzo the Magnificent—the *uomo universale,* the Renaissance Man.

### Hugo van der Goes, *Death of the Virgin,* c. 1470

The long deathwatch is over—their beloved Mary has passed, and the disciples are dazed with grief, as though hit with a spiritual two-by-four. Each face is a study in sadness, all coping differently—lighting a candle, fidgeting, praying, or just staring off into space. Blues and reds dominate, and there's little eye-catching ornamentation, which lets the lined faces and expressive hand gestures do the talking.

Hugo van der Goes (c. 1430-c. 1482) painted this, his last major work, the same year he attempted suicide. He had built a successful career in Ghent, then abruptly dropped out to join a monastery. His paintings became increasingly emotionally charged, his personality more troubled.

Above the bed floats a heavenly vision, as Jesus and the angels prepare to receive Mary's soul. Their smooth skin and serene expressions contrast with the gritty, wrinkled death pallor of those on earth. Caught up in their own grief, the disciples can't see the silver lining.

**Hans Memling, *The Moreel Triptych,* 1484**

Memling (c. 1430-1494), though born in Germany, became Bruges' most famous painter. This triptych (three-paneled altarpiece) fuses the detail of Van Eyck with the balanced compositions of (his probable teacher) Rogier van der Weyden, while introducing his own innovations.

This is perhaps the art world's first group portrait, and everything about it celebrates the family of Willem Moreel, the wealthy two-term mayor of Bruges. In the center is St. Christopher—patron saint of seafarers—who brought wealth to the merchant Moreel family. He's shown (according to the traditional legend) as a gentle giant graciously carrying Baby Jesus across a river. Christopher is flanked by St. Maurus (the black-robed monk with staff and book) and St. Giles (a hermit whose only companion was a red deer). These two saints represent the family names of Moreel (from Maurus) and his wife.

The true stars of the triptych are not the saints but the earthbound mortals who paid for it. Moreel (left panel) kneels in devotion along with his five sons (and St. William, who was Willem's patron saint). Barbara (right) kneels with their 13 daughters (and her patron saint, Barbara). Memling's skills as a portraitist capture 20 different personalities in this large family. He sets all the figures in a single landscape—note that the horizon line stretches across all three panels. Saints and mortals mingle in this unique backdrop that's both down-to-earth (the castle, plants, and St. Barbara's stunning dress) and ethereal (the weird rock formations and unnaturally pristine light). The glowing Christ child sits at the peak of this balanced composition. Memling creates a motionless, peaceful

---

# Oil Paint

Take vegetable oil pressed from linseeds (flax), blend in dry powdered pigments, whip to a paste the consistency of room-temperature butter, then brush onto a panel of whitewashed oak—you're painting in oils. First popularized in the early 1400s, oil eventually overshadowed egg-yolk-based tempera. Though tempera was great for making fine lines shaded with simple blocks of color, oil could blend colors together seamlessly.

Watch a master create a single dog's hair: He paints a dark stroke of brown, then lets it dry. Then comes a second layer painted over it, of translucent orange. The brown shows through, blending with the orange to match the color of a collie. Finally, he applies a third, transparent layer (a "glaze"), giving the collie her healthy sheen.

Many great artists were not necessarily great painters (e.g., Michelangelo). Van Eyck, Rembrandt, Hals, Velázquez, and Rubens were master painters, meticulously building objects with successive layers of paint...but they're not everyone's favorite artists.

---

world that invites meditation. It was perfect for where the triptych originally stood—in the Moreel burial chapel.

### Jan Provoost, *Death and the Miser*, c. 1515

A Bruges businessman in his office strikes a deal with Death. The grinning skeleton lays coins on the table and, in return, the man—looking unhealthy and with fear in his eyes—reaches across the divide in the panels to give Death a promissory note, then marks the transaction in his ledger book. He's trading away a few years of his life for a little more money. The worried man on the  right (the artist's self-portrait) says, "Don't do it."

Jan Provoost (also known as Provost; c. 1465-1529) worked for businessmen like this. He knew their offices, full of moneybags, paperwork, and books. Bruges' materialistic capitalism was at odds with Christian poverty, and society was divided over whether to praise or condemn it. Ironically, this painting's flip side is a religious work bought and paid for by...rich merchants.

### Gerard David, *Judgment of Cambyses,* 1498

That's gotta hurt.

A man is stretched across a table and skinned alive in a very businesslike manner. The crowd hardly notices, and a dog just scratches himself. According to legend, the man was a judge arrested for corruption (left panel) and flayed (right panel), then his skin was draped (right panel background) over the new judge's throne.

Gerard David (c. 1455-1523), Memling's successor as the city's leading artist, painted this for the City Hall. City councilors could ponder what might happen to them if they abused their offices.

By David's time, Bruges was in serious decline, with a failing economy and struggles against the powerful Austrian Habsburg family. The Primitive style also was fading. Italian art was popular, so David tried to spice up his retro-Primitive work with pseudo-Renaissance knickknacks—*putti* (baby angels, over the judgment throne), Roman-style medallions, and garlands. But he couldn't quite master the Italian specialty of 3-D perspective. We view the flayed man at an angle from slightly above, but the table he lies on is shown more from the side.

### Hieronymus Bosch, *Last Judgment,* c. 1500

It's the end of the world, and Christ descends in a bubble to pass judgment on puny humans. Little naked people dance and cavort in a theme park of medieval symbolism, desperately trying to squeeze in their last bit of fun. Meanwhile, some wicked souls are being punished, victims either of their own stupidity or of genetically engineered demons. The good are sent to the left panel to frolic in the innocence of paradise, while the rest are damned to hell (right panel) to be tortured under a burning sky. Bosch paints the scenes with a high horizon line, making it seem that the chaos extends forever.

The bizarre work of Bosch (c. 1450-1516)—who, by the way, was not from Bruges—is open to many interpretations, but some see it as a warning for the turbulent times. He painted during the dawn of a new age. Secular ideas and materialism were encroaching, and the pious, serene medieval world was shattering into chaos. Be aware that this masterpiece is often out on loan; ask the attendant if you can't find it.

## REST OF THE MUSEUM

Breeze through the final rooms to get a quick once-over of Flemish art after Bruges' golden age. (The displays in these rooms change often.) As Bruges declined into a cultural backwater, its artists simply copied the trends going on elsewhere: Italian-style Madonnas, British-style aristocrat portraits, French Realist landscapes, Impressionism, and thick-paint Expressionism.

• *After fast-forwarding through the centuries, you may encounter a couple of Belgium's 20th-century masters.*

### Paul Delvaux, *Serenity,* 1970

Perhaps there's some vague connection between Van Eyck's medieval symbols and the Surrealist images of Paul Delvaux (1897-1994). Delvaux gained fame for his pale nudes, dreamily sleepwalking through moonlit, videogame landscapes.

### René Magritte, *The Assault,* c. 1932

Magritte (1898-1967) had his own private reserve of symbolic images. The cloudy sky, the female torso, windows, and a horsebell (the ball with the slit) appear in other works as well. They're arranged here side by side as if they should mean something, but they—as well as the title—only serve to short-circuit your thoughts when you try to make sense of them. Magritte paints real objects with photographic clarity, then jumbles them together in new and provocative ways.

• *When you're done touring the museum, consider a visit to the nearby Arentshuis Museum (see page 40).*

# SINT-JANSHOSPITAAL MEMLING COLLECTION TOUR

Located in one of Europe's oldest surviving hospital buildings, this museum has two parts. First, you see a few rooms of the former hospital, which operated from about 1150 until 1850. You get a glimpse into medieval medicine, with displays of surgical instruments, archival documents, and visual aids. Then you work your way to the collection's climax: several of Hans Memling's glowing masterpieces.

Memling's art was the culmination of Bruges' Flemish Primitive style (see sidebar on page 77). His serene, soft focus, motionless scenes capture a medieval piety that was quickly fading. The popularity of the style made Memling (c. 1430-1494) one of Bruges' wealthiest citizens, and his work was gobbled up by visiting Italian merchants, who took it home with them, cross-pollinating European art.

## Orientation

**Cost:** €12, includes entry to the skippable old pharmacy (Apotheek) in a nearby building and loaner folding chairs (if you'd like to sit and study the paintings).

**Hours:** Tue-Sun 9:30-17:00, closed Mon. Also expect month-long closures between temporary exhibits.

**Information:** +32 50 448 713, www.museabrugge.be.

**Renovation:** The museum may be closed for renovation during your visit; when open expect changes from what's described here.

**Getting There:** The museum is at Mariastraat 38, across the street from the Church of Our Lady. There are two entrances to the complex—a passageway and a door, 20 yards farther south. The door takes you to the museum.

**Tours:** Scan the QR code at the entrance to download the free audioguide to your mobile device (bring your own earbuds).
**Length of This Tour:** Allow one hour.
**Starring:** The expansive hospital hall (with displays on medieval medicine) and Memling's *St. John Altarpiece.*

# The Tour Begins

• *After showing your ticket, enter a vast hall filled with contemporary art. The displays on medieval medicine are all here, with the Memlings at the far right end. In former days, this hall was the...*

## HOSPITAL

Take in the great hall with its sturdy wood-beamed ceiling, stone pillars, and brick walls. Some 500 years ago, this place would have been bustling with doctors and nurses (that is, monks and nuns) attending to the sick. As Bruges was a large city and a major destination for pilgrims (who came to see the Holy Blood relic), the building had to accommodate a lot of patients.

This hall was lined with beds filled with the sick and dying. At the far end was the high altar, which once displayed Memling's

*St. John Altarpiece* (which we'll see). Bedridden patients could gaze on this peaceful, colorful vision and gain a moment's comfort from their agonies.

Browse the displays. Old paintings scattered among the modern pieces show the hospital in former times, and portraits depict its Isaac Newton-looking doctors. One painting by Jan Beerblock—*Zicht op de Oude Ziekenzalen* (1778)—gives an intimate peek at "the old sick hall" in action: Notice that the soup's on, dogs are welcome, a nun administers last rites, and a sedan chair ambulance taxi awaits a patient. (An actual

sedan chair ambulance still stands nearby.) Snacks and drinks are served in bed. The floor needs mopping. A VIP clergyman drops in to see that all's OK.

You may also see displays of medical implements. There are scalpels, medical books, flasks for testing urine, screws, syringes, and devices more appropriate to a hardware store.

It makes you glad for modern medicine. It's clear that medicine of the day was well-intentioned but very crude. In many ways, this was less a hospital than a hospice, helping the dying make the transition from this world to the next.

Religious art (displayed throughout the museum) was therapeutic, addressing the patients' mental and spiritual health. The numerous Crucifixions reminded the sufferers that Christ could feel their pain, having lived it himself. Paintings of saints gave the suffering hope for a miracle. Visions of heaven offered the terminally ill a light at the end of the tunnel.

That's where Memling came in. The hospital hired him to paint works that could bring serenity to the sick.

• *As you continue through the displays (past ominous slabs marking graves of prominent nuns and friars who worked here), you'll find works by Hans Memling. Start by locating a painted box displayed in a free-standing glass case.*

## MEMLING COLLECTION
### *St. Ursula Shrine*, c. 1489

On October 21, 1489, the mortal remains of St. Ursula were brought here to the church and placed in this gilded oak shrine,

built specially for the occasion and decorated with paintings by Memling. Ursula, yet another Christian martyred by the ancient Romans, became a sensation in the Middle Ages when builders in Germany's Cologne unearthed a huge pile of bones believed to belong to her and her 11,000 slaughtered cohorts.

The church-shaped shrine, carved of wood and covered with gold, has "stained-glass windows" of Memling paintings describing Ursula's well-known legend.

• *"Read" the shrine's story counterclockwise, beginning with the...*

**Left Panel:** Ursula—in white and blue—arrives by boat at the city of Cologne and enters through the city gate. She's on a pilgrimage to Rome, accompanied by 11,000 (female) virgins. That night (look in the two windows of the house in the background, right), an angel appears and tells her this trip will mean her death, but she is undaunted.

**Center Panel:** Continuing up the Rhine (which Memling knew well, having grown up on it), they arrive in Basel and prepare to cross the Alps (background, right). Memling condenses the

---

## Some Memling Trademarks

As you browse the Memling paintings, notice these telltale signs of his work.

- Serene symmetry, with little motion or emotion
- Serious faces that are realistic but timeless, without blemishes
- Eye-catching details such as precious carpets, mirrors, and brocaded clothes
- Glowing colors, even lighting, no shadows
- Cityscape backgrounds

---

11,000 virgins to a more manageable 11, making each one pure enough for a thousand.

**Right Panel:** They arrive at the gates of Rome, where Ursula falls to her knees before the pope. Kneeling behind Ursula is her fiancé. Ursula has agreed to marry him only if he becomes a Christian and refrains from the marriage bed long enough for her to make this three-year pilgrimage as a virgin (making him, I guess, virgin number 11,001).

**Opposite Side—Left Panel:** They board ships to head back home, now joined by the pope. Memling's crowd scenes are hardly realistic—more like a collage of individual poses and faces—but they capture the pomp and ceremony Memling would have seen in Bruges parades.

**Middle Panel:** Back in Cologne, a surprise awaits them—the city has been taken over by vicious Huns. They grab Ursula's hubby, stab him, and he dies in Ursula's arms.

**Right Panel:** The Hun king (in red with turban and beard) woos Ursula, placing his hand over his heart, but she says, "No way." So, a Hun soldier draws his arrow and prepares to shoot her dead. Even here, at the climax of the story, there are no histrionics. Even the dog just sits down, crosses his paws, and watches. The whole shrine cycle is as posed, motionless, and colorful as the *tableaux vivants* that may have inaugurated the shrine here in this church in 1489.

In the background, behind Ursula, a Bruges couple looks on sympathetically. This may be Memling himself (in red coat with fur lining) and his wife, Anna, who bore their three children.

• *Now continue to the right and find a black-and-white tiled room where Memling's paintings are displayed. A large triptych (three-paneled altarpiece) dominates the space.*

### St. John Altarpiece, a.k.a. The Mystical Marriage of St. Catherine, 1474

Sick and dying patients lay in their beds in the hospital and looked at this colorful, three-part work, which sat atop the hospital/church's high altar. The piece was dedicated to the hospital's patron saints, John the Baptist and John the Evangelist (see the inscription along the bottom of the frame), but Memling broadened the focus to take in a vision of heaven and the end of the world.

**Central Panel:** Mary, with Baby Jesus on her lap, sits in a canopied chair, crowned by hovering blue angels. It's an imaginary gathering of conversing saints *(Sacra Conversazione)*, though nobody in this meditative group is saying a word or even exchanging meaningful eye contact.

Mary is flanked symmetrically by the other saints: John the Baptist (to the left) and John the Evangelist (in red); an organist angel (left) matched by a book-holding acolyte; St. Catherine (left) balanced by book-reading St. Barbara. Behind them, classical columns are also perfectly balanced left and right.

At the center of it all, Baby Jesus tips the balance by leaning over to place a ring on Catherine's finger, sealing the "mystical marriage" between them.

St. Catherine of Alexandria, born rich, smart, and pagan to Roman parents, joined the outlawed Christian faith. She spoke out against pagan Rome, attracting the attention of the emperor, Maxentius, who sent 50 philosophers to talk some sense into her—but she countered every argument, even converting the emperor's own wife. Maxentius killed his wife, then asked Catherine to marry him. She refused, determined to remain true to the man she'd already "married" in a mystical vision—Christ.

Frustrated, Maxentius ordered Catherine to be stretched across a large, spiked wheel (the rather quaint-looking object at her feet), but the wheel broke, so they just cut her head off, which is why she has a sword, along with her "Catherine Wheel."

Looking through the columns, we see scenes of Bruges. Just to the right of the chair's canopy, the wooden contraption is a crane used to hoist barrels from barges on Kraanplein.

**Left Panel:** Even this gruesome scene, showing the beheaded John the Baptist with blood still spurting from his severed neck, becomes serene under Memling's gentle brush. Everyone is solemn, graceful, and emotionless—including both parts of the decapitated John. Salomé (in green) receives the head on her silver platter with a humble servant's downcast eyes, as if accepting her role in God's wonderful, if sometimes painful, plan.

**Right Panel:** John sits on a high, rocky bluff on the island of Patmos and, in a vision of the Apocalypse, sees the end of the world as we know it...and he feels fine.

Overhead, in a rainbow bubble, God appears on his throne, resting his hand on a sealed book. A lamb steps up to open the

seals, unleashing the awful events at the end of time. Standing at the bottom of the rainbow, an angel in green gestures to John and says, "Write this down." John picks up his quill, but he pauses, absolutely transfixed, experiencing the Apocalypse now.

He sees wars, fires, and plagues on the horizon, the Virgin in the sky rebuking a red dragon, and many other wonders. In the center ride the dreaded Four Horsemen, wreaking havoc on the cosmos (galloping over either islands or clouds). Horseman number four is a skeleton, followed by a human-eating monster head. Helpless mortals on the right seek shelter in the rocks, but find none.

Memling has been criticized for building a career by copying the formulas of his predecessors, but this panel is a complete original. Its theme had never been so fully expressed, and the bright, contrasting colors and vivid imagery are almost modern. In the *St. John Altarpiece*, Memling shows us the full range of his style, from medieval grace to Renaissance symmetry, from the real to the surreal.

• *In the small adjoining room, find more Memlings.*

### *Diptych of Martin van Nieuwenhove,* **1489**

Three-dimensional effects—borrowed from the Italian Renaissance style—enliven this two-panel devotional painting. Both Mary and Child and the 23-year-old Martin, though in different panels, inhabit the same space within the painting.

Stand right in front of Mary, facing her directly. If you line up the paintings' horizons (seen in the distance, out the room's windows), you'll see that both panels depict the same room—with two windows at the back and two along the right wall.

Want proof? In the convex mirror on the back wall (just to the left of Mary), the scene is reflected back at us, showing Mary and Martin from behind, silhouetted in the two "windows" of the picture frames. Apparently, Mary makes house calls, appearing right in the living room of the young donor Martin, the wealthy, unique-looking heir to his father's business.

• *Before leaving this area, find, to your right, a...*

### *Portrait of a Young Woman,* **1480**

Memling's bread-and-butter was portraits created for families of wealthy businessmen (especially visiting Italians and Portuguese). This portrait takes us right back to that time.

The young woman looks out of the frame as if she were looking out a window. Her hands rest on the "sill," with the fingertips sticking over. The frame is original, but the banner and Van Eyck-like lettering are not.

Her clothes look somewhat simple, but they were high-class in their day. A dark damask dress is brightened by a red sash and a detachable white collar. She's pulled her hair into a tight bun at the back, pinned there with a fez-like cap and draped with a transparent veil. She's shaved her hairline and plucked her brows to get that clean, high-forehead look. Her ensemble is animated by a well-placed necklace of small stones.

Memling accentuates her fashionably pale complexion and gives her a pensive, sober expression, portraying her like a medieval saint. Still, she keeps her personality, with distinct features like her broad nose, neck tendons, and realistic hands. She peers out from her subtly painted veil, which sweeps down over the side of her face. What's she thinking? (My guess: "It's time for a waffle.")

• *Special exhibitions are sometimes displayed in a room up the stairs from the main hall. But it's hard to compete with a waffle.*

# BRUGES SLEEPING, EATING & MORE

Bruges is the most inviting town in Belgium for an overnight. This chapter describes the town's top accommodations, eateries, shopping, and nightlife options, as well as train connections to other cities.

## Sleeping in Bruges

Bruges is a great place to sleep, with Gothic spires out your window, little traffic noise, and the cheerily out-of-tune carillon heralding each new day at 8:00 sharp. (Thankfully, the bell tower is silent from 22:00 to 8:00.) Most Bruges accommodations are located between the train station and the old center, with the most distant (and best) being a few blocks to the north and east of the Markt (Market Square).

B&Bs offer the best value, but hoteliers have lobbied City Hall to make it harder to have more than three "official" rooms. Creative B&B owners have found ways to get around the restrictions. For some travelers, short-term, Airbnb-type rentals can be a good alternative; search for places in my recommended hotel neighborhoods.

Bruges is most crowded Friday and Saturday evenings from Easter through October—July and August weekends are the worst. Many hotels charge a bit more on Friday and Saturday and won't let you stay just one night if it's a Saturday.

I rank accommodations from **$** budget to **$$$$** splurge. For the best deal, contact my family-run places directly by phone or email. When you book direct, the owner avoids a commission and may be able to offer a discount. Book well in advance for peak season or if your trip coincides with a major holiday or festival (see the appendix). For details on reservations, short-term rentals, and more, see the "Sleeping" section in the Practicalities chapter.

## HOTELS

**$$$$ Hotel Heritage** offers 22 rooms, with chandeliers that seem hung especially for you, in a solid and completely modernized old building with luxurious public spaces. Warm and inviting with old-time elegance, it's one of those places that does everything just right—if you can afford it (breakfast extra, iPad and Nespresso machine in every room, air-con, elevator, sauna, fitness room, pay parking, Niklaas Desparsstraat 11, a block north of the Markt, +32 50 444 444, www.hotel-heritage.com, info@hotel-heritage.com). It's run by cheery and hardworking Johan and Isabelle Creytens.

**$$$ Hotel Patritius,** family-run and centrally located, is a grand, circa-1830 Neoclassical mansion with hardwood oak floors in its 22 stately, high-ceilinged rooms. It features a plush lounge, a chandeliered breakfast room, and a courtyard garden. If you get a room at the lower end of the price range, this can be a great value, or skip breakfast for a lower rate (use code "676PPq" when you book direct for a discount, family rooms, air-con, elevator, coin-op laundry, pay parking, Riddersstraat 11, +32 50 338 454, www.hotelpatritius.be, info@hotelpatritius.be, cordial Garrett and Elvi Spaey).

**$$$ Hotel Marcel** has 24 big, boutique rooms with oversized photos of sights around Bruges plastering their ceilings and walls. Breakfast features fresh juice and baked goods served in the hip ground-level café. The location is ideal—on a quiet street a block off the Markt (apartments, some rooms have air-con, elevator, Niklaas Desparsstraat 7, +32 50 335 502, www.hotelmarcel.be, info@hotelmarcel.be, Sophie).

**$$ Hotel Adornes** is small and welcoming—a great value situated in the most charming part of town. This 17th-century canal-side house has 20 rooms with full modern bathrooms, free loaner bikes, and a cellar lounge with games (family rooms, elevator, self-serve pay laundry, limited pay parking—reserve in advance, some street noise, near Carmersstraat at St. Annarei 26, +32 50 341 336, www.adornes.be, info@adornes.be). Nathalie runs the family business.

**$$ Hotel Augustyn,** in a quiet canalside neighborhood 10 minutes from the Markt, offers the best of both worlds: 29 classic wainscoted rooms with updated, contemporary comforts (breakfast

# Bruges Hotels

1. Hotel Heritage & Hotel Marcel
2. Hotel Patritius
3. Hotel Adornes
4. Hotel Augustyn
5. Hotel Botaniek
6. Canalview Hotel ter Reien
7. Hotel Rose Red
8. To Hotel de Pauw
9. Hotel Bla Bla
10. The Townhouse
11. La Maison de Nathalie
12. Gastenhuis Sint-Andriescruyse
13. B&B Amaryllis Dieltiens
14. B&B Setola
15. 't Geerwijn B&B
16. Charlie Rockets Hostel

BRUGES SLEEPING, EATING & MORE

extra, spacious family rooms and a family apartment with kitchen, elevator, limited pay parking—reserve in advance, bike rental, Augustijnenrei 18, www.hotelaugustyn.com, info@hotelaugustyn.com).

**$$ Hotel Botaniek,** located a block from Astrid Park, is a quiet, pint-sized hotel with a comfy lounge, renting nine slightly worn rooms—some of them quite big (RS%, family rooms, elevator, Waalsestraat 23, +32 50 341 424, www.botaniek.be, info@botaniek.be, Veronika and Brend).

**$$ Canalview Hotel ter Reien** is big and basic, with 26 rooms overlooking a canal in the town center—the water is right outside your window. Ask for a renovated room, which has a larger bathroom, for no extra cost (family rooms, elevator, Langestraat 1, +32 50 349 100, www.hotelterreien.be, info@hotelterreien.be, Diederik).

**$$ Hotel Rose Red,** a charming family-run hotel, rents 22 simple, compact, hardwood-floor rooms on a quiet street two blocks off the Markt. It's one of the best deals in town (breakfast extra, family rooms, patio, Cordoeanierstraat 16, +32 50 339 051, http://hotelrosered.be, hotel@rosered.be, Jannetien and Kormeel).

**$$ Hotel de Pauw** is tall, skinny, flower-bedecked, and family-run, with eight straightforward rooms on a quiet street next to a church (pay parking, Sint Gilliskerkhof 8, +32 50 337 118, www.hoteldepauw.be, info@hoteldepauw.be, Philippe and Hilde).

**$ Hotel Bla Bla,** despite its name, is anything but average. This modern hotel is in a charming old-school building with 12 airy rooms and an updated backyard annex. Uppermost-level rooms reward guests with vaulted ceilings and big bathrooms. It's homey and well-run on a central yet quiet street, and two private courtyards can be enjoyed when the weather is nice (includes breakfast when you book direct with hotel, family rooms, Dweersstraat 24, +32 50 339 014, www.hotelblabla.com, info@hotelblabla.com, David).

## BED-AND-BREAKFASTS

These B&Bs, run by people who enjoy their work, offer a better value than hotels. Most families rent out their entire top floor—several rooms and a small sitting area. And most are updated and stylish—they're just in medieval shells. Each is central, on a quiet street, and has lots of stairs. Many places charge a little extra for a one-night stay. It's possible to find parking on the street in the evening (pay 9:00-19:00, two-hour maximum for metered parking during the day, free overnight).

**$$$ The Townhouse** is a classy place about 10 minutes' walk south of the Markt, run by friendly Jason and Sandra. Their four rooms, some with views, are spacious and modern—all with king-size beds. Breakfast is cooked to order and served in the garden in good weather (cash only, family room, air-con, limited onsite pay parking, Werkhuisstraat 18, +32 50 615 852, www.thetownhouse. be, bookings@thetownhouse.be).

**$$$ La Maison de Nathalie** hides impeccable contemporary design behind its historic brick facade. Blond wood graces the three rooms, and one has both a bathtub and shower. The public spaces are just as stylish, and breakfast is available on the lovely backyard terrace (breakfast extra, Molenmeers 34, +32 474 113 777, www. lamaisondenathalie.be, info@lamaisondenathalie.be, Nathalie).

**$$$ Gastenhuis Sint-Andriescruyse** offers three warmly decorated rooms with high ceilings in a spacious, cheerfully red canalside house a short walk from the Old Town action. Owners Luc and Christiane treat guests like long-lost family and proudly share their photo albums with pictures of previous guests (cash only, family room, some rooms with shared toilet but private bath, free soft drinks, limited parking, Verversdijk A15, +32 50 789 168, mobile +32 477 973 933, www.gastenhuisst-andriescruyse.be, luc. cloet@telenet.be).

**$$ B&B Amaryllis Dieltiens,** with four comfortable rooms, is run by Amaryllis (whose parents managed this homey B&B for 27 years) and her husband, Bart, both musicians. You'll eat a hearty breakfast around a big table overlooking their garden (cash or prepayment by wire transfer only, air-con, limited pay parking, Waalsestraat 40, three blocks southeast of Burg Square, +32 50 334 294, www.bedandbreakfastbruges.be, dieltiens@ bedandbreakfastbruges.be).

**$$ B&B Setola,** run by Lut and Bruno Setola, offers three expansive rooms and a spacious breakfast/living room on the top floor of their 18th-century townhouse, just a five-minute walk from the Markt. Wooden ceiling beams give the modern rooms a touch of Old World flair (honor bar, guest kitchen, outdoor terrace, Sint Walburgastraat 12, +32 50 334 977, www.bedandbreakfast-bruges. com, setola@bedandbreakfast-bruges.com).

**$$ Waterside B&B** has two fresh, Zen-like rooms, both with private baths, above a peaceful canal south of the town center (cash only, continental breakfast, 15-minute walk from Burg Square at Kazernevest 88, for location see map on page 29, +32 476 744 525, www.waterside.be, mika.steyaert@gmail.com, run by Mieke of recommended Pink Bear Bike Tours).

**$$ Vegan B&B AM/PM** sports three ultramodern rooms in a residential neighborhood just west of the old town (cash only, vegan breakfast, five-minute walk from 't Zand at Singel 10—see map on page 29, +32 486 327 886, www.bruges-bedandbreakfast.com, ampmbruges@gmail.com, artsy young couple Tiny and Kevin). From the train station, head left down busy Buiten Begijnevest to the roundabout. Stay to the left, take the pedestrian underpass, then follow the busy road (now on your left). Just before the next bridge, turn right onto the footpath called Buiten Boeverievest, then turn left onto Singel; the B&B is at #10.

**$ 't Geerwijn B&B,** run by Chris de Loof, rents three homey rooms in the old center. Check out the fun, lofty A-frame room upstairs (cash only, pleasant breakfast room and royal lounge, Geerwijnstraat 14, +32 475 724 702, www.geerwijn.be, chrisdeloof14@gmail.com).

## HOSTELS

The American-style **¢ Charlie Rockets** hostel (and bar), a backpacker dive, is lively and central. The ground floor feels like a 19th-century sports bar, with a foosball-and-movie-posters party ambience. Upstairs is an industrial-strength pile of hostel dorms (private rooms available, breakfast extra, Hoogstraat 19, +32 50 330 660, www.charlierockets.com, info@charlierockets.com).

**¢ Snuffel Backpacker Hostel** is less central and pretty grungy, but friendly and laid-back (Ezelstraat 42—see map on page 29, +32 50 333 133, www.snuffel.be, info@snuffel.be).

# Eating in Bruges

Bruges doesn't really have any specialties all its own, but restaurants here excel at all the predictable Belgian dishes: mussels cooked a variety of ways (one order can feed two, tastiest when in season—July through Dec), fish dishes, grilled meats, and fries. The town's famous indigenous beers include the prizewinning Brugse Zot ("Bruges Fool"), a golden ale, and Straffe Hendrik, a potent, bitter triple ale. Two other great beers to look out for: St. Bernardus #12 and Tongerlo Dark.

You'll find plenty of affordable, touristy restaurants on floodlit squares and along dreamy canals. I wouldn't blame you for eating at one of these places, but I prefer the candle-cool bistros that flicker on back streets or atmospheric beer halls where the pub grub takes a backseat to those famous Belgian brews.

I rank eateries from **$** budget to **$$$$** splurge. For more advice on eating in Belgium, including ordering, tipping, and cuisine and beverages, see the "Eating" section of the Practicalities chapter.

BRUGES SLEEPING, EATING & MORE

# Bruges Restaurants

1. Restaurant Patrick Devos
2. Rock Fort
3. Bistro den Amand & Medard Brasserie
4. Tom's Diner
5. Bistro Den Huzaar
6. The Flemish Pot
7. Restaurant de Koetse
8. Carlito's
9. L'Estaminet
10. De Plaats Vegetarian
11. Café-Brasserie Craenenburg
12. Le Panier d'Or
13. Chez Vincent
14. 't Brugsch Friethuys
15. Markt Frituur Carts
16. Grocery (3)
17. Chez Albert Waffles
18. Lizzie's Wafels
19. Gelateria Da Vinci

## RESTAURANTS

**$$$$ Restaurant Patrick Devos** is my vote for the best romantic splurge in town. It's a tranquil, spacious, and dressy scene with a hard-working mom (Christine serving) and pop (Patrick cooking). Their creative French fare focuses on tasting *menus,* including a gourmet vegan option, along with wine pairings (reservations required, €70 for four courses, €95 for six courses, €50 for a three-course lunch; open Mon-Tue and Thu-Fri 12:00-13:00 & 19:00-21:00, Sat 19:00-21:00, closed Wed and Sun; Zilverstraat 41, +32 50 335 566, www.patrickdevos.be).

**$$$$ Rock Fort** feels like a food lab with an open kitchen cranking out creative dishes in a chic and modern space. Two chefs, Peter Laloo and Hermes Vanliefde, give their French cuisine a creative and global gourmet twist. Their format is complicated and not cheap. I'd explore their website before venturing here...but it could be a trip highlight (Mon-Fri 12:00-14:30 & 18:30-22:00, closed Sat-Sun, reservations recommended, Langestraat 15, +32 50 960 617, www.rock-fort.be).

**$$$ Bistro den Amand,** with seven tables filling a plain interior and a few outdoor tables, exudes unpretentious quality the moment you step in. Chef An is enthusiastic about her fair-trade ingredients, which she puts to good use in creative dishes, some with a hint of Asian influence. Portions are splittable and good vegetarian options are always available. It's on a bustling pedestrian lane a half-block off the Markt (Tue-Sat 12:00-14:00 & 18:00-21:00, closed Sun-Mon; reservations smart for dinner, Sint-Amandstraat 4, +32 50 340 122, www.denamand.be, An Vissers and Arnout Beyaert).

**$$$ Tom's Diner** is a trendy, cozy little candlelit bistro in a quiet, cobbled residential area a 10-minute walk from the center. Chef Tom gives traditional dishes a delightfully modern twist, such as his signature Flemish meat loaf with rhubarb sauce. You can opt for a series of small, sharable plates or go with "Tom's Choice" (a four-course, €39 meal). If you want to flee the tourists and experience a popular neighborhood joint, this is it—the locals love it. Reserve before you make the trip (Tue-Sat 18:00-23:00, closed Sun-Mon, north of the Markt near Sint-Gilliskerk at West-Gistelhof 23, +32 50 333 382, www.tomsdiner.be).

**$$$ Bistro Den Huzaar** is somewhat touristy but affordable, serving big portions of Belgian classics. The long dining room stretches back on well-worn wooden floors and a few tables are out on the sidewalk. It's dignified but relaxed (daily 11:30-14:00 & 17:30-21:00, five-minute walk north of the Markt at Vlamingstraat 36, +32 50 333 797).

**$$$$ The Flemish Pot** is a busy eatery where enthusiastic chefs Mario and Rik cook up a traditional menu of vintage Flemish specialties—such as rabbit stew—served in little iron pots and skillets. Seating is cluttered, the tourist-oriented menu is pricey, and service can be spotty. But portions are hearty and the atmosphere is cozy (Wed-Sun 17:30-21:30, closed Mon-Tue, just off Geldmunt-straat at Helmstraat 3, +32 50 340 086, www.devlaamschepot.be).

**$$$$ Restaurant de Koetse** is a homey yet dressy place where Piet and his hardworking team serve fine Belgian and French cuisine, with an emphasis on grilled meat, seafood, and mussels (Sat-Wed 12:00-14:30 & 18:00-22:00, closed Thu-Fri, Oude Burg 31, +32 50 337 680, www.dekoetse-brugge.be). Show this book when dining for a local specialty as a free appetizer: a bowl of small gray shrimp from the North Sea.

**$$$ Carlito's** is a good choice for basic Italian fare. The menu covers all the Italian bases and the space is dressier than a pizza joint, with whitewashed walls and candles (daily 12:00-14:00 & 18:00-22:00, patio seating in back, Hoogstraat 21, +32 50 490 075).

**$$ L'Estaminet** is a youthful, jazz-filled eatery with a fun energy. Students flock here for the Tolkien-chic ambience, hearty spaghetti, vegetarian dishes, big dinner salads, and more beer than wine. For outdoor dining under an all-weather canopy, enjoy the relaxed patio facing peaceful Astrid Park (Tue-Sun 12:00-24:00, closed Mon, Park 5, +32 50 330 916).

**$$ De Plaats Vegetarian** offers Bruges' best vegetarian and gluten-free dishes. It's not fancy, but it's welcoming, reasonably priced, and just a bit quirky—like its owner, friendly Piet, who cooks and serves (Tue-Sat 12:00-14:00 & 18:00-21:00, closed Sun-Mon; Wapenmakersstraat 5, +32 50 660 366).

**Eating on the Markt:** Most tourists seem to be eating on the Markt with the bell tower high overhead and horse carriages clip-clopping by. The square is ringed by tourist traps with aggressive waiters expert at getting you to consume more than you intend. Still, if you order smartly, you can have a memorable meal or drink at a reasonable price on one of the finest squares in Europe.

**$$ Café-Brasserie Craenenburg** has a straightforward menu where you can get pasta and beer for €20 and spend all the time you want ogling the magic of Bruges (daily 8:00-22:00, Markt 16, +32 50 333 402). Or come here just to savor a before- or after-meal drink with the view.

**$$ Le Panier d'Or** is reputable with a €25 traditional fixed-price *menu* and good seating inside and out (long hours daily, Markt 28, +32 50 96 29 62).

**Cheaper Restaurants Just Off the Markt:** For a similar but less expensive array of interchangeable, tourist-focused eateries, head a few steps off the Markt up Sint-Amandstraat (through the gap between Café Craenenburg and the clock tower). You'll pop out into a busy little square with lots of choices: sushi, burgers,

Spanish, pasta, and more. The best of these is **Bistro den Amand** (recommended earlier), but if that's full or closed, this is a fine place to browse for something else. **$ Medard Brasserie** is where the grumpiest waiters serve the cheapest hot meal in town—hearty meat spaghetti for only €6.50 (sit inside or out, Mon-Sat 12:00-20:00, closed Sun, Sint Amandstraat 18, +32 50 348 684).

## SWEETS AND QUICK EATS
### Belgian Fries and Fried Flemish Gut Bombs

Belgian fries *(frieten)* are a treat. Proud and traditional *frituren* serve tubs of fries, various deep-fried gut bombs, and local-style shish kebabs. Belgians dip their *frieten* in mayonnaise or other flavored sauces. Ketchup is there for the Yankees, but I encourage you to skip it and try a sauce adventure. Look for these favorites.

**$ Chez Vincent** has an upstairs dining area and pleasant outdoor tables on a terrace facing St. Salvator's Cathedral along the lively Steenstraat shopping drag. Here's your chance to dine with local high schoolers and be adventurous with fry sauces. Philip uses fresh, local ingredients to turn out tasty fries and other Belgian tasties: burgers, sausages, meatballs, croquettes, and so on (Tue-Sun 11:30-14:30 & 17:30-20:00, closed Mon, Sint-Salvatorskerkhof 1, +32 50 684 395).

**$ 't Brugsch Friethuys,** a block off the Markt, is more central but not as pleasant for sit-down dining. Their "Big Hunger menu" includes all the traditional greasy, deep-fried foods (daily 12:00-22:00, at the corner of Geldmuntstraat and Sint Jakobsstraat, Mikhail will explain your options).

**Markt Frituur:** Dueling carts sell fried potatoes to go at the foot of the City Hall tower on the Market Square (daily 10:00-24:00). There are plenty of steps and benches nearby overlooking the action on the square.

## Picnics

A handy location for groceries is the **Carrefour Express** mini supermarket, just off the Markt on Vlamingstraat (daily 8:00-19:00); for a slightly wider selection, **Delhaize-Proxy** is just up Geldmuntstraat (daily 8:30-19:30, Noordzandstraat 4). **Brazi's** serves takeout sandwiches that are worth standing in line for, but same-day preorders are possible before 11:00 (Mon-Fri 8:00-15:00, Sat from 9:00, closed Sun, Sint-Jakobsstraat 2, +32 50 490 954). For midnight snacks, you'll find corner grocery stores scattered around town.

## Belgian Waffles and Ice Cream

**Chez Albert Waffles,** on Breidelstraat connecting the Markt and Burg Square, is pricey, but the quality is good and—thanks to the tourist crowds—turnover is quick, so the waffles are fresh (daily 11:00-18:30, at #18, +32 50 950 009).

**Lizzie's Wafels** is also popular but much less touristy. They make their waffles extra-large; try some drizzled in chocolate (Wed-Sun 13:00-18:00, closed Mon-Tue, Sint-Jakobsstraat 16, +32 50 348 769).

**Gelateria Da Vinci,** the local favorite for homemade ice cream, has creative flavors and a lively atmosphere. As you approach, you'll see a line of happy lickers. Before ordering, ask to sample the Speculoos (cinnamon cookie) and the Ferrero Rocher (chocolate, nuts, and crunchy cookie). It's artfully run by Sylvia from Austria, who for decades has gotten up before dawn to whip up the day's creations (daily 11:00-22:00, Geldmuntstraat 34, +32 50 333 650).

## PUBS AND BEER HALLS FOR DINNER (OR JUST BEER)

My best budget-eating tip for Bruges: Stop in to one of the city's bars for a simple meal and a couple of world-class beers with great Bruges ambience. Among these listings, Cambrinus puts more emphasis on its food; Café Terrastje, Café Vlissinghe, and Pub 't Gezelleke have a small selection of still-substantial meals; and 't Brugs Beertje and De Garre have lighter food and snacks.

**$ 't Brugs Beertje,** where you're welcome to sit at the bar and talk with the staff, is a place I could turn a simple dinner into a late night of convivial beer drinking (more than 300 beers—including seasonal brews, very short menu of spaghetti and a few beer snacks, Thu-Tue 16:00-24:00, closed Wed, Kemelstraat 5, +32 50 339 616).

**$$$ Cambrinus** is a bright, tight, and boisterous *bierbrasserie* serving 400 types of beer, including 15 on tap, and good pub grub. The thick menu is an adventure of main courses (generally cooked with beer), seasonal specials, and pages and pages of beers nicely described in English (daily 11:00-23:00, reservations smart, Philipstockstraat 19, +32 50 332 328, www.cambrinus.eu).

**$$ De Garre** (deh-*H*AHR-reh), rather than a noisy pub scene, has a dressy, sit-down-and-focus-on-your-friend-and-the-fine-beer vibe. It's mature and cozy, with light meals (cold cuts, pâtés, and toasted sandwiches) and a huge selection of beers. Heavy beers are the forte: Beer pilgrims flock here, as it's the only place on earth that sells the Tripel van de Garre beer on tap. As it's 12 percent

# Bruges Beer Halls & Nightlife

**Beer Halls**

1. 't Brugs Beertje
2. Cambrinus
3. De Garre
4. Café Vlissinghe
5. Pub 't Gezelleke
6. Café Terrastje
7. Comptoir des Arts
8. 2Be Bar
9. Duvelorium Grand Beer Café

**Nightlife**

10. To Concertgebouw
11. Municipal Theater
12. Eiermarkt
13. Kupiersstraat
14. To 't Zand
15. To Langestraat
16. Charlie Rockets

alcohol, there's a three-Tripel limit (daily 12:00-24:00, additional seating up tiny staircase, off Breidelstraat between Burg and the Markt, on Garre alley, +32 50 341 029).

**In the *Gezellig* Quarter Northeast of the Markt:** These pubs are tucked in the wonderfully *gezellig* (cozy) quarter that follows the canal past Jan Van Eyckplein, northeast of the Markt. Just walking out here is a treat, as it gets you away from the tourists.

**$$ Café Vlissinghe** is the oldest pub in town (1515). Bruno keeps things basic and laid-back, serving simple plates (lasagna, grilled cheese, and angel-hair spaghetti) and great beer in perhaps the best old-time tavern atmosphere in town. This must have been the Dutch Masters' rec room. The garden outside comes with games (a *boules* court and the uniquely Flemish *krulbollen*)—free for guests to watch or play (Wed-Sat 11:00-21:30, Sun until 19:00, closed Mon-Tue, Blekersstraat 2, +32 50 343 737).

**$$ Pub 't Gezelleke** lacks the mystique of the Vlissinghe, but it's a true neighborhood gastropub offering an inviting selection of traditional plates and great beer (it's where I discovered St. Bernardus #12 and Tongerlo Dark). The service is warm and helpful; the music, always 1940s jazz. Its name is an appropriate play on the word for "cozy" and the name of a great local poet (Mon-Tue and Thu-Sat 16:00-24:00, closed Wed and Sun, terrace seating out back, Carmersstraat 15, +32 470 122 183; Anne cooks, Jean serves).

**$$ Café Terrastje** is a cozy, jazzy pub serving tapas and simple bar food. Enjoy the friendly yet subdued vibe inside or relax on the front terrace overlooking the canal and heart of the district (Fri-Mon 12:00-21:00 but food service stops earlier, Tue until 17:00, closed Wed-Thu; corner of Genthof and Langerei, +32 50 330 919, Ian and Patricia).

**Beer Cellar North of the Markt:** Filling a warm, welcoming cellar, **Comptoir des Arts** has 90 types of Belgian beer, a fine selection of whisky, knowledgeable barkeeps, a big fireplace, and occasional live music (typically on Sunday evenings). It's a short walk from the Markt, away from the worst tourist crowds (bar snacks only—no meals, Wed-Mon 19:00-late, closed Tue, also closed Mon May-Sept, Vlamingstraat 53, +32 494 387 961, www.comptoirdesarts.be).

**Beer with a View and Lots of Tourists:** I wouldn't bother eating at these places—they're all about the beer and the views. The bar at **2Be,** though tucked in back of a tacky tourist shop (see listing under "Shopping in Bruges," later), serves several local beers on tap and boasts a fine scenic terrace over a canal. **Duvelorium Grand Beer Café** is located upstairs from the Historium, with a spiny Gothic terrace overlooking the bustle on the Markt (same hours as Historium, you can enter the pub without paying for the museum, last orders at 18:00, may be open later in summer).

# Shopping in Bruges

Touristy Bruges isn't the place to shop for authenticity or bargains (Brussels, Antwerp, and Ghent are more satisfying). But souvenir shoppers find plenty of options. Shops are generally open from 10:00 to 18:00 and closed Sundays.

## WHAT TO BUY

**Chocolate:** A box of Belgian pralines is at the top of most souvenir shoppers' lists; see my tips and recommended chocolate shops on page 48.

**Beer:** Another consumable souvenir is Belgian beer—either a bottle (or three) for later in your trip, or a prized brew checked carefully in your luggage home. In addition to the pubs listed earlier—a few of which sell bottles to go—the streets of Bruges are lined with bottle shops. At some, you can buy the glass that's designed to go with each type of beer (it's a fragile item to pack, but purists insist). Options include the touristy souvenir store **2Be** (described later) or **The Bottle Shop,** which sells 600 different beers and has a staff that enjoys helping visitors navigate the many choices (daily 11:00-19:00, just south of the Markt at Wollestraat 13, +32 50 349 980).

**Lace:** This is a popular item, but very expensive. **'t Apostelientje** is one good option, conveniently located at Balstraat 11, just down the street from the Lace Center.

## WHERE TO SHOP

Souvenir shops abound on the streets that fan out from the Markt and the ones heading southwest, toward the Church of Our Lady. **2Be,** in a classic old brick mansion overlooking a canal a block south of the Markt, is huge, obvious, grotesquely touristy, and filled with a wide variety of tacky and not-so-tacky Belgian souvenirs: Tintin, Smurfs, beer, and chocolates. The "beerwall" at the entrance shows off over a thousand types of Belgian brew; their cellar bottle shop is remarkably well stocked; and their pub has several rotating draft beers you can enjoy on a relaxing terrace floating over a perfect canal (daily 10:00-19:00, Wollestraat 53, +32 50 611 222, www.2-be.biz).

Two parallel streets running southwest between the Markt and 't Zand squares are lined with shops that cater to both tourists and workaday Bruggians. **Steenstraat,** which becomes **Zuidzandstraat** closer to 't Zand, has lots of affordable clothing chains (H&M, Zara), department stores (Hema), and mobile phone shops. At the Markt end of the street, a few tourist/souvenir shops are mixed in, but the farther you go, the more local it becomes.

More colorful are the shops a block to the north, along **Geldmuntstraat** (which becomes **Noordzandstraat**). Along this atmospheric drag—with perhaps Bruges' most enjoyable window-shopping—are smaller, more expensive chains and upscale boutiques (including L'Héroïne, highlighting Belgian designers with Antwerp cred at Noordzandstraat 32); housewares shops (such as Cook & Serve, a fun kitchen gadgets shop, at Geldmuntstraat 16); and the popular Da Vinci gelato shop (described earlier).

The **old fish market** (Vismarkt) just over the bridge from Burg Square still sells fresh fish most mornings, while souvenir stands fill some of its arcades all day long and into the evening. It's a central place to browse toys, jewelry, accessories, starving artists' depictions of Bruges, and more.

For the highest concentration of tourists (and, consequently, the highest concentration of souvenir, chocolate, lace, and *wafel* shops), head down **Katelijnestraat,** which runs south from the Church of Our Lady and Sint-Janshospitaal. While you'll find no great values here, it's convenient for souvenir shopping.

## Nightlife in Bruges

After dark, Bruges is sleepy but enchanting. While there's entertainment to be found, perhaps the city's most rewarding nighttime experience is strolling its floodlit cobbles and monuments. My favorite way to spend a late-summer evening in Bruges is in the twilight on a rental bike, savoring its back streets, far from the touristic commotion. Another good option is to settle into a characteristic pub (or hop between a few) to enjoy some beer; of the several pubs listed earlier (under "Eating in Bruges"), **Café Vlissinghe** and **De Garre** are particularly memorable places for a drink.

I've suggested some other options for entertainment below (for locations, see the "Bruges Beer Halls and Nightlife" map, earlier).

### CONCERTS

The tiny courtyard behind the bell tower has a few benches where people can enjoy free evening **carillon concerts** (generally mid-June–mid-Sept Mon and Wed at 21:00; also Wed, Sat, and Sun at 11:00—schedule posted on courtyard wall).

Otherwise, see what's on at one of the city's main venues: The **Concertgebouw,** a performance hall on the spacious square called 't Zand, features esoteric dance, classy orchestral music, and other high culture (+32 50 476 999, www.concertgebouw.be). The **Municipal Theater** (Brugse Stadsschouwburg), two blocks north of the Markt on Vlamingstraat, features an eclectic lineup of classical and modern presentations, from ballet to contemporary dance to musical theater to big-name jazz performers (www.ccbrugge.be; check location carefully—some performances take place in smaller venues around town). The TI can give you information for any of these; the booking office inside the 't Zand TI also sells tickets for most events in town.

Luc Vanlaere presents 40-minute harp concerts most days in summer at **Old St. John's Church** (Oud Sint Jan), across from the Church of Our Lady and tucked behind Sint-Janshospitaal (free but donations appreciated, generally Tue-Sat 15:00, 17:00, and 18:30, no concerts Sun-Mon, fewer concerts off-season, Mariastraat 38).

Other churches sometimes host concerts, including **St. Salvator's Cathedral** (organ concerts many Fri and some Tue evenings in summer, just southwest of the Markt along the busy Steenstraat shopping drag, www.sintsalvatorskathedraal.be), **St. Walburga** (Jesuit church on Sint-Maartensplein east of the Markt), or **St. James** (on Sint-Jakobsplein, just northwest of the Markt).

## LIVELY AFTER-HOURS STREETS

Check out the following areas for lively bars, many of which have loud music or DJs late at night:

**Eiermarkt** ("Egg Market"), a tiny, table-clogged lane a few steps off the Markt (follow Geernaartstraat, straight across the square from the bell tower), is a rollicking scene that gets younger as the night gets older; Café Pick anchors the scene with frequent live DJs.

Just to the north, **Kupiersstraat** runs behind the City Theater (Stadsschouwburg), with a smattering of bars that cater to various demographics—from funky dives for teens to elegant cellars with well-dressed retirees (for two suggestions, see "Bars with Live Music," next).

Farther out to the west, the long, broad square called **'t Zand** (dominated by the Concertgebouw) is packed with outdoor tables. The area at the north end of the square is the most youthful scene.

East of the Markt, **Langestraat** is lined with young, borderline-rowdy bars and clubs.

## BARS WITH LIVE MUSIC

In addition to the general areas noted earlier, these places have occasional live music.

**'t Zwart Huis** ("The Black House") is a vast, atmospheric space with a classy, upscale vibe. You can get a good meal here, but the main appeal is the chance to enjoy live jazz and blues in an elegant setting (performances several times a month, usually €7.50 cover for music, closed Mon-Tue, Kuipersstraat 23, +32 50 691 140, www.bistrozwarthuis.be). **'t Under Ground,** in the cellar, is a casual and cozy place for drinks but has no live music; they sometimes have dance music late.

**Comptoir des Arts,** a recommended beer cellar, offers live jazz, soul, and blues music on many Sunday evenings (described earlier, under "Eating in Bruges").

**Charlie Rockets** is an American-style bar—lively and central—with foosball, darts, and five pool tables in the inviting back room (closed Mon-Tue, a block off the Markt at Hoogstraat 19). Because they run a youth hostel upstairs, it's filled with a young, international crowd who take full advantage of the guest-only happy hour prices. It's open nightly with nonstop rock 'n' roll (mostly recorded, sometimes live).

# Bruges Connections

## BY TRAIN

For information on rail travel in Belgium, see www.belgiantrain. be; see also the "Transportation" section in the Practicalities chapter.

**From Bruges by Train to: Brussels** (3/hour, 1 hour), **Brussels Airport** (3/hour, 1.5 hours, some transfer at Brussels Midi), **Ghent** (4/hour, 30 minutes), **Antwerp** (3/hour, 1.5 hours, half the trains change in Ghent), **Ypres/Ieper** (hourly, 1.5 hours, change in Kortrijk), **Ostend** (3/hour, 15 minutes), **Delft** (at least hourly, 2.5 hours, change in Ghent, Antwerp, and Rotterdam), **The Hague** (at least hourly, 2.5 hours, change in Ghent and Antwerp, sometimes also Rotterdam), **Cologne** (8/day, 3 hours, change to fast Thalys train or InterCity Express at Brussels Midi), **Paris** (roughly hourly via Brussels, 3 hours on fast Thalys trains—it's best to book the day before), **Amsterdam** (hourly, 4 hours, with 1-4 transfers; faster connection possible with Thalys, 3 hours with changes in Ghent and Antwerp), **Amsterdam's Schiphol Airport** (at least hourly, 3.5 hours with 3 transfers; faster connection possible with Thalys, 2.5 hours with 1-2 transfers), **Haarlem** (hourly, 4 hours, 2-4 changes).

**Trains from London:** Bruges is an ideal "Welcome to Europe" stop after London. Take the Eurostar train from London to Brussels (10/day, 3 hours, see page 220 for details), then transfer, backtracking to Bruges (3/hour, 1 hour, entire trip just a few dollars more with Eurostar ticket).

## BY CRUISE SHIP

The tiny town of **Zeebrugge,** about 10 miles north of Bruges, has a gigantic port that welcomes cruise ships. For more details, see my *Rick Steves Northern European Cruise Ports* book.

From the port, most cruise lines offer shuttles to the Blankenberge train station, the jumping-off point for hourly trains to Bruges (15 minutes), Ghent (50 minutes), and Brussels (1.5 hours). Otherwise, you can ride the coastal tram called Kusttram to the station.

# NEAR BRUGES: FLANDERS FIELDS

These World War I battlefields, about 40 miles southwest of Bruges, remain infamous in military history. In Flanders Fields, the second decade of the 20th century saw the invention of modern warfare: machine guns, trenches, poison gas, and a war of attrition. The most intense fighting occurred in the area called the Ypres Salient, a nondescript but hilly—and strategic—bulge of land just east of the medieval trading town of Ypres. (Ypres is pronounced EE-preh, but the Flemish call it Ieper and pronounce it EE-per.) Over a period of three and a half years, hundreds of thousands of soldiers drew their last breaths here. Fields and forests turned first into trenches and battlefields, and then into desolate, muddy wastelands, devoid of life.

Today, visitors driving through this part of Flanders will pass countless artillery craters, monuments and memorials, stone markers of this advance or that conquest, and war cemeteries alternating with pastureland. Farmers here pull rusty relics of World War I from the earth when they till their fields. Many locals have their own garage collection of "Great War" debris fished out of a field. Human remains are regularly disinterred, with every effort made to identify the fallen soldier and notify any surviving family.

If you're interested in this chapter of history, you can visit several Flanders Fields sights in a one-day side trip from Bruges (best by car or guided tour). The most important and accessible sights are the pleasant market town of Ypres, with its impressive In Flanders Fields Museum; the town of Passchendaele, with a nearby museum (humble but interesting); and Tyne Cot Cemetery, where thousands of enlisted men from the British Commonwealth are buried and honored. Because most of the fighting here involved British Commonwealth troops, the majority of visitors are Brits, Canadians, Australians, and New Zealanders, for whom the stories of Flanders Fields are etched, like names on gravestones, into their national consciousness. You'll notice on maps that many places have English names—often anglicized approximations of the Flemish names (Passiondale for Passchendaele) or evocative new names (Mount Sorrow, Hellfire Corner).

Between the sights, you'll drive through idyllic Belgian countryside, streaked with cornfields, dotted with pudgy cows, and punctuated by the occasional artillery crater—now overgrown with grass or trees, or serving as a little pond.

## GETTING THERE

It's too difficult to see the scattered sights around Ypres using public transportation, so you'll need to rent a car or take a tour (from Ypres or Bruges). Be aware that road signs and transportation timetables use the Flemish "Ieper," not "Ypres."

**By Tour:** To delve into Flanders Fields, your best bet is to take a tour. These come with a rolling history lecture, taking you to off-the-beaten-path sights you'd likely not find on your own. Several companies based in Ypres run tours of the area (for information, check with the Ypres TI listed later); if you're coming from Bruges, it's more convenient to take the Quasimodo big-bus tour (described on page 34).

**By Car:** Here's a one-day plan for seeing the sights listed in this chapter. From Bruges, to make a beeline to Ypres, head south on the A-17 expressway all the way to A-19 and head west, following *Ieper Centrum* signs. For a slower, more scenic route that takes you past more sights, exit the A-17 expressway at R-32 and circle around the northern edge of Roeselare, then head west on N-36, then south on N-313. This leads to Langemark and the German cemetery there. From Langemark, take Zonnebekestraat southeast to the village of Zonnebeke and the Passchendaele Museum. From there follow the Menin Road (N-37) into Ypres, crossing under the Menin Gate as you enter town. After touring Ypres' museum, you can explore more countryside sights or head back to Bruges (fastest

**Flanders Fields**

To Bruges via N-36, R-32 & A-17

2 Kilometers
2 Miles

KLERKEN

N-313

GERMAN CEMETERY

■ CEMETERY
Poelkapelle

Langemark

N-303

CEMETERY ■

Passchendaele

Pilkem    St. Juliaan

O. L. VROUWE.

TYNE COT CEMETERY

ZONNEBEKESTR.

SCHIP

Ypres Canal

N-38

A-19

Zonnebeke

Broodseinde

N-313

N-37

PASSCHENDAELE MUSEUM

N-8

N-332

Ypres

MENIN ROAD

← To Poperinge

MENIN GATE

KASTEELHOF 'T HOOGHE

HOOGE CRATER

IN FLANDERS FIELDS MUSEUM & (CLOTH HALL)

CEMETERY

N-8    A-19

To Kortrijk & Bruges via A-17

TRAIN STATION

Lake    Zillebeke

Geluveld

To Kortrijk, Ghent, Brussels & Bruges

route between Ypres and Bruges: A-19 expressway east to the A-17 interchange near Kortrijk, then zip north on A-17).

**By Public Transportation to Ypres:** You can get to Ypres by train from Bruges (hourly, 1.5 hours with a transfer in Kortrijk) or from Ghent (direct hourly, 1 hour).

## BACKGROUND

Because American forces played a relatively minor role in the fighting at Flanders Fields, its history is obscure to many visitors from the US. This section will get you up to speed.

From 1830, Belgium was established as an independent and neutral state—an essential buffer zone to protect European peace, surrounded by four big powers: France, Prussia, the Netherlands, and Britain. After defeating France and unifying in 1870, Germany was on the rise—an upstart powerhouse hungry for overseas colonies to fuel its growing economy. Germany amassed an intimidating army while the rest of Europe worriedly watched. Some European nations scrambled to ally themselves with their neighbors against potential German encroachment; others threw in with Germany. Because many alliances were secret, and often conflicting, no one knew for sure exactly where anyone else stood. As H. G. Wells said, "Every intelligent person in the world knew that disaster was impending and knew no way to avoid it."

On June 28, 1914, while on a visit to Sarajevo, the heir to the Austro-Hungarian throne, Archduke Franz Ferdinand, and his wife were assassinated by a teenage terrorist working for Bosnian Serb separatists. The Austrians held Serbia responsible and declared war. Germany joined Austria, and Russia (allied with France) backed Serbia. Through an intricate web of alliances—which ironically had been created to prevent war—soon most of Europe was drawn into the conflict. On August 4, 1914, Germany sent some 800,000 troops across the border into neutral Belgium en route to France. By August 20, they had already taken Brussels, and four days later they were in western Flanders.

The Germans expected to blow through the country quickly. But the small Belgian army—less than a quarter the size of the German army—pushed back hard, as they waited for British reinforcements to come from across the Channel. In the **Battle of the Yser (Ijzer) River,** the Belgians opened a sea gate to flood a low-lying plain just before a German advance. This diverted the German effort slightly to the south, around Ypres.

Ypres was an ordinary town, but its surrounding, mostly flat terrain and modern weaponry turned it into a perpetual battlefield. This conflict saw the advent of the machine gun—an invention that, before the war, was called "the peacekeeper" because it was assumed that no sane commander would ever send his boys into its fire. With the machine gun, even the slightest gain in elevation was a strategic advantage. From any ridge, machine guns and artillery could mow down enemy troops—advancing armies were sitting ducks. Consequently, the low-lying ridges just east of Ypres—which came to be known as the **Ypres Salient** (the French term for "bulge")—saw some of the fiercest fighting of World War I.

The **First Battle of Ypres,** in October and November 1914, began when German troops attempted to invade the town. It became a priority of the Allies—Belgians, French, and British Commonwealth troops—to hold the Germans at bay. Both sides sustained huge losses, but the German troops—mostly inexperienced young conscripts who had underestimated the opposition—were devastated; to this day, Germans call the battle *Kindermord,* "Massacre of the Innocents."

Both sides regrouped and prepared for a harsh winter. They dug trenches, as it was human nature for soldiers ducking machine-gun bullets to burrow down. Separated by as little as 50 yards, enemy

# In Flanders Fields

In Flanders fields the poppies blow
Between the crosses, row on row,
That mark our place; and in the sky
The larks, still bravely singing, fly
Scarce heard amid the guns below.

We are the Dead. Short days ago
We lived, felt dawn, saw sunset glow,
Loved and were loved, and now we lie,
In Flanders fields.

Take up our quarrel with the foe:
To you from failing hands we throw
The torch; be yours to hold it high.
If ye break faith with us who die
We shall not sleep, though poppies grow
In Flanders fields.

—John McCrae, Canadian soldier during the
Second Battle of Ypres who died on the front lines in
1918

armies were close enough to offer each other a *Gesundheit!* after each sneeze. It was during this time that the famous "Christmas Truce" took place, in which German soldiers erected little candlelit *Tanenbaum*s beside their trenches and even approached the English trenches with gifts, kind words, and a pick-up soccer game.

During the **Second Battle of Ypres,** in spring 1915, the Germans used poison gas for the first time on a large scale, catching the Allies off guard. Chlorine gas (a.k.a. bertholite) reacts with moisture in the lungs to form hydrochloric acid—choking soldiers from the inside out. It was also one of the first times flamethrowers were used in battle. Still, the Germans were unable to take the town. By May 1915, the opposing forces were deadlocked near the town of Passchendaele, seven miles east of Ypres; for two years, little progress was made in either direction.

Although the Western Front appeared to be "all quiet," each side fortified its positions. The Germans established an elaborate network of five successive trenches, connected to and supplied by one another with perpendicular "switches." They built stout fortresses with flat tops, designed to protect troops from British artillery while allowing them to quickly emerge to man nearby machine-gun nests. These flat-top German fortresses—which you'll see everywhere—were dubbed "pillboxes" (the Germans used the pillbox design again in World War II, but with a rounded top—

which better withstood artillery blasts). The British opted for underground wooden tunnels, called "dugouts," and reserved concrete bunkers for more specialized use as command posts and shelters for the wounded.

In the summer of 1917, the Allies attempted their own offensive against the newly strengthened German lines. This was the **Third Battle of Ypres** (a.k.a. the Battle of Passchendaele). After a sustained two-week artillery bombardment of German positions, some four million projectiles turned the countryside into a desolate wasteland. One soldier said that "the earth had been churned and rechurned"; another termed it "as featureless as the Sahara."

The British infantry then took to the battlefield, going over the tops of the trenches—only to face barbed wire, machine-gun fire, dangerously exposed high ground, and liquid mud. The devastation of the shelling, combined with historic rainfall, turned the Ypres Salient into a sea of mud. With the ground like quicksand, troops and tanks could barely move, and the British gained only two of the four miles they needed to conquer. This battle was the first time the Germans used mustard gas, which blistered skin on contact.

As fall approached, heavy rains continued to deluge the area, but British soldiers made inroads, bunker by bunker. Their goal was the destroyed village of Passchendaele, perched on a modest ridge with a strategic view over the flat lands below. The village's name literally meant "passing the valley," but the Brits dubbed it "Passiondale"...the valley of suffering. Menin Road, which connected Ypres to Passchendaele (now road N-37), was the focus of much warfare—especially the intersection dubbed "Hellfire Corner."

In the end, British forces never succeeded in taking Passchendaele; Canadian forces finally took it in November 1917. By this point, each side had lost about a quarter of a million men in what had become a battle of attrition.

Two pivotal events took place during the winter of 1917-1918: The United States entered the war on the side of the Allies; and Germany agreed to a separate peace with Russia, allowing it to steer more men and resources to the Ypres Salient. In spring 1918, the **Fourth Battle of Ypres** (a.k.a. the Battle of the Lys) saw German forces trying to push through to the town of Ypres before US troops could arrive. Always innovative on the battlefield, the Germans introduced an elite squad of storm troopers (*Stosstruppen*, literally "shock troops")—lightly armed but well-trained and highly mobile special units tasked with breaking through enemy lines.

But by late April, the German advance stalled for lack of supplies. Meanwhile, American troops had arrived, and by the fall of 1918, in the **Fifth Battle of Ypres,** Allied forces made huge gains. Less than a month later, Armistice Day (November 11, 1918) brought an end to the war to end all wars...until the next war.

## *Dulce et Decorum Est*

Bent double, like old beggars under sacks,
Knock-kneed, coughing like hags, we cursed
    through sludge,
Till on the haunting flares we turned our backs
And towards our distant rest began to trudge.
Men marched asleep. Many had lost their boots
But limped on, blood-shod. All went lame;
    all blind;
Drunk with fatigue; deaf even to the hoots
Of tired, outstripped Five-Nines that dropped
    behind.

Gas! Gas! Quick, boys!—An ecstasy of fumbling,
Fitting the clumsy helmets just in time;
But someone still was yelling out and stumbling,
And flound'ring like a man in fire or lime...
Dim, through the misty panes and thick green
    light,
As under a green sea, I saw him drowning.

In all my dreams, before my helpless sight,
He plunges at me, guttering, choking, drowning.

If in some smothering dreams you too could
    pace
Behind the wagon that we flung him in,
And watch the white eyes writhing in his face,
His hanging face, like a devil's sick of sin;
If you could hear, at every jolt, the blood
Come gargling from the froth-corrupted lungs,
Obscene as cancer, bitter as the cud
Of vile, incurable sores on innocent tongues, —
My friend, you would not tell with such high zest
To children ardent for some desperate glory,
The old Lie: Dulce et decorum est
Pro patria mori.

    —Wilfred Owen, English soldier who died in
battle in 1918

World War I claimed the lives of an estimated nine million people; about one million were killed, wounded, or declared missing in action here in the Ypres Salient. In the century since, Flanders Fields has become a compelling destination for the descendants of the soldiers who fought here. As you tour the place, keep in mind that everything you see—every building, every tree—dates from after 1918.

Poppies were the first flowers to bloom in Ypres' ravaged landscape after the war. And today, this far-western corner of Belgium is blooming once more, having adopted that flower as a symbol of sacrifice and renewal.

## Sights in Flanders Fields

### YPRES TOWN
About 40 miles southwest of Bruges is the town most English speakers call Ypres. By the end of the war, Ypres was so devastated that Winston Churchill advocated keeping it in ruins as a monument to the travesty of warfare. But locals did rebuild, resurrecting its charming main market square (Grote Markt), watched over by the grand and impressive Cloth Hall (which houses the In Flanders Fields Museum). Today's Ypres is a

pleasant market town (Saturday morning is market day), with a steady stream of mostly British tourists interested in the WWI sights.

**Tourist Information:** The helpful TI, downstairs in the Cloth Hall, has information on tours (below the museum, Mon-Fri 9:00-18:00, Sat-Sun from 10:00, shorter hours off-season, +32 57 239 220, www.toerisme-ieper.be).

**Helpful Hints:** There's free **parking** at the train station and pay parking on the main market square, next to the Cloth Hall (3-hour limit). If you're exploring on your own, get a **local guidebook and map** to point you to the many additional sights beyond what I list (several are available at local bookstores and tourist offices). For practical information about the area, see www.flandersfields.be.

### ▲▲In Flanders Fields Museum
Using artifacts and thoughtful presentations, this excellent museum offers a moving look at the battles fought on the Belgian front near Ypres. The focus is not on strategy and commanders, but on the people who fought and died here, and features personal testimony about life in the trenches.

**Cost and Hours:** €10; daily 10:00-18:00; mid-Nov-March Tue-Sun 10:00-17:00, closed Mon and all of Jan; last entry one hour before closing, audioguide-€2, in the Cloth Hall at Grote Markt 34, +32 57 239 220, www.inflandersfields.be.

**Visiting the Museum:** Upon entering the high-tech displays, you'll receive a bracelet. Once you register it, some of the exhibits are tuned to your age, gender, and country. One display shows aerial photos of the region today, which you can then select and swipe to see what it looked like from the air during the war.

Throughout the museum, large video panels show actors portraying eyewitnesses to the events of the war. One panel has Germans justifying gas attacks, followed by a different German describing the aftermath—"even the insects died." In a small theater is a moving exhibit featuring doctors and nurses talking about treating the wounded and dying.

**Nearby:** The Cloth Hall's **belfry** (231 steps to the top, €2 extra) offers a panoramic view of the surrounding countryside.

### ▲Menin Gate

This impressive Victorian archway is an easy two-block walk from the museum (past the end of Grote Markt). Built into the old town wall of Ypres, it's etched with the names of British Commonwealth victims who fought here. It marks the Menin Road, where many Brits, Canadians, Aussies, and Kiwis left this town for the battlefields and trenches, never to return. The gate is formally a mausoleum for "the Missing," 54,896 troops who likely perished at Flanders Fields but whose remains were never found.

To honor the hundreds of thousands of British subjects who gave their lives, every night under the arch at 20:00, a Belgian bugle corps plays the "Last Post" to honor the dead. Arrive under the arch at 19:30 to get the best view.

## NEAR YPRES

Most of these sights are on or near the Menin Road between Ypres and Passchendaele (to the northeast), where the most famous battles took place. The German Cemetery is a bit to the north (but still within a few miles).

The sights listed here are just the beginning. You can't drive a mile or two without passing a monument or memorial. Tranquil forests open into clearings with eerily rippled contours—overgrown trenches, pockmarks, and craters. Certain nondescript ponds and lakes are actually flooded artillery craters. Joining a tour helps you find some of the more out-of-the-way remnants of the war. If you're exploring on your own, get a guidebook on the region.

### ▲Passchendaele Museum

Though a bit old-fashioned, this exhibit supplements the In Flanders Fields Museum nicely, with a focus on strategy and battles.

**Cost and Hours:** €10.50, includes audioguide, daily 10:00-17:30, last entry one hour before closing, closed Dec-Jan, Berten Pilstraat 5a, in Zonnebeke about 5 miles east of Ypres and 2 miles west of Passchendaele, +32 51 770 441, www.passchendaele.be.

**Visiting the Museum:** Presented chronologically on the top floor of a chalet-like mansion, this museum details each advance and retreat, from the first German boot on Belgian soil to Armistice Day. You'll see displays of uniforms, medical instruments, and objects illustrating day-to-day life at the front. One exhibit explains—and lets you sniff—the four basic types of poison gas used here.

An exit takes you through a simulation of the wooden underground "dugout" tunnels used by British forces as their headquarters (built after artillery fire had scorched the ground above so badly there was nothing left). Outside, you'll walk through a reconstruction of the shallow trenches that zigzagged along No Man's Land. Note how later trenches had slotted walkways so that soldiers didn't have to wade through mud.

Finally, back at the museum, you can hear video testimony from WWI veterans—Brits, Aussies, Kiwis, and Canucks—on what it was like at Passchendaele.

### ▲Tyne Cot Cemetery

This evocative cemetery is the final resting place of 11,956 British, Canadian, Australian, New Zealander, South African, and other British Commonwealth soldiers. It was named for a blockhouse on this site that was taken by British forces, who nicknamed it "Tyne Cottage" after the river in North England.

**Cost and Hours:** Free, visitors center open daily 10:00-18:00, closed Dec-Jan, just northeast of Zonnebeke, off of N-37 toward Passchendaele, about 6.5 miles east of Ypres, www.cwgc.org.

**Visiting the Cemetery:** The cemetery grounds hold three German pillbox bunkers and seemingly endless rows of white headstones, marked with a soldier's name and his unit's emblem (such as the maple leaf of Canada). Many graves are marked simply "A soldier of the Great War, known to God." The long list of names and ages of the deceased are announced over speakers.

In the center of the cemetery, near the tallest cross (marking the location of Tyne Cottage), notice the higgledy-piggledy arrangement of graves. During the war, when this cottage was a makeshift medic station, this area became an impromptu burial ground. Any cemetery that's neat and symmetrical—like the surrounding headstones—dates from after the war.

Running along the top of the cemetery is a wall inscribed with the names of 34,857 "officers and men to whom the fortune of war denied the known and honoured burial given to their comrades in death." The visitors center has a few artifacts and exhibits about the fighting here.

## Hooge Crater

This giant flooded crater, about three miles east of Ypres, was created by successive mine explosions detonated in turn by both British and German forces. The strategic high ground around the crater (where a château used for a time as British headquarters once stood) switched hands repeatedly throughout the war.

Today the Hooge Crater area has a large British Commonwealth **cemetery** with about 6,000 graves—about 60 percent of which are "known unto God." Across the road is the **Hooge Crater Museum,** a touristy exhibit with information about the fighting here (€7.50, Wed-Sat 10:00-18:00, Sun until 21:00, closed Mon-Tue, Meenseweg 467, +32 57 468 446, www.hoogecrater.com). Hiding out in the woods just down the road is a hotel/restaurant called **Kasteelhof 't Hooghe,** where you can pay €1 to stroll around the adjacent crater-pond and see some trenches and old bunkers—one of which is accessible (restaurant closed Sat-Sun, Meenseweg 481, www.hotelkasteelhofthooghe.be).

## German Military Cemetery (Deutscher Soldatenfriedhof) at Langemark

A relatively rare site dedicated to the invaders of this region, this is the where 44,324 Central Powers soldiers are buried (along with two Brits who were originally misidentified). Compared with the gleaming British Commonwealth cemeteries nearby, it's dull and drab. That's because the Treaty of Versailles that concluded World War I forbade German WWI cemeteries

FLANDERS FIELDS

from using white stones. Instead, gray basalt and even oak are used to mark the graves. As you wander the cemetery, you'll notice many Slavic names: Troops were sent to fight here from the far eastern corners of the multiethnic Austro-Hungarian Empire. In the center is a mass grave with 25,000 soldiers (cemetery located on the northern outskirts of Langemark, about five miles north/northeast of Ypres).

# BRUSSELS

# ORIENTATION TO BRUSSELS

*Brussel • Bruxelles*

Six hundred years ago, Brussels was just a nice place to stop and buy a waffle on the way to Bruges. With no strategic importance, it grew as a free trading town. Today it's the capital of Belgium, the headquarters of NATO, and the seat of the European Union (EU). It's also a fascinating and vibrant city in its own right, with fun-to-explore neighborhoods, good sightseeing, pleasant pedestrian zones, an impressive selection of restaurants, and a quirky Flemish/French mix.

The Brussels of today reflects its past. The city enjoyed a golden age of peace and prosperity (1400-1550) when many of its signature structures were built. In the late 1800s, Brussels had another growth spurt, fueled by industrialization, wealth taken from the Belgian Congo, and the exhilaration of the country's recent independence (1830). The "Builder King" Leopold II erected grand monuments and palaces. Then, in 1992, 12 countries established the European Union by signing the Treaty of Maastricht, and sleepy Brussels was thrust into the spotlight as the unofficial capital of the new Europe. It started a frenzy of renovation, infrastructure projects, foreign visitors, and world attention.

As a tourist destination, Brussels captivates some visitors and exasperates others. At its best, Brussels mingles French class and Belgian spunk. At its worst, it's a crowded, jaded city of demanding tourists, stuffy bureaucrats, and down-and-out immigrants. Its museums are respectable, but not quite befitting its status as a world capital. But if you make an effort to explore some less-traveled neighborhoods, you'll experience another side of Brussels. The more you see, the more you'll like it.

In Brussels, people speak French. Bone up on *bonjour* and play up the *s'il vous plaît* (see the French survival phrases in the appendix). The Bruxellois are cultured and genteel—even a bit snobby

Greater Brussels

ATOMIUM ■

JETTE

To Antwerp & Amsterdam

Canal

3 Kilometers
2 Miles

To Ghent & Bruges

Charleroi

To Airport, Antwerp & Amsterdam

■ KOEKELBERG BASILICA

KOEKEL-
BERG

SCHAERBEEK

NORD STATION

N-22

See Brussels Center detail map

*Grand Place*

ANDER-
LECHT

CENTRAL STATION

CENTER

Parc de Bruxelles

Cinquantenaire Park

■ EUROPEAN PARLIAMENT

MIDI STATION

PALAIS DE JUSTICE

See Upper Town detail map

MATONGE

See East Brussels detail map

"LITTLE BELT"

Note: Shaded area indicates Central Brussels within the "Little Belt"

To Bruges & Paris

ST. GILLES

N-5

To Waterloo ▾

To AfricaMuseum

compared to their earthier Flemish cousins. The whole feel of the town is urban French, not rural Flemish. And yet there's an impish sparkle and joie de vivre, as evidenced by the Bruxellois love of comic strips (giant comic-strip panels are painted on buildings all over town) and their civic symbol: a statue of a little boy peeing.

Brussels is the cutting edge of modern Europe, but still clothed in its Old World garments. Stroll the Grand Place, snap a selfie with the *Manneken-Pis,* and watch diplomats at work at the EU assembly halls. Then grab some mussels, fries, and a hearty Belgian beer, and watch the sun set behind the Town Hall's lacy steeple.

**Brussels Overview**

To Simonis

To Gare de l'Ouest & Erasmus

Metro #1 & 5

Comte de Flandre

Charleroi

Canal

BLVD. DE NIEUPORT

To Airport, Antwerp & Amsterdam

NORD STATION

Yser

BLVD. D'ANVERS

Metro #2 & 6

"LITTLE BELT"

Rogier

BLVD. DU JARDIN BOTANIQUE

Botanique

STE. CATHERINE

BELGIAN COMIC STRIP CENTER

Sainte-Catherine

Metro #3 & 4

De Brouckère

RAIL TUNNEL

RUE ROYALE

BLVD. BISCHOFFSHEIM

Madou

DANSAERT

Bourse

BLVD. ANSPACH

Grand Place

Gare Central

LOWER TOWN

MANNEKEN-PIS

Anneessens

Bus #38 & 71

CENTRAL STATION

Parc

Metro #1 & 5

Arts-Loi

To Stokkel & Herrmann-Debroux

RUE DE LA LOI

To Cinquantenaire Park

RUE BELLIARD

"PETIT RING"

BLVD. DE L'ABBATOIR

UPPER TOWN

ROYAL MUSEUMS OF FINE ARTS

Parc de Bruxelles

To Simonis & Roi Baudouin

Lemonnier

PALAIS DE JUSTICE

BLVD. DU REGENT

Trône

Bus #27

Bus #27 & 38

R. LUXEMBOURG

EUROPEAN PARLIAMENT

Gare du Midi

Bus to Charleroi Airport

BLVD. DU MIDI

Bus #27

"LITTLE BELT"

Porte de Namur

Bus #71

WAVERSESTEENWEG

MIDI STATION

Metro #2 & 6

"BD. DE WATERLOO"

Louise

AVE. LOUISE

ELSENSESTEENWEG

MATONGE

To Paris

Porte de Hal

Hôtel Des Monnaies

IXELLES

ST. GILLES

1 Kilometer

1/2 Mile

Note: Shaded area indicates "Little Belt" that encircles Central Brussels

## BRUSSELS: A VERBAL MAP

Central Brussels is surrounded by a pentagon-shaped ring of roads, which replaced the old city wall. All hotels and nearly all the sights I mention are within this ring. The epicenter (or *petite ceinture*, literally "little belt") holds the main square (the Grand Place), the TI, and Central/Centraal station (all within three blocks of one another).

What isn't so apparent from maps is that Brussels is a city divided by altitude. A ridgeline splits the town into the Upper Town (east half, elevation 200 feet) and Lower Town (west, at sea level), with Central station in between.

Brussels' bilingual street signs give the French name first, then the Dutch. That, combined with the lack of a regular grid plan, can make navigating the city confusing. It's easy to get turned around. I rely heavily on a good map when exploring this town. Note that in the Brussels chapters of this book, after introducing a name in

French and Dutch, I've used the French names alone to keep things simple.

It's helpful to think of the city as a series of neighborhoods, each with its own character.

**The Lower Town:** This crowded, touristy district—with the Grand Place (in Dutch: Grote Markt, *H*ROH-teh markt), narrow streets, old buildings, modern shops, tourist-trap eateries, and the famous *Manneken-Pis* peeing-boy statue—is squeezed between Central station and Boulevard Anspach.

**West of Boulevard Anspach:** This newly pedestrianized boulevard, which runs over the city's forgotten river, marks the boundary between Brussels' touristy core and its more characteristic neighborhoods. Just beyond Boulevard Anspach—past a block or two of high-rise ugliness—is the lively and youthful market square called **Place St-Géry** (Sint-Goriksplein). The **Dansaert** district (just above Place St-Géry, along Rue Antoine Dansaert) is emerging as a high-fashion district, with a creative "bobo" *(bourgeois-bo-hème)* ambience. Just to the north is the **Ste. Catherine** neighborhood, a charming village-within-a-city huddled around the old fish market, and home to several recommended hotels and restaurants.

**The Upper Town:** This uphill, upper-crust district surrounds the Royal Palace. Traditionally the home of nobility and the rich, this area has big marble palaces, broad boulevards, and the major museums. Compared with other parts of the city, it feels stately and sterile. The zone between the Upper and Lower towns, called **Sablon,** feels French and urbane.

**Beyond the Core:** Everything within the center of town is walkable. Outside that zone, sprawling suburbs and vast green spaces contain attractions that are more easily reached by public transportation or taxi. To the east are the **European Parliament** and, beyond that, the **Park of the Cinquantenaire** (with the Royal Museum of the Armed Forces and Military History and Autoworld). Tucked between the European Parliament and the Upper Town is **Matongé,** an immigrant African neighborhood that has become high-rent. And far to the north is the **1958 World's Fair site,** with the Atomium and Mini-Europe.

## PLANNING YOUR TIME

For a city of its size and prominence, Brussels can be seen quickly: Its main attraction, the Grand Place, is a short walk from Central station; several good museums and neighborhoods are also easily walkable. On a quick trip, a day and a night are enough for a good first taste (but if you have more time, Brussels has enjoyable ways to fill it). Or—if you're in a hurry—Brussels can be done as a day trip by train from Bruges, Ghent, or Antwerp (frequent trains, less than an hour from any of these) or a stopover on the Amsterdam-Paris or Amsterdam-Bruges ride.

## Brussels in Three to Five Hours

Toss your bag in a locker at Central station and confirm your departure time and station (note that fast international trains depart from Midi/Zuid station—not from Central station). Then walk about five minutes into town and do this Brussels blitz:

Head directly for the Grand Place and take my Grand Place Walk. To streamline, skip the *Manneken-Pis* until later, and end the walk at the Bourse (stock-exchange building). From there, walk a few blocks to Place de Brouckère, where you can catch a taxi or Uber to Place Royale (Koningsplein) in the Upper Town. Enjoy the Royal Museums of Fine Arts. If catching a train, make a bee-line to the station; if you have another hour or two, do my Upper Town Walk, which ends near the *Manneken-Pis* and the Grand Place. Buy a box of chocolates and a bottle of Belgian beer, and pop the top as your train pulls out of the station.

## Brussels in One to Two Days

A full day (with one or two overnights) is about right to get a more complete taste of Brussels. With a second day, you can slow down and really delve into the city.

### Day 1

| | |
|---|---|
| 10:00 | Get your bearings with my Grand Place Walk. |
| 12:00 | Walk over to the Ste. Catherine neighborhood for a quick lunch. |
| 13:30 | Tour the Musical Instruments Museum on your way to the Upper Town. |
| 15:00 | Tour the Royal Museums of Fine Arts. |
| 17:00 | Follow my Upper Town Walk. |
| Evening | Relax with a predinner drink on the Grand Place. Then explore some of the interesting neighborhoods away from the touristy core, and find a good place for dinner. Poke around the fun and colorful streets around Place St-Géry and Ste. Catherine. |

### Day 2

If staying for two days, you could do the Grand Place Walk on the first day, and save the art museums and Upper Town Walk for the second day. To fill in the remaining time each day, consider the following options.

Historians enjoy the story of Belgium at the excellent BELvue Museum (very near the Royal Museums). Aficionados of the funny pages head for the Belgian Comic Strip Center (in the Lower Town, a 15-minute walk from the Grand Place). And political-science majors visit the European Parliament complex for a lesson in Euro-civics (best on weekdays).

With more time or a special interest, head to the museums at the Park of the Cinquantenaire. Outside of town, see the Mémorial 1815 museum at the site of the Battle of Waterloo, or venture to Tervuren to tour the AfricaMuseum, set in a big park.

# Overview

## TOURIST INFORMATION

Brussels has two centrally located TIs: inside the Town Hall on the Grand Place (daily 9:00-18:00) and on Place Royale (Mon-Fri 9:30-17:30, Sat-Sun 10:00-18:00, Rue Royale 2). They share a phone number and website: +32 2 513 8940, www.visit.brussels.

The TI offers a good €1 city map with a Métro/train map on the back, and a €5 "Official Guidebook." For concerts and entertainment options in English, grab the free weekly magazine *Bruzz* (and check the "Agenda" page on the TI website).

**Sightseeing Pass:** The **Brussels Card,** sold at TIs and museums, includes entrance to nearly all major sights except the Comic Strip Museum (€29/24 hours, €39/48 hours, €46/72 hours, www.brusselscard.be)—but you'll need to do a lot of sightseeing to get your money's worth.

## ARRIVAL IN BRUSSELS
### By Train

Brussels has three stations (none of which is officially the "main" train station): Central/Centraal (central), Midi/Zuid (south), and Nord/Noord (north). Most Brussels-bound trains (except high-speed international trains) stop at all three stations, but Central station is by far the most convenient for arriving sightseers. The three stations are connected by regular trains (leaving every few minutes).

### Central/Centraal Station

This station, nearest to the sights and my recommended hotels, has handy services: a small grocery store, fast food, waiting rooms, and luggage lockers (between tracks 3 and 4).

You can walk from the station to the Grand Place in about five minutes: Take the escalator to the top floor, leave the station, and walk downhill to a little square nicknamed "Agora." At the far end of this square, turn left to reach the Grand Place.

Hop-on, hop-off tourist buses depart from Central station—a handy way to get oriented to the city (see "Tours in Brussels," later).

# Brussels Center

RUE DE LA BLANCHISSERIE

BLVD. DU JARDIN BOTANIQUE

M Botanique

RUE DU DAMIER

R. DE L'OMMEGANG

N

200 Meters
200 Yards

RUE AUX CHOUX

BRUSSELS
CONGRÈS
STATION

Place des
Martyrs

RUE ROYALE

Place des
Barricades

BELGIAN
COMIC STRIP
CENTER

R. DES SABLES

RUE DU MEIBOOM

BLVD. PACHECO

R. DU GOUVERNEMENT PROVISOIRE

RUE DU MARAIS

RUE DES BOITEUX  RUE DES COMEDIENS

RUE ST. LAUREN

Place du
Congrès

RUE ROYALE

ILOT
SACRE

BLVD. DU BERLAIMONT

RUE DE LA BANQUE

RUE DE LIGNE

RUE DU CONGRES

RUE DE LA PRESSE

RUE DE L'ENSEIGNEMENT

See
Grand Place Walk
detail map

RUE DE LIGNE

D'ARENBERG

RUE D'ASSAUT

Place
Sainte
Gudule

ST.
MICHAEL'S

RUE DE LA CROIX DE FER

MONTAGNE

RUE DE L'IMPÉRATRICE

RUE DE LOUAIN

Gare
Central M

RUE DES COLONIES

M Parc

RUE DE LOUVAIN

BELGIAN
PARLIAMENT

BD. DE L'IMPÉRATRICE

Carrefour
de l'Europe

PUTTERIE

T

B #58 &
71

RUE DE LA LOI

ISABELLE

CENTRAL
STATION

Marché
aux Bois

B
#38 &
71

RUE RAVENSTEIN

Parc de
Bruxelles

RUE ZINNER

Jardin du
Mont
des Arts

RUE ROYALE

RUE DUCALE

MUSICAL
INSTRUMENTS
MUSEUM

BELVUE
MUSEUM

MAGRITTE
MUSEUM

B #58 &
71

Place
Royale

ROYAL
MUSEUMS
OF FINE
ARTS

Place des
Palais

RUE DUCALE

SCULPTURE
GARDEN

B
#27

COUDENBERG
PALACE

ROYAL
PALACE

To
Place du Trône &
European
Parliament

UPPER
TOWN

BLVD. DU REGENT

## Brussels Waffles...Linguistically

Brussels is the one part of Belgium that's neither fully French nor fully Flemish. (It occupies its own bicultural mini province, near the border between Wallonia and Flanders.) While residents spoke mostly Dutch until 1900, today Brussels is officially bilingual and bicultural. In practice, 65 percent of "Bruxellois" speak French as their first language, and only 5 percent speak Dutch (and call themselves "Brusselaar").

The remaining 30 percent aren't Bruxellois, or even Belgian—they're nonnatives who speak their own languages. As the unofficial capital of Europe, Brussels is multicultural. Besides its immigrant population, it hosts politicians and businesspeople from around the globe and features cuisine from around the world in its restaurants. The city is home to over 300 embassies (the US has three here, one each to the EU, NATO, and Belgium). Every sizable corporation has a lobbyist in Brussels.

Most businesspeople, diplomats, and politicians use English as their default. Some predict that in 20 years, English will be the city's de facto first language.

### Midi/Zuid Station

About 1.5 miles southwest of the city center, Midi station serves the fastest high-speed international connections, such as Eurostar, Thalys, and TGV, which stop only at this station (for more on these, see "Brussels Connections" on page 219). All other trains that stop at Midi also stop at Central and Nord.

It's a good idea to know both the French and Dutch names for this station (Bruxelles-Midi and Brussel-Zuid), as you may see signs for either one.

Midi's tracks are connected by a long, gloomy, gray-steel concourse with ample computer screens showing upcoming trains. High-speed trains use tracks 1-6 (1-2 for Eurostar and 3-6 for the others). The station has plenty of luggage lockers (between tracks 6 and 7), as well as three separate Travel Centre ticket offices (for domestic, international, and international/immediate departures). The area around the station is a rough-and-tumble immigrant neighborhood.

**Getting from Midi Station to the Center:** If you must disembark at Midi station, it's easy to make your way to **Central station** and on to Grand Place. Trains run every few minutes, and the fare is covered by any train ticket into or out of Brussels (or an active rail pass). Scan the departure boards—even if "Central" isn't listed as a destination, trains headed for many places (the airport, Antwerp, Leuven, Liège, Namur, etc.) will stop there. Note that trains headed in the opposite direction—including those to Ghent and Bruges—have *already* stopped at Central station.

Alternatively, you can take a **taxi** or Uber from Midi into the city center. It should cost no more than €15, but cabbies from this station are notorious for taking a roundabout route. Insist on the meter, follow the route on a map, and if the total fare seems too high, enlist the help of your hotel receptionist.

### Nord/Noord Station
Any train that goes through Nord station will also stop at the other two. Don't bother getting off at this station (surrounded by a seedy red light district)—disembark at Central station instead.

## By Plane
Brussels is served by two airports. Most flights use the primary Brussels Airport, a.k.a. Zaventem. No-frills carriers use the Brussels South Charleroi Airport. For details on both, see "Brussels Connections" on page 219).

## HELPFUL HINTS
**Theft Alert:** The tourist zone—the area within the pentagon-shaped ring road—is basically safe at any hour of day or night, but as in any big city, low-level street crimes (bag snatching/pickpocketing) do occur. Be aware of your surroundings in the Métro, train stations, or any crowded zone.

**Festivals and Events:** Check www.agenda.brussels for a calendar of concerts, festivals, markets, and more.

**Money:** As fewer people are using cash these days, there are fewer ATMs around town. Get cash when you have a convenient opportunity.

**Sightseeing Schedules:** Brussels' most important museums are closed on Monday. Of course, the city's single best sight—the Grand Place—is always open. You can also enjoy a bus tour any day of the week, or visit the more far-flung sights (which are open daily), such as the Atomium/Mini-Europe, the European Parliament's Parlamentarium museum, or the 1815 Mémorial museum commemorating the Battle of Waterloo.

**Travel Bookstore: Anticyclone des Açores** has a wide selection of maps and travel books, including many in English (Tue-Sat 11:00-18:00, closed Sun-Mon, Rue Fossé aux Loups 34, +32 2 217 5246, www.anticyclonedesacores.be).

**Bilingual Brussels:** Because the city is officially bilingual, Brussels' street signs and maps are in both French and Dutch. Because the languages are so different, many places have two names that barely resemble each other (for example, Marché aux Herbes/Grasmarkt, or Place Royale/Koningsplein). In

## Brussels Public Transportation

Metro

Rail

Bus Routes

Not all lines or stations are shown

■ ATOMIUM

Roi Baudouin — Heysel

Belgica

Elisabeth — Simonis

Ribaucourt — Yser

Ossegem

Etangs Noirs — Sainte-Catherine

STE. CATHERINE

Beekkant

Gare de l'Ouest

Jacques Brel — Delacroix — Clemenceau

Erasme

Not to Scale

this book—due to space constraints—I've generally given only the French name.

**Laundry: Wash Club** is near the Grand Place, along the shopping street Rue du Marché au Charbon (at #68, daily 7:00-22:00). **Maximousse** is convenient for those sleeping in the Ste. Catherine neighborhood (daily 7:00-22:00, no change machine, Rue Flandre 51). For locations see the "Brussels Hotels" map on page 204.

**Car Rental:** All major agencies have offices at Midi/Zuid station and Brussels Airport.

## GETTING AROUND BRUSSELS

Most of central Brussels' sights can be reached on foot. But public transport is handy for connecting the train stations, climbing to the Upper Town, visiting sights outside the central core (the European Parliament, Autoworld, Atomium, or Matongé neighborhood), and getting to Ste. Catherine neighborhood hotels. The city-run Villo system has public bike stations around town.

### By Public Transportation

Brussels' extensive public transport network includes a Métro, trams, and buses (www.stib-mivb.be). Transit stops are labeled in both French and Dutch (though sometimes just one name works in both languages). A downloadable Métro(train) map is available at www.brussels.be/public-transport (and is on the back of the official map sold at the TI). Maps of Brussels' bus routes are available at www.stib-mivb.be, but it's easiest to navigate with Google Maps on your mobile device.

**Buying and Using Tickets:** A single-fare €2.60 **ticket** is good for one hour on all public transportation—Métro, buses, trams, and even trains shuttling between the city's train stations. An **all-day pass** (Discover Brussels 24H) is €8—cheaper than four single tickets—and on Saturday, Sunday, and holidays, this pass covers two people.

Buy individual tickets from vending machines at Métro stations and many central bus stops. When you enter the Métro, a bus, or a tram, validate your ticket by touching the scanner until you hear the beep. You can also pay by tapping your credit card as you board.

**Métro:** Lines 1 and 5 travel east-west through the city, with stops at Sainte-Catherine/Sint-Katelijne (recommended hotels), De Brouckère (hotels near the Bourse and Grand Place), Gare Central/Centraal Station (trains), Parc/Park (Upper Town), and continuing east to Merode (Cinquantenaire). The other Métro lines are less helpful for travelers. Lines 3 and 4 run north and south, with stops at De Brouckère, Bourse/Beurs, and Gare du Midi/Zuidstation. Métro line 6 takes you to sights far north of downtown (Atomium, near Métro stop Heysel/Heizel).

**Buses:** Buses #38 and #71 travel roughly east-west, connecting the Lower Town (near Central station), the Upper Town (Royal Museums), and sights farther east (#38 to the European Parliament, #71 to Matongé). Bus #27 connects the Royal Museums with the European Parliament and the Park of the Cinquantenaire. Hop-on, hop-off buses (described later) can be helpful to get to some outlying sights.

## By Bike

The city of Brussels subsidizes the **Villo** network of cheap rental bikes for short rides within the city. After you register online or at the kiosk, you can borrow bikes at will, then drop them off at any other station. You must know your credit-card PIN to pick up a bike from a rental station (a €150 hold on your credit card ensures you return the bike; free for up to 30 minutes, €0.50/30-60 minutes, €1/1-1.5 hours, €2/1.5-2 hours, www.villo.be).

## By Taxi or Uber

Cabbies charge a €2.40 drop fee, then €1.80 per additional kilometer (€2 surcharge after 22:00). You'll pay about €15 for a ride from the Place de Brouckère to the Royal Museums of Fine Arts, or about €10 from Central station to the Ste. Catherine neighborhood. Figure €12 to ride from the center to the European Parliament. Convenient taxi stands near the Grand Place are at Place de Brouckère and at the "Agora" square (Rue du Marché aux Herbes). In the Upper Town, try Place du Grand Sablon. For short trips within the central core, the tangled one-way streets make taxis inefficient; it's easier to just walk. To call a cab, ring **Taxi Bleus** (+32 2 268 0000) or **Autolux** (+32 2 512 3123). If you use **Uber,** it works in Brussels just like it does in the US (UberX service).

# Tours in Brussels

### Hop-On, Hop-Off Bus Tour

**Tootbus** offers two loops with recorded narration: The red route serves the far-flung European Parliament and Parc du Cinquantenaire; the blue serves the Atomium. Choose between the two-hour express tour or a full-day pass to hop on and off at leisure. Tickets are available onboard or online; the handiest starting point is Central station (€24.30/24 hours, €20/2-hour express tour, daily 9:30-18:00, hourly; Oct-May shorter hours and 3-4/day; www.tootbus. com, customerservice-brussels@tootbus.com).

### Bus Tour

**Brussels City Tour's** 2.5-hour guided bus tour (in up to five languages) provides an easy way to get the grand perspective on Brussels. You start with a walk around the Grand Place, then jump on a tour bus (€30; runs year-round Tue, Thu, and Sat at 9:30; meet at their office a block off Grand Place at Rue du Marché aux Herbes 61; buy tickets there, online, or at TI; +32 2 513 7744, www. brussels-city-tours.com).

### Local Guides

**Roger van Buynder** is a good local guide who does history enthusiastically, but not chocolate (€200/3 hours, €230/4 hours, also does excursions in his car, +32 495 120 517, www.rogervanbuynder. be, tourguide.be@gmail.com).

**Taste the City** (run by Erwin Liekens and his knowledgeable team) offers good walks, including tours focused on Belgian food and drink (€180/3 hours, €350/day, +32 495 625 215, www. tastethecity.be, info@tastethecity.be).

**Visit Brussels** is an agency with plenty of good guides available for private hire (€170/3 hours, +32 2 548 0448, guides@ visitbrussels.be; I enjoyed the guiding of Didier Rochette).

**BRUSSELS ORIENTATION**

# SIGHTS IN BRUSSELS

The Grand Place may be Brussels' top sight, but the city offers a variety of museums, big and small, to fill your time here. I've divided the sights between the Lower Town, the Upper Town, and the outskirts.

## LOWER TOWN
### On the Grand Place
📖 The Grand Place and some of the sights fronting it, including the Town Hall, City Museum, and chocolate shops, are described in more detail in the Grand Place Walk chapter.

### ▲▲▲Grand Place
Brussels' aptly named Grand Place (grahn plahs; in Dutch: Grote Markt, *H*ROH-teh markt) is the heart of the old town and the city's greatest sight. Any time of day, it's worth swinging by to see what's going on. Concerts, festivals, sound-and-light shows, endless people-watching—it entertains.

### Town Hall (Hôtel de Ville)
With the Grand Place's tallest spire, this is the square's centerpiece, but its interior is no big deal. Admission is only possible with a one-hour English tour, which also covers city history and the building's tapestries and architecture.

**Cost and Hours:** €8; English tours offered Wed at 14:00, Sun at 10:00, 15:00, and 16:00; tickets available at www.visit.brussels (search for "Hôtel de Ville") or in the TI shop on Grand Place; 25-person limit—assure a spot by buying tickets three days in advance.

## ▲City Museum (Musée de la Ville de Bruxelles)

Inside the King's House (Maison du Roi) building on the Grand Place, this mildly interesting museum has city history exhibits, the original *Manneken-Pis* statue, models of old Brussels, and some old tapestries, altarpieces, and paintings. Posted information and info sheets in English are available, and a free downloadable audioguide provides more in-depth information on select items. (The BELvue Museum in the Upper Town is better for Belgian history.)

**Cost and Hours:** €10, ticket also valid for GardeRobe MannekenPis—described later; Tue-Sun 10:00-17:00, closed Mon; download free audioguide with QR code at museum, Grand Place, +32 2 279 4350, www.brusselscitymuseum.brussels.

**Visiting the Museum:** Begin your visit on the ground floor and work your way up.

**Ground Floor:** Here you'll see the original statues that once adorned the Town Hall. The limestone is no match for the corrosive acidic air, so they were brought inside for protection. Also on this floor are a few old paintings (one may be by Jan Brueghel the Elder), fine carved altarpieces, and porcelain. Spend some time with a Brussels specialty—tapestries. With access to great materials (via the thriving cloth trade) and great artists (like Peter Paul Rubens), Brussels cranked out these wall hangings that adorned Europe's homes as both functional insulators and artistic masterpieces.

**Middle Floor:** Watch the 20-minute video (in English) for a bite-sized introduction to Brussels history. Find the model of the

city in the 13th century. (Get oriented: Uphill is east.) The largest structure back then was St. Michael's Cathedral. At the top of the model is the Upper Town—which, at this point, hasn't even a hint of its monumental future. At the bottom of the hill is the (former) River Senne, which was the city's trading lifeline. In between stands the fledgling Grand Place—only a small clearing amid a cluster of houses.

The city was a port town—see the crane unloading barges—since it was at this point that the shallow Senne became navigable. Grain from the area was processed in the watermills, then shipped downstream to Antwerp and on to the North Sea.

By the 1200s, Brussels—though tiny by today's standards—was an important commercial center, and St. Michael's was the region's religious hub. Still, most of the area inside the 2.5-mile-

# Brussels at a Glance

▲▲▲**Grand Place** Main square and spirited heart of the Lower Town. See page 136.

▲▲▲**Royal Museums of Fine Arts of Belgium** Museums displaying Old Masters, turn-of-the-century art, and works by Belgian Surrealist René Magritte. **Hours:** Tue-Sun 10:00-17:00, closed Mon. See page 145.

▲▲*Manneken-Pis* World-famous statue of a leaky little boy. **Hours:** Always peeing. See page 140.

▲▲**BELvue Museum** Belgian history with a focus on the popular royal family. **Hours:** Tue-Fri 9:30-17:00 (July-Aug until 18:00), Sat-Sun 10:00-18:00, closed Mon. See page 146.

▲▲**European Parliament** Soaring home of Europe's governing body. **Hours:** Parlamentarium and House of European History—Tue-Fri 9:00-18:00, Sat-Sun from 10:00, Mon from 13:00; Parliament tours offered Mon-Fri. See page 149.

▲▲**Mémorial 1815** State-of-the-art museum at the site of the Battle of Waterloo. **Hours:** Daily 10:00-18:30, July-Aug 9:30-19:30, Nov-March 10:00-17:30. See page 162.

▲**City Museum** Models and exhibits of Brussels' history, plus the original *Manneken-Pis* statue. **Hours:** Tue-Sun 10:00-17:00, closed Mon. See page 137.

▲**Fashion and Lace Museum** World-famous Brussels lace and embroidery. **Hours:** Tue-Sun 10:00-17:00, closed Mon. See page 140.

▲**St. Michael's Cathedral** White-stone Gothic church where Belgian royals are married. **Hours:** Mon-Fri 7:00-18:00, Sat-Sun from 8:30. See page 141.

▲**Musical Instruments Museum** Exhibits with more than 1,500 instruments, complete with audio. **Hours:** Tue-Fri 9:30-17:00, Sat-Sun from 10:00, closed Mon. See page 145.

▲**Autoworld** Hundreds of historic vehicles. **Hours:** Mon-Fri 10:00-17:00, Sat-Sun until 18:00. See page 154.

▲**Royal Museum of the Armed Forces and Military History** Vast collection of weaponry and uniforms. **Hours:** Tue-Sun 9:00-17:00, closed Mon. See page 155.

▲**AfricaMuseum** Ethnography and natural history of Central Africa, and an examination of Belgium's colonial past. **Hours:** Tue-Fri 10:00-17:00, Sat-Sun until 18:00, closed Mon. See page 161.

**Belgian Comic Strip Center** Homage to the Smurfs, Tintin, Lucky Luke, and more. **Hours:** Tue-Sun 10:00-18:00, closed Mon. See page 142.

long city wall was farmland, dotted with a few churches, towers, markets, and convents (such as the Carmelite convent hugging the south wall).

Another model (at the far end of the room) shows the city a couple of centuries later—much bigger, but still within the same wall. By this time, the Upper and Lower Towns are clearly defined. In the Upper Town, the huge palace of the dukes of Burgundy marks the site of today's Royal Palace.

**Top Floor:** The main hall—under an interesting wood-carved roof—showcases the original *Manneken-Pis* statue that stood near the Grand Place. The exhibit explains that a *Manneken-Pis* was first mentioned in a 1451 administrative text about water pipes—though this brass statue is from the 17th century. This floor also generally has temporary exhibits highlighting the city's history.

### Brewery Museum

This little basement-level, bar-like place has one room of old brewing paraphernalia and one room of new (beer video in English). It's pretty lame...skip it unless you're really thirsty.

**Cost and Hours:** €5 includes a local beer; Wed-Sat 11:00-18:00, closed Sun-Tue; Grand Place 10, +32 2 511 4987, www.belgianbrewers.be.

### ▲Chocolate Shops on the Grand Place

For many, the best thing about the Grand Place is the chocolate sold at its venerable chocolate shops: Godiva, Neuhaus, Mary, Galler, and Leonidas (shops generally open daily until 18:00, later on weekends). It takes a lot of sampling to judge. For more, see the sidebar on page 170.

## South of the Grand Place
### Choco-Story: The Chocolate Museum

This museum is a deep dive into all aspects of Belgium's favorite confection, beginning with the cultivation of cacao in the Amazon basin by the Mayas. Hundreds of fascinating chocolate-related artifacts and tools from around the globe—accompanied by an audioguide, video, and corny mannequins—illustrate the introduction of chocolate to Europe and its subsequent history. You'll also watch a chocolate master at work (live demos 2/hour) and taste some samples.

**Cost and Hours:** €11—book online in advance in peak season to avoid the ticket line, includes essential audioguide; daily 10:00-18:00, last entry one hour before closing; between Grand Place and *Manneken-Pis* at Rue de l'Etuve 41, +32 2 514 2048, https://choco-story-brussels.be.

### ▲▲*Manneken-Pis*

Brussels is a great city with a cheesy mascot: a 17th-century statue of a little boy urinating (apparently symbolizing the city's irreverence and love of the good life). Read up on his story at any postcard stand. His facsimile is three short blocks off the Grand Place: For directions, take my Grand Place Walk; look for small, white *Manneken-Pis* signs; or just ask a local, *"Où est le Manneken-Pis?"* (oo ay luh man-uh-kan pees). The little squirt may be wearing some clever outfit, as costumes are sent for him from around the world. (For more about his fashion statements, visit the museum described next.) The tourist hubbub and frantic selfie derby on this street corner is as much of a sight as the statue itself.

### GardeRobe MannekenPis

That little bronze boy with the bladder control problem is also a clothes horse. For three centuries, it's been a tradition for the statue to be outfitted in clothing—the little guy pees through several costume changes each week. Many of the outfits you see here were donated by other countries. There are some 1,000 costumes in the archives, including a Civil War Union soldier, an El Salvadorian farmer, a Polish hussar, a Japanese samurai, an Indian maharajah, a Spanish bullfighter, a Maasai herder, and a Fiji islander.

**Cost and Hours:** €5, free with City Museum ticket; Tue-Sun 10:00-17:00, closed Mon; about a half-block from the little squirt at Rue du Chêne 19, +32 2 514 5397, www.mannekenpis.brussels.

### ▲Fashion and Lace Museum
### (Musée Mode et de la Dentelle)

This fine little museum showcases rotating exhibits of historic fashion as well as the art of lace. You'll enjoy exquisite costumes, feathery fans, and baby baptismal gowns. As the lace is fragile, much of it is stored in drawers—be sure to pull them out. At the entry, borrow the necessary English booklet that describes each showpiece.

**Cost and Hours:** €8, Tue-Sun 10:00-17:00, closed Mon, Rue de la Violette 12, a block off the Grand Place, +32 2 213 4450, www.fashionandlacemuseum.brussels.

## West of the Grand Place

These two fun-to-explore spots, just across the busy Boulevard Anspach from the Bourse and minutes apart on foot, offer some of Brussels' most appealing restaurants (far less touristy than those near the Grand Place). If you're looking for a bustling nighttime neighborhood full of inviting eateries and bars, you'll enjoy strolling these two areas.

## Ste. Catherine and the Old Fish Market
## (Vieux Marché aux Poissons)

Two blocks northwest of the Bourse is the ragtag Church of Ste. Catherine, which marks an inviting "village in the city" area with great eating options. The church itself is falling apart—during its construction, the architect got the commission for the Place of Justice in the Upper Town and rushed to complete this church so he could begin the more lucrative new job as quickly as possible. In front of the church stretches the long, skinny former fish market, lined with a range of upscale fish restaurants. Alongside the church is Place Ste. Catherine (Sint-Katelijneplein), with more restaurants, bars, and the city's best cheap-and-fast lunch options (see page 212 for recommended eateries). Place Ste. Catherine also hosts an organic market on Wednesdays (7:30-15:00) and a zero-waste market on Saturdays (8:00-17:00).

### Place St-Géry

This square—called *Sint-Goriksplein* in Dutch—is a lively scene, especially at night, when its bars are busy. It was actually once an

island in the now covered-up Senne River, Brussels' former trading lifeline. The market hall in the middle of the square evokes a time when goods were offloaded a few blocks away, at the old fish market, and brought here for sale. Today the hall houses a café and special exhibits. Across from the southwest corner of the hall, at #23 (next to the *Ô Lion d'Or* information board), duck through the little gateway to find a relaxing oasis of a courtyard—you might see businesspeople dozing on their lunch breaks here. At the far end of the courtyard, there's even a small exposed stretch of the Senne.

## East of the Grand Place
### ▲St. Michael's Cathedral

One of Europe's classic Gothic churches, built between roughly 1200 and 1500, Brussels' cathedral is made from white stone and topped by twin towers. For nearly 1,000 years, it's been the most important church in this largely Catholic country. (Whereas the Netherlands went in a Protestant direction in the 1500s,

Belgium remains 80 percent Catholic—although only about 20 percent attend Mass.)

**Cost and Hours:** Free to enter church, small fees to visit the underwhelming crypt and treasury; Mon-Fri 7:00-18:00, Sat-Sun from 8:30; www.cathedralisbruxellensis.be.

**Visiting the Cathedral:** The white-themed nave is bare but impressive, with a few nice stained-glass windows and a marvelous carved pulpit of Adam and Eve supporting the preacher. On top, Mary and Jesus stab Satan in serpent form.

This church is where royal weddings and funerals take place. Photographs (to the right of the entrance) show the funeral of the popular King Baudouin, who died in 1993, and the wedding of Boudouin's nephew, Philippe, who became king when his father, Albert II, abdicated in 2013. Traditionally, the ruler was always a male, but in 1992 the constitution was changed to allow the oldest child of either gender to take the throne. Elisabeth, born in 2001 to King Philippe and his wife, Queen Mathilde, is next in line for the throne.

Before leaving, pause on the outer porch to enjoy the great view of the Town Hall spire with its gold statue of St. Michael.

## Belgian Comic Strip Center
## (Centre Belge de la Bande Dessinée)

Belgians are as proud of their comics as they are of their beer, lace, and chocolates. Something about the comic medium resonates with the wry and artistic-yet-unpretentious Belgian sensibility. Belgium has produced some of the world's most popular comic characters, including the Smurfs, Tintin, and Lucky Luke. You'll find these, and many less famous local comics, at the Comic Strip Center. It's not a wacky, lighthearted place but a serious museum about a legitimate artistic medium.

Even if you don't have the time or interest to visit the museum's collection, pop into the lobby to see the groundbreaking Art Nouveau building (a former department store designed in 1903 by Belgian architect Victor Horta), browse through comics in the bookshop, and snap a photo with a three-foot-tall Smurf. That's enough for most people—especially for kids, who will likely find the museum itself boring. But those who appreciate art in general may enjoy this sometimes  humorous, sometimes probing, often beautiful medium. Most of the cartoons are in French and Dutch, but descriptions come in

# Tintin 101

The Belgian comic character Tintin is beloved by several generations of Europeans. Translations of his adventures and Steven Spielberg's 2011 animated Tintin film have endeared him to Americans as well.

In 1929, Brussels cartoonist Georges Rémi (1907-1983), using the pseudonym Hergé, created a dedicated young re-

porter with a shock of blond hair who's constantly getting into and out of misadventures. A precise artist, Hergé used a simple, uncluttered style with clear lines and appealing color.

Combining fantasy, mystery, and sci-fi with a dash of humor, the Tintin stories quickly found an appreciative audience. *The Adventures of Tintin* spanned 47 years and 24 books (selling some 200 million copies—and counting—in 50 languages). Tintin's popularity continues even today, as nostalgic parents buy the comics they grew up on for their own kids.

Tintin is the smart, upbeat, inquisitive, brave-but-not-foolhardy young man whose adventures propel the plot. His newspaper sends him on assignments all over the world. Snowy, Tintin's loyal fox terrier, is his constant companion—and often saves the day. The grizzled, grouchy, heavy-drinking Captain Haddock is as cynical as Tintin is optimistic, with a penchant for colorful curses ("Blistering barnacles!"). Professor Calculus is as brilliant as he is absentminded and hard of hearing, and comic relief is provided by the bumbling, nearly identical detectives called Thomson and Thompson.

Throughout his swashbuckling adventures, Tintin travels far and wide to exotic destinations. Hergé has been acclaimed for his meticulous research—he studied up on the places he portrayed and tried to avoid basing his stories on assumptions or stereotypes (though by today's standards, some of the comics betray an ugly Eurocentrism—one of the earliest, *Tintin in the Congo,* Hergé himself later acknowledged was regrettably racist).

And though the supporting characters are dynamic and colorful, Tintin himself has a rather bland personality. His expressions are usually indistinct (Hergé wanted young readers to project their own emotions onto Tintin's blank-canvas face). While presumably a teenager, Tintin's age is unclear—at times we imagine him to be a young boy, while at others he's seen drinking a beer, piloting a plane, or living in his own apartment (we never meet his family, if he has one). All of this is intentional: Hergé's style subconsciously encourages readers to put themselves in Tintin's everyman shoes.

English. Borrow the free English guidebooklet to read short bios of famous cartoonists.

**Cost and Hours:** €12; Tue-Sun 10:00-18:00, closed Mon, last entry one hour before closing; café, 10-minute walk from the Grand Place to Rue des Sables 20, +32 2 219 1980, www.comicscenter.net.

**Getting There:** From Central station, walk north along the big boulevard, then turn left down the stairs at the roundabout with the shipping container on its end.

**Visiting the Museum:** The collection changes often, but no matter what's on, you'll see how comics are made and watch early animated films. The heart of the collection is the golden age of comics in the 1950s and 1960s. You'll likely see an exhibit on Tintin, the intrepid young reporter with the button eyes and wavy shock of hair, launched in 1929 by Hergé and much loved by older Europeans. Brussels' own Peyo (a.k.a. Pierre Culliford, 1928-1992) invented the Smurfs—the little blue forest creatures that stand "three apples high," known as Les Schtroumpfs in Belgium. Displays don't go much beyond the comics themselves and descriptive panels, though there are some photo ops with life-size characters.

The top floor's temporary exhibits are often dedicated to "serious" comics, where more adult themes and high-quality drawing aspire to turn kids' stuff into that "Ninth Art" (*neuvième art*—the French term for comics as fine art). These works can be grimly realistic, openly erotic or graphic, or darker in tone, often featuring flawed antiheroes. The museum's bookstore is nearly as interesting, giving you the chance to page through reproductions of classic comics.

**Nearby:** The related **Marc Sleen Museum,** across the street, is dedicated to the oh-so-typically Belgian cartoonist whose big-nosed, caricatured drawings are recognizable even to many Americans. Sleen's *Adventures of Nero and Co.*, which he churned out in two strips a day for a staggering 55 years, holds the record for the longest-running comic by a single artist. Still, the collection is worth a visit only to his fans (free, Wed-Sun 10:00-18:00, closed Mon-Tue, Zandstraat 33, www.marc-sleen.be).

**Other Comic Sights:** If you're a Belgian comics completist, consider visiting the **Museum of Original Figurines** (MOOF), at the entrance to the Horta Gallery at the lower end of Central station (a few steps from "Agora" square). It features changing exhibits of colorful figurines of your favorite Belgian characters (closed Mon-Wed, www.moofmuseum.be). A handy **Smurf Store** is next door.

## UPPER TOWN

Brussels' grandiose Upper Town, with its huge palace, is described in the ▢ Upper Town Walk chapter. Along that walk, you'll pass the following sights (for locations, see the map in that chapter). An antiques market is held on Place du Grand Sablon on Saturdays (9:00-17:00) and Sundays (9:00-15:00).

### ▲▲▲Royal Museums of Fine Arts of Belgium
### (Musées Royaux des Beaux-Arts de Belgique)

This sprawling complex houses a trio of museums showing off the country's best all-around art collection. The **Old Masters Muse-**

**um**—featuring Flemish and Belgian art of the 14th through 18th century—is packed with a dazzling collection of masterpieces by Van der Weyden, Bruegel, Bosch, and Rubens. The **Fin-de-Siècle Museum** covers art of the late 19th and early 20th centuries, including an extensive Art Nouveau collection. The **Magritte Museum** contains works by the Surrealist painter René Magritte. Although you won't see many of Magritte's most famous pieces, you will get an unusually intimate look at the life and work of one of Belgium's top artists.

**Cost and Hours:** €15 for Magritte, €15 combo-ticket covers Old Masters and Fin-de-Siècle, €20 version covers all three; all are free first Wed of the month after 13:00; open Tue-Sun 10:00-17:00, closed Mon; audioguides-€4 each, Rue de la Régence 3, +32 2 508 3211, www.fine-arts-museum.be, www.musee-magritte-museum.be.

### ▲Musical Instruments Museum
### (Musée des Instruments de Musique)

One of Europe's best music museums (nicknamed "MIM") is housed in one of Brussels' most impressive Art Nouveau build-

ings, the beautifully renovated Old England department store. This museum has more than 1,500 instruments—from Egyptian harps, to medieval lutes, to groundbreaking harpsichords, to the saxophone (invented by Belgium's own Adolphe Sax).

**Cost and Hours:** €15, includes multimedia guide; Tue-Fri 9:30-17:00, Sat-Sun from 10:00, closed Mon; mandatory free bag check, Rue Montagne de la Cour 2, just downhill and toward Grand Place from the Royal Museums, +32 2 545 0133, www.mim.be.

**Visiting the Museum:** With your included multimedia guide, you're free to wander through exhibits on several levels. Using the guide, just punch in the number next to any instrument you want to hear or know more about (now I know what a hurdy-gurdy sounds like!), or follow the one-hour highlights tour. The basement level displays musical mechanisms, including a musical grandfather clock with automation. The ground floor has folk instruments from around the world; the first floor covers the history of Western musical instruments; and the second floor is filled with keyboards. The third floor has an exhibit about the history of the building and Brussels Art Nouveau in general—plus great city views from the turret-shaped alcove in thef right corner.

## ▲▲BELvue Museum

This 21st-century museum is the best introduction to modern Belgian history (1830-present) that you'll find in Brussels. It's well described in English, artfully arranged, and spiced up with touchscreens, video, and a timeline of 200-plus objects, from a lace collar to a rolling suitcase. But it's also Belgian history—so it is what it is. The museum sits over the (skippable) archaeological remains of the 12th-century Coudenberg Palace. If you do tour the palace ruins, see the BELvue Museum first, because you'll exit the Coudenberg downhill, near the Musical Instruments Museum.

**Cost and Hours:** Museum-€10, includes audioguide; palace remains-€10; €18 combo-ticket covers both; Tue-Fri 9:30-17:00 (July-Aug until 18:00), Sat-Sun 10:00-18:00, closed Mon; adjacent to the Royal Palace at Place des Palais 7, +32 2 500 4554, www.belvue.be.

**Visiting the Museum:** You'll get a QR code with your ticket to download the audioguide (bring your own earbuds). Start in the first-floor hallway, where you'll get a brief overview of how Belgium achieved independence from the Netherlands in 1830. From there, each room explores a theme of Belgian history through artifacts, exhibits, and even commentary from everyday Belgians (shown on video screens).

**First Floor:** In Room 1 you'll explore "Democracy" (women didn't get the vote until 1948) and see a timeline of the Belgian royal family. It's clear the dynasty is generally appreciated, even loved. Since these imported German monarchs arrived in 1830, each of the seven "Kings of the Belgians" (as they're officially known) has had his own style and claim to fame. Leopold I was the visionary who united the young nation. Leopold II was the "Builder King" and Congo exploiter. Albert I guided Belgium through World War I—only 30,000 Belgian troops died. Controversial World War II-era Leopold III was tainted after his attempt to negotiate with Hitler, and later abdicated in disgrace. He was followed by Baudouin, who restored respect for the monarchy. His equally popular brother became King Albert II. Albert II's son Philippe now reigns as king; the royal family includes his wife Mathilde, two princes (Gabriel and Emmanuel), and two princesses (Elisabeth and Eléonore).

Next comes "Prosperity" (Room 2), which covers how Belgium welcomed the Industrial Revolution (it had the first railroad on the Continent), thrived by exploiting its colony in Africa, and embraced the idea of a united Europe after World War II. The following room explores "Solidarity" and the rise of the labor movement (look for quotes from Vincent van Gogh and Karl Marx, both of whom lived in Brussels for a time). One of the major battles inside Belgium was over religion and who would run the schools: The "Pluralism" exhibit (Room 4) explores the "school wars" over two centuries.

**Second Floor:** The "Migration" exhibit covers both the departure of Belgians for better lives (more than 200,000 emigrated to the US in the 19th and early 20th centuries) as well as the tide of immigration into Belgium after World War II as Belgium's booming economy attracted foreign workers. Perhaps the most fascinating issues are examined in "Language" (Room 6). An excellent video tries to explain the back story of the festering Flemish-Walloon conflict and the bitter struggle to prevent Belgium from splitting completely in half. The final room focuses on postwar efforts to launch the European Union.

**Coudenberg Palace:** Below the museum, long, vaulted cellars are all that's left of this 12th-century royal palace. Although well-lit and explained, the archaeological remains require too much imagination to make them meaningful. The best part is the free orientation video you see before descending underground.

### Notre-Dame du Sablon Church

This 15th-century church in the Flamboyant Gothic style retains some of its original stained-glass windows. It also holds a little statue of the Virgin Mary that's been venerated by Bruxellois since the 1300s.

**Cost and Hours:** Free, daily 9:00-18:30, Rue de la Régence 3, +32 2 511 5741.

## EAST OF DOWNTOWN

Two clusters of sights lie just east of the city center: the European Parliament (museums about the European Union and European history plus tours of the parliament complex) and the Park of the Cinquantenaire (with three museums: cars, the military, and art). Between these sights and central Brussels is the Matongé neighborhood—a fascinating blend of Congolese influences and Belgian *bohème*, and a fun place to grab a bite to eat.

## Planning Your Time

Because the areas are connected by a quick bus ride, it's easy to visit both in a single half-day excursion. The best days to visit are Tuesdays through Fridays, as some Cinquantenaire museums are closed on Mondays, and the European Parliament is pretty dead on weekends. Here's a suggested itinerary:

Start with the **Park of the Cinquantenaire** (details on getting to the park are later).

After visiting the museums, take a bus to the **European Parliament.** To get there, catch bus #27 behind the Autoworld building on Avenue des Gaulois (bus stop: Gaulois/Galliërs, direction: Gare du Midi/Zuidstation, 4/hour Mon-Fri, 2/hour Sat-Sun) to the Luxembourg stop. Arriving at Place du Luxembourg, you immediately see the modern gray-and-glass buildings that make up the EU complex.

After your European Parliament visit, catch bus #38 to the city center (or walk to the **Matongé** district).

## ▲▲European Parliament

Europe's governing body welcomes visitors with an exhibit about the European Union and its parliament. You can also follow an

audioguide tour of the actual parliament chamber—the Hemicycle. The parliament's sprawling complex of modern glass buildings is a babel of black-suited politicians speaking 24 different Euro-languages. It's exciting just to be here—a fly on the wall of a place that aspires to chart the future of Europe "with respect for all political thinking...consolidating democracy in the spirit of peace and solidarity."

**Getting There:** The European Parliament is next to Place du Luxembourg (a skippable info office called "Station Europe" is in the Neoclassical former train station). Bus #38 heads here from Central station or the Royal Museums; bus #27 comes from the

# The European Union

Brussels is the capital of one of the biggest, most powerful, and most idealistic states in the world (and, arguably, in history): the European Union (EU). In just one generation, more than two dozen European countries have gone from being bitter rivals to compatriots. This union of such a diverse collection of separate nations—with different languages, cultures, and soccer teams—is almost unprecedented. And it all started in the rubble of a war.

World War II left 40 million dead and a continent in ruins, and it convinced Europeans that they had to work together to maintain peace. Poised between competing superpowers (the US and the USSR), they also needed to cooperate economically to survive in an increasingly globalized economy. Just after the war ended, visionary "Eurocrats" began the task of convincing reluctant European nations to relinquish elements of their sovereignty and merge into a united body.

The transition happened gradually, in fits and starts. It began in 1948, when Belgium, the Netherlands, and Luxembourg—jointly called "BeNeLux"—established a free-trade zone. That evolved into an ever-broadening alliance of states (the European Coal and Steel Union, then the European Economic Community, or "Common Market"). In 1992, with the Treaty of Maastricht, the 12 member countries of the Common Market made a leap of faith: They created a "European Union" that would eventually allow for free movement of capital, goods, services, and labor.

In 2002, most EU members adopted a single currency (the euro), and for all practical purposes, economic unity was a reality. There are now 27 member states—encompassing nearly all of Western Europe, and much of Eastern Europe and Scandinavia. Almost all EU members have joined the open-borders Schengen Agreement, making passport checkpoints obsolete. This makes the EU the world's seventh-largest "country" (1.6 million square miles), with the third-largest population (around 450 million peo-

Royal Museums or the museums at the Park of the Cinquantenaire. Place du Luxembourg is a seven-minute walk from the Trône/Troon Métro stop (straight ahead up Luxembourg street—Europe's "K" Street, teeming with lobbyists). From Place du Luxembourg, signs direct you to the complex's main visitor sights: the Parlamentarium, the House of European History, and the Hemicycle tour. To return to the city center, catch bus #38 from Place du Luxembourg.

ple), and an economy slightly smaller than the US (around $16 trillion GDP).

The EU is governed from Brussels. While it has a parliament, the EU is led primarily by the European Commission (with commissioners appointed by individual member governments and approved by its parliament) and the Council of Ministers. Daily business is conducted by an army of bureaucrats and policy wonks.

Unlike America's federation of 50 states, Europe's member states retain the right to opt out of some EU policies. Denmark, for example, belongs to the EU but hasn't adopted the euro as its currency. While the 2009 Lisbon Treaty streamlines EU responses to conflicts and issues, there's no unified foreign or economic policy among the member countries. The EU also lacks a powerful chief executive—the president of the European Council, appointed for 2.5-year term, is much weaker than the US president, as EU laws require consensus on taxes, foreign policy, defense, and social programs.

The goal is to create a competitive, sustainable, environmentally friendly economy that improves the quality of life for all Europeans. Still, many "Euroskeptics" remain unconvinced that the EU is a good thing. There's no clearer evidence than Britain's stunning 2016 vote to leave the EU ("Brexit"). Other EU countries have debated similar referendums, and leaders in Hungary and Poland are unabashed Euroskeptics. These EU critics chafe at the highly regulated business environment and high taxes, complain about the bureaucracy, and worry that their national cultures will be swallowed up. Some countries want to control their own borders rather than leave immigration decisions to Brussels. And wealthier member countries (mostly in the north) are reluctant to bail out economically troubled compatriots (mostly in the south), while poorer countries resent the cuts demanded by the richer ones.

Still, despite these problems, Europeans don't want to go back to the days of division and strife. Even after Brexit, most agree that a strong, unified Europe is necessary to keep the peace and compete in a global economy.

## Parlamentarium

This high-tech, informative museum is designed to let you meet the European Union and understand how it works. Pick up your free multimedia guide and wander through its many exhibits. You'll learn about how the EU came to be and the many challenges it has faced; "meet" virtual EU parliamentarians; find out about some of Europe's most powerful political parties and movements; cast your own vote regarding recent hot-button EU issues; and get a rundown of each EU country's culture, commerce, and contemporary challenges. The interactive exhibits are rather dry, and the pro-EU propaganda, while expected, can be heavy-handed. Still, it's good introduction to the EU; it's smart to visit before your parliament tour.

**Cost and Hours:** Free; Tue-Fri 9:00-18:00, Sat-Sun from 10:00, Mon from 13:00; https://visiting.europarl.europa.eu.

## Parliament Tours

The only way to get inside the European Parliament itself is to take the free one-hour multimedia tour. You'll tour the complex at your own pace, learn about the world's largest transnational parliament, and get a look at the Hemicycle, the semicircular chamber where EU members debate issues and cast votes. Reservations are not taken—simply drop by the starting point about 10 to 15 minutes before the tour to register (bring ID—passport or driver's license).

**Cost and Hours:** Free; tours offered on the hour Mon-Thu 9:00-16:00, Fri until 13:00; no tours Sat-Sun.

**Getting There:** The Parliament building is behind the main complex, a five-minute walk from the circular main square—follow *Visit Hémicycle* signs. You'll walk through an arcade and down a long set of stairs. When you see the statue of the woman holding a euro sign, turn left and follow along the building. The parliament tour entrance will be on your right—near a piece of the Berlin Wall.

**Visiting the Parliament:** When you check in, you'll be sent through security and given a multimedia guide. You'll learn how early visionary utopians (like Churchill, who, in 1946, called for a "United States of Europe" to avoid future wars) led the way as Europe gradually evolved into the European Union (1992).

From the balcony overlooking the building's lobby, you can see the giant *Confluence* sculpture with moving metal-wire pieces—representing people coming together for a common purpose. The building itself is in line with EU idealism: It's functional, transparent, and very "green."

The grand finale is the vast "Hemicycle," where the members of the European Parliament sit. Here you'll listen to a political-science lesson about the all-Europe system of governance. The parliamentarians who hash out pan-European issues in this hall represent 160 different national political parties and are organized into seven different voting blocs—based on political ideals rather than nationality.

With the president facing them, they're seated from left to right—both literally and politically—which means that from their perspective, they sit on the "wrong" side of the hall. This is done to foster empathy. Although most parliamentarians can speak English, in this setting they are encouraged to talk in their mother tongues—ensuring they will be fully comfortable in expressing their thoughts. That makes this the largest multilingual operation on the planet, with a very busy army of translators, who simultaneously translate every word into all 24 official languages.

### House of European History

This high-tech museum does its part in the grander project to foster European unity. Its main theme is how history has shaped Europeans' memories and daily lives from the 19th century to today. It works hard to show how fundamental characteristics of European culture—such as cooking, leisure activities, and politics—are distinctive in each country but also broadly similar. While well intentioned, it's a little underwhelming, though still worth visiting for history buffs.

**Cost and Hours:** Free, includes multimedia guide; Tue-Fri 9:00-18:00, Sat-Sun from 10:00, Mon from 13:00; in Léopold Park behind the main EU buildings at Rue Belliard 135, +32 2 283 1220, www.historia-europa.ep.eu.

**Visiting the Museum:** After passing through security, leave any bags in lockers on the ground floor. Head one floor up to pick up the multimedia guide (essential, as most exhibits are not labeled). The initial floors skim big-picture topics such as Europe as a global power and a geographical entity; as you go up the floors, the museum focuses on history.

Exhibits explore European unification efforts post-World War II, as visionary leaders tried to overcome the continent's many divisions. The Cold War's brutal severing of Europe into eastern and western halves receives a lot of attention, as well as the dramatic fall of communist regimes in 1989 that stitched the halves back together. All of this is thoughtfully illustrated with historical objects, such as the cap worn by the "Irish liberator" Daniel O'Connell or a wall of class photos from the 1950s, '60s, and '70s from both sides of the Iron Curtain.

**Nearby:** The worthwhile **Royal Belgian Institute of Natural Sciences** (Institut Royal des Sciences Naturelles de Belgique) sits practically next door to the European Parliament. Dinosaur enthusiasts come here for the world's largest collection of iguanodon skeletons (€13; Tue-Fri 9:30-17:00, Sat-Sun 10:00-18:00, closed Mon; Rue Vautier 29, +32 2 627 4211, www.naturalsciences.be).

## Park of the Cinquantenaire Museums

Standing proudly in a big park in eastern Brussels is a trio of sprawling museums housed in cavernous halls: the Royal Museum of the Armed Forces and Military History, Autoworld, and the Museum of Art & History. These attractions thrill specialists but bore most others.

The complex itself is interesting to see. There's a huge Neoclassical triumphal arch, and the place is surrounded by a spacious park (Parc du Cinquantenaire). It has a grandiose history: The ambitious 19th-century Belgian king Leopold II wanted Brussels to rival Paris. In 1880, he celebrated the 50th anniversary *(cinquantenaire)* of Belgian independence by building the arch flanked by massive exhibition halls, which today house the museums.

**Getting There:** Take Métro line 1 or 5 from the city center to Métro stop Merode. Exit the Métro station following signs to *Yser/ IJzer*, then cross the street toward the big arch. Other options: Take bus #27 from the Upper Town (Royale/Koning) to the Gaulois/ Galliërs stop or consider a hop-on, hop-off bus (see page 135).

### ▲Autoworld

A cavernous hall filled with 400 historic cars shows the vast array of motorized vehicles built over the last century-plus. The place is made for browsing—each car is clearly labeled. Besides historic cars, Autoworld always features some of the latest and hottest designs. Vroom.

There's an audioguide and some English descriptions, but for much of it, you're left to either bring your own knowledge or simply admire the high-polish gleam.

**Cost and Hours:** €13, includes audioguide; Mon-Fri 10:00-17:00, Sat-Sun until 18:00; in Palais Mondial, Parc du Cinquantenaire 11, +32 2 736 4165, www.autoworld.be.

**Visiting the Museum:** Start by tracing the history of automobiles, decade-by-decade, along the right wall. (But first up, admire the humongous green 1929 Minerva sedan at the entrance—a rarity by Belgium's best-known automaker, which went defunct in the 1950s.)

As you work your way counterclockwise through the ground floor, you'll see the first handmade cars—basically converted horse carriages. Then comes mass production (introduced by America's Henry Ford) and the big luxury cars of the 1920s. During the Great Depression, small economy cars were in vogue—France's Citroën and Hitler's brainchild, the Volkswagen. It was Hitler and Mussolini who built the first freeways to quickly mobilize troops in wartime. The postwar years produced monstrous gas-guzzling cars for the suburban masses—particularly in America.

Head upstairs to the sporty '60s, the fuel-efficient '70s (after the Arab oil embargo of 1973), and the international brands of the '80s and '90s. Then just browse the rest of this vast collection.

## ▲Royal Museum of the Armed Forces and Military History (Musée Royal de l'Armée et d'Histoire Militaire)

Wander through this enormous collection of weaponry, uniforms, tanks, warplanes, and endless exhibits about military history, fo-

cusing on the 19th and 20th centuries. The museum is filled with real, tangible history. This impressively complete museum is nirvana for fans of military history and aviation (but skippable for those who think a "panzer" is a pretty flower).

**Cost and Hours:** €11, credit card only; Tue-Sun 9:00-17:00, closed Mon, last entry one hour before closing; audioguide-€3, Parc du Cinquantenaire 3, +32 2 737 7811, https://klm-mra.be.

**Visiting the Museum:** Exploring the whole place is exhausting, so be selective. Some good English descriptions are available; to get the most out of your visit, renting the audioguide is essential.

Here's how I'd organize my visit. From the entrance, go straight ahead, through the Belgian military history section—seeing Belgian flags, cannons, uniforms, and Leopold II's tricycle (midway along). This leads to exhibits on World War I and World War II (which, naturally, are strong on the role of Belgium). The grand finale is the vast (and I mean vast) aviation hall filled with warplanes. You'll see WWI biplanes and WWII fighters, plus a Soviet MiG fighter (with camouflage paint) that crashed in Belgium in 1989 (one of the last airspace violations of the Cold War). Some of these planes are one-of-a-kind relics—including a French Nieuport fighter, a Schreck seaplane, and two German observation planes from World War I. There's much more to the museum including the arms and armor section (access it through the gift shop near the entrance).

Finish your visit at the Panorama—the stunning viewpoint atop the Cinquantenaire arch (free, open in summer only). The elevator is near the museum's entrance lobby and gift shop—follow signs to *Arcades* and *Panorama*. You'll enjoy Napoleonic views over the park complex and the Brussels skyline—some of the best in the city. Find the distant Atomium and the curved glass arch of the European Parliament.

## Museum of Art & History

This varied, decent (but not spectacular) collection features artifacts from many cultures—both European and non-European—ranging from prehistoric times to the present. As you wander the almost-empty halls, you'll see fine tapestries, exquisite altarpieces, impressive Islamic and antiquities collections, gorgeous Art Nouveau and Art Deco, and a "museum of the heart" (featuring various creative depictions of everyone's favorite organ, donated by a local heart doctor).

**Cost and Hours:** €10; Tue-Fri 9:30-17:00, Sat-Sun from 10:00, closed Mon; some galleries closed for renovation—check website, audioguide-€3, limited English information; hiding behind Autoworld at Jubelpark 10, Parc du Cinquantenaire, +32 2 741 7211, www.artandhistory.museum.

**Visiting the Museum:** The collection is arranged somewhat haphazardly; pick up the brochure at the entry to figure out which items you'd like to find. As you enter and stand under the rotunda, to the left is the Non-European wing (Native American, Mayan, Asian), and to the right is European (Gothic-Renaissance-Baroque tapestries, altarpieces, and jewels).

A highlight is the Antiquities wing: From the rotunda, head left, then turn left at the totem pole. Start in Rome, in a spacious hall with a vast floor mosaic of an animal hunt, overseen by a bronze statue of Emperor Septimius Severus. There's a room-sized model of ancient Rome (on the same level as the floor mosaic)—find the Colosseum, the Circus Maximus chariot-race course, and the grand buildings of the Forum in between. (Ask when the next model demonstration takes  place.) On other floors, you'll find Greek pottery and a reconstructed Egyptian tomb you can walk inside.

## ▲Matongé Neighborhood

About one of every 10 Brussels residents claims African ancestry. Wedged between the campus of the European Parliament and the royal sights of the Upper Town is the Matongé (mah-tong-gay) district, a mélange of African immigrant culture, turn-of-the-century architecture, and young Bruxellois in search of a trendy scene in an "emerging" neighborhood. Consider riding the Métro to Matongé, exploring the neighborhood, and staying for lunch or dinner. I've recommended several restaurants in this section; for detailed listings see page 215.

**Getting There:** Take the Métro to Porte de Namur/Naamsepoort. If you're starting at the European Parliament, it's a 15-minute walk to Porte de Namur.

**Background:** Matongé, part of the Ixelles district of Brussels, had ties to Africa even before any Africans lived here. Back when the Belgian Congo was a colony, many of its administrative offices were located in this part of Brussels. A Congolese choir was invited to perform at the 1958 World's Fair, and soon after, several of the performers decided to return to Belgium to study at the university. A local aristocrat bought them a residential building in this neighborhood. More and more immigrants arrived—from Congo and throughout Africa—and soon the neighborhood was nicknamed Matongé (after a market district in the Congolese capital, Kinshasa). For decades, Matongé was a center of "Belgican" (Belgian African) culture, although more recently it supports large Indian, Pakistani, and Latin American communities. And now, drawn by fine old buildings and a central location near the European Parliament, a younger, richer clientele is easing into the neighborhood, and rents are on the rise.

### Matongé Walk

To trace the route of this walk, see the map on the following page.

From the Porte de Namur/Naamsepoort Métro station, exit toward *Chaussée d'Ixelles/Elsensesteenweg* and *Chaussée de Wavre/Waversteenweg*. Riding the escalator up into the square, head uphill, up Chaussée d'Ixelles (with your back to the giant traffic circle and modern monument). As this busy street becomes pedestrianized, the character of the neighborhood is becoming more inviting. Notice the street art mural (*Porte de Namur!, Porte de L'Amour?*) high above on the right, celebrating this immigrant community and the diversity brought by the 180 nationalities that come together in Brussels.

Take the first left down **Chaussée de Wavre.** You'll pass the landmark Cinéma Vendôme art house theater on your left. Soon after, on your right, look for the entrance to the bustling African market. The sign *Souriez, vous êtes à Matongé* means "Smile! You are

# Matongé Neighborhood

**Eateries**

1. Le Clan des Belges
2. Hope House African
3. Au Soleil d'Afrique
4. Restaurant Volle Gas
5. Il Nobile Ristorante Pizzeria
6. Le Cocq Bar

in Matongé." You can enter the market, or if that's too intense, simply keep strolling down the street—passing exotic taste-of-Africa grocery shops (displaying cassava, plantain, and other ingredients used in Congolese cooking), call shops offering cheap rates for phone calls to Africa, boutiques selling colorful batik fabric, and neighborhood-gathering-place barbershops and hair salons.

After two blocks, you reach a little crossroads. A statue here is called ***Beyond Hope.*** Made of spent cartridges welded into the shape of a woman and a child and splattered with red paint, it remembers the real victims and the hopelessness of the ongoing strife in Congo.

Turn right down Rue Ernest Solvay to find a collection of multicultural shops under neglected **Art Nouveau facades.** Soon you'll arrive at the cross-street of **Rue Saint-Boniface.** This energetic café row, which dead-ends at the front door of St. Boniface Church, is one of Matongé's most gentrified drags. It has a decidedly urbane-Bruxellois vibe, with busy brasseries and cafés and an eclectic range of eateries in both directions. Explore a bit, and don't miss the lovely Art Nouveau facades at #17 (housing the Comptoir Florian teahouse) and #19.

Wander slowly up toward the church—window-shopping for a drink or meal—to a green statue just before the church. The statue remembers **Charles Woeste,** a Catholic prime minister who died in 1922. He supported the brutal colonial policies of Leopold II and was anti-socialist and anti-Flemish—an all-around hard-right conservative. Like statues commemorating Confederate heroes in the US, this statue is controversial and will likely be taken down soon. Pause to imagine this neighborhood a hundred years ago.

Facing the church, turn left on **Rue de la Paix.** Halfway down the block on the right is **Inzia** (at #37), a Congolese restaurant. At the end of the block, you'll run into **Rue Longue Vie.** On a nice evening, this street is the buzzing center of Matongé, with two popular African restaurants to your left (**Au Soleil d'Afrique** and **Hope House African**).

Turn right down Rue Longue Vie, then immediately right again on Rue Bouré. At the cute little square behind the church, take a left, then a right down "Tulip Street" to find your way to charming **Place Fernand Cocq.** This leafy, triangular square—facing the Town Hall of the district of Ixelles—feels a world away from the African vibe just a few streets away. A dozen cafés, bars, and restaurants compete for your attention, all with inviting sidewalk tables.

When you're ready to head back, head away from the Town Hall and up Chaussée d'Ixelles all the way back to the Métro.

## NORTH OF DOWNTOWN
## 1958 World's Fair Grounds Sights

These sights are next to each other about four miles north of the Grand Place at Heysel.

**Getting There:** It's a 20-minute Métro ride from the center to Heysel/Heizel; from there, walk about five minutes toward the can't-miss-it Atomium. To reach Mini-Europe, follow the *Bruparck* arrows.

### Atomium

This giant, silvery scale model of a steel molecule, with escalators and stairs connecting the various "atoms" and a view from the top sphere, was the über-optimistic symbol of the 1958 World's Fair. It's Brussels' answer to Paris' Eiffel Tower, Seattle's Space Needle, and St. Louis' Gateway Arch.

Your ticket includes an elevator ride to the panorama deck, with views over the fairgrounds and Mini-Europe (which looks *really* mini from up here). From there, you'll meander on endless escalators and stairs through five of the nine balls on your way back down. The audioguide provides a good explanation of the building and the 1958 World's Fair, including sound clips from people who attended.

**Cost and Hours:** €16, daily 10:00-18:00, free downloadable audioguide, overpriced restaurant inside, +32 2 475 4775, www.atomium.be.

**Nearby:** Your Atomium admission also covers entry into the ADAM: Brussels Design Museum, with changing exhibits on 20th-century style (€10 without Atomium ticket, includes audioguide, +32 2 669 4929, www.adamuseum.org).

### Mini-Europe

This kid-pleasing sight, sharing a park with the Atomium, has 1:25-scale models of 350 famous European landmarks such as Big Ben, the Eiffel Tower, and Venice's canals. The "Spirit of Europe" indoor exhibit has educational interactive games about the EU.

**Cost and Hours:** €17.30; daily 9:30-18:00, July-Aug until 19:00, shorter hours off-season, closed Jan-mid-March, last entry one hour before closing; +32 2 474 1313, www.minieurope.com.

## OUTSIDE BRUSSELS
### ▲AfricaMuseum
This worthwhile museum, housed in an immense palace surrounded by a vast park in the town of Tervuren, focuses on Central Africa, including its ethnography, sculpture, jewelry, flora, and fauna. Besides cataloging the region's abundant natural wonders, the exhibits confront Belgium's colonial history in the Congo and incorporate contemporary art and commentary.

**Cost and Hours:** €12, Tue-Fri 10:00-17:00, Sat-Sun until 18:00, closed Mon, +32 2 769 5211, www.africamuseum.be.

**Getting There:** The museum is at Leuvensesteenweg 13 in the town of Tervuren. By public transit, Tervuren is about an hour east of Brussels. Take Métro line 1 (direction: Stockel/Stokkel) to Montgomery, and then catch tram #44 and ride it about 20 minutes to its final stop, Tervuren. From there, walk 300 yards through the park to the palace.

## Battle of Waterloo Sights
For anyone who lived through 9/11, it's clear that history can pivot in just one day. On June 18, 1815, the fate of Europe was decided on farm fields about 10 miles south of Brussels. More than 40,000 men were killed or wounded in a day-long struggle that ended the reign of Napoleon and made Britain the superpower of the 19th century.

**Planning Your Time:** While it's called the Battle of Waterloo, the action really took place about a mile south of the town. If you have time for only one sight, make it the **Mémorial 1815** museum, with spectacular displays and a movie experience not to be missed. Those with more time can consider visiting the ho-hum town of Waterloo and the Duke of Wellington's headquarters (Wellington Museum, of most interest to British military aficionados, www.museewellington.be), or Hougoumont Farm, a decisive battlefield site (described later). Another sight in Waterloo, Napoleon's Last Headquarters, is a sad attempt to give equal time to the emperor—skip it.

**Getting There:** A **car** works best, as the battlefield sites are scattered. The Mémorial 1815 museum is about a 30-minute drive south of Brussels. Leaving central Brussels, take the E-19 motorway toward Charleroi, exit onto the R0 ring road (direction: Waterloo), and get off at exit 25 (signed *Lasne/Braine-l'Alleud*). Turn right at the end of the ramp and park in the lot on the left.

By **public transit,** you can take a train/bus combo to the museum: Ride the train from Brussels to Braine-l'Alleud (2/hour, 20 minutes, direction: Charleroi Sud). Outside the station in Braine-l'Alleud, hop on the W bus (usually 2/hour). Get off at the fifth stop, marked *Lion, Route de Nivelles* (look for an Esso gas station across the street). Head for the traffic lights, where signs will point you to the *Butte du Lion;* it's a five-minute walk to the museum.

**Background:** By 1815, the Grand Alliance (England, Prussia, Austria, and Russia) had defeated Napoleon, sending him into exile on Elba and putting Louis XVI's brother on the French throne. It was as if the French Revolution never happened. But on March 1, 1815, Napoleon escaped and returned to France, driving out the king and restoring his army to its former glory. His rise sent shockwaves throughout Europe, and members of the alliance pledged 150,000 troops to rout him.

Napoleon's best chance was to attack the allied armies separately, before they had a chance to unite. On the day of the Battle of Waterloo, 72,000 French faced off against 68,000 British and Dutch troops under the Duke of Wellington. Within marching distance of the battlefield were 45,000 Prussians under General Gebhard von Blücher.

Wellington, a master of defense, took the high ground and hunkered down atop a ridge. Napoleon advanced, but then paused to let the field dry from the previous night's rainfall. This, some say, was his fatal mistake. Napoleon finally attacked, and Wellington pushed back. Meanwhile, the Prussians attacked the nearby village of Plancenoit.

Napoleon realized he had to act quickly or he'd have to fight both armies on the battlefield. He had no choice but to send in his elite Imperial Guard. But the British surprised the guard by rising up from the cover of a wheat field. As the French corps retreated in chaos, Wellington swooped down from the ridge while Blücher's soldiers punched through. By nightfall, the British and Prussian armies had come together. The Prussians even captured Napoleon's abandoned carriage, chock full of diamonds—the booty later became part of the Prussian crown jewels. Napoleon's reign of glory was over, and Waterloo became a metaphor for a crushing defeat.

## ▲▲Mémorial 1815

Built for the 200th anniversary of the battle, Mémorial 1815 is an ultramodern museum that doles out its history in small doses.

With its smart design, you can skim the surface with your audioguide or plunge into the arcane depths of the Napoleonic wars for hours.

**Cost and Hours:** €17 ticket includes downloadable audioguide app (use your own smartphone and earbuds)—covers Mémorial 1815, Panorama, and Lion's Mound; daily

10:00-18:30, July-Aug 9:30-19:30, Nov-March 10:00-17:30; +32 2 385 1912, www.waterloo1815.be. Don't bother getting the Pass 1815 (€23), unless you're also visiting the Wellington Museum.

**Visiting the Museum:** Use the excellent audioguide and begin your tour with a series of rooms charting the French Revolution, Napoleon's rise to power, and his conquest of most of Europe. Next is a brilliant display of military equipment and uniforms that also serves as a timeline leading up to the battle.

The star of the museum is the "4-D" movie that clearly explains the events of the day. It's really a 3-D movie augmented by special effects. You'll feel the ground tremble during a cavalry charge and smell the smoke of a burning farmhouse. Best of all, you'll clearly understand the major turning points in the battle: Napoleon's delay, relentless cavalry attacks, the siege of a crucial farm complex, the Prussians' arrival, and the final charge of the Imperial Guard—and how the British soldiers surprised them. The concluding scenes of the post-battle carnage send a not-very-subtle message that this must never happen again.

Your visit ends with exhibits on the aftermath of the battle and how Waterloo is perceived today.

**Panorama:** Your ticket includes this 360-degree painting of the battle. Skip it unless you want to see a static Victorian rendering of what happened here.

**Lion's Mound** (Butte de Lion): This hill on a ridge where Wellington made his stand was also the likely site where the future King William II of the Netherlands was wounded by a musket shot. The Dutch commemorated their contribution to the battle by building a huge mound that ruined the battlefield geography—so most historians hate it. For visitors, it provides a sweeping view of the battlefield (after climbing 226 steep stairs).

### Hougoumont Farm

This farm is one of the few relics of the battle to survive to this day—though much of it burned during the fighting (what you see is mostly a restoration). A fine, 20-minute movie in English explains why the farm was key to Wellington's victory. Just prior to the battle, the British fortified its brick buildings. French troops could not make a direct attack on British lines without facing withering fire from the farm. Somehow the British troops and their Hanoverian allies managed to hold it despite repeated French assaults. At one legendary moment, 40 French soldiers started pouring in, but 10 English and Scottish soldiers somehow closed the gates behind them. All the French soldiers inside were killed except for their 10-year-old drummer boy. When the day was over, more than 6,000 soldiers perished at the farm. Wellington later said, "The success of the battle turned upon closing the gates at Hougoumont."

**Cost and Hours:** €8; July-Aug daily 10:00-19:00; Sept-June Sat-Sun 10:30-18:00 plus some Wed 14:00-18:00 only. A free horse-drawn shuttle runs from Lion's Mound at least hourly. It's also possible to walk from the visitors center (about 30 minutes)—battlefield buffs enjoy this chance to see the lay of the land away from crowds.

# GRAND PLACE WALK

Like most European cities, Brussels has a main square, but few are as "Grand" as this one. From its medieval origins as a market for a small village, the Grand Place has grown into a vast public space enclosed by Old World buildings with stately gables. Today, the "Place" is the place to see Europe on parade. If Brussels is indeed the "capital of Europe," there's no better evidence than the crowds that flock here from every nation. Visitors come to bask in the ambience, sample chocolate, and relax with a beer at an outdoor café.

This walk allows all that, but also goes a bit beyond. We'll take in the spectacular (if heavily touristed) square, browse an elegant shopping arcade, run the frenetic gauntlet of restaurant row (Rue des Bouchers), stand at the center of modern Brussels at the Bourse, and end at the grand finale (he said with a wink): the one-of-a-kind *Manneken-Pis*.

## Orientation

**Length of This Walk:** Allow two hours.
**Town Hall:** €8; English tours offered Wed at 14:00, Sun at 10:00, 15:00, and 16:00; get tickets in advance—see page 135.
**City Museum:** €10, Tue-Sun 10:00-17:00, closed Mon.
**Brewery Museum:** €5, Wed-Sat 11:00-18:00, closed Sun-Tue.
**Chocolate Shops on the Grand Place:** Generally open daily until 18:00, later on weekends.

## The Walk Begins

### ❶ Grand Place

The Grand Place has long been the commercial and geographical heart of Brussels. A thousand years ago, this was where farmers and merchants sold their wares in open-air stalls, enticing travelers from the main east-west highway across Belgium, which ran just north of the square.

The dominant building on the Grand Place is also the oldest: The **Town Hall** (Hôtel de Ville). While it was built in the 1400s in Gothic style, the statues and orna-mentation are mostly neo-Gothic icing, added in the 1800s. The grand tower, which dates from 1455, is topped with St. Michael, patron and protector of the city.

The fancy smaller buildings giving the square its unique character are for-mer **guild halls** (now mostly shops and restaurants). In the Middle Ages, Brus-sels consisted of two zones: The king and the Church were on the hill (up-town), and the traders and merchants were on the riverbank (downtown). To assert themselves in a world controlled (until the French Revolu-tion) by an alliance of Church and king, the merchants organized into guilds and built headquarters on this square.

In 1695, during the Nine Years' War, French King Louis XIV's troops took the high ground east of the city, sighted their cannons on the Town Hall spire, and managed to level everything around it (4,000 mostly wooden buildings) without ever hitting the spire itself. The "Bombardment of Brussels" was the most destruc-tive event in the city's history.

As a matter of pride, Brussels' brewers, bakers, and *Manneken-Pis* corkscrew makers rebuilt their offices better than ever. They completed everything within seven years—in stone, taller, and topped with ornamented gables and classical statues. Richer guilds had the money to hire top architects and show off with even more lavish buildings, trimmed with gold. The Brussels governor invited the lesser guilds—millers, tanners, and the like—to set up shop here as well, and provided a common facade for their offices on the uphill side of the square.

The many differences in style reflect the independent spirit of the people and the many cultural influences that con-verged in this crossroads trading center. The entire square comes with a little extra sparkle, thanks to a 2014 restoration proj-ect. The result is that you're completely surrounded by centuries-old buildings, free from any hint of a modern skyscraper, and immersed in historic ambience.

Pan the square to get oriented. Face the **Town Hall** with its skyscraping spire. The **TI** is on your right, under the Town Hall's arches. To your right, a block away (downhill), is the Bourse building. The Upper Town is to your left, rising up the hill beyond Central train station. Over your left shoulder a short walk away is St. Michael's Cathedral. And the *Manneken-Pis* is three blocks ahead, down the street that runs along the left side of the Town Hall.

Opposite the Town Hall is the impressive, gray **King's House** (Maison du Roi), which now houses the **City Museum.** The structure has gone through several incarnations in its 800-year history. First it was the medieval square's bread market—hence, the building's Dutch name—Broodhuis. Then (early 1500s) it became the regional office for the vast Habsburg empire of Charles V—hence its French name—Maison du Roi. Its lacy, prickly Gothic facade dates from the late 1800s, when it was renovated to be the City Museum (for details on visiting the museum, see page the "Sights in Brussels" chapter).

The **Swan House** (#9, just to the left of the Town Hall) housed a bar where Karl Marx and Friedrich Engels met in February 1848 to write their *Communist Manifesto*. Later that year, when the treatise sparked socialist revolution around Europe, Belgium exiled Marx and Engels. Next door (#10) is the Maison des Brasseurs, home of the brewers' guild and the **Brewery Museum.**

Today, the grand buildings of Grand Place host shops and cafés selling chocolates, *gaufres* (waffles), beer, mussels, fries, *dentelles* (lace), and flowers. And the Town Hall hosts weddings—it's where King Philippe got married in 1999. (The Belgian government demands that all marriages are first performed in simple civil ceremonies.)

Imagine this already glorious square filled with a carpet of flowers. Every other August, florists create a colorful 19,000-square-foot pattern of tightly packed begonias—that's about three-quarters of a million individual flowers (www.flowercarpet.be). Begun in 1971 by a begonia salesman as a way to promote his wares, this gorgeous display has become a biennial Brussels fixture that makes this grand space even grander. If you're here in August on the off-year, there is a massive floral display inside the Town Hall (see www.floralientime.be).

• *Exit the Grand Place next to Godiva (from the northeast, or uphill, corner of the square), and go north one block on Rue de la Colline. Along the way, you'll pass a popular* **Tintin boutique** *(at #9), selling merchandise of the popular Belgian comic-strip hero (see sidebar on page 143). Continue to Rue du Marché aux Herbes, which was once the main east-west highway through Belgium. The little parklike square just to*

# Grand Place Walk

1. Grand Place
2. Galeries Royales St. Hubert
3. Rue des Bouchers
4. Church of St. Nicolas
5. The Bourse
6. Place de la Bourse & Boulevard Anspach
7. Two Monuments
8. Manneken-Pis Statue

GRAND PLACE WALK

DE LA FOURCHE

RUE DES

R. DES DOMINICAINS

PETITE R.D. BOUCHERS

BOUCHERS

3

RUE CHAIR ET PAIN

R. DU MARCHÉ AUX HERBES

GALERIES ROYALES ST. HUBERT

N

RUE DE LA MONTAGNE

KING'S HOUSE & CITY MUSEUM

R. HARENGS

2

GODIVA, MARY & NEUHAUS CHOC.

TIN-TIN SHOP

R. COLLINE

WALK BEGINS

"Agora" Square

DON QUIXOTE STATUE

Place d'Espagne

MAISON DUCS DE DE BRABANT

AGORA GALLERY

BRASSERIE

RUE DES ÉPERONNIERS

RUE DE LA MADELEINE

T

MADELEINE CHURCH

R. DE L'INFANTE ISABELLE

RUE DU QUESNOY

Square de la Putterie

To Upper Town

# Tasty Treats Around the Grand Place

Brussels' grand square (and the surrounding area) offers plenty of places to sample Belgium's culinary specialties.

## Cafés

Mussels in Brussels, Belgian-style fries, yeasty local beers, waffles...if all you do here is plop down at a café on the square, try some of these specialties, and watch the world go by—hey, that's a great afternoon in Brussels.

The outdoor cafés are casual and come with fair prices (a decent Belgian beer costs €5, and a really good one is more like €7—with no cover or service charge). Have a seat, and a waiter will serve you. The half-dozen or so cafés on the downhill side of the square are all roughly equal in price and quality for simple drinks and foods—check the posted menus. As they are generally owned by breweries, you won't have a big selection of beers.

## Choco-Crawl

The best chocolate shops lie along the north (uphill) side of the square, starting with Godiva at the high end (higher in both altitude and price). The cost goes down slightly as you descend to the other shops. Each shop has a mouth-watering display case of chocolates and sells 100-gram mixes (six or so pieces) for about €9, or individual pieces for about €1.50 (for more on buying chocolate in Belgium, see page 49).

**Godiva** is synonymous with fine Belgian chocolate. Now owned by a Turkish company, Godiva still has its management and the original factory (built in 1926) in Belgium. This store, at Grand Place 21, was Godiva's first (est. 1937).

**Mary,** at #23, was founded in 1919 by the first woman chocolatier, Mary Delluc. She shot to stardom when the royal family began favoring her chocolates. Today, the store and its treats' packaging are faithful to her original designs.

**Neuhaus,** at #27, has been encouraging chocoholics since 1857 and claims to have invented the praline. Their main store is in the Galeries Royales St. Hubert. Neuhaus publishes a good little pamphlet explaining its products. The "caprice" (toffee with vanilla crème) tastes like Easter.

**Galler,** just off the square at Rue au Beurre 44, proudly serves less sugary dark chocolate. The top-end choice, 85 percent pure chocolate, is called simply "Black 85"—and worth a sample if you like chocolate without the sweetness. Galler's products are well described in English.

**Leonidas,** four doors down at Rue au Beurre 34, is where cost-conscious Bruxellois get their fix, sacrificing 10 percent in quality to nearly triple their take (machine-made, only €3.10/100 grams). White chocolate is their specialty.

*your right—a modest gathering place with market stalls—is nicknamed "Agora" (after the nearby covered shopping area). Looking to the right, notice that it's all uphill from here to the Upper Town, another four blocks (and 200-foot elevation gain) beyond. Straight ahead, you enter the arcaded shopping mall called...*

## ❷ Galeries Royales St. Hubert

Built in 1847, one of Europe's oldest still-operating shopping malls served as the glass-covered model that inspired shopping galleries in Paris, London, and beyond. It celebrated the town's new modern attitude (having recently gained its independence from the Netherlands). Built in an age of expansion and industrialization, the mall demonstrated efficient modern living, with elegant apartments

upstairs above trendy shops, theaters, and cafés—handy for fancy people who wanted to go to the theater without muddying their boots or dealing with the rougher world sprawling alongside this elegant gallery. This mall was the center of upwardly mobile Brussels—home to progressive newspapers and French expats (Hugo, Dumas, Baudelaire), and where the first Belgian motion picture was screened.

Looking down the arcade, you'll notice that it bends halfway down, designed to lure shoppers farther in. Its iron-and-glass look is still popular, but the decorative columns, cameos, and pastel colors evoke a more elegant time. It's Neo-Renaissance, like a pastel Florentine palace.

In this shopping mall, there's no Gap, no Foot Locker, no Cinnabon. Instead, you'll find hat, cane, and umbrella stores that sell...hats, canes, and umbrellas—generally handmade on the premises. **Ganterie Italienne** (immediately on the right) has been making ladies' leather gloves since 1890. Since 1857, **Neuhaus** (near the end of the first section, on the right) has sold chocolates here at its flagship store, where many Brussels natives buy their pralines—filled chocolates were invented in this very shop in 1912. Next to Neuhaus is its competition—the avant-garde chocolatier **Pierre Marcolini.** Across from Neuhaus, the **Taverne du Passage** restaurant serves the same local specialties that hometown singer-songwriter Jacques Brel used to come here for: *croquettes de crevettes* (shrimp croquettes), *tête de veau* (calf's head), *anguilles au vert* (eels with herb sauce), and *fondue au fromage* (cheese croquettes).

• *Midway down the mall, where the two sections bend, turn left and exit the mall onto...*

### ❸ Rue des Bouchers

Yikes! During mealtimes, this street is absolutely crawling with tourists browsing through wall-to-wall, low-quality restaurants. Brussels is known worldwide for its food, serving all kinds of cuisine, but specializing in seafood (particularly mussels). You'll have plenty to choose from along this table-clogged restaurant row, where hustlers will try to draw you into their eateries. Don't count on getting a good value here—better restaurants are just a few steps away (for specifics, see page 211).

Many diners here are day-trippers. Colin from London, Marie from Paris, Maartje from Holland, and Dietrich from Frankfurt could easily all "do lunch" together in Brussels—just three hours from home.

The first intersection, with Petite Rue des Bouchers, is the heart of the restaurant quarter, which sprawls for several blocks. The street names reveal what sorts of shops used to stand here—butchers *(bouchers)*, herbs, chickens, and cheese.

• *At this intersection, turn left onto Petite Rue des Bouchers and walk straight back to the Grand Place. (You'll see the Town Hall tower ahead.) At the Grand Place, turn right on Rue au Beurre. Comparison-shop at the Galler and Leonidas chocolate stores and pass by the little "Is it raining?"* **fountain** *(one of a series of fountains you'll see around town, each featuring a scene from a painting by local boy Pieter Bruegel). At the intersection with Rue du Midi is the...*

### ❹ Church of St. Nicolas

Since the 12th century, there's been a church here. Because of a 1954 restoration, the church looks younger than it is. Inside, along the left aisle, see rough stones in some of the arches from the early church. Outside, notice the barnacle-like shops, such as De Witte Jewelers, built right into the church. Medieval churches often built tiny structures against their walls and rented them out as shops and apartments.

• *Just beyond the church, you run into the back entrance of a big Neoclassical building.*

### ❺ The Bourse and Art Nouveau Cafés

The Bourse (stock exchange) was built in the 1870s in the Historicist style—a mix-and-match, Neo-everything architectural movement. Plans are in the works for the former stock exchange to host a big beer museum.

Several historic cafés huddle around the Bourse in a car-free zone. To the right is the woody **Le Cirio,** with its delightful circa-1900 interior. Many Brussels cafés, like Le Cirio, are still decorated in the early 20th-century Art Nouveau style. Ironwork columns twist and bend like flower stems, and lots of Tiffany-style stained glass and mirrors make them light and spacious. Slender, elegant, willowy Gibson Girls decorate the wallpaper, while waiters in vests and bowties glide by.

• *Circle around to the front of the Bourse, toward Boulevard Anspach.*

## ❻ Place de la Bourse and Boulevard Anspach

Brussels is the political nerve center of Europe (with as many lobbyists as Washington, DC), and the city sees several hundred demonstrations a year. When the local team wins a soccer match or some political group wants to make a statement, Place de la Bourse is where people flock to wave their flags.

It's also where the old town meets the new. To the right along Boulevard Anspach are two shopping malls and several first-run movie theaters. Rue Neuve, which parallels Anspach, is another bustling pedestrian-only shopping street.

Boulevard Anspach was once the city's main drag, choked with cars. Since 2015, it's been closed to car traffic, creating one of the largest pedestrian zones in Europe. And under your feet is the still-flowing Senne River. Remember that Brussels was once a port, with North Sea boats coming as far as this point to unload their goods. But with frequent cholera epidemics killing thousands of its citizens, in 1870 the city decided to cover up its stinky river.

Beyond Boulevard Anspach—down Rue Paul Devaux—is the charming **Ste. Catherine** neighborhood, clustered around the former fish market and the Church of Ste. Catherine. This village-like zone is the easiest escape from the bustle of downtown Brussels and features several recommended lunch stops.

• *For efficient sightseeing, consider catching bus #71 from Place de Brouckère, a few blocks north on Boulevard Anspach, to the Place Royale, where you can follow my Upper Town Walk (see next chapter), ending near the* Manneken-Pis. *But if you'd rather stay on foot in the Lower Town, walk back to the Grand Place.*

## From the Grand Place to the *Manneken-Pis*

• *Leave the Grand Place kitty-corner, heading south down the street running along the left side of the Town Hall, Rue Charles Buls. Just five yards off the square, under the arch, are* ❼ *two monuments honoring illustrious Brussels notables:*

The first monument is a leafy scene on the wall featuring a beautiful young man. It's an Art Nouveau allegory of knowledge and science (which brings illumination, as indicated by the Roman oil lamp) designed by Victor Horta. It honors **Charles Buls,** mayor from 1888 to 1899. If you enjoyed the Grand Place, thank him for saving it. He stopped the "Builder King" Leopold II from blasting a grand esplanade from Grand Place up the hill to his palace.

A few steps farther you'll see locals rubbing a **brass statue of a reclining man.** This was Alderman Evrard 't Serclaes, who in 1356 bravely refused to surrender the keys of the city to invaders, and so was tortured and killed. Touch him, and his misfortune becomes your good luck. Judging by the reverence with which locals treat this ritual, I figure there must be something to it.

From here, the street becomes a gauntlet of Belgian clichés: lace, waffles, *frites,* chocolate, and tapestries. The **N. Toebac Lace Shop** shows off some fine lace and gives travelers with this book a 15 percent discount. For more on lace, visit the Fashion and Lace Museum (a block away and just around the corner—see page 140).

Continuing down the street, notice a **comic strip panel mural** on the wall ahead, depicting that favorite of Belgian comic heroes, Tintin. Known and beloved by virtually all Europeans, Tintin is the intrepid boy with the wavy hair. In this scene, he's fleeing yet another misadventure, scrambling down a fire escape. He's accompanied by his faithful dog Snowy, and his friend

# Tapestries

In 1500, tapestry workshops in Brussels were famous, cranking out high-quality tapestries for the walls of Europe's palaces. They were functional (as insulation and propaganda for a church, king, or nobleman) and beautiful—an intricate design formed by colored thread. Even great painters, such as Rubens and Raphael, designed tapestries, which rivaled Renaissance canvases. The best Belgian tapestries are in Madrid, because the golden age of Belgian tapestries was under Spanish rule in the 16th and 17th centuries. Also impressive are the Brussels-made tapestries of the Sistine Chapel, which some say were so extraordinary that they sparked the Northern Renaissance.

To make a tapestry, neutral-colored threads are stretched vertically over a loom. (In Renaissance Belgium, the threads were made from imported English wool.) The design of the tapestry is created with the horizontal weave, from the colored threads that (mostly) overlay the vertical threads. Tapestry making is much more difficult than basic weaving, as each horizontal thread is only as long as the detail it's meant to create. A single horizontal row can be made up of many individual pieces of thread. Before weaving begins, an artist designs a pattern for the larger picture, called a "cartoon," which weavers follow for guidance as they work.

Flanders and Paris (in the Gobelins workshop) were the two centers of tapestry making until the art died out, mirroring the decline of Europe's noble class.

Captain Haddock, who always keeps an eye out for him. Dozens of these building-size comic-strip panels decorate Brussels, celebrating the Belgians' favorite medium (if interested in tracking them down, buy a map from the TI or search online for "comic street art Brussels"). Just as Ireland has its writers, Italy its painters, and France its chefs, Belgium has a knack for turning out world-class comic artists.

• *Follow the crowds, passing the* **Choco-Story Museum** *on the right. Notice the excitement building, because in another block you reach the...*

## ❽ *Manneken-Pis*

Even with low expectations, this bronze statue is smaller than you'd think—the little squirt's under two feet tall, practically the size of a newborn. Still, the little peeing boy is an appropriately low-key symbol for the unpretentious Bruxellois. The statue was made in 1619 to provide drinking water for the neighborhood. Notice that the baby, sculpted in Renaissance style, actually has the musculature of a man instead of the pudgy limbs of a child. The statue was knighted by the occupying King Louis XV—so French soldiers had to salute the eternally pissing lad when they passed.

It's tradition for visiting VIPs to bring the statue an outfit—and he also dresses up for special occasions—so you can often see the *Manneken* peeing through a colorful costume. A sign on the fence lists the month's festival days and how he'll be dressed. For example, on January 8, Elvis Presley's birthday, he's an Elvis impersonator; on Prostate Awareness Day, his flow is down to a slow drip. He can

also be hooked up to a keg to pee wine or beer. The collection of costumes he's worn for three centuries—GardeRobe Manneken-Pis—is just up the hill on Rue du Chêne.

There are several different legends about the *Manneken*—take your pick: He was a naughty boy who peed inside a witch's house, so she froze him. A rich man lost his son and declared, "Find my son, and we'll make a statue of him doing what he did when found." Or—the locals' favorite version—the little tyke loved his beer, which came in handy when a fire threatened the wooden city: He bravely put it out. Want the truth? The city commissioned the

*Manneken* to show the freedom and joie de vivre of living in Brussels—where happy people eat, drink...and drink...and then pee.

The gathering crowds make the scene more interesting. Hang out for a while and watch the commotion this little guy makes as tour groups come and go. When I was there, a Russian man marveled at the statue, shook his head, and said, "He never stop!"

# UPPER TOWN WALK

The Upper Town has always had a more aristocratic feel than the medieval, commercial streets of the Lower Town. It's the Brussels of the late 1800s, when it was a cosmopolitan European city and capital of a colonial empire. With broad boulevards, big marble buildings, palaces, museums, and so many things called "royal," it also seems much newer and a bit more sterile. But the Upper Town has plenty to offer and even a bit of personality poking out from behind its stuffy veneer.

Use this walk to get acquainted with this less-touristed part of town, sample some world-class museums, see the palace, explore art galleries, and get the lay of the land from a panoramic viewpoint. The tour starts at Place Royale, a half-block from the one essential art sight in town, the Royal Museums of Fine Arts of Belgium—consider a visit while you're here (see the next chapter). The Musical Instruments Museum is also in the neighborhood.

From Place Royale, we'll walk south along the ridge, pop into a stained-glass-filled Gothic church, continue on to the towering Palace of Justice (next to the best view of the city), descend through the well-worn tapestry of the Sablon quarter's antique stores, art galleries, and cafés, and end in the Lower Town at a homey little square right near the *Manneken-Pis*, the pride and joy of Brussels.

## Orientation

**Length of This Walk:** Allow 1.5 hours.

**Getting There:** The walk begins at Place Royale in the Upper Town. You have several ways to get there: **Walk uphill** (about 15 minutes from the Grand Place); catch a **taxi** (about €19 from Rue Orts, near Place de la Bourse); ride frequent **bus** #38 or #71 two stops to Royale/Koning (catch from Putterie

street just north of Central/Centraal station, direction: Héros/
Helden or Delta); or take a **hop-on, hop-off** bus tour (hop off
at Place Royale).

**Royal Museums of Fine Arts of Belgium:** €15 for Magritte, €15
combo-ticket covers Old Masters and Fin-de-Siècle, €20 for
all three; all are free first Wed of the month after 13:00; open
Tue-Sun 10:00-17:00, closed Mon.

**Musical Instruments Museum:** €15, Tue-Fri 9:30-17:00, Sat-Sun
from 10:00, closed Mon.

**BELvue Museum:** €10, Tue-Fri 9:30-17:00 (July-Aug until
18:00), Sat-Sun 10:00-18:00, closed Mon.

**Notre-Dame du Sablon Church:** Free, daily 9:00-18:30.

**Giant Wheel:** €9, daily 11:00-23:00.

# The Walk Begins

## ❶ Place Royale

At the crest of the hill sits Place Royale (Koningsplein), encircled
by cars and trams and enclosed by white Neoclassical buildings
forming a mirror image across a cobblestone square. A big, green
statue of a horseman stands in the center.

The **statue** depicts local hero Godfrey de Bouillon, one of
the leaders of the First Crusade (in 1096). The ultimate Catholic
knight, he rides forward with his
flag, gazing down on the Town
Hall spire. Godfrey, a patriarch of
the House of Flanders, established
his family's rule over what would
become Belgium. This statue dates
from 1830—the year of Belgian
independence. It was one of a class
of statues designed to celebrate (or
dream up) deep roots of the Bel-
gian people to give their new nation legitimacy. (Today, about the
only thing that stirs Belgian nationalistic sentiment is a victory by
the Belgian soccer team.)

This hilltop in Brussels became home to the region's rulers. In
the 12th century, a castle called the Coudenberg Palace was built
(over Godfrey's right shoulder, just outside the square). Today, it's
the **Royal Palace,** where modern Belgium's king still lives.

Behind Godfrey is the **Church of St. Jacques-sur-Cou-
denberg,** with its imposing cupola, dominating the square's ring
of buildings. This building (from 1787) stands on the spot of the
original church built here next to the 12th-century castle. Locals
remember that it was on the porch of the Church of St. Jacques,

on July 21, 1831, that their first king took the oath that established modern Belgium.

In the 1870s, as Belgium industrialized and modernized, this tight ensemble of buildings and squares was given a makeover. It signaled that Brussels had arrived as a world capital. Old buildings were refurbished and new ones built to create a planned neighborhood on a grand scale. If Godfrey turned and looked left down Rue de la Régence, he'd see the domed Palace of Justice at the end of the boulevard. This Neoclassical look—broad vistas down wide boulevards, ending at gleaming white, Greek-columned monuments—was all the rage, seen not only here but in Paris, London, and Washington, DC.

The square has several worthwhile museums. The main entrance to the **Royal Museums of Fine Arts of Belgium** is a half-block to the right (for a tour, see the next chapter). The **Musical Instruments Museum** is straight downhill from the square—if Godfrey spurred his horse straight ahead, he'd pass it on his right (for details on visiting, see page 145). It's housed in an early 20th-century iron-and-glass former department store whose Art Nouveau facade was a deliberate attempt to get beyond the retro Greek columns and domes of the Place Royale.

• *Before heading south, exit Place Royale on the north side, which opens up to the large, tree-lined...*

## ❷ Parc de Bruxelles

Copying Versailles, the Habsburg empress Maria Theresa of Austria (Marie-Antoinette's mom) had this symmetrical park laid out in 1776 (she ruled, but never visited, the city). This is just one of many large parks in Brussels, which started with an awareness of the importance of city planning.

At the far (north) end of the park (directly opposite the Royal Palace, no need to actually walk there) is the Parliament building. Which parliament? The city hosts several: the European Parliament, the Belgian Parliament, and several local, city-council-type parliaments. This is the Belgian Parliament, seen on nightly newscasts as a backdrop for talking heads and politicians.

In 1830, Belgian patriots rose up and converged on the park, where they attacked the troops of the Dutch king. This was the

# Upper Town Walk

first blow in a short, almost bloodless revolution that drove out the foreign-born king and gave the Belgians "independence"...under a different foreign-born king.

• *The long building facing the park (to your right) is the...*

## ❸ Royal Palace (Palais Royale)

Belgium struck out twice trying to convince someone to be its new king. Finally, Leopold I (r. 1831-1865), a nobleman from Germany,

**UPPER TOWN WALK**

1. Place Royale
2. Parc de Bruxelles
3. Royal Palace
4. Notre-Dame du Sablon Church
5. Place du Petit Sablon
6. Palace of Justice
7. Viewpoint from Place Poelaert
8. Place du Grand Sablon
9. Rue de Rollebeek
10. Tour d'Angle
11. Place de la Vieille Halle aux Blés

agreed to become "King of the Belgians." Leopold was a steadying influence as the country modernized. His son rebuilt this palace—near the site of earlier palaces, dating back to the 10th century—by linking a row of townhouse mansions with a unifying facade (around 1870).

Leopold's great-great-great-great-grandnephew, King Philippe (b. 1960), today uses the palace as an office. (His head is on Belgium's euro coins.) Philippe and his wife, Queen Mathilde, live in a palace north of here (near the Atomium), at several country estates, and on the French Riviera. If the Belgian flag (black-yellow-red) is flying from the palace, the king is somewhere in Belgium.

Philippe is a figurehead king, as in many European democracies, but he serves an important function as a common bond between bickering Flemish and Walloon citizens. The king—regarded by some as awkward and standoffish—is not as popular as Queen Mathilde, also a Belgian native. Their daughter, Elisabeth, born in 2001, is first in line to become the next Belgian monarch.

The palace is off-limits to tourists except from late July through August (visit www.koninklijk-paleis-palais-royal.be to book advance tickets; gardens open April-May). The adjacent **BELvue Museum** has a well-presented exhibit on Belgian history (see page 146).

• *Return to Place Royale, then continue south along Rue de la Régence, passing the main entrance to the Royal Museums of Fine Arts of Belgium complex. This grand boulevard—cut through a tangle of medieval buildings in the 19th century—connects the Royal Palace with the grand Palace of Justice at the far end. Continue ahead, passing grand government administration buildings (including those that ran the affairs of Belgian colonies), to the Gothic church (on the right).*

## ❹ Notre-Dame du Sablon Church

This is the Church of the Archers, built in the 14th century in the Flamboyant Gothic style. In the Middle Ages, archers and cross-bowmen were vital defenders of the realm, and the royals made sure they were taken care of very well. While the church was built six centuries ago, the exterior highlights were added in the 1880s and are Neo-Gothic. It's worth a look inside.

**Visiting the Church:** The church is made of simple gray stone lit by the warm light of the **stained-glass windows.** The windows in the nave (which date from the 19th and 20th centuries) are notable for their symmetry—rows of saints in Gothic niches topped by coats of arms. The glorious apse behind the altar—bathed in colorful light from some original 15th-century windows—is what Gothic is all about.

Midway up the nave is an artistically **carved pulpit,** supported by an angel and animals, the symbols of the Evangelists. The left transept has relics of the last Habsburg emperor, Karl I (1887-1922). Karl's legendary Catholic devotion inspires many devoted people to pray here, and he was beatified in 2004.

The church's claim to fame is next to the altar—a small wooden **statue of Mary** dressed in white with a lace veil. The statue is near

and dear to the hearts of the people of Brussels. This is a copy, but the original statue was thought to have had miraculous powers that saved the town from plagues. In 1348, the statue spoke to a godly woman named Beatrix, prompting her to steal the statue away from Antwerp on a boat. (That's why the church is decorated with several images of boats, including the small **wooden boat** high up in the right transept.) When the citizens of Antwerp tried to stop Beatrix, the Mary statue froze them in their tracks.

When Beatrix and the statue arrived here, the Bruxellois welcomed Mary with a joyous parade—the Ommegang. Now, every summer, the citizens re-create the procession by dressing up in tights and flamboyant costumes and parading the streets with colorful banners and large puppets. The Ommegang begins here, threads downhill, and culminates in a climax on the Grand Place.

• *Exiting the church, head to the other side of Rue de la Régence from the church, where you'll find a leafy, fenced-off garden called the...*

### ❺ Place du Petit Sablon

Step into this charming little park, a pleasant refuge from the busy street and part of why this neighborhood is considered so livable. Its central fountain, a fine example of 19th-century Romanticism, honors two local nobles who were executed because they promoted tolerance during the Inquisition. Good friends, one Catholic and the other Protestant, they were beheaded on the Grand Place in 1568.

Check out the other statues. The 48 small figures atop the wrought-iron fence represent the craftsman guilds—weavers, brewers, and butchers—of 16th-century Brussels. And inside the garden, the 10 large statues represent hometown thinkers of the 16th century—a time of Humanism and great intellectual accomplishments in Brussels. Gerardus Mercator (1512-1594), the Belgian mapmaker who devised a way to more accurately show the spherical earth on a flat surface, holds a globe.

This collection of statues is a reminder that, although Belgium was never a great power, Belgians have much to be proud of as a people. From here, look back at the church and enjoy its flamboyant Neo-Gothic lines.

• *Continue along Rue de la Régence. You'll pass (on the left) the **Music Academy** and Brussels' main **synagogue**, with its towering facade and tight security (notice the closed front entrance and protective bollards). Across the street is the **Benelux building**, three flags flying. Benelux, which integrated the trade and industry of Belgium, the Netherlands, and Luxemburg in the late 1940s, was the nucleus of today's European Union. Both have a similar mission: to promote the trade, security, and well-being of their member states. Continue another block to reach the long-scaffolded...*

## ❻ Palace of Justice (Palais de Justice)

This domed mountain of marble sits on the edge of the Upper Town ridge, dominating the Brussels skyline. Built in wedding-cake layers of Greek columns, it's topped with a dome taller than St. Peter's in Rome, rising 340 feet. Covering more than six acres, it's the size of a baseball stadium and extends seven floors underground.

The palace dates from the late 19th century, when tiny Belgium was a global power. It was built under King Leopold II (son of Leo I, r. 1865-1909) and epitomizes the brassy, showy grandeur of his reign. Leopold became obscenely wealthy by turning Africa's Congo region—80 times the size of Belgium—into his personal colony. Whip-wielding Belgian masters forced enslaved Congolese people to tend lucrative rubber plantations, exploiting the new craze for car tires. Leopold spent much of this wealth expanding and beautifying the city of Brussels.

Today the building (which stands on the historic site of the town gallows) serves as a Hall of Justice, where major court cases are tried. If you pop in to the lobby, you may see lawyers in black robes buzzing about. The building is perennially scaffolded—for more than 20 years so far and likely a decade more. At the end of World War II, the Nazis set fire to it as they left town, compromising the cupola's structure, and the palace has never quite recovered.

Notice the rack of city bikes. Like many European cities, Brussels subsidizes a public-bike system, designed for riders to pick up a bike in one part of town and drop it off anywhere else. But these bike racks are often empty, since this is a popular place to grab a bike for the easy ride back down to the Lower Town.

• *One of the best views of Brussels awaits from a perch immediately to the right of the Palace of Justice (to get even higher, ascend the 180-foot-tall* **Great Wheel** *ferris wheel).*

### ❼ Viewpoint from Place Poelaert

Place Poelaert is 200 feet above the former Senne River Valley. Gazing west over the Lower Town, pan the valley from right (north) to left:

Near you is the stubby **clock tower** of the Minimes Church. To the left of that, in the distance past a tall square skyscraper, is the lacy, white Town Hall **spire** (marking the Grand Place).

Twinkling in the far distance, six miles away, you can see one of the city's landmarks, the **Atomium.** (No doubt, someone atop it is looking back at you.) The Atomium's nine shiny steel balls form the shape of an iron molecule that's as tall as the Palace of Justice behind you. Built for the 1958 World's Fair, it's now a middle-aged symbol of the dawn of the Atomic Era.

Next (closer to you) rises the **black clock tower** of Notre-Dame de la Chapelle. The great painter Pieter Bruegel the Elder is buried here, in the city's oldest church (from 1134, with a tower that starts Gothic and ends Baroque). On the distant horizon (behind the spire), see **four boxy skyscrapers,** part of the residential sprawl of this city of more than a million, which now  covers 62 square miles. Breaking the horizon to the left is a **green dome,** which belongs to the Basilica of Koekelberg (fourth-biggest church in the world). And finally (panning quickly to the left), you see a **black glass skyscraper** marking the Midi/Zuid train station, where you can catch high-speed train lines, such as the Eurostar to London.

At your feet lies the **Marolles neighborhood.** Once a funky, poor place where locals developed their own quirky dialogue, today it can be either seedy or colorful, depending on the time of day and your perception. The area is famous for its sprawling flea market (daily 7:00-14:00, best on weekends). Two of the streets just below you—Rue Haute and Rue Blaes—are lined with secondhand shops. A free **elevator** (see the skywalk entry on your left) connects Place Poelaert with the Marolles neighborhood, which is worth a 10-minute detour to its café-lined square.

Gazing off into the distance to the far left (south), you can't quite see the suburb of **Waterloo,** 10 miles away. It was there that the tide of 19th-century European history turned: Napoleon suffered a crushing defeat on the Waterloo battlefield, his rule of Europe ended, and Belgium was placed under a Dutch king—until the Belgians won their independence in the 1830 revolution.

Behind you, in Place Poelaert, is a **memorial** to the two world wars. Both conflicts slashed through Belgium with deadly force, and both were tragic. In World War II the blitzkrieg blew through Belgium. But World War I, with its trenches and mustard gas, took a bigger toll on this country and left greater scars.

• *Backtrack east, descending by walking down Rue Ernest Allard and turning left onto Rue des Sablons. Passing lots of antique shops and galleries, you'll eventually reach Place du Grand Sablon, the square below the Notre-Dame du Sablon Church. (For a light meal, $$ Le Pain Quotidien—on the square at Rue des Sablons 11—offers a fine value with delightful seating and baked goods right out of the oven.)*

## ❽ Place du Grand Sablon

The Sablon neighborhood that surrounds this square and its church features cafés and restaurants, antique stores, and art galleries. Every weekend, there's an antique market on the square. The 1740 statue celebrates how Brussels gave refuge to Catholics who fled Protestant England.

On warm summer evenings, the square sparks magic, as sophisticated locals sip aperitifs at the café tables. **Chocolatier Wittamer** (on the far side of the square, at #6) often has elaborate window displays. And at the bottom of the square is the shop of the innovative celebrity choco-chef **Pierre Marcolini**—one of the world's top chocolatiers—with a tempting buffet upstairs.

• *Sloping Place du Grand Sablon funnels downhill into the pedestrian-only street called...*

### ❾ Rue de Rollebeek

Today it's a delightful traffic-free lane lined with sidewalk cafés, art galleries, shops, midrange restaurants, and boutiques—a pleasant place to press "Pause" before returning to the bustle of Brussels. This is an easy place to comparison-shop for a drink or meal. About 100 yards down the street, a few surviving brick buildings give you a taste of the city before its 1695 bombardment by France's Louis XIV (during the Nine Years' War—fought between France and just about all the rest of Europe).

• *Rue de Rollebeek leads down to the busy Boulevard de l'Empereur. To the right on the boulevard, just past the bowling alley, is the...*

### ❿ Tour d'Angle

The "Corner Tower" is a rare surviving section of Brussels' medieval city wall. It stood over one of seven gates along the 2.5-mile-

UPPER TOWN WALK

long wall that enclosed 13th-century Brussels. Notice the slash through the city here that marks where underground trains connect Central station (to your right) and Midi station (to your left, with the black skyscraper). Six tracks under you are kept busy with about a thousand trains a day. This ambitious bit of city infrastructure was a project started in 1902 and not finished until 1952—two occupations by Germany slowed things down.

Notice the charm of the 1950s-era buildings that lined this street after the completion of the Métro line. Across the street from the bowling alley (with red flags and balconies) is the **Socialist Party headquarters** building. Part of its mission: finding a way for the two leading socialist parties—representing Flemish- and French-speaking Belgians, respectively—to work together for their shared liberal values. (Brussels is historically an island of liberalism amid more conservative small towns and countryside.)

• *Cross the street, head right, and take the first left at Rue de l'Escalier, which leads downhill to a pleasant square at the T-intersection.*

## ❶ Place de la Vieille Halle aux Blés

Do a 360-degree sweep from the center of this little square—circled by nice apartments and lined with cafés that hum on a sunny day. Imagine what a delight it would be to call this neighborhood home. A few decades ago, this was a derelict slum—a good reason why Brussels was famous as a fine place to work but a lousy place to live. People were moving out, leaving the down-and-out downtown. But in 1989 Brussels became its own political region and got its own government. Since then, its policy has been to revitalize the center of town; tearing down homes to build office space is no longer allowed. Consequently, new construction is reserved for residences, and people are moving into the area again. As in so many European cities, government policies are spurring the revitalization of old town centers.

The statue in the middle of the square celebrates **Jacques Brel,** a beloved singer-songwriter. You could say he was to the Belgians what Edith Piaf was to the French. Brel, a Frank Sinatra-like crooner from the 1950s, sang in French but was beloved by both the Dutch- and French-speaking communities. The Jacques Brel Foundation, across the street, works to protect and promote his legacy.

• *Your walk is finished. From here, the* Manneken-Pis *is about a five-minute walk and his costume collection at GardeRobe Manneken-Pis is along the way (both described in the Sights in Brussels chapter). Grand Place is about a 10-minute walk. If you're hungry or thirsty, return to Rue de Rollebeek, with several options for a meal, or try the nearby recommended* **La Fleur en Papier Doré,** *a classic Belgian café.*

# ROYAL MUSEUMS OF FINE ARTS TOUR

*Musées Royaux des Beaux-Arts de Belgique*

This museum complex, spread throughout three large buildings, covers much of the history of Western painting. We'll visit a trio of interconnected museums: the Old Masters Museum (pre-1850); the Fin-de-Siècle Museum (1850-1910); and the Magritte Museum, which celebrates the work of the popular Belgian Surrealist painter. The collections, while enjoyable, can be overwhelming, so this chapter highlights the museums' strengths: Flemish and Belgian artists. But don't limit your visit to these works—let the museums surprise you.

## Orientation

**Cost:** €15 for Magritte, €15 combo-ticket covers Old Masters and Fin-de-Siècle collections, €20 for all three. All are free the first Wed of the month after 13:00.

**Hours:** All three museums are open Tue-Sun 10:00-17:00, closed Mon.

**Getting There:** The main entrance, with access to all three museums, is at Rue de la Régence 3 in the Upper Town, a five-minute walk uphill from Central/Centraal station, or take bus #38 or #71 from Putterie street. Bus #38 or #27 connects this area with the European Parliament, with #27 continuing to the Park of the Cinquantenaire.

**Keep Your Magrittes Straight:** Don't confuse this Magritte Museum with the much smaller René Magritte Museum, located in the artist's former home on the outskirts of Brussels. This is clearly the place to enjoy his art.

**Information:** +32 2 508 3211, www.fine-arts-museum.be or www.musee-magritte-museum.be.

**Tours:** Consider the €4 audioguides for the Old Masters Museum or Magritte Museum (it's helpful here) and the €4 videoguide for the Fin-de-Siècle Museum.

**Length of This Tour:** Allow one hour for the Old Masters and Fin-de-Siècle museums, and another hour for the Magritte Museum. A complete visit involves a lot of walking.

**Cuisine Art:** There's a **$$** café and a fancy **$$$** brasserie on site.

**Starring:** Bruegel's *Census at Bethlehem;* Post-Impressionist works by Seurat, Gauguin, and Ensor; and Magritte's *The Treachery of Images.*

## The Tour Begins

Enter at Rue de la Régence 3 and buy your ticket. Continue into the large entrance hall and get oriented. The Old Masters Mu-

seum is on level 1 (in the galleries you can see above you); reach it through the doorway directly ahead. The Fin-de-Siècle Museum is through the passageway to the right, down several levels. The Magritte Museum is also to the right, through the same passageway. While it's a confusing floor plan, it's well signed.

Pause at the information desk to pick up a free map and consider renting an audioguide. Now let's dive in.

## Old Masters Museum

• *Go up to level 1 and start with the Flemish masters. The art is displayed in (roughly) chronological order, working counterclockwise around the central gallery. So, turn right, enter the corner room (70), and find a small canvas with a portrait.*

### ❶ Rogier van der Weyden, *Portrait of Anthony of Burgundy,* c. 1456-1465

Anthony and his cultured family—the dukes of Burgundy—are largely responsible for the art we're about to see in this first museum.

In this sensitive portrait, young Prince Anthony of Burgundy wears a black cloak, a bowl-cut hairdo, and a dark-red cap, with his pale face and hand emerging from a dark background. Anthony was a well-known Renaissance Man—soldier, scholar, and patron of the arts—whose sense of style impressed other European princes, like Florence's young Lorenzo the Magnificent.

In the 1400s, Anthony and the dukes of Burgundy helped make

# Royal Museums of Fine Arts—Old Masters

WC
ESCALATOR
STAIRS

❶ ROOM 70
❷
❸
❹ ROOM 68

MAIN FLOOR BELOW

❺
ROOM 53 ❻
ROOM 54
ROOM 55
❼

Not to Scale

Ｎ

ROYAL MUSEUMS

❶ VAN DER WEYDEN – Portrait of Anthony of Burgundy

❷ BOSCH – Triptych of the Temptations of St. Anthony

❸ MEMLING – Martyrdom of St. Sebastian

❹ BRUEGEL – The Census at Bethlehem

❺ Rembrandt & Frans Hals Paintings

❻ RUBENS – The Ascent to Calvary

❼ DAVID – The Death of Marat

Brussels one of the richest and most progressive cities in Europe, rivaling Florence and Venice. They built the Coudenberg Palace (100 yards from here) and the magnificent Town Hall (on Grand Place), and turned a gangly collection of French and Dutch-speaking and Dutch-speaking provinces into the nation we know today as Belgium. The Burgundian court attracted Europe's greatest artists, who chronicled this aristocratic family so famous across Europe.

Van der Weyden (c. 1399-1464), Brussels' official portrait painter, captures the prince in all his glory. Anthony fingers an arrow like a bowstring, indicating his re-nown as a great archer. From his gold neck-lace dangles a Golden Fleece, one of Europe's more prestigious knightly honors. You can even see the wrinkles in Anthony's neck and the faint shadow his chin casts on his Adam's apple. Anthony gazes into the distance, his clear, sad eyes lit with a speckle of white paint.

Anthony was known in his day as the Great Bastard, the brave and distinguished (but illegitimate) son of Philip the Good. Compare this portrait with that of Philip, whom Van der Weyden had also painted—see the photo on page 79. The two mens' long, elegant faces and full lips are a mirror image—pretty convincing DNA evidence in a paternity suit.

• *Continue counterclockwise around the central gallery. As you head up the long right side, stop in the first section and find...*

## ❷ Hieronymus Bosch, *Triptych of the Temptations of St. Anthony*, c. 1501

The explosion of art in the Low Countries produced the eccentric and visionary artist named Hieronymus Bosch. He added a fanciful strain to the sober realism of Flemish art.

In the center panel, find the central figure of St. Anthony—the Christian hermit who withdrew to the desert, where he was haunted by demonic apparitions. Anthony (in gray robe and beard) looks out with an expression that says, "What have I gotten myself into?"

All around are bizarre supernatural creatures who try to divert Anthony from his faith. There are humans with animal heads, animals with human heads, boats that look like fish, and birds that look like boats. In the right panel, a haggard-looking Anthony tries to block the visions out by reading his Bible. In the left panel, he's carried off by airborne devils (above) and tended to by friends (below). According to legend, Anthony persevered through it all to become an inspiration to others plagued by demons of the mind.

• *Continue up the long right side to the third section.*

## ❸ Hans Memling, *Martyrdom of St. Sebastian (Le Martyre de Saint Sébastien)*, c. 1475

Memling's Sebastian is as placid as Bosch's Anthony is turbulent. Sebastian—an early Christian killed by pagans—looks peaceful as he's punctured with arrows by a serene firing squad in a serene landscape. (In fact, Sebastian miraculously survived, so they clubbed him to death.)

Hans Memling (c. 1430-1494) was a student of Rogier van der Weyden and his "Flemish Primitive" style (for more, see the sidebar on page 77). Memling purposely disregarded the 3-D realism so admired in Italy at the time. For example, Sebastian's arm is tied to a branch that's not arching overhead, as it should be, but instead is behind him. And an archer aims slightly behind, not at, Sebastian. The other archer strings his bow in a stilted pose.

Nevertheless, Memling is clearly a master of detail. He freezes this dramatic scene so we can admire the colorful costumes, expressive faces, hazy landscape, and the cityscape in the background. Altogether it creates a meditative mood appropriate to where the painting originally stood—in a church in Bruges.

• *Next, head for the far-right corner of the gallery and find Room 68, where paintings by Pieter Bruegel the Elder are displayed.*

### ❹ Pieter Bruegel the Elder, *The Census at Bethlehem (Le Dénombrement de Bethléem)*, 1566

Bruegel sets a Bible scene—the birth of Jesus—in a typical snow-covered village near Brussels. Perched at treetop level, you have

a bird's-eye view over the action. Kids throw snowballs and sled across the frozen canals. A crowd gathers at the inn (lower left), where a woman holds a pan to catch blood while a man slaughters a pig. Most everyone has their back to us or head covered, so the figures speak through poses and motions.

Into the scene rides a woman on a donkey led by a man—it's Mary and husband Joseph. They're hoping to find a room at the inn (or at least a manger), because they didn't reserve ahead and now Mary's going into labor.

The year is 1566—the same year that Protestant extremists throughout the Low Countries were vandalizing Catholic churches and tearing down "idolatrous" depictions of the Virgin Mary. In a similar vein, Bruegel brings Mary down to earth—she's in the humble here and now. The busy villagers put their heads down and work, oblivious to the future Mother of God and the wondrous birth about to take place.

This room may also contain other works by Bruegel I (c. 1527-1569). He's famous for his crowds of everyday peasants going about their daily lives. He also dabbled in flights of bizarre fancy and obscure symbolism in the style of Bosch. You may also see works by his less famous sons—Pieter Brueghel the Younger (who copied his dad's style and even some exact paintings) and Jan the Elder (who did glossy still life paintings of flowers).

• *Continue your counterclockwise circuit around the gallery of the Old Masters collection. As you round the corner and head up the other long side, pause midway along, in the fourth alcove, with a few works by* ❺ *Rembrandt and Frans Hals. From here, enter the big adjoining Room 54, and then left into Room 53, full of large paintings by Rubens, including the massive...*

## ❻ Peter Paul Rubens, *The Ascent to Calvary* *(La Montée au Calvaire), c. 1636*

Life-size figures scale this 18-foot-tall canvas on the way to Christ's Crucifixion. The scene ripples with motion, from the windblown clothes to steroid-enhanced muscles to billowing flags and a troubled sky. Christ stumbles—he might get trampled by the surging crowd. Veronica kneels to gently wipe his bloody head.

This 200-square-foot canvas was manufactured at Rubens' studio in Antwerp. Hiring top-notch assistants, Rubens (1577-1640) could crank out large altarpieces for the area's Catholic churches. First, Rubens himself did small-scale sketches and studies in oil (like the studies you may see in Room 60). His assistants would reproduce them on the large canvas, and Rubens would then add the final touches.

This work is from late in Rubens' long and very successful career. He got a second wind in his fifties, when he married 16-year-old Hélène Fourment. She was the model for Veronica, who consoles the faltering Christ in this painting.

• *Backtrack to Room 54, turn left, and enter Room 55, where you'll find...*

## ❼ Jacques-Louis David, *The Death of Marat* *(Marat Assassiné), 1793*

In a scene ripped from the day's headlines, Jean-Paul Marat—a well-known crusading French journalist—has been stabbed to death in his bathtub by Charlotte Corday, a conservative fanatic.

Marat's life drains out of him, turning the bathwater red. With his last strength, he pens a final, patriotic *"Vive la Révolution"* message to his fellow patriots. Corday, a young noblewoman angered by Marat's campaign to behead the French king, was arrested and guillotined three days later.

Jacques-Louis David (1748-1825), one of Marat's fellow revolutionaries, set to work painting a tribute to his fallen comrade right after the 1793 assassination. (He signed the painting: *"À Marat"*—"To Marat.")

David makes it a secular pietà, with the brave writer portrayed as a martyred Christ in a classic dangling-arm pose. Still, the deathly pallor and harsh lighting pull no punches, creating in-your-face realism.

David, the official art director of the French Revolution, supervised propaganda and the costumes worn for patriotic parades. A year after finishing this painting, in 1794, his extreme brand of revolution (which included guillotining thousands of supposed enemies) was squelched by moderates, and David was jailed. He emerged later as Napoleon's court painter. When Napoleon was exiled in 1815, so was David, spending his last years in Brussels.

• *To get to the Fin-de-Siècle Museum, return to the ground floor and the large main entrance hall of the Old Masters Museum, where a passageway leads to the Fin-de-Siècle and Magritte Museums. Immediately after entering the passageway, you'll pass by the tiny Modern Museum (included in the combo-ticket). Go down the escalators and through the passageway (noting the entrance to the Magritte Museum), then continue down into the Fin-de-Siècle wing.*

## Fin-de-Siècle Museum

Brussels likes to think of itself as the capital of Art Nouveau and the crossroads of Europe, and this space presents a convincing case. Around the year 1900—the "turn of the century," or *fin-de-siècle*— many cultural trends converged in Brussels to create great art. The collection features a handful of high-powered paintings by notable Impressionists, Post-Impressionists, Realists, and Symbolists. It also houses an assemblage of Art Nouveau glassware, jewelry, and furniture.

• *You enter on level -3. On your visit, you'll go down, down, down through several levels. (Pray the elevator is working for the trip back up.) Keep the big picture. I've pointed out a few specific paintings, but don't*

ROYAL MUSEUMS

*worry so much about finding them all. Enlist the help of nearby guards if you must find a particular piece.*

## Welcome to the Fin-de-Siècle (Level -5)

Paintings of distinguished men in suits and ladies in gowns introduce you to the elegance of the era. Nearby, black-and-white photographs of Brussels show that it was also a time of great technological progress—the train, camera, and telegraph. As you browse the rest of the museum, keep in mind that the art was paid for and consumed by these wealthy industrialists and their trophy wives.

• *Continue down to the next level, which often displays the museum's best-known masterpieces.*

## Impressionism and Post-Impressionism (Level -6)

In the late 1800s, there was a revolution in painting—Impressionism. The displays start with traditional Academic paintings of the usual subjects—serene landscapes, Greek gods, and stuffy aristocrats. But as the next rooms show, painters burst out of the studio to paint the "real" world. They captured the harsh reality of peasant life and factory workers. They hung out in cafés, sketchbook in hand, capturing the bustle of modern life, or set up their can-

vases in the open air to paint a landscape. Here you'll find some classic examples.

**Georges Seurat** (1859-1891) painted a Sunday-in-the-park view from his favorite Parisian island in *The Seine at Grande-Jatte (La Seine à la Grande-Jatte).* Taking Impressionism to its extreme, he builds the scene out of small points of primary colors that blend at a distance to form objects. The bright colors capture the dazzling, sunlit atmosphere of this hazy day.

**Paul Gauguin** (1848–1903), though schooled in Impressionism, soon developed his own unique style. In *Breton Calvary (Calvaire Breton;* a.k.a. *The Green Christ/Le Christ Vert),* he returned to the bold, black, coloring-book outlines of more Primitive (pre-3-D) art. The Christian statue and countryside look less like Brittany and more like primitive Tahiti, where Gauguin would soon settle.

ROYAL MUSEUMS

Finally, find paintings by Belgium's own **James Ensor** (1860-1949). At 22, Ensor, an acclaimed child prodigy, proudly presented his lively Impressionist-style works to the Brussels Salon for exhibition. They were flatly rejected.

The artist withdrew from public view and, in seclusion, painted *Shocked Masks (Les Masques Scandalisés),* a dark and murky scene set in a small room of an ordinary couple wearing grotesque masks. Once again, everyone disliked this disturbing canvas and heaped more criticism on him. For the next six decades, Ensor painted the world as he saw it—full of bizarre, carnival-masked, stupid-looking crowds of cruel strangers who mock the viewer.

• *Descend to the next floor, enjoying exhibits on...*

## Opera (Level -7)

Opera played a central role in turn-of-the-century life. Painters collaborated with writers, composers, and directors to create lavish sets, costumes, and art design.

Among the paintings, it's hard not to notice *The Caress of the Sphinx (Des Caresses),* where a young man cozies up to a cheetah-girl. The painter, **Fernand Khnopff** (1858-1921), was James Ensor's college buddy. Khnopff championed the Symbolist movement, presenting arresting images (often of women as femme fatales) intended to provoke primeval emotions.

• *Now head for the bottom floor.*

## Art Nouveau (Level -8)

The collection's final paintings show how turn-of-the-century Post-Impressionism led the way to more abstract styles of Modernism.

The Gillion Crowet Collection is a stunning assemblage of Art Nouveau paintings, jewelry, woodwork furniture, and flowery vases (by the likes of Emile Gallé). You'll also see pieces by Brussels' own Victor Horta, whose influential architecture (such as the Belgian Comic Strip Center—see listing in the Sights in Brussels chapter) steered the curvaceous Art Nouveau style toward simpler Art Deco and Modernism.

• *Which is the perfect segue to Magritte. Return to the Fin-de-Siècle entrance on level -3, then go up the stairs to find the entrance to the...*

# Magritte Museum

Bowler hats, clouds, birds...these are the iconic images that have become associated with Belgium's great Surrealist, René Magritte.

Magritte's puzzling works are perhaps best described in his own words: "My paintings are visible images which conceal nothing. They evoke mystery, and indeed, when one sees one of my pictures, one asks oneself this simple question: 'What does that mean?' It does not mean anything, because mystery means nothing either, it is unknowable." If that brainteaser titillates you, you'll love this museum.

The exhibits take you on a chronological route through Magritte's life and art. Each of the three floors is devoted to a period of his life. Timelines (in English) put the art in its historical context. Fascinating quotes from Magritte are posted around the museum (but only in French and Dutch, so pick up the English translation as you enter). The audioguide is helpful.

The following tour follows the layout of the museum, but it's not really intended as a room-by-room analysis. It's best to read this tour ahead of time for background, then enter the darkened rooms and let Magritte transport you to his world.

• *From the entrance, you'll take an elevator up to level +3.*

## The Struggling Artist, 1898-1929 (Level +3)

Born to a middle-class Belgian family, Magritte moved to Brussels at age 17. He studied at the Academy, where he learned to draw meticulously and got a broad liberal arts education. In the 1920s, he eked out a living designing advertisements, posters, and sheet music. Meanwhile, he wrote for the avant-garde *7 Arts* **magazine** (you'll see samples posted). He explored **various styles**—Post-Impressionism, Futurism, Cubism—in search of his own voice.

In 1922, he married his childhood sweetheart, **Georgette,** who became his lifelong companion, artist's model, and muse. It's said that all the women he would paint were versions of Georgette. (It's touching to think that he found a soul mate who could truly understand and encourage his weirdness.)

Influenced by the Dada and Surrealist movements coming out of Paris (Salvador Dalí, Marcel Duchamp, Giorgio de Chirico), Magritte became intrigued with the idea of painting dreamscapes that capture an air of mystery.

For Magritte, 1927 was a watershed year, when he painted his first truly Surrealist work—*The Man from the Sea.* It featured a man on a beach with a wood-block head, pulling a lever.

Together, René and Georgette mingled in sophisticated, bohemian circles. He and his friends took **photographs,** striking wacky tableaux and distorted poses.

## The Art of René Magritte

René Magritte (1898-1967) is Belgium's most famous 20th-century artist. He trained and worked in Brussels, but also

lived for a time in Paris, where he connected with other Surrealist painters. Though he's well-known now, it took decades before his peculiar brand of Surrealism caught on. He painted real objects with photographic clarity, and then jumbled them together provocatively. Or he confounded the viewer's expectations by presenting ordinary items as something altogether different (as in his iconic painting of a smoker's pipe, which he labeled "This is not a pipe").

Magritte had his own private reserve of symbolic images. You'll see clouds, blue sky, open windows, the female torso, men in bowler hats, rocks, tobacco pipes, spheres with slits (sleigh bells), birds, castles, and turtles. All of these are placed side by side as if the arrangement means something. He heightens the mystery by making objects unnaturally large or small. People morph into animals or inanimate objects. The juxtaposition short-circuits your brain only when you try to make sense of it. Magritte's works are at once playful and disorienting...and, at times, disturbing.

Magritte began writing words on paintings. This culminated in his most famous work, of a **tobacco pipe** (in the Los Angeles County Museum of Art, though there's a similar version here). On the picture, Magritte wrote (in French) "This is not a pipe." Of course it's not a pipe, Magritte always insisted—it's a *painting* of a pipe. It forces the viewer to ponder the relationship between the object and its name—between the "signified" and the "signifier," to quote the deconstructionist philosophy that Magritte's paradoxical paintings inspired. Some credit this work for planting the seeds of Postmodernism. By the way, two decades later, Magritte did another version with the message: "This is still not a pipe."

• *Head downstairs to the next phase of Magritte's life.*

### Recognition—and the War, 1930-1950 (Level +2)

After a time in Paris, Magritte returned to Brussels, where he struggled through the Depression years by doing ad work and portraits.

He now had his **signature style:** combining two arresting images to disrupt rational thought and produce an emotion of mystery. The paintings have his now-familiar motifs such as clouds and bowler hats. The background and foreground seem to shift.

The paintings' **weird titles**—*Forbidden Literature, God Is No Saint*—added another layer of disruption. These were intentional nonsequiturs, which he and his Surrealist friends made up during regular Sunday-night get-togethers.

Then came World War II, and Brussels was under Nazi occupation. Magritte began using **birds** as a metaphor for the longing to be free.

He also dabbled in a **variety of styles:** Impressionistic colors and rough brushwork, tongue-in-cheek "portraits" of animals, a Technicolor nude of Georgette. He went through a childlike period of comic-book-inspired paintings (like the green man with a long nose), which are quite different from his normal photorealistic style.

• *Continuing to the final floor, note that it has two different sections, with two different entrances from the landing.*

## Mature Years, 1951-1967 (Level +1)

These two rooms are like a victory lap for all of the symbols and styles we've seen. Nearing the end of his prolific life, Magritte had a quiver full of artistic arrows to shoot at the canvas. He mixed his **trademark symbols**—doves, clouds, balls, open windows, forlorn landscapes—in recombinant ways.

The collection culminates at his *Empire of Lights.* This painting of a typical bourgeois home at twilight suggests that even well-scrubbed suburbia can possess an ominous air of mystery. Magritte loved night-sky tones. He often created several versions of the same work, which explains why there are several *Empire of Lights* canvases in the world.

By the end of his life, Magritte was well known, especially in America. His use of everyday objects and poster-art style inspired Pop Art. His mix of words and images inspired Postmodernist philosophers. His bizarre imagery inspired the psychedelia of the '60s. And the mystery his canvases evoke is timeless.

• *Exit to the bookshop and an appropriately perplexing 50-minute film about Magritte (plays constantly, English subtitles). From here you can find your way either back to the other museums or to the exit...and real.*

# BRUSSELS SLEEPING, EATING & MORE

As the capital of Belgium—and of the European Union—Brussels is a great place to spend some time. This chapter provides suggestions for the best places to sleep and eat; tips for shopping and after-hours fun; and a rundown of connections to points throughout Belgium, the Netherlands, and beyond, as well as tips for getting to and from the city's two airports.

## Sleeping in Brussels

Hotel prices are high in central Brussels. This popular business destination tends to be busiest and most expensive on weekdays, especially in spring and fall. Brussels' fancy business-class hotels can be desperately empty most of July and August and on most Friday and Saturday nights. During these slow times, rates drop. You may be able to rent a double room at a three-star hotel in the center with enough comforts to keep a diplomat happy, including a fancy breakfast, for about €110.

Conversely, Bruges—a pleasure destination—has higher demand on weekends. If your trip is flexible, consider arranging your overnights in these two towns with these patterns in mind.

### NEAR THE GRAND PLACE
**$$$$ Hotel Le Dixseptième,** with sleek, 21st-century rooms behind its luxurious lounges and entryway, is ideally located a block

below Central station. Prim, proper, and peaceful, with chandeliers and squeaky hardwood floors, the hotel's 37 rooms are each themed after a different painter (air-con, elevator, Rue de la Madeleine 25, +32 2 517 1717, www.ledixseptieme.be, info@ledixseptieme.be).

**$$$ The Dominican Hotel,** with 150 rooms, provides a high-end sanctuary on a quiet street just minutes from the touristic chaos. The original monastery (bombed flat in World War I, rebuilt in 2007) inspired the hotel's high ceilings, arcaded courtyard, and sedate color palette. When you step into the hotel's elevator, Gregorian chants remind you this is your refuge (RS%, extravagant breakfast extra, air-con, laundry service available, gym, sauna, dressy cocktail lounge and public spaces, Rue Leopold 9, +32 2203 0808, www.thedominican.be, info@thedominican.carlton.be, Bert).

**$$$ Art de Séjour** is a classy splurge B&B a few blocks from the Grand Place (farther than the others listed here...but worth it). Well run by Mario, it fills a gorgeously restored building with five thoughtfully appointed rooms that are an engaging mix of new (air filters and iMacs in every room) and old (original woodwork). Mario's training as an engineer shows in all the special touches (air-con, elevator and a few stairs, Rue des Bogards 12, +32 2 513 9755, www.artdesejour.com, concierge@artdesejour.com).

**$$$ NH Brussels Carrefour de l'Europe** offers 65 rooms—some with lovely views. What the hotel lacks in personality it makes up for in predictable comfort and location (family room, air-con, elevator, pay parking, Rue du Marché aux Herbes, +32 2 504 94 00, www.nh-hotels.com, nhcarrefourdeleurope@nh-hotels.com).

**$$ Hotel Ibis off Grand Place,** well situated halfway between Central station and the Grand Place, is the best of several Ibis locations around Brussels. It's a big, modern hotel offering 184 simple, industrial-strength-yet-comfy rooms (breakfast extra, air-con, elevator, Marché aux Herbes 100, +32 2 514 4040, www.ibishotel.com, h1046@accor.com).

**$$ Hotel La Légende** rents 26 small, straightforward rooms a block from the *Manneken-Pis* statue. Although it's on a busy road, its classic lobby sits back on a pleasant courtyard. The furnishings are basic, but the location and price are right, and the rooms are modern and comfortable (breakfast extra, request a quieter courtyard room, elevator, Rue du Lombard 35, +32 2 512 8290, www.hotellalegende.com, info@hotellalegende.com).

**$ Hotel the Moon** is an efficient budget option, with 17 barebones rooms and no public spaces. It's noisy (thin walls and on a square), but it's just steps from the Grand Place—and it's the cheapest centrally located hotel this side of a youth hostel (no breakfast, ask for a quieter room in the back, stairs but no elevator, on the small "Agora" square at Rue de la Montagne 4, +32 2 508 1580, www.hotelthemoon.com, info@hotelthemoon.com).

## IN STE. CATHERINE, NEAR THE OLD FISH MARKET

The following listings are a 10-minute walk from the intensity of the old center, near the Sainte-Catherine/Sint-Katelijne Métro stop (two stops from Central station). This charming neighborhood, "the village in Brussels," faces the canalside fish market and has many of the town's best restaurants.

**$$$ Citadines Sainte-Catherine Apart'hotel,** part of a Europe-wide chain, is a huge apartment-style hotel with modern, functional rooms and an outdoor courtyard. Choose from efficiency studios with double beds or two-room apartments with a bedroom and a foldout couch in the living room. All 169 units come with a kitchen, dishware, and dishwasher. This is a good option for families staying several nights (breakfast extra, self-serve laundry, pay parking, Quai au Bois à Brûler 51, +32 2 221 1411, www.citadines.com, stecatherine@ citadines.com).

**$$$ Hotel Ibis Brussels City Centre** is a big, impersonal, perfectly comfortable place with 236 rooms in a great location (breakfast extra, air-con, elevator, laundry service, Rue Joseph Plateau 2 at Place Ste. Catherine, +32 2 550 1110, www.ibishotel.com, h1454@accor.com).

**$$ B&B Druum,** in a 19th-century mansion, is artsy and cool—but with a laid-back, unpretentious vibe. Its six rooms, each designed by a different artist, have lofty ceilings and creaky wide-plank floors. Some have doorless bathrooms, some have wild and creative light fixtures, while others feel more sedate—but all come with a contemporary, minimalist flair (pay parking, Rue du Houblon 63, +32 472 054 240, www.druum.be, sleep@druum.be).

## HOSTELS

Four classy and modern hostels in drab buildings are within a 10-minute walk of Central station. Each accepts people of all ages and serves cheap and hot meals.

**¢ SafeStay Hostel,** on a people-filled street near the Grand Place, is a popular option (private rooms available, elevator, Rue Grétry 53, +32 2 219 4343, www.safestay.com, safestaybrussels@ safestay.com).

**¢ Bruegel Hostel,** an "official" hostel and a fortress of cleanli-

ANSPACH
FOUNTAIN

To Nord/Noord
Station

RUE DU GRAND HOSPICE

RUE MARCQ

RUE DU CIRQUE

RUE DE LA FIANCEE

BLVD. ADOLPHE MAX

NOTRE-
DAME
DU FINISTERE

Pond

QUAI AUX BRIQUES

RUE DE FLANDRE

RUE DE ROULEAU

Place de
Beguinage

ST.
JEAN

RUE VANDER ELST

RUE DU FLEURS

RUE SAINT-MICHEL

Sainte-
Catherine

8

15

SAINTE-
CATHERINE

R. DES HIRONDELLES

Place de
Brouckère

RUE NEUVE

To
10

Place du
Nouveau
Marché aux Grains

SAINTE-
CATHERINE

Place
Sainte-Catherine

9

R. DES AUGUSTINS

RUE DE L'EVEQUE

RUE DU FOSSÉ AUX LOUPS

RUE D'ARGENT

RUE ANTOINE DANSAERT

RUE SAINTE-
CATHERINE

RUE VIERGE NOIRE

RUE DES HALLES

BLVD. ANSPACH

RUE GRETRY

De Brouckère

71

Place
de la
Monnaie

THEATRE
ROYAL

2

RUE LEOPOLD

RUE DES CHARTREUX

RUE DU MARCHE AUX POULETS

RUE DES FRIPIERS

RUE DE L'ECUYER

RUE SAINT-CHRISTOPHE

RUE SAINT-

Place
St-Géry

R. J. V. PRAET

R. DE LA BOURSE

Bourse

BOURSE

RUE HENRI MAUS

11

ST.
NICOLAS

RUE DE LA FOURCHE

RUE DES DOMINICAINS

RUE DES BOUCHERS

RUE DE LA

R. DES RICHES
CLAIRES

RUE DES PIERRES

PETITE R.D. BOUCHERS

R. AU BEURRE

COLL

CITY
MUSEUM

GALERIES
ST. HUBERT

7

RUE DES
SIX JETONS

GRANDE ÉCLIPSE

BLVD. ANSPACH

RUE DU MIDI

TOWN
HALL

Grand
Place

BREWERY
MUSEUM

"Agora"
Square

Place
d'Espagne

5

4

HORTA
GALLERY

Place
Fontainas

RUE DU MARCHE AUX CHARBON

15

CHOCO-
STORY

6

FASHION &
LACE MUSEUM

RUE DE LA VIOLETTE

RUE DES EPERONNIERS

1

RUE DE LA MADELEINE

R. DE L'INFANTE

3

R. DES MOINEAUX

R. VAN HELMONT

RUE DU MIDI

RUE DES BOGARDS

RUE DE CHAMPAGNE

RUE TERRE NEUVE

MANNEKEN-
PIS STATUE

RUE DU LOMBARD

RUE DUQUESNOY

RUE SAINT-JEAN

Square
de la
Putterie

GARDEROBE
MANNEKEN-PIS

TOWN

Place
du Vieille Halle
aux Blés

RUE DE L'HOPITAL

Place de
l'Albertine

CANTERSTEEN

Place
Rouppe

RUE D'ACCOLAY

RUE DES
ALEXIENS

Place de
Dinant

BD. DE L'EMPEREUR

TOUR
D'ANGLE

RUE LEBEAU

RUE DU
RUYSBROECK

Place du
Grand
Sablon

RUE DE LA ROUE

RUE DU POINCON

BRUSSELS
CHAPELLE
STATION

Place de
la Chapelle

R. DE ROLLEBEEK

To
Midi/Zuid
Station

R. DES URSULINES

NOTRE-DAME
DE LA CHAPELLE

R. JOSEPH STEVENS

12

LOWER

# Brussels Hotels

1. Hotel Le Dixseptiéme
2. The Dominican Hotel
3. Art de Séjour B&B
4. NH Brussels Carrefour de l'Europe
5. Hotel Ibis off Grand Place
6. Hotel La Légende
7. Hotel the Moon
8. Citadines Sainte-Catherine Apart'hotel
9. Hotel Ibis Brussels City Centre
10. To B&B Druum
11. SafeStay Hostel
12. Bruegel Hostel
13. Sleep Well Hostel
14. Jacques Brel Hostel
15. Launderette (2)

BRUSSELS SLEEPING, EATING & MORE

ness, is handy and comfortable (private rooms available, midway between Midi and Central stations, behind Chapelle church at Rue de St. Esprit 2, +32 2 511 0436, www.youthhostels.be, brussel@vjh.be).

¢ **Sleep Well Hostel,** surrounded by high-rise parking structures, is also comfortable (private rooms available, no curfew, Rue de Damier 23, +32 2 218 5050, www.sleepwell.be, info@sleepwell.be).

¢ **Jacques Brel Hostel** is a little farther out, but it's still a reasonable walk from everything (private rooms available, no curfew, Rue de la Sablonnière 30, +32 2 218 0187, www.hihostels.com, brussels.brel@hostelbrussels.be).

# Eating in Brussels

Brussels is known for both its high-quality, French-style cuisine and its multicultural variety. Seafood—fish, eel, shrimp, and oysters—is especially well prepared here.

When it comes to choosing a restaurant, many tourists congregate on the Grand Place or at Rue des Bouchers, the city's restaurant row. While the Grand Place is undeniably magnificent for enjoying dessert or a drink, go elsewhere to eat well, such as the international and trendy zone past the Bourse near Place St-Géry or the area around Place Ste. Catherine.

## OLD CENTER
### Dining on the Grand Place
My vote for northern Europe's grandest medieval square is lined with hardworking eateries that serve predictable dishes to tourist crowds. Of course, you won't get the best quality or prices—but, after all, it's the Grand Place.

**$$$$ L'Estaminet du Kelderke**—with its one steamy vault under the square and small patio of tables on the square—is packed with both natives and tourists and is a real Brussels fixture. It serves local specialties, including mussels, fish soup, beef stew, and horse steak (daily 12:00-24:00, no reservations taken, Grand Place 15, +32 2 513 7344, Kam).

### Lunches near the Grand Place
The super-central square dubbed the "Agora" (officially Marché aux Herbes, just between the Grand Place and Central station) is lined with low-end eateries—Quick, Subway, Panos sandwich shop, Exki health-food store—and is especially fun on sunny days. On

## Mussels in Brussels

Big, fresh mussels (*moules*) are available all over town. Mostly harvested from aqua farms along the North Sea, they are available for most of the year (except from about May through mid-July, when smaller ones are brought in from Denmark). The classic Belgian preparation is *à la marinière,* cooked in white wine, onions, celery, parsley, and butter. Or, instead of wine, cooks use light Belgian beer for the stock. For a high-calorie version, try *moules à la crème,* where the stock is thickened with heavy cream.

You order by the kilo (just more than 2 pounds), which is a pretty big bucket. While restaurants don't promote these as splittable, they certainly are. Your mussels come with Belgian fries (what we think of as "french fries"—dip them in mayo). To accompany your mussels, try a French white wine such as Muscadet or Chablis, or a Belgian blonde ale such as Duvel or La Chouffe. When eating mussels, you can feel a little more local by nonchalantly using an empty mussel shell as a pincher to pull the meat out of other shells. It actually works quite nicely.

the other side of the Grand Place is Rue du Marché aux Fromages, jammed with mostly Greek and gyros places, with diners sitting elbow-to-elbow at cramped tables out front. For something fresher and more interesting, stroll a few blocks to one of the following alternatives:

**$$ Yummy Bowl** is a fun-loving little vegetarian/vegan place with inventive, delicious salads and flavorful soups. It feels like a group of college friends got together one day and decided to open a healthy salad joint. Grab a rickety chair and sit inside or out (daily 10:30-17:00, between the Grand Place and Central station at Rue des Eperonniers 49, +32 2 265 1802).

**$$ Bia Mara** ("Sea Food" in Irish Gaelic) offers five different styles of fish-and-chips made with sustainable ingredients. The industrial-mod interior is small, so lines can be long at peak times (long hours daily, around the corner from the Grand Place at Rue du Marché aux Poulets 41, +32 2 502 0061).

**Groceries:** Big and practical **Carrefour Express** supermarkets are near the Bourse at Rue du Marché aux Poulets 52, along the street between the Grand Place and the Bourse at Rue au Beurre 27, and near Central station on Rue de l'Infante Isabelle (all daily 7:00-23:00). **AD Delhaize** is another major supermarket, at the

**Brussels Restaurants**

## Eateries

1. L'Estaminet du Kelderke
2. Yummy Bowl
3. Bia Mara
4. La Roue d'or Brasserie
5. Arcadi Café
6. La Maison des Crêpes
7. Yaki
8. La Fleur en Papier Doré
9. Waffle Factory
10. Maison Dandoy
11. Restaurant de l'Ogenblik
12. Restaurant Chez Leon
13. Restaurant Vincent
14. A la Mort Subite
15. Wolf Sharing Food Market
16. Selecto Bistronomique & Restaurant La Marée
17. Bij den Boer
18. La Villette Restaurant
19. Mer du Nord/Nordzee
20. Nona
21. Gaston
22. La Fin de Siècle & Le Greenwich
23. Publico
24. Groceries (4)

## Beer

25. Le Cirio
26. A la Bécasse
27. Poechenellekelder Estaminet
28. Moeder Lambic
29. A l'Imaige Nostre-Dame & Au Bon Vieux Temps
30. Delirium Tap House
31. De Biertempel Shop

BRUSSELS SLEEPING, EATING & MORE

intersection of Rue du Marché aux Poulets and Boulevard Anspach (Boulevard Anspach 63). And small late-night minimarkets ("night shop") dot the town.

## More Eateries near the Grand Place

These restaurants are good for a sit-down meal day or night.

**$$$$ La Roue d'Or Brasserie** (The Golden Wheel), a block off the Grand Place, is a classic bistro with a between-the-wars ambiance and Magritte murals. Traditions are honored—on the menu and in the decor (Rue des Chapeliers 26, +32 2 514 2554).

**$$ Arcadi Café** is a delightful little eatery serving daily plates, salads, and a selection of quiche-like tortes. The interior comes with a fun, circa-1900 ambience; grab a table there, on the street, or at the end of Galeries St. Hubert (Tue-Sun 9:00-23:30, closed Mon, 1 Rue d'Arenberg, +32 2 511 3343).

**$ La Maison des Crêpes,** a half-block south of the Bourse, looks underwhelming but serves delicious crêpes (both savory and sweet varieties) and salads, as well as good beers and fresh mint tea. There's been a crêpe shop at this address since 1898. Even though it's just a few steps away from the tourist bustle, it feels laid-back and local (cash only, sidewalk seating, daily 11:30-23:00, Rue du Midi 13, +32 475 957 368, George).

**$$ Yaki** is a tempting Vietnamese and Thai noodle bar in a stately old flatiron building tucked between the Grand Place and the Rue du Marché au Charbon café/nightlife zone. Choose between the tight interior and the outdoor tables (daily 12:00-23:00, Rue du Midi 52, +32 2 503 3409).

**$$ La Fleur en Papier Doré** is a homey café covered in old-fashioned paintings and memorabilia that looks a bit like your eccentric great-aunt's house. René Magritte was a regular and held his wedding reception here (see the big picture of him in the back). A selection of *stoemp* specialties—mashed potatoes with vegetables—makes this a good spot for a casual meal (Tue-Sat 11:00-24:00, Sun until 19:00, closed Mon, Rue des Alexiens 55, +32 2 511 1659).

## Waffles near the Grand Place

As you walk from the Grand Place to the *Manneken-Pis* (along Rue Charles Buls) you'll pass a crass gauntlet of tourist shops—including a bevy of places selling Belgian waffles. Most are suspiciously cheap (€2)—but the big stack of stale waffles in the window clues you in that these are far from top-quality.

For a better experience, the most glitzy and touristy is **Waffle Factory** (American fast-food ambience, big variety, quieter upstairs seating); closer to Grand Place, **Maison Dandoy** is more upscale and pricey. Both sell Liège-style and Brussels-style waffles (for details on both types, see page 345). Both places have crowds and fast turnover, so you're sure to get a fresh waffle.

## Near but Not on Rue des Bouchers (Restaurant Row)

Brussels' restaurant streets, two blocks north of the Grand Place, are touristy and notorious for touts who aggressively suck you in and predatory servers who greedily rip you off. It's hard to justify dining here when far better options sit just a block or two away (see later listings). If you are seduced into a meal here, order carefully, understand the prices thoroughly, and watch your wallet.

**$$$$ Restaurant de l'Ogenblik,** a remarkably peaceful eddy just off the raging restaurant row, fills an early 20th-century space in the corner of an arcade. The waiters serve well-presented, near-gourmet French cuisine. This mussels-free zone has a great, splittable rack of lamb with 10 vegetables. Their sea bass with risotto and truffle oil is a hit with return eaters. Reservations are smart (Tue-Sat 12:00-14:30 & 18:30-24:00, closed Sun-Mon, Galerie des Princes 1, +32 2 511 6151, www.ogenblik. be, Yves).

**$$ Restaurant Chez Leon** is a legendary, if touristy, mussels factory, slamming out piles of cheap buckets since 1893. It's a sprawling place with a sprawling menu featuring lots of seafood. The €17 "Formula Leon" is a light meal consisting of a small bucket of mussels, fries, and a beer (daily 12:00-23:00, kids under 12 eat free, Rue des Bouchers 18, +32 2 511 1415, www.chezleon.be).

**$$$$ Restaurant Vincent** has you enter through the kitchen to enjoy their dressy 1905-era ambience. This place is better for meat dishes than for seafood (Mon-Sat 12:00-14:30 & 18:30-23:30, closed Sun, across from Restaurant de l'Ogenblik—listed earlier—at Rue des Dominicains 8, +32 2 511 2607, www.restaurantvincent. be, Julien).

**$$ A la Mort Subite,** also recommended for its great beer (see sidebar) is perfect for a very simple meal amid wonderful old-time ambiance. A typical lunch or light dinner here is an omelet with a salad, *croque monsieur/madame,* or a *tartine* spread with *fromage blanc* (cream cheese) or pressed meat (daily 10:00-23:00, Rue Montagne aux Herbes Potagères 7, +32 2 513 1318).

**$$ Wolf Sharing Food Market** fills a vast former bank building with a food circus of 18 eateries (mostly from serious Brussels restaurants) and a youthful energy. Choose from Vietnamese, dim

## Sampling Belgian Beer in Brussels

Brussels is full of atmospheric cafés to savor the local brew. The places lining the Grand Place are touristy, but the setting—plush, old medieval guildhalls fronting all that cobbled wonder—is hard to beat.

All varieties of Belgian beer are available, but Brussels' most distinctive beers are *lambic*-based. Look for *lambic doux, lambic blanche, gueuze* (pronounced "kurrs"), and *faro,* as well as fruit-flavored *lambics,* such as *kriek* (cherry) and *framboise* (raspberry—*frambozen* in Dutch). These beers look and taste more like a dry, somewhat bitter cider. The brewer doesn't add yeast—the beer ferments naturally from wild yeast floating in the marshy air around Brussels. For more on Belgian beer, see the "Eating" section of the Practicalities chapter.

The following places are generally open daily from about 11:00 until late but aren't really good for a full meal—though you can usually get lighter fare, such as a cold-meat plate, a *tartine* (open-face sandwich), or a salad.

**A la Mort Subite,** a few steps above the top end of the Galeries St. Hubert, is a classic old bar that has retained its 1928 decor...

and its loyal customers seem to go back just about as far. The decor is simple, with wood tables, grimy yellow wallpaper, and some-other-era garland trim—it's a great scene with great waiters and the best beer. This is a good place to try the *kriek* beer (Rue Montagne aux Herbes Potagères 7, +32 2 513 1318). I've listed it separately for a handy meal.

**Le Cirio,** across from the Bourse, feels a bit more upscale, with a faded yet still luxurious gilded-wood interior, booths with velvet padding, and dark tables that bear the skid marks of over a century's worth of beer glasses.

sum, *frites*, fish, salad, Ethiopian, vegetarian, waffles, and more. Order a meal from your venue of choice, get a drink from the central bar, and grab a seat anywhere (daily 12:00-22:00, Rue du Fossé aux Loups 50).

## STE. CATHERINE, NEAR THE OLD FISH MARKET

A 10-minute walk from the old center puts you in "the village within the city" area of Ste. Catherine (Métro: Sainte-Catherine/Sint-Katelijne). The historic fish market here has spawned a tradition of fine restaurants specializing mostly in seafood. The old

The service is jaded—perhaps understandably given its touristy location (Rue de la Bourse 18, +32 2 512 1395).

**A la Bécasse** keeps a lower profile than Le Cirio, with a simple wood-panel and wood-table decor that appeals to both poor students and lunching businesspeople. The *lambic* has been artfully blended with other beers and served in clay jars here since 1825. It's just around the corner from Le Cirio, toward the Grand Place, hidden away at the end of a tight lane (Tabora 11, +32 2 511 0006).

**Poechenellekelder Estaminet** is a great bar with lots of real character located right across the street from the *Manneken-Pis*. As the word *estaminet* (tavern) indicates, it's not brewery-owned, so they have a great selection of beers. Inside tables are immersed in *Pis* kitsch and puppets. Outside tables offer some fine people-watching (Rue du Chêne 5, +32 2 511 9262).

**Moeder Lambic** has a modern industrial feel, with owners who are maniacs about craft beer and sell only traditional brews from independent producers. With a knowledgeable staff, this is an excellent place to start exploring the acquired tastes of *lambic, gueuze,* and *kriek* (on a square off Boulevard Anspach at Place Fontainas 8, +32 2 503 6068).

Two tiny and extremely characteristic bars are tucked away down long entry corridors just off Rue du Marché aux Herbes. **A l'Imaige Nostre-Dame** (closed Sun, at #8) and **Au Bon Vieux Temps** (at #12) both treat fine beer with great reverence and seem to have extremely local clientele, whom you're bound to meet if you grab a stool. Au Bon Vieux Temps stocks the legendary Trappist brew Westvleteren 12, which is hard to find outside Belgium.

**Delirium Tap House** is a sloppy frat party nightly with no ambience, a noisy young crowd, beer-soaked wooden floors, rock 'n' roll, and a famous variety of great Belgian beers on tap (near Rue des Bouchers, not far from Chez Leon at Impasse de la Fidélité 4). It's an unforgettably raucous scene.

fish canal survives, and if you walk around it, you'll see plenty of enticing places to eat, including these very good, yet very different, options.

**$$$$ Selecto Bistronomique** is my choice for a dressy, gourmet splurge. It's a young, smart, and sophisticated scene with a focus on great food—modern, creative dishes mixing Mediterranean and Belgian tastes. The *menu* is inviting, with one course for €26, two courses for €38, and three courses for €44. You may need to reserve days in advance to get a table (Tue-Sat lunch 12:00-14:30, dinner seatings at 19:00 and 21:30, closed Sun-Mon, Rue de Flandre 95, +32 2 511 4095, https://leselecto.com).

**$$$ Restaurant La Marée** is a classic local spot a couple of blocks away from the trendy places on the square. With an older clientele, an open kitchen, and an inviting menu, this untouristy bistro specializes in mussels and seafood—their only boast is their insistence that it's fresh. Reservations are smart—request the ground floor (Tue-Sat 12:00-14:00 & 18:30-22:00, closed Sun-Mon, near Rue du Marché-aux-Porcs at Rue de Flandre 99, +32 2 511 0040, www.lamaree-sa.com, Mario).

**$$$$ Bij den Boer,** a fun, noisy eatery popular with locals and tourists, has inviting tables out on the esplanade and feels like a traditional and very successful brasserie. Their specialty: fish (Mon-Sat 12:00-14:30 & 18:00-22:30, closed Sun, Quai aux Briques 60, +32 2 512 6122, www.bijdenboer.com).

**$$$ La Villette Restaurant** is a romantic, subdued alternative, serving traditional Belgian cuisine: meaty stews, eels, *stoemp* (mashed potatoes and vegetables), and dishes with beer. The chef proudly makes the sauces from scratch, and can match your order to the right beer. The restaurant has a charming red-and-white-tablecloth interior and good outdoor seating facing a small square (Mon-Sat 12:00-14:00 & 18:30-22:30, closed Sun, Rue du Vieux Marché-aux-Grains 3, +32 2 512 7550, Adrian).

## Economic, Fast, and Tasty Lunches in Ste. Catherine

Place Ste. Catherine, which branches off from the side of Ste. Catherine Church, is lined with enjoyable cafés with outdoor seating.

**$$ Mer du Nord/Nordzee** is as delicious as it is inexpensive. This seafood bar—basically a grill attached to a fresh fish shop—cooks up whatever it catches and serves it on small tapas-like plates with glasses of wine to an appreciative local crowd. Just belly up to the counter and place your order, then eat standing at the counter or sit outside at a table on the square. Plates are just seafood with no sides. I enjoyed the grilled shrimp, *scampi à la plancha* (Tue-Sun 11:00-18:00, closed Mon, Rue Ste. Catherine 45, at corner with Place Ste. Catherine, +32 2 513 1192). The similar **ABC Poissonerie,** across the street, has a comparable but less crowded operation.

**$ Nona** makes traditional Neapolitan pizza using only ingredients from local farms. You might find Brussels sprouts or kale on your pizza—or opt for the seasonal special (daily 12:00-22:00, Rue Ste. Catherine 17, www.nonalife.com).

**$ Gaston** is *the* choice for waffles, artisan ice cream, and coffee away from the tourist crush around the Grand Place. Taking your sugar or caffeine injection here is civilized and delicious (daily 11:00-22:00, shorter hours in winter, Quai aux Briques 86, +32 2 223 4306).

## ON OR NEAR PLACE ST-GÉRY

For a trendier and youthful scene, head to Place St-Géry (a.k.a. Sint-Goriksplein). The epicenter is at the intersection of Pont de la Carpe and Plétinckx street. This area is more about drinking than about dining, but mixed in among the bars are several eateries: sushi, Italian, Thai, Vietnamese, Indian, and so on. Rue Jules van Praet is lined mostly with interchangeable Asian and Indian restaurants.

**On Rue des Chartreux:** Just across Rue Van Artevelde from the Place St-Géry action, this street has several enticing options. **$$ La Fin de Siècle** is a bohemian place serving basic, unpretentious Belgian/French fare. With an appropriately turn-of-the-century atmosphere, mismatched secondhand furniture, and long, shared tables, it has a youthful energy (food served daily 18:00-24:00, at #9, +32 2 512 5123). Next door, at #7, **$$$ Le Greenwich** has an even more exquisite Art Nouveau facade. Just up the street, **$$$ Publico** is hip but accessible, with a black-subway-tile interior and well-priced Belgian and Mediterranean fare. Reservations are smart on weekends (daily 12:00-23:00, at #32, +32 2 503 0430, www.publicobxl.be).

## MATONGÉ: AN AFRICAN NEIGHBORHOOD AND A TRENDY SQUARE

The neighborhood of Matongé—just past the royal sights of the Upper Town—is a fun-to-explore mix of vivid African immigrant culture and Belgian trend seekers. Ride the Métro to Porte de Namur/Naamsepoort and explore the neighborhood, then hang around for a meal. For locations, see the "Matongé Neighborhood" map on page 157.

**On and near Rue Saint-Boniface:** **$$$ Le Clan des Belges** serves Belgian classics in the center of Matongé, with a rustic, cozy interior and a lively, leafy outdoor dining zone with tables in the shadow of the church steeple. They are serious about their burgers and beer (daily roughly 12:00-14:30 & 18:00-23:00, Rue de la Paix 20, +32 2 511 1121, www.leclandesbelges.com).

**$$ Hope House African** is a charming family-run place serving dishes from Cameroon, Congo, and Senegal. It feels both authentic and dressy (11:00-23:00, closed Sun, Rue Longue Vie 13, +32 465 41 50 18).

**$ Au Soleil d'Afrique,** across the street from Hope House, is a more adventurous and cheaper option for African cuisine (Mon-Sat 12:30-late, Sun from 17:30, Rue Longue Vie 10, +32 486 302 640).

**Place Fernand Cocq:** A few blocks from the heart of Matongé, this grassy square feels more traditionally Belgian—like a neighborhood's shared front yard. Here are my three favorites on the square:

**$$$ Restaurant Volle Gas,** which means "full throttle," is an energetic brasserie with old-fashioned woody ambience and a fun and accessible menu, serving crank-'em-out Belgian standards (daily, lunch from 12:00, dinner from 18:00, Place Fernand Cocq 21, +32 2 502 8917).

**$$ Il Nobile Ristorante Pizzeria** is a good Italian place popular for its pizza and pasta (Place Fernand Cocq 24, +32 2 540 8077).

**$$ Le Cocq Bar** is the neighborhood hangout, where trendy couples sip quality beer and people-watch on the sidewalk while families enjoy simple bar food—burgers and fries—inside (daily 12:00-23:00, Place Fernand Cocq 12).

## Shopping in Brussels

The obvious temptations—available absolutely everywhere—are chocolate and lace. Other popular Brussels souvenirs include EU gear with the gold circle of stars on a blue background (flags, T-shirts, mugs, bottle openers, hats, pens, and so on) and miniature reproductions of the Manneken-Pis or the Atomium. Belgian beers are a fun, imbibable souvenir that you can either enjoy at a picnic while traveling, or pack (carefully) in your checked luggage to take home.

### Souvenirs near the Grand Place

The streets immediately surrounding the Grand Place are jammed with Belgium's tackiest souvenir stands, with a few good shops mixed in. In my Grand Place Walk, I've listed some good places to pick up chocolates (page 170) and to browse for tapestries and lace (page 175).

**De Biertempel,** on the street that runs below the Grand Place, stocks not only hundreds of types of Belgian beer but an entire wall of beer glasses—each one designed to highlight the qualities of a specific beer (Rue du Marché aux Herbes 56—for location, see the "Brussels Restaurants" map, earlier, +32 2 502 1906).

### Fashion on Rue Antoine Dansaert

While Antwerp is the epicenter of Belgian design, Brussels has worked hard in recent years to catch up. To browse the best selection of Belgian boutiques, start by heading up Rue Antoine Dansaert (from the big Bourse building, cross Boulevard Anspach and continue straight up Rue Auguste Orts, which becomes Rue Antoine Dansaert). Along here, you'll see an eclectic array of both Belgian and international apparel. While specific designers seem to come and go, the genteel vibe persists. Window-shopping this street, you'll pass fine parks. After Place du Nouveau Marché aux Grains, the high-fashion focus downshifts, and the rest of the street feels like an emerging neighborhood with some funkier, lower-rent shops. You could return the way you came, or cut a few blocks northeast to the long fish market square at Ste. Catherine, which runs roughly parallel to Rue Antoine Dansaert.

### Funky Design Shops near Place St-Géry

Brussels has its own term for what we might call "hipsters": *bobo*, short for *bourgeois-bohème*...bohemian middle-class kids with enough money and free time for creative endeavors. You'll find *bobo* pockets around town, but these two streets are a good place to start.

**Rue des Chartreux,** which angles off Rue Antoine Dansaert, has a decidedly lower-rent aura and a lineup of creative shops, such as **Blender 01** (style and gadgets, at #18). A bit closer to the Grand Place, the lively, café-lined **Rue du Marché au Charbon** and the streets nearby (especially Plattesteen) are another good browsing area.

### Big Chains on Rue Neuve

This street, a few blocks north of the Grand Place, is where you'll find big department stores and other international shops. The giant City2 complex on this street is the downtown's primary modern shopping mall.

### Secondhand Shops in Marolles

This somewhat seedy neighborhood is well known for its second-hand shops. Rue Blaes and Rue Haute, which run southwest from near the old Tour d'Angle (described in the Upper Town Walk chapter) to the Midi train station, are lined with several characteristic stores. There's a lively flea market each morning (7:00-14:00, best on weekends) on Place du Jeu de Balle, just off Rue Blaes.

### A Taste of Africa in Matongé

Browse the neighborhood of Matongé (described in the Sights in Brussels chapter) for colorful fabrics and exotic ingredients at the many African grocery stores (you'll find the highest concentration along Chaussée de Wavre).

# Nightlife in Brussels

At the TI, pick up the free *Bruzz* weekly magazine, which lists events including opera, symphony, and ballet; and the *Be Nightlife* guide, which lists bars and music venues by neighborhood. Also check the Agenda page of www.visit.brussels. Make a point to savor the Grand Place at night, when it becomes even more magical—as day-tripping tourists are gone and the Town Hall spire is floodlit.

### Films

At one time, Brussels had a wide range of characteristic little cinemas. These days, most Bruxellois flock to the multiplexes; a handy one is the **UGC** cinema on De Brouckère square (look for *v.o.* for the original version; *v.f.* means it's dubbed in French). A small arthouse cinema in the Galeries St. Hubert plays international films in their original language (generally not English), with Dutch and French subtitles.

### Music and Dance

The **Ancienne Belgique** concert hall, right by the Bourse, is a major venue for up-and-coming international pop, folk, and singer-songwriter acts (Boulevard Anspach 110, www.abconcerts.be).

**Theatre Royal de la Monnaie** hosts orchestral concerts, opera, and dance performances (5 Place de la Monnaie—entrance on Rue des Princes, +32 2 222 1211, www.lamonnaiedemunt.be).

### After-Dark Neighborhoods

Just a few steps west of the Grand Place, **Rue du Marché au Charbon** (Kolenmarkt) is the center of Brussels' gay scene, with many lively cafés and restaurants with outdoor seating. The trendy eateries, shops, and businesses along here change so fast, the locals can't keep track.

Across Boulevard Anspach is **Place St-Géry**, where you'll find a raucous collection of lively bars with rollicking interiors and a sea of outdoor tables. Mappa Mundo anchors the area, with two levels of scenic tables. Zebra Bar, across the street by the market hall, is another fun scene. And inside the market hall is the Café des Halles, with chichi cocktails in an elegantly airy, open-feeling, steel-beamed space, and DJs on the weekends.

A five-minute walk northeast is the pleasant **Ste. Catherine** district, with lively local restaurants and hotels huddled around the Church of Ste. Catherine and the old fish market. On Place Ste. Catherine, a red truck adorned with brightly painted birds sells tropical drinks to an appreciative local crowd; in warm weather, young people sip mojitos while socializing on the square.

Farther from the center, the **Matongé** African immigrant neighborhood is lively after dark. Rue Saint-Boniface, leading up to the front door of the neighborhood church, is "café row"—with plenty of choices for an al fresco drink. The widest selection of bars and cafés clusters around Place Fernand Cocq.

# Brussels Connections

## BY TRAIN

Brussels has three train stations: Central/Centraal, Midi/Zuid, and Nord/Noord. Most trains stop at all three stations, but high-speed international trains serve only the Midi station. Any train ticket to any Brussels station includes a transfer to any other Brussels train station (but not the airport). For more details on the three stations—and tips on connecting between them—see page 127. For schedules, see www.belgiantrain.be or www.bahn.com. For general information on rail travel in Belgium, see the "Transportation" section of the Practicalities chapter.

## Within Belgium and the Netherlands

**From All Brussels Stations by Train to: Bruges** (3/hour, 1 hour, catch InterCity train—direction: Ostend or Knokke-Blankenberge), **Antwerp** (3/hour, 40-50 minutes), **Ghent** (3/hour, 35 minutes), **Ypres/Ieper** (hourly, 2 hours, change in Gent St. Pieters). The following destinations are in the Netherlands: **Haarlem** (hourly, 3 hours, change in Amsterdam), **Delft** (almost hourly, 2.5 hours, change in Breda), **The Hague** (almost hourly, 2.5 hours, change in Breda).

**Getting Between Brussels and Amsterdam:** Slower, regional trains leave about hourly for Amsterdam and Amsterdam's Schiphol Airport from all three Brussels stations (3 hours to Schiphol, 3.5 hours to Amsterdam's Centraal station). For a faster (but more expensive) connection, the high-speed Thalys train goes direct from Brussels' Midi station to Amsterdam's Centraal station and Schiphol Airport (about hourly, 2 hours).

**BRUSSELS SLEEPING, EATING & MORE**

## Outside Belgium and the Netherlands

The following special, high-speed train lines depart only from Midi station, tracks 1-6. Rail-pass holders must book a seat reservation for Thalys and TGV trains. For schedules, see Bahn.com or www.b-europe.com (the Belgian rail website for cross-border trains).

**From Brussels by Thalys Train to: Paris** (almost hourly, 1.5 hours), **Cologne** (8/day, 2 hours). Thalys also operates the slower but cheaper IZY train on this route (2-3/day, 2.5 hours, rail passes not accepted, www.izy.com). Train info: Toll +32 7 066 7788, Thalys.com.

**By TGV Train to France:** French TGV trains connect to **Paris' Charles de Gaulle Airport** (8/day, 1.5 hours, www.tgv-europe.com) and then continue to various destinations in France; to reach downtown Paris you must transfer at the airport.

**By ICE Train to Germany:** Germany's InterCity Express trains zip to **Cologne** (3/day, 2 hours) and **Frankfurt** (3/day, 3 hours), with onward connections to the rest of the country. Reservations are not required except for advance-ticket discounts (besides Midi, these trains make a quick stop at Brussels' Nord station).

**By Eurostar to/from London:** Brussels and London are about 2 hours apart by Eurostar train (6/day). Trains to London leave from tracks 1 and 2 at Brussels' Midi station. Arrive early to go through security and passport control (must be completed at least 45 minutes before departure).

A one-way ticket between Brussels and London can vary widely in price; for instance, $60-275 (Standard class), $150-375 (Standard Premier), and $400 (Business Premier). Fares depend on how far ahead you reserve and whether you're eligible for any discounts—available for children (under 12), youths (under 26), and adults booking months ahead or purchasing round-trip. You can book tickets up to six months in advance. Tickets can be exchanged before the scheduled departure for a fee (about $55, may be waived for early exchanges) plus the cost of any price increase, but only Business Premier class allows any refund. Buy tickets ahead at RickSteves.com/rail or at Eurostar.com (Belgian +32 2 400 6731, with €14 phone handling fee).

If you have a Eurail Global Pass, seat reservations are avail-

# Brussels Area

To Antwerp & Amsterdam

OUTER RING FREEWAY

A-12

R-0

A-1

HEYSEL

**BRUSSELS AIRPORT** ✈

ATOMIUM ■

Canal

DIEGEM

N-22

To Ghent & Bruges

A-10

KOEKELBERG BASILICA ■

Charleroi

SCHAERBEEK

A-3

To Liège & Cologne

KOEKELBERG

**NORD STATION**

R-0

ANDERLECHT

*Grand Place* ■

See detail maps

**CENTRAL STATION**

Cinquantenaire Park

**MIDI STATION**

EUROPEAN PARLIAMENT

MATONGE

R-0

"LITTLE BELT"

ST. GILLES

To Ghent & Bruges

N-5

To AfricaMuseum

A-7

To Namur

CHAUSSÉE D'ALSEMBERG

N-275

N-5

R-0

E-19

Note: Shaded area indicates Central Brussels within the "Little Belt"

**Waterloo** ●

N-253

CHAUSSÉE DE TUBIZE

Braine-l'Alleud ●

MEMORIAL 1815 ■

3 Kilometers

2 Miles

N-2

N-5

HOUGOUMONT FARM ■

N-271

R-0

To Charleroi & Paris

able at Eurostar departure stations, Eurail.com, or by phone with Eurostar (generally harder to get at other train stations and travel agencies; $35 in Standard, $45 in Standard Premier, can sell out).

A Eurostar ticket between Brussels and London can also cover a regional train connection to/from any Belgian station for $13/€11 more, if you choose the "ABS option" (or specify your end point) at the time of purchase. Show your ticket when boarding the connecting train(s) within 24 hours of the reserved Brussels arrival or departure (as long as the connecting train is not a Thalys).

## BY BUS

You can save money—but not time—by traveling by BlaBlaCar bus to Paris or London or Flixbus to Paris (BlaBlaCar—www. blablacar.co.uk; Flixbus—UK tel. +44 178 829 8784, www.flixbus. com).

**From Brussels by Bus to: Paris** (€10-42 one-way, 8/day, 4-5 hours), **London** (€30-60 one-way, 2/day, 7-11 hours).

## BY PLANE
### Brussels Airport (a.k.a. Zaventem)

Brussels' main airport is nine miles north of downtown. Terminals A and B are connected by an underground walkway; the train station is in the basement at level -1 (code: BRU, +32 2 753 7753, www.brusselsairport.be).

Brussels Airport has stringent security measures, especially for those arriving by private car or taxi. Plan to arrive three hours before your flight.

The clear winner for getting to and from the airport is the **train** that runs between the airport and all three Brussels train stations (€9.30, 8/hour, 25 minutes, daily 6:00-23:00). If you're connecting the airport with Bruges, take this shuttle train and transfer at Brussels' Nord station (about 1.5 hours total). There's also a direct train connection from the airport to Ghent (1 hour). For a **taxi,** figure on spending around €45 between downtown Brussels and the airport.

Brussels Airlines flies between Brussels and several European cities, including Athens, London, Milan, Florence, Zürich, Nice, Lisbon, Barcelona, and Madrid (Belgian +32 7 035 1111, www. brusselsairlines.com).

### Brussels South Charleroi Airport

Discount airlines Ryanair (www.ryanair.com) and Wizz Air (www. wizzair.com) use this smaller airport, located about 30 miles from downtown Brussels in the town of Gosselies, on the outskirts of the city of Charleroi (code: CRL, +32 9 020 2490, www.brussels-charleroi-airport.com).

The easiest way to connect to downtown Brussels is to take the **shuttle bus** to Brussels' Midi station (€14-17, 2/hour, about 1 hour, runs 4:00-22:30; stops right in front of airport terminal; if you're taking the bus from Brussels' Midi station, look for it at the corner of Rue de France and Rue de l'Instruction—the bus stop is not clearly marked, www.brussels-city-shuttle.com). You can also take a **bus-plus-train** connection: Bus #A connects Charleroi Airport and Charleroi station (2/hour, 20 minutes), where you can take the train into Brussels (2/hour, 40 minutes). A **taxi** from the airport into the city center is costly (figure around €90 and 45-90 minutes travel time), but from Brussels to Charleroi you can catch a cheap taxi from Midi station—taxis compete with the airport shuttle and are willing to go as low as €12/person if you're willing to share.

## BY CRUISE SHIP

The cruise port of Zeebrugge—near Bruges—is often billed by cruise lines as "Brussels." While Bruges is the easier choice for an excursion from that port, Brussels is also doable. For more on Zeebrugge, see page 108.

# ANTWERP

# ANTWERP

*Antwerpen • Anvers*

Antwerp (*Antwerpen* in Flemish, *Anvers* in French) is Belgium's up-and-coming "second city" after Brussels, with a half-million people. Where Brussels dominates French-speaking Wallonia, Antwerp is the biggest city and de facto (if not official) capital of Dutch-speaking Flanders.

Antwerp has enjoyed an illustrious history. Once Europe's most important trading city, it later was the hometown of accomplished painter Peter Paul Rubens. It was partially destroyed during World War II and then rebuilt. The drab air of heavy industry has been supplanted by an edgy, creative spirit. Like Barcelona, Liverpool, and Rotterdam, it's been reborn as a city of tech and European fashion.

Antwerpenaars (as locals are called) have a love of life, and the city has a funky urbanity. Antwerp's big-city bustle is the yang to Bruges' cutesy-village yin. And while Brussels has become international, Antwerp has retained more of a local identity—it's an honest, what-you-see-is-what-you-get place that feels more Flemish.

Antwerp has an especially strong "pop-up" culture: The people here love spontaneity and see everything as temporary. Here more than in most places, restaurants come and go, and major museums close for multiyear renovations with little notice. Expect changes to some things described in this book, confirm hours online, and be prepared for new discoveries.

The sights here are easily on par with the best in Belgium. Antwerp is renowned for the art of Rubens (and fellow Flemish artists Anthony van Dyck and Pieter Bruegel), a soaring cathedral, several other interesting churches packed with great art, and a red light district that boxes puritan ears. Historians enjoy the Museum Plantin-Moretus, art lovers savor the Snijders-Rockox House, fashionistas love the window shopping (and MoMu, a museum of fashion and design), children of immigrants are moved by the Red Star Line Museum, and architecture fans drool over the building housing the Museum aan de Stroom (Museum on the River, or MAS for short).

Antwerp is equally enjoyable without a sightseeing agenda, offering fun-to-explore neighborhoods, abundant al fresco café tables, and an inviting main market square with a carillon that jingles the hour.

## PLANNING YOUR TIME

You could easily fill two days touring all the sights here, but selective visitors can see the highlights in a few hours as a day trip from Bruges or Brussels (each less than 1.5 hours away by train), or on the way between other Belgian and Dutch destinations.

On a **quick visit** of just a few hours, take parts 1 and 2 of my Antwerp City Walk from the train station to the Old Town, tour the cathedral, ogle the Grote Markt, and add any sights that intrigue you (if you're really short on time, skip straight to part 2). Then zip back to the train station on underground trams known as the "Metro."

With **more time,** follow all three parts of my Antwerp City Walk and dip into more of the museums. Antwerp's diverse restaurant scene and lively nightlife make it well worth spending a night. And with a variety of quirky boutiques and cafés on each street, it's a delightful place to simply linger.

As in most of Belgium, sights tend to be closed on Mondays (though that day may change, so confirm the latest hours online). Many sights are free the last Wednesday of the month.

# Orientation to Antwerp

Antwerp sits along the east bank of the Scheldt River (*Schelde* in Flemish). The main tourist area is fairly compact. On a quick trip, narrow your focus to these main zones: the Old Town along the river; the train station area and Diamond Quarter to the east, and the Meir shopping district between the Old Town and train station; the newly rejuvenated Little Island (Eilandje) zone and the red light district to the north; and, to the south, the Sint-Andries fashion district and, beyond that, the happening nightlife zone aptly called 't Zuid ("The South"). All these areas are within about a 30-minute walk (or a quick tram or taxi ride) of one another.

## TOURIST INFORMATION

Antwerp's TI has two branches: inside the **train station** (at the head of the tracks, on level 0, daily 9:00-17:00); and in the **waterfront castle,** or Het Steen, near Grote Markt (daily 10:00-18:00;

# Antwerp's History

Owning a prime location where the major Scheldt River meets the North Sea, Antwerp established itself in Roman times as a river-trade town. In the late 15th century, as Bruges' harbor silted up, Antwerp became a major trading center and the Low Countries' top city. As the Age of Exploration dawned, Portuguese and Spanish ships returning from the New World laden with exotic goods docked here in Antwerp, making it a center of world trade. During Antwerp's 16th-century golden age, it became Europe's wealthiest city, with a population of about 100,000.

In the mid-16th century, Antwerp was pulled into the Eighty Years' War between the Dutch rebel Protestants and the ruling Spanish Catholics. In 1576, after growing impatience at not being paid by Habsburg King Philip II, Spanish troops relentlessly sacked Antwerp for three days—massacring thousands of its residents and destroying hundreds of homes. The outraged public response to this so-called "Spanish Fury" elevated Antwerp to the capital of the Dutch Revolt. (The event also irrevocably damaged Antwerp's trade ties with partners who wanted no business with a war zone.) But the crushing, Spanish-led Siege of Antwerp in 1584-1585 wore down the independence movement, and the city fell under Spanish/Catholic control. In a postwar "brain drain," more than half of the city's population fled to Amsterdam...and took prosperity with them.

Seeking to rehabilitate its image in the aftermath of the bloody warfare, the Catholic Church invested mightily in building and decorating churches in Antwerp. A local artist named Peter Paul Rubens (1577-1640)—while arguably less talented than some of his contemporaries—found himself in the right place at the right time. A brilliant salesman, Rubens allied himself with the Church to win one big commission after another. His style epitomized exactly what the Church was looking for: bold, bombastic images trumpeting the glory of God (and his Church on earth).

The treaty that ended the Eighty Years' War in 1648 imposed rigid regulations on shipping on the Scheldt River, restricting Antwerp's outlet to the North Sea. The city devolved from an international port to a regional one. Antwerp's industry, led by an elite group of pro-Catholic traders, began to specialize in luxury goods—cabinets, paintings, tapestries, and so on. The city would languish as a Catholic backwater and second-rate shipping city for centuries, although its industry was kept alive by Napoleon, then by Belgian independence, and later by Belgium's colonization of the Congo. By the 20th century, Antwerp ranked as Europe's second-busiest port (just after Dutch rival Rotterdam). Damaged in both world wars, Antwerp has recently begun to enjoy a new gentrification that's making it one of Europe's most exciting young cities.

+32 3 221 1333, phone answered Mon-Fri only, www.visitantwerp. be). Peruse their racks of fliers and pick up a free town map. The **Antwerp City Card**—which includes transit, museum admissions, and additional discounts—can be a good value for very busy sightseers; grab a brochure and do the math (€29/24 hours, €40/48 hours, €48/72 hours).

## ARRIVAL IN ANTWERP

**By Train:** Antwerp's Central rail station (Antwerpen Centraal)— with a refurbished grand century-old shell and modern under-ground zone—feels like a cathedral of travel. (Some people stop off here just to see one of Europe's most impressive train stations.) While big, it's fairly easy to navigate, with three well-signed levels of tracks connected by escalators and elevators.

Level 0 is the hub of activity, where you'll find a TI and lug-gage lockers tucked under the stairs (pay by card). Carrying on straight ahead, you'll pass through the gorgeously restored great hall (with ticket windows). Exiting out the front door puts you in the vast and somewhat seedy Koningin Astridplein, with the city's zoo on your immediate right.

To reach the city center **by foot**—following my Antwerp City Walk—turn left and walk down busy De Keyserlei boulevard. It's about 20 minutes to the Grote Markt. (To easily find De Keyserlei from inside the station's main hall, face the ticket offices and big clock, turn left, and pass by the pharmacy to exit under the *Keyser-lei/Meir/Centrum* sign.)

For a speedier trip, take the **Metro:** From next to the TI, take the escalator marked *Metro* down to the Diamant stop. Buy a ticket from the easy-to-miss yellow machines in the passageway, then find the tracks and hop on tram #9 or #15 (direction: Linkeroever or Regatta; validate your ticket in the yellow machine when you board). Ride just three stops to Groenplaats for the Grote Markt and the historical center.

## HELPFUL HINTS

**Tours:** The TI organizes a two-hour historical walking tour through town combining English and French (€10—or €8 if you book at least a day in advance, July-Aug daily at 14:00, Sept-June Sat-Sun only, departs from TI at the castle). You can also find

# Antwerp

Scheldt River

To Red Star Line Museum

SINT LAUREIKAAI

T #7 MAS

LITTLE ISLAND

**WALK ENDS**

14 **MUSEUM AAN DE STROOM**

SINT-ALDEGONDISKAAI

SCHOONBEKEPLEIN

VAN

BROUWERSTRAAT

BROUWERSVLIET

OUDE

BROUWERSVLIET

OUDE

B #17, #30

SCHIPPERSSTR

VING

FALCONPLEIN

VILLA TINTO

12 VERVERGRUI

13

Falconplein

OUDE MANSTR

**RED LIGHT DISTRICT**

KLAPDORP

MUTSAARDSTRAAT

KAASBRUG

KLAPDORP

**QUICK RETURN ROUTE**

GORTERSTR

11 KEISTR

NOSBSTR

T #7 Sint-Paulusplaats

SINT-PAULUSSTRAAT

**ST. PAUL'S**

MINDERBROEDERSRUI

Veemarkt

JORDAENSKAAI

VAN DIJKKAAI

ZAKSTR

ZIRKSTRAAT

10 **OLD BUTCHERS HALL** (MUSICAL INSTRUMENTS MUSEUM)

19TH C. STEEL CANOPIES

CASTLE

i 9

KUIPERSTR

OUDE

B #30

BEURS

**OLD TOWN**

KORTE

KOEPOORTSTR

WOLSTRAAT

**QUICK RETURN ROUTE**

AMBTMANSTR

**CHURCH OF CAROLUS BORROMEUS**

**WALK PART 3 BEGINS**

BOAT TRIPS

8 Steenplein

19TH C. STEEL CANOPIES

ERNEST

DIVA DIAMOND MUSEUM

ZILVER CITY HALL

6 **Grote Markt**

**WALK PART 2 BEGINS**

KAASRUI

KORTE NIEUWESTRAAT

Hendrikconscienceplein

P

PLANTINKAAI

GR. PIET

SUIKERRUI

7

Handschoenmarkt

5 **CATHEDRAL**

EIERMARKT

SINT-KATELIJNEVEST

**HANDELS-BEURS**

HAARSTRAAT

HOOGSTRAAT

OUDE KOORNMARKT

RUBENS STATUE

**Groenplaats**

**FARMERS TOWER**

SPTAVL

MEIRBRUG

VLASMARKT

REYNDERSSTRAAT

PELGRIMS

LEUWEN

#9, 15 T M Groenplaats

SCHOENMARKT

T #7

M Meir

STOOFSTRAAT

**MUSEUM PLANTIN-MORETUS** Vrijdagmarkt

STEENHOUWERSVEST

GEEF

SCHRIJNWERKERSSTR

HUIDEVETTERSSTRAAT

KROMME ELLEBOOGSTR

MUNTSTRAAT

**MOMU** (MODEMUSEUM)

NATIONALESTRAAT

KAMMENSTRAAT

LOMBARDENVEST

**SINT-ANDRIES**

Munthof

To T'Zuid District & Royal Museum of Fine Arts

SLEUTELSTRAAT

ST. ANTONIUS-STR

To A-1 Motorway & Brussels

N

200 Meters

200 Yards

ANTWERP

a variety of tours and other activities through the TI's partner company, Experience Antwerp (www.experienceantwerp.be).

For a private tour, Erwin Liekens and his team from **Taste the City** lead tours in Antwerp as well as Brussels (€240/3 hours, €80 per additional hour, +32 495 625 215, www.tastethecity.be, info@tastethecity.be).

**Markets:** The most entertaining market is on Saturday, when Theaterplein (by the giant city theater), Oudevaartplaats, and surrounding streets are enlivened by food stalls and other vendors (Sat 8:00-16:00); a smaller version, with a bird market, fills the same area on Sunday mornings (8:00-13:00). At the charming square called Vrijdagmarkt—**"Friday Market"**—antiques and other secondhand items are auctioned off in Flemish (Fri 9:00-13:00).

**Laundry:** The most central launderette is just off the **Grote Markt** (daily 7:00-22:00, Wisselstraat 2, +32 489 119 2090). **Wassalon Oase** is not far away, just to the south (daily 7:00-21:00, Oever 6, +32 477 693 434).

## GETTING AROUND ANTWERP

**By Public Transportation:** Sprawling Antwerp is walkable, but using the city's public transit network saves time and sweat (operated by De Lijn, www.delijn.be).

Visitors make good use of the Metro, which is actually a series of underground trams. The handiest lines are #9 and #15, which run under the city's main east-west axis, with key stops at Diamant (train station; so named for the surrounding Diamond Quarter), Opera (at east end of Meir shopping street), Meir (at west end of Meir shopping street), and Groenplaats (near the cathedral and Grote Markt). If you're heading from the train station to the Old Town, look for *Linkeroever* or *Regatta;* in the opposite direction, from the Old Town to the train station, look for *Eksterlaar* or *Boechout.* Surface trams and buses can be useful for reaching zones to the north (Little Island/Eilandje) and south ('t Zuid).

A **single ticket** costs €2.50 and is good for an hour (including a transfer). Buy tickets at the machines in the passages near the platforms (cards accepted); trams and buses have ticket machines on board. If you're going to Bruges and/or Ghent and plan to use public transportation there as well, consider the shareable **10-ride ticket** for €17—valid on local transit throughout Flanders. Other options are a **day pass** (€7.50) and a **three-day pass** (€15). Validate your ticket when you board. Day passes need validation only once. Smart travelers buy their return ticket at the same time to avoid later hassles.

**Hop-On, Hop-Off Bus:** Connect the major sights with

# Antwerp at a Glance

▲▲**Cathedral of Our Lady** Cavernous church packed with fine artwork, including paintings by Rubens. **Hours:** Mon-Fri 10:00-17:00, Sat until 15:00, Sun 13:00-17:00. See page 246.

▲▲**Museum Plantin-Moretus** Early printing presses, workshops, and memorabilia from Antwerp's golden age. **Hours:** Tue-Sun 10:00-17:00, closed Mon. See page 256.

▲**Red Star Line Museum** Illustrates the "other end" of the Ellis Island experience, where emigrants were processed on their way to the New World. **Hours:** Tue-Sun 10:00-17:00, closed Mon. See page 254.

▲**Snijders-Rockox House Museum** Aristocratic 17th-century home with impressive art, furniture, and delightful garden courtyard. **Hours:** Tue-Sun 10:00-17:00, closed Mon. See page 251.

▲**Museum aan de Stroom (MAS)** Displays focusing on Antwerp's and Belgium's history of trade and cultural exchange—plus a rooftop viewpoint. **Hours:** Building open Tue-Sun 9:30-24:00, off-season until 22:30, closed Mon; exhibits open Tue-Sun 10:00-17:00, closed Mon. See page 253.

▲**Royal Museum of Fine Arts** Many of Antwerp's art treasures, all under one (recently renovated) roof. **Hours:** Mon-Fri 10:00-17:00, Thu until 22:00, Sat-Sun 10:00-18:00. See page 258.

**ModeMuseum (MoMu)** Newly renovated museum celebrating Antwerp's role in the world of fashion and design. **Hours:** Tue-Sun 10:00-18:00, closed Mon. See page 258.

**Rubens House** The richly decorated home, studio, and garden of Peter Paul Rubens, with a few of his paintings to boot. **Hours:** Closed for renovation, likely through 2027.

**Cabrio Sightseeing** (€14/all day, +32 470 999 352, www.antwerp-citytourbus.be).

# Antwerp City Walk

This three-part, L-shaped walk starts at the train station, turns right at the Old Town, and ends at the harbor to the north (follow the route on the "Antwerp" map, earlier). With this walk, you can say you've "seen" Antwerp, as it laces together many of the city's main sights. It's ideal for day-trippers who want to see everything in a few hours' blitz from the train station.

You can also enjoy the different parts at your leisure, and in any order: Part 1 of the walk is an easy stroll from the train station down a modern, pedestrian-friendly shopping street to the heart of town. Part 2 covers the historic core—the towering cathedral, the Grote Markt, and the riverfront where the city was born. Part 3 takes you where fewer tourists go—through a residential neighborhood, the red light district, and to the modern dockyards, with two great museums.

Along the way, you'll see the city's historic architecture, youthful citizens, trendy restaurants, and a high-tech brothel. You can also take this opportunity to stop in and tour several sights, including the cathedral or the Museum aan de Stroom (MAS). The walk ends with a view back over the towers, steeples, cranes, and skyscrapers of this teeming city.

**Length of This Walk:** The whole walk covers two miles. Allow at least 30 minutes for each part, plus another 20-30 minutes to return to your starting point. Budget additional time if you go inside any sights along the way. With limited time, skip to Part 2 by riding the Metro directly from the train station to the Old Town (Groenplaats stop). You could also skip Part 3 and visit the MAS separately.

## PART 1: FROM THE TRAIN STATION TO THE OLD TOWN
### ❶ Antwerp's Train Station

• *Start on level +1—the highest level of tracks (under the 19th-century steel and glass arch). They dead-end under the ornate old-timey clock.*

The city's central train station is not merely a convenient transportation hub, it's a work of art and a loud-and-clear comment on a confident new age. Built between 1895 and 1905 and expanded a century later, it's an eclectic mix of historical art styles: Industrial Age meets Art Nouveau, giddy with steel and glass.

Look down through the center of the station to see the various levels of train tracks. The original station was all on one level—you'd walk from your wheezing steam train directly to the place you're standing now. But dead-end stations are just too slow for today's express trains, so they've excavated these several layers of tracks. Today's fastest trains, on the lowest level, pass straight through a tunnel beneath the station—connecting Antwerp with Amsterdam or Paris in just an hour or two.

Look up at the vintage **clock** in the center of the hall. Set into a facade of gray marble and gold trim, towering high above the tracks, this is a temple of time. Timekeeping was crucial in the age of train schedules. Belgium was a busy new colonial power, speeding into the modern age fueled by ivory and rubber from its colony in the Congo. The station is the work of the "builder king" Leopold II. You'll see his *L* monogram everywhere.

The **Royal Café,** to the left of the big clock, is first-class, yet economical and elegant...a fine place for a quiet cup of coffee or light bite.

• *Let's start walking. Pass underneath the big clock, into the main lobby with even more grandiose architecture. Antwerpen Centraal may be the best-decorated train station in Europe.*

*Facing the ticket office and big clock, turn left, passing by the pharmacy to exit under the* Keyserlei/Meir/Centrum *sign. Once in the open air, you can see our route: From here, we'll walk basically straight ahead on the Keyserlei pedestrian mall, past the ugly gold skyscraper, all the way to the Old Town. Your destination is in the distance—the lacy spire of the cathedral.*

## ❼ Upper Main Drag: Train Station to Rubens House

Stroll three blocks gradually downhill on the bustling, sand-colored boulevard called **De Keyserlei,** lined with chain restaurants and shops. Following European trends, this boulevard is becoming a bike-and-pedestrian zone.

You'll pass by a few diamond and jewelry stores. This area is known as the **Diamond Quarter**—one of the world's top centers

where diamonds are sold wholesale and cleaved into smaller pieces to prepare them for cutting. While you could explore more of the "Diamond Square Mile" (stretching to the left, in the old Jewish Quarter), it's mostly just more diamond shops and extremely casual-looking people with briefcases handcuffed to their wrists.

When you cross the tram tracks at **Frankrijklei** (marking the former town wall), you're also crossing a massive highway underfoot (notice the offramp to your left). This was moved underground,

ANTWERP

## Antwerp's Diamond Quarter

The area around the train station is known as the Diamond Quarter—one of the world's top centers for commerce in these gems. Although the industry is highly secretive, experts guess that four out of every five of the world's rough diamonds pass through Antwerp at some point. The diamond industry is located in the train-station neighborhood for good reason: If you're carrying millions of dollars' worth of precious jewels in your briefcase through a strange city, you don't want to have to venture too far to reach a trader or diamond cutter.

Beginning in the 16th century, the diamond industry in Antwerp was dominated by Sephardic Jews from Spain, but under Catholic rule, they fled to Amsterdam. Then, in the late 19th century, Hasidic Orthodox Jews fleeing the pogroms in Russia settled here and took up the trade. In the streets around the train station, you'll likely see men wearing tall hats and black coats, with long beards and curly locks at their temples, and women with long dresses and hair covers. More recently, the industry here has been increasingly dominated by Indians.

The history of the diamond trade focuses on Africa, where diamond seekers dug the world's biggest man-made hole, the Kimberley Crater in South Africa. In some parts of Africa, the exploitative conditions for finding these gems haven't improved much since the early days of Belgian colonialism. A strict diamond-certification process, introduced in Antwerp in 2000, attempts to block the sale of so-called "blood diamonds"—stones sold by rebels fighting governments in war zones in central and western Africa.

then covered up, just a few years ago. Over your right shoulder, look for the glorious **opera house,** no longer engulfed in ugly traffic.

Just beyond, a noble bronze statue of **David Teniers**—one of several big Antwerp painters—marks a classic Antwerp street scene, bookended with grand facades built in the late-19th-century style called Historicism. This style cobbled together all the best, most bombastic, bits and pieces from past styles to wow the viewer.

Passing the statue of **Anthony van Dyck** (1599-1641)— another talented Antwerp artist who worked with Rubens—you reach the pleasant pedestrian shopping street (and neighborhood) called the **Meir** (pronounced "mare"). This showcase shopping zone was built, like the train station, in the boom times around 1900.

A long block ahead on the

left is the grand **Stadsfeestzaal shopping mall** (with the gold niche over the door). Venture inside for a glimpse at its astonishing interior.

Back out on the Meir, keep strolling; it's great for people-watching. Antwerp is diverse, including lots of Muslim citizens (the trendiest of whom are nicknamed "Mipsters"). Along with the biggest Jain temple outside India and a sizable Buddhist community, about 40 mosques call Antwerp home. Antwerp also has many Black residents. Some came here generations ago from former colonies (the Belgian Congo, 1908-1960; Rwanda and Burundi, 1916-1962); others are more recent arrivals.

One block later, look left down Wapper Square, featuring (a block down) one of the city's top sights, the ❸ **Rubens House.** This former home of Peter Paul Rubens introduces visitors to the artist's work and lifestyle. However, it's closed through 2027 for an extensive renovation. Starting about 2024, they hope to add some temporary exhibits; Rubens fans can detour here to take a look.

## ❹ Lower Main Drag: Rubens House to Cathedral

Just past Wapper Square is an ornate gray building on the left—the **Paleis op de Meir.** This gorgeous Rococo palace, built in 1745, was later purchased by Napoleon, who decorated it in Empire Style. With Belgium's independence in 1830, this became one of the official residences of the king of the Belgians.

But what really matters is chocolate. At the Paleis entrance, step into the **Chocolate Line** shop. Notice the *grisailles*—the monochrome illustrations that look like 3-D carved reliefs but are actually flat paintings. Here, you can see the creative work of the crazy "shock-o-latier" Dominique Persoone (€4 for your choice of three wacky flavors, daily until 18:30). Past the shop, you can see a kitchen where truffles are being made.

Farther along, the Meir opens up. Continue about 150 yards and, nearing the end of the street (just before you cross to the corner with the giant skyscraper), turn right up the little lane called Twaalfmaandenstraat (between the first and second underground staircases to the Metro). Straight ahead at the end of the block, the building marked *Anno 1872* is the **Handelsbeurs.** If it's open, step inside (free, likely daily 10:00-17:00 in summer, often open unexpectedly at other times—just give the door a try, www.handelsbeursantwerpen.be).

Translated as "Stock Exchange," the Handelsbeurs evokes Antwerp's glory days as a trading power. This genteel hall—rebuilt after fires in 1583 and in 1858—feels like a gigantic vaulted cloister covered by a glass-and-steel roof, which bathes the space in light. (The current Neo-Gothic structure dates from 1872, with some very early echoes of Art Nouveau.) Historically, this was where

Belgians would bring VIPs, including Winston Churchill, who visited after World War II. It later fell into disuse; locals recall the time when this neglected space was seedy and dangerous. Now fully restored as a public meeting and events space, it's a fun place to wander around and simply take in the sparkling details. Ninety-six columns (each with a unique pattern— I checked) support two layers of galleries. Under the arcades, peruse the highly detailed maps, painted in oil by an actual sea captain in the 1870s. Even the wrought-iron ceiling supports are lacy with delicate floral motifs.

Back out on the Meir, cross the tram tracks and continue straight toward the Art Deco, Gotham City-style skyscraper called the **Farmers Tower** (or *Boerentoren*, though it's officially named after its current occupant, KBC—a bank). Completed in 1932, this was considered the first Chicago-style skyscraper in Europe. It held the title of Europe's tallest skyscraper for 20 years.

At the Farmers Tower, bear left along Schoenmarkt. This leads to the square called **Groenplaats.** Here you'll find a handy Metro stop, a statue of **Rubens**—the third Antwerp artist we've seen on this walk—and the cathedral spire hovering just beyond. The high-fashion district is to your left, and the Old Town is beyond the cathedral.

• *Stroll through the square toward the cathedral. Bear left up a narrow street of restaurants (Jan Blomstraat) known as "Little Italy Lane." It spills out at Handschoenmarkt in front of the cathedral. You've arrived at the historic center of Antwerp.*

## PART 2: FROM THE CATHEDRAL TO THE RIVERFRONT
### ❺ Cathedral of Our Lady

Antwerp's biggest church, with its lacy 400-foot-tall spire—still the tallest structure in the city—dominates the Old Town. Its mismatched towers tell Antwerp's story in a nutshell. The church was begun in 1352 and consecrated in 1521, when Antwerp was at its peak, and there were grandiose plans to make the already huge church even bigger—the biggest on earth. But then a 1533 fire gutted the church, and in 1576, the Spanish Catholics sacked the city, causing Protestants to flee (mostly to Amsterdam) and Antwerp's fortunes to plummet. The church was left with only one completed tower—once the tallest in the Low Countries; the other is a stump of thwarted dreams.

Though much of the facade was left undecorated, the tympanum (archway) over the main door is remarkable. It's the Last Judg-

ment, and Christ raises his hand to divide the righteous from the wicked. Below him, St. Michael weighs souls. One naughty lady is led away by a gleeful demon to be tormented for eternity. Farther down (between the doors) is a statue of Mary—"Our Lady"—who smiles, willing to save us from that grim fate.

The church's richly ornamented interior is packed with fine art, including four masterpieces painted by Peter Paul Rubens (for details on visiting the church interior, see the listing under "Sights in Antwerp," later).

• *Now, as you face the church, turn left and exit the square by walking up Maalderijstraat. You'll emerge in the...*

## ❻ Grote Markt

Antwerp's main square is dominated by the stately **City Hall** (Stadhuis). Dating from Antwerp's golden age (16th century), it's adorned with flags from many different countries—representing the importance of international trade to the city. The central tower sports the golden coats of arms of great medieval powers that shaped Antwerp: the lion of the Duchy of Brabant, the gilded coat of arms of the city's Spanish rulers, and the two-headed eagle of the Habsburgs.

The other buildings fronting the square are **guild houses,** celebrating the trade associations of each of the city's industries. Each one is topped with a golden statue, which usually represents that guild's patron saint. There's a man on a rearing

**ANTWERP**

horse, a cat (or is it a wolf?), and (between those) a saint with a migraine. Some of these are over-the-top, exaggerated rebuilt versions from the Romantic period in the 19th century. The many ground-floor cafés (especially the venerable Den Engel and Den Bengel, which catch the most sun) are inviting places for a drink with a view. Locals say that when the outdoor terraces open up, they know summer has arrived in Antwerp.

The unusual **fountain** in the middle of Grote Markt illustrates a gruesome story from Flemish folklore. Supposedly, a giant named Druon Antigoon collected tolls along the Scheldt River. If someone was unable or unwilling to pay, the giant would sever their hand. His reign of terror finally ended when a brave young Roman soldier named Silvius Brabo defeated Antigoon, then cut off the giant's hand. Here we see Brabo in his wind-up, ready to toss Antigoon's blood-spouting hand into the river. (You can circle around behind to see the giant's bloody stump.) Tour guides love to explain that *hand werpen* ("to throw a hand") evolved into "Antwerpen"... though scholars prefer less glamorous alternatives: "Antwerp" probably comes from *an*  *'t werf,* "on the wharf"; or *ando verpis,* "where land is thrown up against land" (because the river deposits sludge along the bank here).

• *From the Grote Markt, exit the square along the left side of the City Hall. Now head toward the river up the big street called...*

## ❼ Suikerrui

Along Suikerrui you get your first sense of Antwerp's origins as a river-trading port town. Today's paved street was once an open canal that flowed to the river. You'll pass the much-loved statue to the unknown dockworker, whose insolent pose is both carefree and defiant. Created in 1890 by Constantin Meunier, it was put here after World War II to symbolize the heroic workers who kept the harbors open during the war (*Arbeid Vrijheid* means "Work Is Freedom"). It instantly became a  symbol of the city. Farther along, near the river on the right, the building at #5 is adorned with big green statues. This is the former Hansahuis, where the German guild of traders had their regional headquarters. Also along here, you may spot—if it has reopened to the public—the **DIVA Museum,** featuring exhibits on diamonds and silver (described later, under "Sights in Antwerp").

• *Suikerrui street leads to the river. The best place to view the water is up the ramp to the promenade.*

## ❽ Riverfront

Antwerp was born on the Scheldt River. The river flows north-ward 200 miles, from France to Belgium, where it begins bearing northwest to the North Sea. The city began right along the riverbank back in Roman times. Antwerp's location was perfect for commerce: where the river trade to the interior met the oceangoing trade to the North Sea. The port was fortified with a castle, which, as you can see, still stands nearby.

During Antwerp's golden age (early 1500s), the Scheldt brought more than a hundred ships a day, carrying goods from all over the world: sugar and silver from America, pepper and cinnamon from Asia. The city was completely cosmopolitan, full of international businessmen. But when Antwerp fell to the Spanish in 1585, everything changed suddenly. The Dutch gained control of the Scheldt's river trade and Antwerp declined. It wasn't until Belgium gained its independence in the 19th century that sea trade recovered.

Today, the port of Antwerp is Europe's second largest—but you'd hardly know it standing here, because the main docks have moved to the north (see the forest of cranes in the distance to the right), and the focus of the city has shifted away from the river to the train station. Now the original riverfront is dingy and drab—tucked behind a busy boulevard and basically ignored by the city. The steel canopies nearby are former 19th-century warehouses, today used for covered parking or to shelter old boats (and a WC below). Cruise ships dock right here (along the canopies) to disgorge their passengers into town.

From the promenade, backtrack down the ramp, turn left, and head north along the riverfront, through the park 100 yards. As you walk, notice the waist-high concrete **retaining wall** that runs along the busy street. Because the Scheldt is a tidal river, there's a huge risk of flooding—made more serious by rising sea levels. This retaining wall is equipped with orange steel doors that can roll along railroad tracks to open or close. Antwerp's new vision is to control flooding by building raised parklike dikes and revitalizing the entire riverfront.

• *Straight ahead, you can't miss the...*

## ❾ Castle (Het Steen)

Once part of a city wall that fortified the heart of town, this is all that's left from the medieval era. Billed as "Antwerp's oldest building," it was begun in the 800s, and parts of today's structure date from the 1200s. Today it houses a sprawling gift shop with TI counters and free WCs, and an overpriced high-tech exhibit called "The Antwerp Story." Before taking the entry ramp into the castle, enjoy the photogenic anchor and the statue of the legendary giant intimidating two poor traders. (Or, perhaps, he's being diagnosed by a pair of medieval urologists.)

**Cost and Hours:** Free to enter TI/shop, €7 for skippable exhibit, both daily 10:00-18:00, www.hetsteen.be.

**"Antwerp Story" Exhibit:** Visitors who pay for the exhibit see an impressive modern tapestry illustrating Antwerp's history with a series of comic book-like panels; a celebration of the city's diversity, inviting you to see Antwerp through the eyes of nine residents from different walks of life; exhibits on the city's fashion, design, and diamond industries; and a chance to virtually "fly" over the rooftops of Antwerp (projected onto the floor). While lightly entertaining, the experience feels like paying to watch a slickly produced chamber of commerce video promoting other sights in town. Feel free to skip it.

• *Part 2 of our walk is finished. If you're short on time and want to do some sightseeing in the Old Town, feel free to bail out now. Or, to return to the train station, make your way back to the cathedral and Groenplaats, and hop on tram line #9 or #15.*

*If you stick with Part 3, you'll wander through Antwerp's generally safe and well-patrolled red light district before reaching the rejuvenated old dockyards, with super-modern buildings. (If you'd like to see the dockyards, but not the red lights, simply walk north along the riverbank for about 15 minutes, then turn right at the harbor.)*

## PART 3: FROM THE RIVERFRONT TO THE RED LIGHT DISTRICT AND OLD DOCKYARDS

• *From the castle, find the modest little staircase that takes you up and over the concrete retaining wall (or use the orange gates, farther along). Cross the busy street at the crosswalk and climb the stairs by the recommended Restaurant de Bomma. At the top of the stairs, make a U-turn left, walk 20 yards (enjoying a nice view of the castle), then turn right on Kuipersstraat. Follow Kuipersstraat as it curves through brick row houses. After two blocks, turn left on Vleeshouwersstraat to find a big old building.*

## ⑩ Old Butchers Hall

This hall was built in 1504 to house one of Antwerp's guilds—the butchers. The impressive red-and-white stone structure (which lo-

cals say reminds them of bacon) was the neighborhood meat market. It now houses the Musical Instruments Museum (see listing later, under "Sights in Antwerp").

Notice that the building stands on something quite rare in Antwerp: a small hill. As the hill was always a desirable place to live, this is one of the oldest neighborhoods. But the area today is mostly modern, sterile brick buildings. It was bombed heavily by Nazi V-2 rockets in World War II. Only the Old Butchers Hall survived. Then, in the 1970s, whatever remained was replaced by these modern brick "projects"—subsidized housing. Notice there are no pubs or shops in this poor neighborhood. But if you poke around you'll discover pleasant public courtyards tucked back in-

side many of these buildings, with benches that are inviting on a sunny day (and sinister on a cold, dark night).

• *With the Old Butchers Hall on your left, head gently downhill on Vleeshouwersstraat. Walk two blocks. At a pleasant residential square (Veemarkt), cut diagonally across the basketball court, turn left, and continue on Nosestraat, passing a church. Then you'll angle right to reach the square called...*

## ⑪ Sint-Paulusplaats

This used to be a medieval harbor, then a bustling sailors' quarter with red lights in the windows. The area now has its share of trendy, youth-oriented restaurants.

At this point, you could cut this walk short and opt out of the red light district. Follow the tram tracks to the Sint-Paulusplaats stop, where tram #7 (direction: Mortsel) can take you back to the Old Town.

If you're continuing into the red light district, take a few minutes to read ahead (especially the directions) before tucking your book away and walking boldly through.

• *The route through the red light district is simple: It's basically a straight shot—two long blocks. So, start walking past the big anchor and over*

ANTWERP

*the tram tracks, up the pedestrian street Oudemanstraat, which becomes Vingerlingstraat, and into the heart of the red light district. Follow the road as it curves to the right (through another block of the red light district) and eventually spills out on peaceful Falconplein. See you there.*

## ⓬ Red Light District

Enter Antwerp's red light district—Belgium's biggest hub of legalized prostitution. There are sex shops, sleazy bars, peep shows, and sex workers shimmying in windows. (It feels more comfortable during the day but is livelier after dark.) City leaders believe that legalizing prostitution and concentrating it here makes things safer for sex workers, their clients, and city residents at large.

In the 19th century, Antwerp's red light district was notorious the world over; these days, it's a much tamer place, but still provocative. Most people who come here aren't "lookie-loos"—they're all business. You'll see a few rowdy "stag parties" making a racket, but mostly lonely men silently prowling the pedestrian zone.

Near the end, on the right, is an alleyway marked **Villa Tinto**—essentially a shopping mall of ladies in windows. Designed by prominent artist Arne Quinze, it's a state-of-the-art brothel. It has a high-tech system of "panic buttons" that sex workers can use to call for help and a police station right in the middle. If a prostitute needs help, it's considered better that a policeman answers the call than a pimp.

• *You'll pop out on a long, narrow square called...*

## ⓭ Falconplein

Falconplein is a nice landing spot after the sleaze of the red light district. It used to be pretty seedy—dubbed "Red Square" for its Russian mafia-style thugs—but city leaders cracked down and gentrified the space.

• *At Falconplein, turn left. Cross busy Brouwersvliet (a former canal where cargo ships unloaded their goods). Continue straight ahead, on Van Schoonbekeplein, toward the red buildings with our final sight: the museum called MAS. Had enough? No MAS? You could end the walk now and return to the center of town (for details, see the end of the walk).*

## ⓮ Old Dockyards and MAS (Museum aan de Stroom)

You've reached Antwerp's old industrial port area—once thriving, then dreary, and now revitalized. The port was built by Napoleon in the early 1800s and became the world's first Industrial Age harbor. It was a bustling area of brick warehouses and towering cranes. But by the 1950s and 1960s, the city's shipping industry relocated to larger ports farther north, and it fell into decline. In the mid-1980s, city leaders decided to reclaim and gentrify this prime real estate.

Today it's home to a tidy little yacht marina, a row of desirable condos, some trendy restaurants, and a state-of-the-art museum in an eye-catching tower. A few masted ships and old floating cranes keep alive the memory of this harbor's 19th-century heyday.

The **Museum aan de Stroom** (Museum on the River), or **MAS** for short, is housed in a 210-foot-tall blocky tower, encased in

hand-cut red stone and speckled with silver hands (the symbol of Antwerp). Designed to resemble the spiraling stacks of goods in an old maritime warehouse, the museum emphasizes the way Antwerp's status as a shipping center has made it a crossroads for people from around the world. Since you've made it this far, it would be a shame not to check it out. The building itself is free to enter and wander around in (but you need to buy a ticket if you want to enter the exhibit). It's free to ride the escalators up 10 stories to the museum's rooftop. It takes a while, but the view is good. (Visitors with disabilities can ascend by elevator.) After this long walk, you've earned a look back over all you've traversed. For a description of

the view, the building, and the museum exhibits, see "Sights in Antwerp," later.

The museum's global focus is a fitting end to this walk through Antwerp—a city built on global trade. • *You're done. The **Red Star Line Museum** (with its impressive coverage of emigration from here to America) is*

*a 10- to 15-minute walk beyond the MAS (see "Sights in Antwerp," later).*

**Getting Back to the Center:** To **walk** back to the Old Town, the quickest route (15 minutes, see the "Antwerp" map, earlier) is to return to Falconplein and exit the square at the far end, heading south down Kaasbrug street, which quickly becomes Mutsaardstraat. After about four blocks, you reach an intersection at a small square. Turn right on Minderbroedersstraat and begin following signs to the Grote Markt (or jog straight from the intersection another block to reach the Snijders-Rockox House—see "Sights in Antwerp," later).

To return to the Old Town or train station by **tram,** cross the water on the pedestrian bridge north of the MAS and turn left, where you'll find the MAS stop for tram #7. Hop on and get off five stops later at Meirbrug, where you can transfer to the Metro (Meir station, lines #9 or #15).

To return to the train station by **bus,** backtrack from the MAS to the wide Brouwersvliet, cross it, and look for the bus stop on your right. From here you can catch bus #17 (direction: UZA) to the train station.

# Sights in Antwerp

Antwerp offers an eclectic array of sightseeing, so if you have just one day (or less), you'll need to be selective. Every sight is either in the old center or within walking distance, and many are stops on my Antwerp City Walk.

Note that many of Antwerp's attractions are in flux. Some major museums (including the Rubens House) have closed for extensive renovations; others (including the Royal Museum of Fine Arts and the fashion-forward ModeMuseum) are finally open again after years of rehabbing. Expect lots of changes, and confirm locally that the sights you want to visit are open.

## OLD TOWN
### ▲▲Cathedral of Our Lady
### (Onze-Lieve-Vrouwekathedraal)

Antwerp's biggest church has a spire that shoots like a Gothic rocket 400 feet up from the middle of the Old Town. Its cavernous interior is packed with fine artwork, including four paintings by Rubens.

**Cost and Hours:** €12, Mon-Fri 10:00-17:00, Sat until 15:00, Sun 13:00-17:00, Handschoenmarkt, +32 3 213 9951, www.dekathedraal.be.

**Tours:** Free English tours are sometimes offered—ask or check the website.

**Self-Guided Tour:** Stepping inside, notice how remarkably wide the cathedral is (250 feet), with three aisles on either side of the nave.

• *Take a seat in the nave.*

**Nave:** Looking up, you'll see that the Gothic design is also dramatically vertical—everything stretches upward (90 feet) toward heaven. The stained-glass windows (some of them original) colorized the light emanating from inside, drawing worshippers like moths to a flame. After dark, in medieval times, the interior was filled with countless candles, and this was the only place to find bright light.

Sitting here, ponder the cathedral's troubled history: It was gutted by the fire of 1533, then stripped of its medieval decoration by iconoclastic Protestants (in 1566). A few fragments of colorful murals remain on the underside of the vaults, where the iconoclasts couldn't reach. After the Catholics came to power (1585), they redecorated the church in bubbly Baroque, including several pieces by Rubens. Napoleon's troops (late 18th century) turned the church into a stable and carried off several Rubens paintings (returned from Paris much later). Church leaders redecorated with a hodgepodge of ecclesiastical art brought here from elsewhere.

One of these later additions, along the right side of the nave, is the Rococo **pulpit** (1713)—a riot of birds, foliage, and cupids symbolizing the spread of the faith and the word. All that amazing carving is supported by four figures: allegories of the four main continents, with Europe in front and Africa around back...pointedly in the dark.

• *Cross over to the left side of the nave, where a long, skinny chapel fills the left aisle.*

**Chapel:** Stand at its entrance (only those here to pray may enter) and look all the way to the far end to see a 16th-century devotional statue depicting the **"Madonna of Antwerp"**—one of many depictions of St. Mary you'll find inside her namesake church. Notice, in the ceiling above this chapel, some of the surviving decorations from pre-iconoclast times.

Along the wall on your left, look at the life-size **wood figures,** which were relocated here from a countryside church. There are two dozen figures in all, all mixed together: the 12 apostles, as well as 12 female figures that transition from vice to virtue, by way of confession and repentance. Try to figure out which vice or virtue is which, and notice how the woman ages as she evolves from bad to good—a poignant reminder that self-improvement is a lifelong journey, and time is limited.

• *Now walk up the left aisle (with the Madonna of Antwerp chapel on your left) until you reach the transept. Here you'll find two of the church's four paintings by hometown boy Peter Paul Rubens. The first one you reach—face to face, in the left transept—is the...*

**Raising of the Cross** (1610-1611): Biblical bodybuilders strain to upright the cross, which is heavy with the swooning body of Christ. The painting

## Peter Paul Rubens (1577-1640)

Born in Germany in 1577, Rubens at age 12 moved with his family to Antwerp, where he was apprenticed to a local painter. During

his twenties, he studied in Rome, where he picked up the Italian fad of painting giant compositions on huge canvases. He returned to Antwerp in 1608, married, and settled down, buying today's Rubens House in 1610. He would live and work there for the remainder of his life, churning out painting after painting.

Rubens' paintings run the gamut, from realistic portraits to lounging nudes, Greek myths to Catholic altarpieces, pious devotion to rough sex. Rubens painted anything that would raise your pulse: battles, miracles, hunts, rapes, and especially, fleshy "Rubenesque" women with dimples on all four cheeks. An expert of composition, Rubens could arrange a pig pile of many figures into a harmonious unit. Each painting was powered with an energy that people called his "fury of the brush."

Everything is on a larger-than-life scale in Rubens' work. Many canvases almost fill entire walls—you can see the seams

is emotive, sumptuous, and almost sensual. Rubens had just returned from eight years in Italy, and the influence is obvious—Michelangelo's twisting poses and bulky musculature and Caravaggio's light-dark contrast. Notice how lifelike Jesus' skin appears—a Rubens forte. The bold diagonal composition, thickly muscled bodies in motion, bright (almost garish) colors, and illusion of movement are vintage Rubens. The painting is the inner panel of

a hinged altarpiece; it was normally kept closed, and opened to reveal this scene only on special occasions—when its color and motion must have been even more striking to churchgoers unaccustomed to this sort of spectacle. Even the baby (lower left) looks up from the important work of breastfeeding to take it all in.

• *Cross over to the other side of the nave. In the right transept is Rubens'...*

**Descent from the Cross** (1612-1614): This diagonal composition—the mirror image of *Raising of the Cross*—is a freeze-frame of an action-packed moment...just as where the cloth pieces were stitched together—and approximately 2,500 canvases bear his name. How could he paint so many enormous canvases in one lifetime? He didn't. His house was an art factory, designed to mass-produce masterpieces. As was standard at the time, his assistants did much of the work: After he laid out a painting, his apprentices painted the background and filled in minor details. Rubens orchestrated the production from a balcony, and before a painting was carried out his tall, narrow door, he would put on the finishing touches, whipping each figure to life with a flick of his furious brush.

Rubens' fascination with plus-size models, and his skill at capturing their rippling folds of fat, are the reasons we now describe certain figures as "Rubenesque." The sweet faces and ample proportions of the damsels he painted were inspired by Hélène Fourment, 37 years Rubens' junior, whom the artist married after his first wife died.

Rubens distinguished himself as a smart businessman who knew how to provide wealthy benefactors with exactly what they wanted. In his long career, he was rich, famous, well traveled, and the friend of kings and princes. A true Renaissance Man in the Baroque Age, Rubens was even an accomplished diplomat—he helped to negotiate peace between England and Spain (and was knighted by the kings of both countries in appreciation).

workers strained to erect the cross with Christ's limp body, now they struggle to lower him from it. But at this somber moment, everyone seems to be moving more slowly, methodically. Notice the pallor of Christ's dead skin—a strong contrast to the lifelike luster of the other painting. The details make the poignancy of this moment come to life: the man in the top-right corner who's holding on to the shroud with his teeth; Mary's outstretched arm, in a tender matronly effort to comfort her son even in death; and, in the lower-right section, a blood-filled bronze basin holding the crown of thorns and the nails. This main canvas is flanked by side panels showing people "carrying" Christ in two very different ways: on the left, a pregnant Mary, and on the right, presenting the Baby Jesus at the temple. You may see Japanese tourists admiring this painting, as it figured into a novel that's popular in Japan.

• *To continue the story through the eyes of Rubens, proceed farther up the right aisle, next to* Descent from the Cross *(with the altar and choir area on your left). Enter the second chapel on the right side. Look right to see—on the back wall of the chapel—Rubens'*...

**Resurrection** (1611-1612): A radiant Christ strides vigorously out of the tomb, offering hope of revival to the deceased. Rubens painted this for some prominent Antwerpenaars buried here. Note the names on the plaque: Plantin and Moretus, of the well-known printer families (whose names also adorn the city's best history museum).

• *Back in the ambulatory, head a few steps farther toward the back of the church, then go up the stairs on your left into the elevated choir/altar area. Here we find Rubens' final chapter.*

*The Assumption* (1626): Rubens captures the moment that Mary—the cathedral's namesake, in a position of honor over the altar—was brought up to heaven. Beneath Mary are the 12 apostles (after the Resurrection, the faithful disciple Matthias replaced Judas) and the three women who were present at her death. The role of Mary in church doctrine was one of the major dividing lines between Catholics and Protestants; whereas the Catholic Church considered her a saint to be venerated, the Protestants embraced the notion that she was an ordinary woman called to do God's work. The gauzy heroine-worship of this canvas makes it clear who finally controlled the turf here.

• *Head back the way you came.*

**More Sights in the Church:** You can cross over to the **sacristy** (with historic portraits of the church's 21 local bishops, plus a modest café and WCs for customers); nearby, you can descend to the **crypt** to see foundations of earlier structures, as well as five old tombs painted with red crosses, uncovered during excavation.

On your way out of the church, pause in the middle of the transept and gaze up to the **painted dome** of the cupola high above the center (which looks domed yet is flat) for one last image of the saint to whom the church is dedicated...Mary.

Finally, as you exit the church toward the shop, you can't miss the glittering *Man Who Bears the Cross* (2015), which ponders that challenge of balancing one's faith in a complicated, modern, increasingly secular world.

## Musical Instruments Museum at the Old Butchers Hall (Museum Vleeshuis)

This restored brick palace, home to Antwerp's butchers during the city's glory days, now houses a collection of musical instruments. The Klank van de Stad ("Sound of the City") exhibition presents two floors of instruments and old music manuscripts (don't miss the cellar). The collection is decent and well presented. You'll stroll from medieval bagpipes, hurdy-gurdies, drums, and sackbuts, to church bells and carillons, to weird early versions of modern instruments, to some classic harpsichords, pianos, and even a "glass organ." The downstairs shows how music fit in with dance and theater. English information is limited, but a free app brings the exhibits to life. Even without a ticket, you can step into the (free) entry area for a peek at the impressive brick vaults (or to use the WC).

**Cost and Hours:** €8, Thu-Sun 10:00-17:00, closed Mon-Wed, Vleeshouwersstraat 38, +32 3 292 6100, www.museumvleeshuis. be. To get here from the Grote Markt, face the City Hall and turn right up Braderijstraat, take the first left on Kuipersstraat, then look right.

## DIVA (Diamond and Silver Museum)

Antwerp has long been a center of the diamond trade—and over the years, a variety of exhibits and museums have attempted to tell that story. The latest iteration, called DIVA, opened to much fanfare in 2018 before closing for further renovations; it may reopen in time for your visit. DIVA's high-tech experience showcases both a diamond and silver collection (including examples of some exquisite and over-the-top jewelry) with demonstrations of diamond cutting and silversmithing. If it's not open, they may have a temporary "pop-up" exhibit nearby. Ask locally or check the website for current offerings.

**Cost and Hours:** Likely €12, Thu-Tue 10:00-18:00, closed Wed, Suikerrui 17, +32 3 360 5253, www.divaantwerp.be.

## ▲Snijders-Rockox House Museum (Snijders&Rockoxhuis)

Nicolaas Rockox (1560-1640) was a mayor of Antwerp and a friend of Peter Paul Rubens. His neighbor was Frans Snijders, a painter of still lifes and also a friend of Rubens. Today their adjoining houses—buried amid a residential zone a 10-minute walk northeast of the cathedral and Grote Markt—have been transformed into a lovely museum. Exploring here, it's amazing to think of the interplay of personalities and ideas in 17th-century Antwerp. You'll get a truly authentic look at aristocratic homes from the period (unlike the Rubens House, which was rebuilt), while viewing impressive artwork, furniture, and a beautiful garden courtyard. Exhibits draw from the men's vast personal art collections and include works by Rubens, Van Dyck, and Breughel.

**Cost and Hours:** €10, Tue-Sun 10:00-17:00, closed Mon, Keizerstraat 10, +32 3 201 9250, www.snijdersrockoxhuis.be.

**Visiting the Museum:** The paintings are not labeled or described; rather, you'll be given a tablet computer that you can point at any item to get more information. Here's a quick orientation to the collection to help you find your way.

Most of the works are in the Rockox house. But first you'll cross next door into the Snijders house, to begin in...

**Room 1:** This hall displays some large-scale still lifes, includ-

ANTWERP

ing one of an impressive hanging dead deer. This is the work of Frans Snijders, noted for his realistic animals. You'll also find biographical sketches of the two men who gave this museum its name. Head back through the ticket area and go up a few stairs into...

**Room 2:** You're introduced to the world of Antwerp in the 1600s by several portraits. Over the fireplace, Rockox is shown from the ruff-collar up. Nearby, a portrait by Rubens shows two more ruff-wearers: Albert and Isabella, the Habsburg (Spanish) rulers of the Low Countries. The portrait of Antwerp's bishop is by Anthony van Dyck.

**Room 3:** Appreciate Rockox's fine fireplace and beautiful art cabinets, where he kept his collection of curios. He would bring these objects out at dinner parties as conversation pieces. Van Dyck's *Study of a Man's Head* demonstrates the artist's skill in bringing ordinary people to life.

Pass through **Room 4,** then cross the courtyard to...

**Room 5:** Spend some time with Pieter Brueghel the Younger's fun *The Proverbs.* This is one of 20 copies he made of his father's famous work. The painting makes literal more than a hundred Flemish sayings and figures of speech. There's your basic "banging your head against a wall" (lower left). Find other well-known proverbs: "the die is cast" (in the window, upper left), "don't cry over spilled porridge" (lower right), "the blind leading the blind" (upper right), and "casting pearls (roses) before swine" (lower middle). Some scenes have multiple meanings; one in the lower left is a three-fer, with "armed to the teeth," "bell the cat," and "not a cat to handle without gloves." Others don't make literal sense, but you get the drift: "He's so rich he tiles his roof with tarts" (upper left) or "He's so poor he's stretched between two bread loaves" (lower right). And many more make no literal sense at all, like the unfaithful wife (lower middle) who cuckolds her husband by "putting on the blue cloak." And, "Who knows why the geese go barefoot?" To learn more, use the touchscreen.

**Room 6** has an old rifle and a *Last Judgment* altarpiece commissioned by Rockox: That's the nobleman himself, praying in the left panel; and in the right panel, his wife, Catherine, and her 10 daughters.

**Room 7** has a small but insightful portrait by Rubens of an old woman, and **Room 8** is the former kitchen.

Finally, go **upstairs** (Rooms 9-10, in the neighboring Snijders house) for a look at the music room and a collection of period instruments. Here Rockox, Snijders, Rubens, and Van Dyck might have gathered to enjoy good music and the fruits of the golden age.

### ▲▲Rubens House (Rubenshuis)

This museum is closed through at least 2027 for an extensive renovation; some small exhibits may open in the meantime, likely in 2024. When open, the museum offers Europe's best look at the artist Peter Paul Rubens. By touring the house he lived and worked in (more a replica than "authentic"), you get a sense of both the man and his art. For updates on the renovation project, see www. rubenshuis.be.

## AT THE OLD DOCKYARDS, NORTH OF DOWNTOWN

The dockyards—an easy 15-minute walk north from the Grote Markt—have been boldly redeveloped and now house a pair of fine museums: the Museum aan de Stroom (MAS) and the Red Star Line Museum. For the most interesting approach here, through Antwerp's red light district, see Part 3 of my Antwerp City Walk (earlier). Otherwise, from the train station, take Metro lines #9 or #15 (direction: Linkeroever or Regatta) to the Meir stop. Go above ground there and take tram #7 (direction: Eilandje); get off at MAS, which is the final stop. If you're short on time, the Red Star Line Museum is more worthwhile than the Museum aan de Stroom.

### ▲Museum aan de Stroom (MAS)

The Museum aan de Stroom (Museum on the River)—housed in a strikingly modern building—hosts an eclectic collection that's fitting for this global-crossroads city. In addition to exhibits on Antwerp, you'll also see pre-Columbian stone heads (world-class, but probably not what you came to Antwerp to see), African masks, Polynesian fertility statues, weapons, and an array of temporary exhibits. In this city of excellent museums, this collection is nothing special, but the building itself and its roof terrace—which are free to enter—make it worth the trip.

**Cost and Hours:** Building—free to enter and explore, Tue-Sun 9:30-24:00, off-season until 22:30, closed Mon; exhibits—€10, extra for temporary exhibits, open Tue-Sun 10:00-17:00, closed Mon; informative English booklets in most rooms; top-floor top-class restaurant (by reservation only), 15-minute walk north of Groenplaats at Hanzestedenplaats 1, +32 3 338 4400, www.mas. be.

**Visiting the Museum:** In the lobby, buy your ticket (if you want to enter the exhibits) and pick up information brochures, then ride the escalators up, up, up through 10 levels. The escalators and hallways often feature free exhibits such as poems celebrating Antwerp or photographs of the city's people and history.

The museum's **permanent exhibits** are on floors 4-8. Two

floors are dedicated to Antwerp (floors 5 and 6): In "Antwerp à la Carte" (floor 5), you learn the story of food in this busy port town; "Freight" (floor 6) displays models of the many kinds of ships that docked here and traces the evolution of the port through videos and photos. From there, the museum goes global. "Celebration!" (back down on floor 4) explores how rites of passage are observed around the world. "Life and Death" (floor 7) considers how world cultures wrestle with these big questions—from Egyptian mummies to a roomful of Buddhas to Catholic symbols. And finally, floor 8 is an excuse to show off the museum's exquisite collection of pre-Columbian artifacts.

Finish your visit by ascending to the **rooftop panorama** (floor 10). Find the soaring spire of the Cathedral of Our Lady. To the left of that is the unmistakable Farmers Tower skyscraper. To the right of the cathedral is the Scheldt River. And around you is the harbor—the huge cranes, barges, container ships, tugs, and vast warehouses. It stretches into the distance and is one of the busiest ports in the world.

**Nearby:** The low-lying, long building just in front of the MAS houses a small, free exhibit on the **Port of Antwerp,** where you can walk across a blown-up aerial view of the sprawling port area for a sense of its astonishing scale (Tue-Sun 9:30-17:30, closed Mon).

### ▲Red Star Line Museum

Is there anything more poignant than a person willing to sacrifice everything in pursuit of a better life? That's the story of hardscrabble Europeans heading off to dreamed-of opportunities in far-off America. This cutting-edge museum tells the story of the Red Star shipping line that brought European emigrants to the Americas from 1873 to 1935. The route passed through the port of Antwerp, and many emigrants were processed in the very hall where the exhibits now stand. The museum combines personal stories with high-tech presentation to detail the "other end" of the Ellis Island experience. This sight is rated ▲▲ for any North

Americans descended from European immigrants, and it is worth the 10- to 15-minute walk beyond the MAS.

**Cost and Hours:** €10, more for temporary exhibits, Tue-Sun 10:00-17:00, closed Mon, Montevideostraat 3, +32 3 298 2770, www.redstarline.be.

**Getting There:** From the MAS, cross the drawbridge and head up Nassaustraat, past the two-tone green skyscrapers. Just after those buildings, turn left down Montevideostraat. This part of Antwerp's docklands is still being redeveloped, so it's not easily accessible by public transportation.

**Background:** In the late 19th century, Europe was changing. The Industrial Revolution, the end of traditional peasant lifestyles, and a tremendous population boom led to political instability and economic turmoil. Across the Atlantic, the United States and Canada symbolized a hope for a better life. And during the great migration between 1873 and 1935, the Red Star shipping line brought some two million emigrants from Antwerp to New York City. This was the point of exit not only for Belgians but also for people from all over Europe—especially Germany and Eastern Europe—who rode in rickety trains all the way across the Continent to get here. (By the 1930s, many of the emigrants were Jews fleeing the Nazi regime in Germany.) The 10-day steamer journey transported cargo, luxury travelers, and "steerage-class" peasants alike. In these red-brick warehouses, emigrants underwent humiliating health exams and nervously waited while clerks processed their paperwork. (Because arriving passengers who were ill were immediately deported at the shipping line's expense, screening procedures were stringent.)

**Visiting the Museum:** Your visit is a one-way route: ground floor, upstairs, and then the elevator to the view terrace. The displays have good English information, and there's a free info booklet.

First up is a powerful exhibit—using wraparound video screens—that drives home the point that immigration is as common today as it was in the heyday of Ellis Island. Displays profile different kinds of immigrants through history—from the first humans who left Africa in 40,000 BC to Ellis Island to the migrant workers of today.

Next, you follow in the footsteps of individuals who passed through this very building to board ships for the prospect of a new start in the New World. A 10-minute video introduces you to some of the Red Star Line's passengers, and touchscreens let you zoom in on stories in the emigrants' own words (including Albert Einstein's). You'll see the (deceptively) glossy brochures that the shipping lines used to lure customers. A map of Europe demonstrates how far many immigrants had to travel by train even before stepping on the ship. And there are period photos of Antwerp—the last European city many of these soon-to-be-former-Europeans would ever see.

The next section details the invasive processing procedures for passengers before they were allowed on board: They were stripped of their baggage and clothes—which were disinfected—then required to shower and be inspected for lice and disease.

Upstairs, you'll learn about the actual voyage. With steam power replacing sails, the trip to America went from 40 days down to 10. You'll see models of various Red Star Line ships through the years. Some were floating cities of 2,500 passengers. You'll also see the harsh contrast between life in first class and the miserable world in steerage.

The museum culminates with the stirring moment when immigrants first saw the Statue of Liberty. The final room emphasizes that Antwerp today is a city not of emigrants but of immigrants—people from other countries flocking here to pursue their dreams.

Before leaving, you can ride the elevator (and avoid the seemingly endless stairs) up to the **panorama tower** for a glimpse at the last view many Europeans enjoyed of their home continent before leaving forever.

## SOUTH OF THE OLD TOWN

These museums line up south of the Grote Markt. The first two are a short and easy stroll away, in the fashion district of Sint-Andries. The third is farther south (a long walk or a quick tram or taxi ride) in the pretty, lively zone called 't Zuid. Both of these areas have great eateries, farther from the touristy zone around the Grote Markt. For suggestions, see "Eating in Antwerp," later.

### ▲▲Museum Plantin-Moretus

In the digital age, it's easy to forget how revolutionary printing books once was. Antwerp of the 1500s was a wide-open city, dis-

seminating ideas from its new-fangled presses. This museum is named for two influential Antwerp printers: Frenchman Christoffel Plantin, who began a printing business here in 1546; and his son-in-law Jan Moretus, who carried on the family business. (Eventually, they were the official court printer for the Spanish monarchs of the Low Countries.) This building was both the family's home and their workshop. It's a remarkably well-preserved look at 16th- and 17th-century aristocratic life, while also illustrating several aspects of Antwerp's golden age. You'll see early printing presses, the printer's historic workshop and house, old books, and art and memorabilia owned by the prominent printing family. Every Flemish kid comes here on a field trip to understand their enlightened heritage. If you love books, this place is worth ▲▲▲.

**Cost and Hours:** €12, includes audioguide, Tue-Sun 10:00-17:00, closed Mon, Vrijdagmarkt 22, +32 3 221 1450, www.museumplantinmoretus.be.

**Visiting the Museum:** There's a lot to see in this meandering maze of rooms. I'd suggest following my tour to hit the highlights, while using the excellent—and humorous—audioguide for the whole story. Allow at least one hour to appreciate the place. Though the building is large and sprawling, you follow an easy, one-way route. From the ticket desk, begin by heading to the base of the old stairs to enter the exhibit.

**Ground Floor:** This floor tries to re-create the house as it looked in the 16th and 17th centuries. Even the lighting is low to simulate a candlelit glow. Room 1 has tapestries on the walls; in Room 2, a large and elaborately decorated hall, find Rubens' portrait of Plantin (right of the fireplace). In Room 3, find portraits from nine generations of the family—each generation represented by a book in the display case.

Step into the courtyard, and—to the right—find Room 4, a reconstructed bookshop. On the wall is a list of books forbidden by the Catholic Church: The list was printed by, and includes books sold by, Christoffel Plantin. Continue through this wing to Room 6, which offers you a chance to handle paper similar to the type used when printing was young.

Back through the courtyard, Room 7 has a printing press and displays on how it worked—one man inking it up, another lowering a blank paper onto it, then rinsing and repeating every 20 seconds. If you're lucky, a volunteer will be running the press during your visit—ask if you can help. In the proofreaders' room (Room 9), you can imagine diligent editors huddled around the enormous, shared oak desk, debating the 17th-century equivalent of whether "email"

takes a hyphen. The publisher's private leather-bound office (Room 10) is classy and surprisingly small.

Finally, you reach the actual workshop. Neatly stacked in Room 13 are some 10 tons of lead letters, with racks of complete sets of fonts and different type sizes. In Room 14, you'll see several presses, type cases, and other printer's tools. At the far end stand some of the oldest printing presses in the world (c. 1600).

**Upstairs:** Exhibits here represent the impact Plantin's books had on the world, organized around the themes of language, science, society, and religion. Look for the vertical red labels by some of the books—these mark what curators feel are the top 10 books in the collection, such as the first Dutch dictionary and the world's first atlas.

At the end of the first wing, you'll go down a few stairs into smaller, darker, more lived-in-feeling rooms, including Plantin's bedroom...with a tiny bed (Room 24). Down yet a few more steps, the next wing includes fine drawing rooms (and some of the creakiest floors yet).

Finally, near the end of the loop, Room 31 displays religious works, including a (possible) Bible by the founder of modern printing, Johannes Gutenberg (c. 1460). You'll also see the best Bible that Plantin produced—a beautifully illustrated version from 1583; if you read Latin, it's still perfectly legible today.

Room 32 displays a polyglot Bible, with five languages on one page, printed by Christoffel Plantin. It took five years to compile the text in Latin, Greek, Hebrew, Chaldean (Aramaic), and Syriac. The result is a masterpiece in eight volumes: four for the Old Testament, one for the New Testament, and three of commentary—weighing a total of 106 pounds.

**Nearby:** The museum is on a charming square called Vrijdagmarkt, where there really is a "Friday market" (as well as some recommended restaurants).

## ModeMuseum (MoMu)

Antwerp is synonymous with fashion and design, and this newly renovated museum is perhaps the best place in this city to learn about those topics. The museum celebrates Belgian designers and owns an extensive collection of clothing, textiles, accessories, and historic tools and machines for textile production.

**Cost and Hours:** €12, Tue-Sun 10:00-18:00, closed Mon, Nationalestraat 28, +32 3 470 2770, www.momu.be.

## ▲Royal Museum of Fine Arts (Koninklijk Museum voor Schone Kunsten Antwerpen, or KMSKA)

Following a decade-long renovation, this grand and hulking museum reopened in fall 2022. Anchoring the 't Zuid neighborhood, it displays some of the finest works of art in this city of artists.

**Cost and Hours:** €20, Mon-Fri 10:00-17:00, Thu until 22:00, Sat-Sun 10:00-18:00, Leopold de Waelplaats 2, +32 3 224 7300, www.kmska.be.

**Visiting the Museum:** The collection is particularly strong in works by **Peter Paul Rubens**—the famously prolific Antwerpaar who generated some 10,000 works of art (including 2,500 paintings) throughout his career. If you didn't get your fill of Rubens in the Cathedral of Our Lady, this is a good opportunity to scratch that itch—especially with the Rubens House closed for renovation.

The museum has an extensive catalog of works by **James Ensor** (1860-1949), an Oostend-born Modernist who dabbled in a variety of styles ranging from Expressionism to Surrealism. He was among the founders of *Les XX* ("The Twenty")—Belgium's homegrown avant-garde movement. Ensor is best known for his paintings of colorful carnival masks, but he was equally happy painting slices of life featuring middle-class women *(The Oyster Eater)* or gauzy beach scenes.

The collection also features works by Quentin Matsys, who founded the Antwerp School of painters that eventually produced Rubens; Rubens' talented students Anthony van Dyck and Erasmus Quellinus the Younger; Jan van Eyck (*Saint Barbara*, a dreamy, unfinished drawing); Rogier van der Weyden (*Seven Sacraments* altarpiece); Hans Memling *(God the Father with Singing Angels)*; pointillist Théo van Rysselberghe; and Surrealist René Magritte. Non-Belgian artists are represented by the likes of Titian, Modigliani, and Rodin.

**Nearby:** The streets surrounding the museum are an enticing nightlife and dining zone; for recommendations, see listings later in this chapter.

## Sleeping in Antwerp

Because it's a commercial center and a major European port, Antwerp has an abundance of business-class hotels. On summer weekends, it's also a popular party town—so prices can go even higher. While I've listed a few options oriented to business travelers, most of my recommended lodgings are more homey establishments concentrated in the Old Town and the high-fashion Sint-Andries district. If you want to look elsewhere, consider 't Zuid, but avoid the somewhat seedy train station neighborhood.

**$$$$ Hotel Julien,** a chic boutique hotel, is Antwerp's most enticing splurge. Located in a renovated 16th-century building on a drab street just outside the Old Town, its 21 rooms are a perfectly executed combination of old and new. The public areas, with high ceilings and lots of unfinished wood, feel like an art gallery. If you want to pretend you're royalty—or a rock star—rent the "experience plus" suite (breakfast extra, air-con, elevator, spa in basement, Korte Nieuwstraat 24, +32 3 229 0600, www.hotel-julien.com, info@hotel-julien.com).

**$$$$ Hotel Rubens** is a solid choice for fresh, predictable, business-class comfort. Its 36 rooms are on a quiet street just a block

# Antwerp Hotels, Restaurants & Nightlife

200 Meters
200 Yards

Scheldt River

To
Red Star Line
Museum
SINT LAUREIKAAI
MAS

LITTLE ISLAND

MUSEUM AAN DE STROOM

TAVENIERKAAI

SINT-ALDEGONDISKAAI

VAN SCHOONBEKEPLEIN

BROUWERSTRAAT

BROUWERSVLIET          OUDE

BROUWERSVLIET          OUDE

SCHIPPERSSTR.          B #17, #30

VILLA TINTO

VERVERSRUI

FALCONPLEIN

Falconplein

RED LIGHT DISTRICT

KEISTR.

KLAPDORP

KAASBRUG

HUISAARDSTRAAT

19TH C. STEEL CANOPIES

JORDAENSKAAI

OUDE MANSTR.

GORTEKSTR.

NOSESTR.

SINT-PAULUSSTRAAT

Sint- #7
Paulusplaats

Veemarkt          ST. PAUL'S

MINDERBROEDERSRUI

CASTLE

VAN DIJKAAI

ZAKSTR.          6

ZIRKSTRAAT

OLD BUTCHERS HALL
(MUSICAL INSTRUMENTS MUSEUM)

KUIPERSTR.          OUDE

AMBTMANSTR.

BOAT TRIPS

Steenplein

ERNEST

B #30
10    OLD TOWN          2          WOLSTRAAT

ZILVER     BEURS

24          LAUNDRY          CHURCH OF CAROLUS BORROMEUS

DIVA DIAMOND MUSEUM          Grote Markt          19

CITY HALL          KAASRUI          KORTE KOEPOOKSTR.

Hendrikconsciencieplein

19TH C. STEEL CANOPIES          12

SUIKERRUI          7          5          14

HAARSTRAAT          Handschoenmarkt          25          1

PLANTINKAAI          GR. PIET          17          16          CATHEDRAL

P          HOOGSTRAAT          15          KORTE NIEUWSTR.

OUDE KOORNMARKT          13          HANDELS-BEURS

VLASMARKT          11          EIERMARKT

REYNDERSSTRAAT          RUBENS STATUE

STOOFSTRAAT          PELGRIMSTR.          Groenplaats          FARMERS TOWER

8          3          Groenplaats          SINT-KATELIJNEVEST

MUSEUM PLANTIN-MORETUS          LEEUWENSTR.          18          #9, 15          SCHOENMARKT          MEIRBRUG #7

Vrijdagmarkt          20          Meir

LAUNDRY          4          GEEF.

STEENHOUWERSVEST          23

MOMU (MODEMUSEUM)          LOMBARDENVEST

KROMME ELLEBOOGSTR.          MUNTSTRAAT          NATIONALESTRAAT          KAMMENSTRAAT          SCHRIJNWERKERSSTR.          HUIDEVETTERSSTRAAT

21

SINT-ANDRIES          Munthof

To T'Zuid District & Royal Museum of Fine Arts          SLEUTELSTRAAT          To          To
A-1 Motorway & Brussels

22          ST. ANTONIUS-          STR.          9          26

ANTWERP

## Accommodations

1. Hotel Julien
2. Hotel Rubens
3. Antwerp Business Suites
4. Aplace/Antwerp Boutique Flats
5. Hotel O Kathedral
6. CityStay Antwerp
7. Matelote Hotel
8. B&B Sablon
9. Pulcinella Youth Hostel

## Eateries

10. Restaurant de Bomma
11. Kartini
12. Maritime
13. Pasta-Hippo-Vino
14. Bia Mara, Meat Factory & Compagnie Belgie
15. Pelgrimstraat Eateries
16. Handschoenmarkt Eateries
17. Frituur No. 1
18. Billie's Bier Kafétaria
19. Hendrik Conscienceplein Eateries
20. Vrijdagmarkt Eateries
21. Maarten Lutherplein Eateries
22. Frituur Chips
23. Désiré de Lille

## Nightlife

24. Den Engel
25. De Muze Jazzcafé
26. To Kapitein Zeppos

ANTWERP

off Grote Market (air-con, elevator, Oude Beurs 29, +32 3 222 4848, www.hotelrubensantwerp.be, booking@hotelrubensantwerp.be).

**$$$ Antwerp Business Suites** has eight bright, classy, smartly appointed, neat-as-a-pin rooms above a business center and gallery just a few minutes' walk from the Grote Markt. While the rooms—equipped with good desks—are designed for businesspeople, they're also a comfortable option for tourists and a good value on weekends. Conscientious mother-and-daughter team Anny and Lindsey offer a personal touch (breakfast extra, air-con, elevator, Reynderstraat 30, +32 3 502 1000, www.abs-antwerp.be, info@abs-antwerp.be).

**$$$ Aplace/Antwerp Boutique Flats** offers two stylish suites and two apartments overlooking charming Vrijdagmarkt and the Museum Plantin-Moretus. Expertly decorated with a lifetime's worth of vintage finds, the spacious suites have a shared "coffee corner"; the apartments offer full-size kitchens (apartments require minimum 3-night stay, last-minute shorter stays sometimes possible, Vrijdagmarkt 1, +32 473 735 650, www.aplaceantwerp.be, sleep@aplace.be, knowledgeable Karin makes you feel at home).

**$$$ Hotel O Kathedral** is a modern boutique hotel with a hip lounge, a swanky wine bar, and 35 rooms on the small square facing the Cathedral of Our Lady. Superior rooms are plastered with oversized Rubens prints and have see-through showers (air-con, elevator, breakfast extra, Handschoenmarkt 3, +32 3 500 8950, www.hotelokathedral.com, info@hotelokathedral.com).

**$$ CityStay Antwerp,** a great value warmly and conscientiously run by Tobias, has seven tidy, well-appointed rooms on a quiet back street just behind the Butchers Hall, a short walk from Grote Markt (air-con, Burchtgracht 43, +32 472 525 297, www.citystay.be, tobias@citystay.be).

**$$ Matelote Hotel** ("Sailor") enjoys a central location on a characteristic street deep in the Old Town, just a few steps from... everything. Its 10 well-worn rooms overlook a quiet central courtyard, mix heavy old beams with modern flourishes, and offer some nice extras such as electric kettles and minifridges with free mineral water (air-con in some rooms, Haarstraat 11a, +32 3 201 8800, www.hotel-matelote.be, info@matelote.be).

**$$ B&B Sablon** rents three rooms above a café near the river. Two rooms have a private bath across the hall, and one has the bath en suite. While the rooms are a bit plain, host Gea offers a warm welcome and the location is handy (cash only, breakfast served in café, Zand 25, +32 468 104 917, http://sablon-bbb.hotelb3.com).

**¢ Pulcinella Youth Hostel** is Antwerp's most modern official hostel, with 162 beds. In addition to 4- to 6-bed dorms, it also has 21 doubles—offering privacy and bargain prices (fee for nonmembers, in the fashion district at Bogaardeplein 1, +32 3 234 0314, www.jeugdherbergen.be, antwerpen@vjh.be).

# Eating in Antwerp

In this trendy, youthful city, the range of options is as impressive as it is ever-changing. What's good one year is old news (or closed) the next. While I've tried to recommend some reliable standbys, the best strategy may be to browse appealing streets or squares and choose the menu and ambience that stand out.

## ON OR NEAR GROTE MARKT

On a balmy summer evening, a sea of outdoor tables—each one perfectly positioned to catch every last fleeting moment of sunshine—gives this zone a nearly Mediterranean vibe and attracts both tourists and locals. Many options here are Italian, Greek/Turkish, and French. At most places, you can choose your view, then overpay for forgettable food. I've selected a few well-established eateries that offer decent value for this high-rent location. Skip these places if you can't snag an outdoor table in nice weather—the interiors are nothing special. For less touristy, less expensive alternatives, see the later sections.

**$$$ Restaurant de Bomma,** as the name indicates, is like eating at Grandma's. The menu of rib-sticking Belgian classics (robust stews, potatoes, mayonnaise-heavy salads) is designed to be shared, family-style. They have a big terrace overlooking the riverfront road, with great views to the castle. And the sprawling interior is done up country-cutesy. The theme? Grandma, of course (daily 12:00-21:30, closed Mon off-season, Willem Ogierplaats 3, +32 3 773 32 01).

**$$$ Kartini,** an Indonesian restaurant named for a beloved women's rights activist, sits just a half-block above the most touristy stretch of Antwerp's most touristy eating zone, Oude Koornmarkt. Compared to the hubbub nearby, it feels sane and cozy, with two tight floors of indoor seating and a few outdoor tables. While Indonesian food is more associated with the Netherlands, this is an excellent place to sample a top-quality rijsttafel—a dizzying variety of small dishes—giving you the chance to taste the full range of Indonesian classics. The staff is helpful in explaining your options (reservations smart on weekends, Tue-Sun 17:30-22:00, closed Mon, Oude Koornmarkt 61, +32 3 226 4463, www.kartiniantwerp.be).

**$$$$ Maritime** fish restaurant, just down the street from the Grote Markt toward the river, is a fixture among locals for a seafood splurge. While the interior is dressy, the outside tables are plain (Fri-Tue 12:00-14:00 & 18:30-21:00, closed Wed-Thu, Suikerrui 4, +32 3 233 0758).

**$$$ Pasta-Hippo-Vino,** with a ridiculous name and what appears to be the most touristy location in town, has somehow cultivated a loyal following of Antwerpaars who appreciate its good-value Italian cuisine (daily 11:30-14:30 & 17:00-21:30, Oude Koornmarkt 32, +32 3 213 1686).

**On Grote Markt:** Two places are tucked back in a little corner facing City Hall on Grote Markt; they both have nondescript indoor and big-view outdoor seating: **$$ Bia Mara** is an outpost of the Brussels-based eatery, founded by an Irishman (the name means "Sea Food" in Irish Gaelic), serving a variety of sustainable fish-and-chips (Tue-Sun 12:30-14:30 & 18:00-20:30, Mon 18:00-20:30, Maalderijstraat 1, +32 3 707 2387). **$$$ Meat Factory** adds turf to the surf, focusing on beef; while the steaks are pricey, the good-quality burgers are an affordable choice (Mon-Fri 17:00-22:00, Sat-Sun from 12:00, Grote Markt 28, +32 460 977 510). The nearby waffle-and-ice-cream place, **Compagnie Belgie,** turns out good-quality but grossly overpriced desserts (closed Mon-Wed, Grote Markt 16).

**Pelgrimstraat:** There's not much else along Oude Koornmarkt worth getting excited about, but Pelgrimstraat—which branches off the wide main drag at the recommended Pasta-Hippo-Vino—has some more interesting choices. Head south on this street for a tempting variety of options ranging from tapas bars and rustic taverns to sushi, Thai, and South American restaurants.

**Handschoenmarkt:** This small, attractive Old World square, directly in front of the Cathedral of Our Lady's main entrance, has a variety of scenic options. Browsing here—and along **Blauwmoezelstraat,** which curls around the left side of the cathedral—can turn up some lovely outdoor dining options with characteristic ambience.

**Fries:** The handiest place to get a cone of *frieten*, or fries, **$ Frituur No. 1** offers the full array of fried, meaty gut-bombs and lots of sauces. While most of their business is takeaway, they also have ample seating (open long hours daily, Hoogstraat 1; for tips on Flemish fast food, see "Belgian Cuisine" in the Practicalities chapter).

## MORE CHARACTERISTIC SPOTS IN THE CENTER

If you're willing to stroll just a few minutes beyond the Grote Markt and cathedral, you'll find abundant options with lower prices, plenty of personality, and a more local clientele. Many of these are to the south, moving toward the Sint-Andries fashion zone.

**$$$ Billie's Bier Kafétaria** is a tiny gastropub popular with locals for its good food and even better beer (11 on tap, another 250 in bottles and cans). The small menu covers Flemish basics like pork cheeks, plus a few other hearty helpings such as chili. You might even meet Billie—who isn't the owner, but the dog (Mon and Wed-Fri 16:00-24:00, Sat-Sun from 14:00, closed Tue, Kammenstraat 12, +32 3 226 3183).

**Hendrik Conscienceplein:** This delightful, Italian-feeling cobbled square—dominated by a towering Baroque Jesuit church—sits just a five-minute walk behind the cathedral. Several restaurants have inviting outdoor seating here; it's worth a browse. Options include **$$$$ Bohm & Berkel,** a French-style brasserie with high prices but perhaps the best seating on the square (at #3; Wed-Sun 11:00-23:00, closed Mon-Tue); and, a few doors down, **$$ Simply Marie,** a café that, true to its name, turns out handmade soups, quiches, wraps, snacks, and cakes at a reasonable price (at #11; Tue-Sat 11:30-16:00, closed Sun-Mon).

**Vrijdagmarkt:** A short walk south of the Old Town core, "Friday Market Square" is just that; the other six days a week, it's simply a tidy, leafy, welcoming square with a nice variety of al fresco restaurants. This area is lively midday and quieter at night. Among the options are **$$$ In de Roscam,** an old-school pub (at #12; Wed-Mon 11:00-21:00, closed Tue), and **$$ Goodie Foodie,** an amiable brunch spot renowned for its American-style pancakes (Tue-Sun 10:00-16:00, closed Mon, Leeuwenstraat 23).

**Maarten Lutherplein:** This humble square, with the fine Munthof hedged park in its center, is less cutesy than some but feels more local because of it. Here you'll find a pair of good-quality, low-key eateries with lots of inviting outdoor tables (and less appealing, tight interiors). **$$$ Camino** turns out a variety of Asian small plates (Tue-Sat 12:00-15:00 & 18:00-21:00, closed Sun-Mon, Muntstraat 4), while **$$$ Pici** presents an enticing variety of fresh Italian pastas (daily 12:00-14:00 & 17:30-21:30 except dinner only Sat, Muntstraat 2).

**Interesting** *Frituur:* Of the many *frieten* places in Antwerp, **$ Frituur Chips** has a particularly loyal following. Its thoughtful owner takes pride in the caliber of his chips and sauces, and he sources quality local meat for his burgers. With a few basic tables out on the humble square on a quiet back street, it's a magnet for Antwerp's *frieten* pilgrims (Wed-Sun 17:00-22:00, closed Mon-Tue, Sint-Antoniusstraat 35).

**Top-Quality Waffles:** A short walk south of Groenplaats, **$$ Désiré de Lille** is the local favorite for waffles. If you want a Belgian waffle cooked to order or an old-fashioned decadent dessert, this historic waffle house is your best bet—it's been keeping people happy for a century (daily 12:00-18:00, Schrijnwerkersstraat 16, +32 3 233 6226).

## 'T ZUID

For a more authentic Antwerp experience, head south to 't Zuid. Literally "The South," this is Antwerp's top restaurant and night-life zone. Frequented mostly by urbanites, this is where you'll find many of the city's hot new restaurants. Options are scattered around a several-block area, with one or two tempting eateries on each block. It's about a 15-minute walk south of the Grote Markt (along entertaining Kloosterstraat, lined with antique and home-decor shops). Or, from Groenplaats, catch tram #4.

**Marnixplaats:** The confluence of eight streets facing a dramatic column dedicated to Neptune creates a circle of corner buildings made-to-order for al fresco drinking and dining. While many of these places are drinks-only (sometimes with light snacks), a few are suitable for a full meal. **$$$$ Fiskebar** is done up like a fish market (as its name implies) and lists a wide range of specialties on its chalkboard menu; it's worth reserving ahead (lunch daily from 12:00, dinner seatings at 18:00 and 20:30, at #12, +32 3 257 1357, www.fiskebar.be). **$$ Lucy Chang,** part of a small and upscale Belgian chain, serves up tasty Asian noodle and rice dishes (daily 12:00-23:00, at #17, +32 3 248 9560).

**Other Options in 't Zuid:** Find some well-regarded places on **Volkstraat,** including two interesting Vietnamese choices. **$$$$ BÚN** is upscale, pricey, and refined, with fixed-price meals (reservations recommended, closed Sun-Mon, at #43, www.bunantwerp.be); farther down and across the street, **$$$ Nuoc Mam** is more casual and affordable, and quite tasty (closed Tue, at #72G).

On the other side of the Royal Museum of Fine Arts, **$$$ Elsie's** offers a great opportunity to sample Ethiopian and Eritrean cuisine. While Antwerp has a large African emigre community, few restaurants are near the center—except this one. It features a few outdoor tables, cheery murals inside, and delicious home cooking (Fri-Tue 18:00-22:00, closed Wed-Thu, Verschansingstraat 59, +32 484 309 329).

# Shopping in Antwerp

As a capital of both fashion and avant-garde culture, Antwerp is a shopper's delight, with a seemingly endless array of creative little corner boutiques selling unique items, as well as outlets for big-name international designers. Serious fashionistas and window shoppers will both find Antwerp's quirky browsing culture one of the most delightful in Europe. Note that most shops open between 9:00 and 10:00 and close by the relatively early hour of 18:30.

**Shopping Streets:** Given the abundance of "pop-up" boutiques in town, it makes little sense to list specific shops; instead, I've focused on streets or neighborhoods worth a browse. As you explore, you'll discover that each street has its own personality and specialties.

**Schuttershofstraat** and **Hopland** are where you'll find famous-label international couture, while **Kammenstraat** is better for young, trendy, retro-hipster fashions.

I enjoy strolling the starburst of traffic-free streets that spin off from the leafy square along **Lombardenvest** (just south of the Farmers Tower). Each street has a different focus, such as shoe stores on Groendalstraat and clothing on Lombardenvest.

**Kloosterstraat,** which sticks closer to the river as it heads south from the Grote Markt area all the way to 't Zuid, focuses on home furnishings—from antiques to minimalist furniture to home decor and gadgets. You'll wish you had an unlimited budget to furnish an avant-garde Belgian flat.

A large upscale shopping center, **Stadsfeestzaal,** is on the boulevard called **the Meir,** between the train station and the Old Town. South of the Rubens House, streets like **Leopoldstraat, Sint-Jorispoort,** and **Mechelsesteenweg** are noted for antiques and home decor. Near the train station, the street called **De Keyserlei** is known for its jewelry and diamond stores.

**Fashion District:** Antwerp's status as a fashion mecca is a relatively recent development. In 1988, six students from the Royal Academy of Fine Arts' fashion department traveled to a London show, where they got a lot of attention. Because their Flemish names were challenging to pronounce, the English press simply dubbed them the "Antwerp Six." Each one opened a shop in **Sint-Andries,** which at the time was a very poor neighborhood. They

put this area on the map, other designers began to move in, and now it's one of Europe's top fashion zones. The academy is still up and running; it has a small enrollment and a strong focus on creativity (www.antwerp-fashion.be).

Sint-Andries is a few minutes' walk south of the Old Town along Nationalestraat. While it's a three-star destination for couture lovers, anybody would have fun window shopping here. In the shops along the streets of Sint-Andries, you'll find top-name international designers, funky hole-in-the-wall boutiques, vintage shops, jewelers, and more. The TI offers thoughtfully designed resources for people interested in delving into Antwerp's high fashion scene, including guided walks.

# Nightlife in Antwerp

**Old Town Spots:** After hours, Antwerp's touristy core (around the Grote Markt and cathedral) hums with activity. Find a café or bar with outdoor tables, order a drink, and people-watch. Below are some favorites; note that most of these serve little or no food—go for the ambience and entertainment, not for dinner.

**Den Engel,** an old-fashioned pub at the corner of the Grote Mark (near the City Hall), is an obvious choice but also a local fixture. The cozy interior oozes authentic charm and feels like it's been the family living room of Antwerpenaars for generations. Outside, it boasts my favorite view in Antwerp, of the dramatic cathedral tower rising behind a row of fine facades (a few bar snacks, long hours daily, Grote Markt 3, +32 3 233 1252). **Den Bengel,** next door, has equally good views but a lesser interior.

**De Muze Jazzcafé** is outrageously atmospheric, with happy drinkers filling antique wooden booths on three levels overlooking the bar. Most come for the live jazz (open long hours daily; free jazz usually Mon-Thu from 21:00 or Fri-Sat from 22:00, schedule at www.jazzcafedemuze.be; Melkmarkt 10, +32 3 226 0126).

**Billie's Bier Kafétaria,** recommended earlier under "Eating in Antwerp," is an ideal spot to sample Belgian brews (a short walk south of Grote Markt at Kammenstraat 12).

**Kapitein Zeppos,** a 10-minute walk from the central square, is a big and inviting beer hall with good basic food (mussels and salads) and a serious appreciation for beer. On hot days, the square is filled with tables. Late in the evening the beer hall is filled with locals (Vleminckveld 78).

**In 't Zuid:** A 15-minute walk or 5-minute bus or tram ride south of the Grote Markt, this area is the more local, somewhat younger alternative to the old core. Bars with outdoor tables cluster around two areas: Marnixplaats and in front of the art museum, at Leopold de Waelplaats (for details, see "Eating in Antwerp," earlier). Along this square, **Hopper** feels urbane and untouristy—like you're in on an insider's tip. The interior is stark but dignified, and they have live jazz a few times a week (open long hours daily, Leopold de Waelstraat 2, +32 3 248 4933, www.cafehopper.be).

# Antwerp Connections

**From Antwerp by Train to: Brussels** (3/hour, 40-50 minutes), **Ghent** (3/hour, 1 hour), **Bruges** (2/hour, 1.5 hours, half change in Ghent), **Ypres/Ieper** (hourly, 2.5 hours), **Amsterdam** (hourly by pricey Thalys, 1.75 hours; also hourly by slower IC train, 2.25 hours), Amsterdam's **Schiphol Airport** (hourly, 1 hour by Thalys, 2 hours by IC train), **Delft** (hourly, 1 hour, most change in Rotterdam), **Paris** (about hourly direct on Thalys, 2 hours; more possible with a transfer at Brussels Midi/Zuid/South to Thalys, 2.5 hours). For train information, see www.belgiantrain.be; see also the "Transportation" section in the Practicalities chapter.

# GHENT

# GHENT

*Gent • Gand*

Made terrifically wealthy by the textile trade, medieval Ghent was a powerhouse, once one of the biggest cities in Europe. Ghent erected grand churches and ornate guild houses to celebrate its resident industry. It was a gathering spot for VIPs and the birthplace of Holy Roman Emperor Charles V (known as Charles I in Spain), who would become one of the most powerful people in Europe. But like its rival Bruges, eventually Ghent's fortunes fell, leaving it with a well-preserved historic nucleus surrounded by a humdrum modern shell.

Ghent doesn't ooze with cobbles and charm, as Bruges does; this is a living place—home to one of Belgium's biggest universities and a vibrant student population. While it has plenty of canals and gables, Ghent also enjoys just the right amount of urban grittiness, with a welcome splash of creative hipster funkiness. It's also a browser's delight, with a wide range of characteristic little shops that aren't aimed squarely at the tourist crowds.

Explore the historic quarter, ponder the breathtaking Van Eyck altarpiece in the massive cathedral, tour an impressive art museum, stroll picturesque embankments, bask in finely decorated historic halls, and prowl the revitalized Patershol restaurant quarter. Ghent is the kind of town that you visit for a few hours—and find yourself wishing you had a few days.

## PLANNING YOUR TIME

Ghent, about halfway between Brussels and Bruges and a half-hour from either, is ideally located for day-tripping. It's easy to get the gist of the town in a few hours. Either toss your bag in a locker at Ghent's train station on your way between those two cities, or side-trip here from either one. With limited time, focus on the historical center: Follow my self-guided walk, tour the cathedral, and dip into a museum or two. With more time or a strong interest in art, also visit the art museums in Citadelpark, closer to the train station. Museums are closed either Mondays or Wednesdays (though the cathedral and other churches remain open). Note that the city's worthwhile Design Museum is closed for renovation until 2024.

Ghent also makes a handy home base for side-tripping to the other destinations in this book. See "Sleeping in Ghent," later, for ideas on where to stay.

### Blitz Tour of Ghent

Day-trippers to Ghent can use my Ghent City Walk to weave together the main sights in as little as three hours. From the train station, take tram #1 to Korenmarkt, where the walk begins. Stop along the way to visit whichever sights interest you: Climb the belfry, tour St. Bavo's with the Ghent Altarpiece, browse the House of Alijn Museum, and scramble up the ramparts of the Castle of the Counts. Tram #1, your ride back to the station, stops right in front of the castle.

# Orientation to Ghent

Although it's a mid-sized city (pop. 250,000), Ghent's historic core is appealingly compact—you can walk from one end to the other in about 15 minutes. The train station (with several museums nearby) is a 15-minute tram ride south of the  center. Its Flemish residents call the town Gent (gutturally: *h*ent), while its French name is Gand (sounds like "gone").

### TOURIST INFORMATION

Ghent's TI is in the Old Fish Market (Oude Vismijn) building next to the Castle of the Counts (daily 10:00-18:00, +32 9 266 5660, www.visitgent.be).

Busy sightseers might save a few euros with the **CityCard Gent,** but on a day-trip blitz with this book, it's probably not worth it (€38/48 hours, €44/72 hours, includes entrance to most major museums, a €10 discount on the Ghent Altarpiece, public transit, and the canal cruise).

GHENT

# Ghent

ZILVERHOF

Lieve Canal

PRINSENHOF

ABRAHAMSTRAAT

GEWAD

ST-MAGRIETSTR.

LANGE STEENESTRAAT

Langesteen-straat

VROUWE

ZEUG.

PLOTERS.

PATERSHOL

HARING.

BALLEN.

CORD.

KRAANLEI

HOUSE OF ALIJN

GELDMUNT

CASTLE OF THE COUNTS

Gravensteen #1 (to stn.)

Sint-Veerleplein

Leie River

LANGE

To Museum Dr. Guislain

Burgstraat #1

BURGSTRAAT

JAN BREYDELSTR.

OLD FISH MARKET

BUTCHERS HALL

Groenten-markt

HOOG-

DESIGN MUSEUM (CLOSED UNTIL 2024)

DRABSTR.

BROUWERSSTR.

RAMEN

POEL

KORENLEI

GRASLEI

CANAL CRUISES

DONKERSTEEG

ST.MICHAELSTR.

FORMER POST OFFICE

Korenmarkt

ST. NICHOLAS

OUDE HOUTLEI

ST. MICHAEL'S

ST. MICHAEL'S BRIDGE

CATALONIE-

MASON'S GUILD HOUSE

Korenmarkt #1 (from stn.)

Korenmarkt #1 (to stn.)

ST-NIKLAASSTR.

SCHUURKEN-STR.

ZWARTEZUSTERSTR.

JAKOBIJN.

VOLDERSTR.

ONDERBERGEN

AJUINLEI

Leie River

VELDSTRAAT

KORTE MEER

200 Meters

200 Yards

To Citadel Park Museums, Ghent City Museum & Train Station

GHENT

GHENT

## ARRIVAL IN GHENT

**By Train:** Ghent's main train station, Gent-Sint-Pieters, is about 1.5 miles south of the city center. A long-delayed renovation (currently slated to wrap up around 2024) has things in flux. If you need to store bags, the station has lockers—ask where they are. Or you can drop bags at the recommended De Draecke hostel, a few minutes' walk from the Castle of the Counts and its handy tram #1 stop (free storage; tips are appreciated).

On arrival at the train station, make your way to the main hall, and be sure to look up at the meticulously restored **frescoes** celebrating great Flemish cities and regions.

It's a dull 30-minute **walk** to the city center. Instead, take the **tram** (€2.50, about 15 minutes). It's easy to pay as you board the tram by tapping your contactless credit card on the white panel. You can also buy tickets in advance from the Lijnwinkel transportation office in the train station or at ticket machines at the tram stop (once on board, validate your ticket by tapping it against the yellow machine). If you're going to Antwerp and/or Bruges and will be using public transportation there as well, consider the 10-ride ticket for €17. It's good in all three cities (and anywhere else in Flanders), and you can share the ticket with others. There's also a €7.50 day pass. Both can be purchased at the Lijnwinkel office or at ticket machines, but not on board.

Find the stop for tram #1: It's out the front door and 100 yards to the left, under the big, blocky, modern building on stilts. Board tram #1 in the direction of Wondelgem/Evergem (departs about every 10 minutes, 15-minute ride). Get off at the Korenmarkt stop and continue a few steps straight ahead to Korenmarkt, where you can see most of the city's landmark towers (and where my Ghent City Walk begins). Figure about €10 for a **taxi** or **Uber** into town.

**By Car:** Exit the E-40 expressway at the Gent Centrum exit, then follow the *P-route* (parking route) to various pay garages in town; the most central include P1 (Vrijdagmarkt) and P5 (Kouter). There's also ample parking at the Gent-Sint-Pieters train station, with its easy tram connection into town.

## HELPFUL HINTS

**Market Day:** Sunday is the main market day in Ghent, with small markets filling squares around town: a flower market at Kouter, secondhand books along Ajuinlei, clothes and pets on Vrijdagmarkt, and more. There are also smaller markets on Fridays and Saturdays.

**Festivals:** Ghent is proud of its **Gentse Feesten** (Ghent Festivities), which last for 10 days and begin around the city holiday of July 21 (www.gentsefeesten.be). This open-air music festival features everything from jazz to techno in venues around

## Ghent at a Glance

▲▲**St. Bavo's Cathedral and Ghent Altarpiece** Main church housing treasures by Peter Paul Rubens and Jan van Eyck. **Hours:** Church open daily 8:30-17:30; altarpiece viewable Mon-Sat 10:00-17:00, Sun from 13:00. See page 289.

▲**Castle of the Counts** Restored fortress with typical castle ramparts, a dungeon, and good tower views. **Hours:** Daily 10:00-18:00. See page 299.

▲**Ghent Design Museum** Enjoyable display of Belgian design from the 17th to 21st centuries. Closed for renovation until 2024. See page 301.

▲**Fine Arts Museum** Accessible collection of Northern European art. **Hours:** Tue-Fri 9:30-17:30, Sat-Sun 10:00-18:00, closed Mon. See page 301.

▲**Ghent City Museum** High-tech museum tracing the city's history through multimedia exhibits and historic artifacts. **Hours:** Mon-Tue and Thu-Fri 9:00-17:00, Sat-Sun 10:00-18:00, closed Wed. See page 304.

town, and lots of boozing. Book hotels during this period well in advance. Other events include a jazz festival (the week before the big festival) and a film festival in mid-October.

**Laundry:** A handy, unstaffed coin-op **launderette** is in the heart of the Patershol restaurant neighborhood (daily 7:00-22:00, corner of Oudburg and Zwaanstraat—for location see the "Ghent Hotels and Restaurants" map later in this chapter, +32 473 977 173).

**Bike Rental:** The city's "bike embassy," **De Fietsambassade Gent,** rents bikes at various points around town, including at the train station and under the Stadshal next to the belfry downtown (+32 9 266 7700, www.fietsambassade.gent.be).

## Tours in Ghent

### Local Guide
Cheerful **Mieke Thienpont** is devoted to sharing her city's history and charm (€135/2 hours, €170/3 hours, €35/additional hour, +32 49 751 6528, miekethienpont@gmail.com).

### Walking Tours
**Ghent Guides** runs historic city walks and themed tours. You can book them for a private tour (€80/2 hours), or contact them to see

if you can join a group English tour for a reduced price (+32 9 233 0772, www.gentsegidsen.be, info@gentsegidsen.be).

▲**Canal Cruises**

Lazy little **tour boats,** jammed with tourists listening to a live guide's spiel in several languages, cruise Ghent's waterways. On a sunny day, this can be a fun way to get a mellow introduction to the city. You'll cruise up and down the main embankments—places you'll see on foot anyway—but the boats take you farther afield for a grand view of the Castle of the Counts; the former site of the palace where Charles V was born; and the stout, fortified, twin-turreted tower called Het Rabot. Several companies offer essentially the same tour for the same price; boats line up along the Korenlei or Graslei embankments—take your pick and hop on the one departing soonest (€9, about 45 minutes).

On weekends during the high season, a hop-on, hop-off **water tram** connects some of the major sights (€15/1 day, €20/2 days, covered by CityCard, April-Nov Sat-Sun 11:00-18:30, www.hoponhopoff.be).

# Ghent City Walk

The heart of Ghent still looks much like it did circa 1500, when this was one of Europe's greatest cities: bristling with skyscraping towers, rich with art, and thronged with upscale citizens.

This self-guided walk starts at the former harbor, where this city of clothmakers plugged in to the global economy. Next we pass by the towers for which the city became known. The grandest is the soaring steeple of St. Bavo's, home to the main art sight in town, Van Eyck's famous altarpiece. Then it's down main street (Hoogpoort) through the heart of town, where these shops make clear that this city of traders lives on. The last part of the walk winds along small lanes, making its way through the trendy residential district. We'll end with the fun-to-tour Castle of the Counts and several photogenic squares.

**Length of This Walk:** Allow 1.5 hours to traverse this mile-long walk, plus more time to go inside sights along the way. You can see it all in about three hours. With limited time, end the walk at the Castle of the Counts, then catch tram #1 back to the station.

## ❍ SELF-GUIDED WALK

• *Take tram #1 from the train station to Korenmarkt (for details, see "Arrival in Ghent," earlier). From the Korenmarkt tram stop, walk straight ahead, turn left at the gray church, and you'll soon reach the bustling square where our walk begins.*

**Ghent City Walk**

PATERSHOL

ZEUG. PLOTERS. TEMMERMAN CANDY RED FACADE ONS HUIS WAAISTR. GARENSTEEG BAUDELOSTRAAT

CASTLE OF THE COUNTS GELDMUNT HARING. CORDUWANIER HOUSE OF ALIJN MEERSEN BEAUTIFUL GABLES

BALLEN. KRAANLEI Leie River Vrijdag-markt

Gravensteen #1 Sint-Veerleplein OLD FISH MARKET LANGEMUNT ONDER ST. JACOB'S KAMMERSTR. SERPENT STR.

BUTCHERS HALL HOOGPOORT "GRAFFITI STREET" WERREGAREN PINK FLAMINGO'S PUB BELFORTSTR.

Groenten-markt WALK ENDS BAKERY, WAFFLE & MUSTARD SHOPS Public Garden NEDERPOLDER

CANAL CRUISES DONKERSTEEG Korenmarkt FORMER POST OFFICE ST. NICHOLAS CITY HALL BOTERMARKT CHOC. VAN HOOREBEKE BIEZEKAPEL.

Emile Braunplein STADSHAL DUTCH THEATER ST. BAVO'S

WALK BEGINS CATALONIE STR. BELFRY Sint-Baafsplein

MASON'S GUILD HOUSE Korenmarkt #1 (from stn.) Korenmarkt #1 (to stn.) LIMBURGSTR.

To Citadel Park Museums & Train Station

200 Meters
200 Yards

1. Korenmarkt Square
2. St. Michael's Bridge
3. Church of St. Nicholas
4. City Market Hall
5. Belfry
6. St. Bavo's Square
7. St. Bavo's Cathedral
8. Hoogpoort
9. Graffitistraatje
10. Vrijdagmarkt & Van Artevelde Statue
11. Patershol
12. Castle of the Counts
13. Groentenmarkt Square

GHENT

# ❶ Korenmarkt Square

You're at the center of historic Ghent. The square is enclosed by the big gray-stone church, a prickly medieval-looking facade, and several historic townhouses with classic gables. The scene captures the glory of Ghent in its heyday.

The city boomed in the Middle Ages, when the wool trade made it wealthy. By the 14th century, Ghent's population was around 65,000—positively massive in an age when most of Europe was rural farmland (north of the Alps, only Paris was larger). Two-thirds of the city's population were textile workers, making Ghent arguably Europe's first industrial city. Imagine Ghent at its peak around the year 1500, flush with guilders from weaving high-fashion cloth and shipping it around Europe. With its wealth, Ghent became a proud city of soaring towers. In fact, Ghent was so big that, unlike lesser cities in Belgium, it didn't have just one single "Great Market" (Grote Markt). It had many squares, each specializing in a different trade. For instance, this square, the "Grain Market," was where citizens flocked to buy food.

The big building with prickly steeples (opposite St. Nicholas) is the **former post office,** now transformed into a ritzy shopping complex. While it seems medieval, it's actually much newer—eclectic Neo-Gothic and Neo-Renaissance, completed in 1910. Ghent was thriving once again and used this retro style that captured the feel of its glory days. Over the entrance you'll see symbols glorifying Belgium, Flanders, Wallonia, and the Belgian Congo. In the window friezes you can find the coat of arms of all the Belgian provinces and major cities. The busts over the windows are leaders of all the nations who joined the International Postal Union—a big deal back when the global economy was laced together by letters and mailed documents. On the side of the building, you can find a bust of Florence Nightingale, the famed English nurse of the Victorian era.

• *Circle around the left side of the post office building, and out onto...*

## ❷ St. Michael's Bridge (Sint-Michielsbrug)

The city was founded at the confluence of two rivers: the Lys (Leie in Dutch) and the Scheldt (Schelde in Dutch, to the south of here). The waterway under your feet—now plied by tourist-laden boats—was the city's busy harbor. Lining the embankment are several ornately decorated guild houses—meeting halls for the town's boatmen, grain traders, and weighers.

This viewpoint offers Ghent's best 360-degree panorama. At one end of the canal, find the imposing tower of the

Castle of the Counts, rising above the Old Fish Market. That's where we'll end this tour.

Now turn 90 degrees right and look back down Cataloniëstraat. View the spires of Ghent's three main buildings: the rectangular tower of the Church of St. Nicholas, the belfry (with a dragon rather than a cross on top), and St. Bavo's Cathedral. We'll see all three, then circle around through town to the Castle of the Counts.

• *Return to the Korenmarkt and turn your attention to the big gray church.*

## ❸ Church of St. Nicholas (Sint-Niklaaskerk)

This stout church was built mostly during the 13th century, a boom time for Ghent. It's dedicated to St. Nicholas, the patron saint of sailors, so it was only natural that it became the favorite of the river traders who sold their goods on the Korenmarkt. The church is a textbook example of Scheldt Gothic style, which marks the transition from Romanesque to Dutch Gothic: bluish-gray stone, turrets, and a single tower in the center (rather than twin towers on the facade).

The church's exterior is a microcosm of Ghent's rise and fall. The bluish-gray limestone of its tower tells you it was built before 1400, when Ghent was rolling in wool money and could afford to float the valuable stone down the Scheldt River from the distant city of Tournai. The yellow sandstone of one of the portals along the right side dates this section to between 1400 and 1500, when the economy was slowing and builders quarried local stone. The red brick along the church's right wall was locally produced after 1500, when competition from Brussels and England, combined with a conservative guild leadership that was slow to adapt to changing markets, caused Ghent's economy to tank. (Proud Ghent natives gleefully point out that their rival, Bruges, is built mostly of brick—indicating that city's lowlier economic status in medieval times.)

**Cost and Hours:** Free, daily 10:00-16:00, on Cataloniëstraat at the corner of Korenmarkt, +32 9 234 2869.

**Visiting the Church:** Enter through the side door facing the tram stop. You can tell the church was built from the front to the back, as the stone transitions from the blue-gray limestone used first to the yellow sandstone used later.

While the building itself is Gothic, the decorations inside—like most in Ghent—are much newer. As this region was at the forefront of the Protestant Reformation in the 16th century, the interior of Ghent's churches suffered at the hands of the iconoclasts—Calvinist Protestants who stripped Catholic churches of all adornments to mark their difference with Catholic "idolatry" and wealth. The church interior was redecorated during the Counter-Reformation with the very Baroque altar of corkscrew columns (painted wood, not marble) and in the 19th century with an impressive organ. Iconoclasts destroyed essentially all the medieval glass in Ghent—the modern stained glass above represents the seven sacraments.

• *Exiting the church, look across the street and notice the statue-topped gable of the* **Masons' Guild House.** *This 15th-century facade was only revealed in 1976, when renovators discovered the old facade behind a brick wall. During the renovation, they added the six statues of twirling dancers.*

*Turn left and head down Cataloniëstraat (away from the river). Beyond St. Nicholas (across the plaza to your left) stands the big, wooden roof of the...*

## ❹ City Market Hall (Stadshal)

Just a few years ago, this space was an ugly parking lot. But city leaders decided to beautify and turn this prime real estate into a 21st-century social hub. Now there's a public square, partially sheltered by a modern twin-gabled timber roof meant to evoke the rooftops of medieval Ghent. While many residents embrace the new market hall, some hate it (especially as it obscures the view of City Hall) and have dubbed it the "Sheep Shed" and the "Hall of Shame." Take a moment to wander beneath the gables, where light filtering in through hundreds of slits scatters in ever-changing patterns. On the lower level is a café, free WCs, and a bicycle parking garage. You'll also see an original 17th-century bell from the adjacent belfry. Nearby cafés, wine bars, and (often) food trucks cater to office workers on their lunch breaks.

• *The next tall building is the...*

GHENT

## ❺ Belfry (Belfort)

This tower has stood here since the 14th century, built to house and protect the parchment record of Ghent's favored privileges,

granted to the city by the counts of Flanders in exchange for financial support. The Neo-Gothic spire (from the gargoyles up) was added when Ghent proudly hosted the World's Fair in 1913. The dragon at the top symbolizes not the devil (as was typical in the Middle Ages), but a protector who never sleeps as it watches over the city's rights. It was also a fire watchtower, represented by the four sentries positioned at the corners. The carillon in the tower often plays the Ghent town anthem at the top of the hour. The long building at the base of (and behind) the belfry is the **Cloth Hall,** which was important to this textile center.

**Cost and Hours:** €10, daily 10:00-18:00, last entry one hour before closing, Sint-Baafsplein, +32 9 233 3954, www.belfortgent.be.

**Visiting the Belfry:** You can ascend the belfry for a decent, if not stunning, view over town. It's just a couple of flights of stairs, then an elevator most of the way. The entrance is on the side facing the tram tracks: Buy your ticket in the shop below the staircase, then head up the stairs to enter. Ogle the gorgeous wall painting of old Ghent in the main hall, then explore the tower. For crowd-control reasons, they may ask you to take the elevator up to the top floor first, then walk down, stopping along the way to see various exhibits. Here's some of what you'll see:

Level 0 shows off models of the former spires that topped the tower (including an original dragon, from 1380).

Level 1 includes a bell museum with a film about how bells are cast.

Level 2 displays the giant bell called "Roland."

Level 3 contains a big rotating drum with pegs used to program short carillon melodies.

• *The square beyond the belfry is...*

## ❻ St. Bavo's Square (Sint-Baafsplein)

This square became a symbolic battleground between Belgium's Dutch-speaking and French-speaking factions during the 1800s and 1900s. Belgium

GHENT

was dominated by the French-speaking bourgeoisie, even though Dutch speakers were in the majority. So, when the ornate **Dutch Theater** (Koninklijke Nederlandse Schouwburg, or NT Gent) was built in 1899, it finally gave the town's Dutch speakers a place to perform plays of their own. By embracing Dutch as a language worthy of theater, the spunky Flemish were asserting their cultural legitimacy. The golden mosaic depicts Apollo returning to Mount Parnassus, much as the Flemish felt they were coming home to their ancestral language.

The **statue** in the middle of the square—of a muscular man and comely woman—also celebrates the resurrection of the Dutch language here. Notice the lion, a symbol of Flanders, on their flag. The relief on the base (facing the theater) depicts Jan Frans Willems, one of the founders of the Flemish revival.

By the way, it took a full century before Ghent's prestigious university was allowed to teach courses in Dutch, rather than in French and Latin. To protest the change, the French-speaking industrialist who owned the local electric company spitefully cut power to mourn, in his eyes, the university's rejection of enlightened thinking. For more on the Flemish-Walloon conflict, see the sidebar in the Belgian: Past & Present chapter.

To the left of the theater is **Chocolatier Van Hoorebeke,** a producer of fine pralines. To see the chocolate makers hard at work, look through the glass floor inside the shop.

• *At the end of the square is Ghent's top sight.*

## ❼ St. Bavo's Cathedral (Sint-Baafskathedraal)

Ghent's Gothic cathedral can claim plenty of history (Holy Roman Emperor Charles V was baptized here), and it has a beautifully carved pulpit and a Rubens altar painting. But the showstopper is the monumental *Adoration of the Mystic Lamb* altarpiece by Jan Van Eyck and his brother, Hubert. For details on visiting the cathedral and altarpiece, see the self-guided tour later, under "Sights in Ghent."

• *Facing the cathedral, turn left and head down the curving street called Biezekapelstraat. You'll pass the medieval turrets and arcades of the back of the Achtersikkel mansion—the former home of a powerful family of patricians, now restored to house a music academy (you may hear students rehearsing). Exiting this street, turn left on Nederpolder. You're now heading up the main street of medieval Ghent.*

GHENT

## ❽ Hoogpoort

This "High Gate" street connects Ghent's two rivers. As you walk, notice you're on a slight hill; Ghent was founded at a high point between the rivers, which people made ample use of for trade.

Crossing Belfortstraat, you'll see the giant, slightly run-down **City Hall** (Stadhuis) on your left. As Ghent in its heyday had

negotiated special privileges from the counts of Flanders, the City Hall was a prestigious symbol, serving as a monument to self-rule. Notice how it's been augmented over the years. The ornate Gothic core (along Hoogpoort) dates from the early 16th century. The blocky, black-and-gold-columned Neoclassical section (down Botermarkt) was added a century later, following the fashion of the time.

• *Continue along Hoogpoort, observing the many facets of this one building—Gothic statues, then banded columns. A few steps beyond the end of City Hall (across from the Novotel), find the narrow passageway on the right called Werregarenstraat. It's better known as...*

## ❾ Graffitistraatje

Once used to drain water away from this high ground, this passageway now has a different purpose and an apt nickname: "Graffiti

Lane." Walk down the lane, enjoying the artwork provided by the people of Ghent. This is a typically pragmatic Belgian solution to a social problem: Rather than outlawing graffiti entirely, the police have designated this one street to give would-be artists a legal, controlled outlet for their impulses.

Halfway down the lane, notice the beautiful fenced-in garden on your right. This restful, city-owned, picnic-perfect space is open to the public. (The entrance is farther ahead, at Onderstraat #22.)

• *Emerging from Graffitistraatje, turn right on Onderstraat—passing the green door where you can enter that pretty park—then take the next left, down narrow Serpentstraat. This street is lined with some fun boutiques and colorful secondhand stores (for details, see "Shopping in Ghent," later). At the end, turn left and you'll be in...*

## ❿ Vrijdagmarkt

This large square represents Ghent as a city of the common people, and several days a week, it hosts a market. While traditionally the big town market was on Friday (as the square's name—Vrijdag—indicates), these days the primary market day is Sunday, when six different locations around the old center are lively with antiques, secondhand books, and—on this square—chirping birds, among other things. Vrijdagmarkt also hosts a smaller market on Friday mornings and Saturday afternoons. But any day, it's a great place to pause for a beverage at one of the cafés ringing the spacious square.

The statue in the square depicts **Jakob van Artevelde,** a clever businessman who saved the day in the 14th century, when Ghent was caught between powerful France (which controlled the city) and England (which provided it with wool). Van Artevelde—not an aristocrat, but an ordinary citizen—boldly negotiated directly with the king to keep Ghent neutral in the conflict and keep the wool coming

in. Van Artevelde's memory was resurrected during the nationalism of the late 19th and early 20th centuries, as a symbol of the Flemish people of Ghent asserting their independence from the Francophones. Today he's still celebrated by the people of Ghent, who sometimes call their city "Artevelde-Stad."

Directly behind the Van Artevelde statue is **Baudelostraat,** a street worth a peek for some particularly beautiful gables dating to the early 20th century. It's also home to a fun antique mall (see "Shopping in Ghent," later).

Towering in a corner of the square is the eclectic **Ons Huis** ("House of the People," with the sign for *Bond Moyson*—a socialist health insurance); it's the headquarters for the region's socialist movement. Not surprisingly for a city with a long industrial heritage, Ghent is a hotbed of left-leaning politics and the birthplace of the original Belgian Labor Party. Above the door, notice the rooster—crowing to wake up the workers.

• *Exit the square down the narrow street just left of the workers' hall (Meerseniersstraat). In a block you reach a bridge. As you cross the bridge, notice the walkways that line the riverbank, allowing you a scenic and uncrowded stroll just above the water. Now, enter the district called...*

## ⓫ Patershol

Until recently a run-down and dangerous district, today this neighborhood is one of Ghent's trendiest. And though it's predominantly residential, Patershol is also a great place for restaurant-hunting (see "Eating in Ghent," later).

As you cross the bridge, you'll see two particularly fine (if well-worn) gabled **facades.** The red facade features panels with figures symbolizing the five senses: monkey = taste; eagle = sight; deer = hearing; dog = smell; and humans = touch (since we have no hair on our hands). The other building has panels demonstrating six virtuous acts (the seventh—burying the dead—was deemed too gruesome to depict, so it's symbolized by the urn on top). The ground floor of this building houses a favorite old-fashioned candy shop, **Temmerman,** with some unique Ghent treats (closed Sun-Tue). Wippers are toffee with a sugar coating, marshmallowy Lieve Vrouwkes are shaped like the Virgin Mary, and cone-shaped Cuberdons—the local favorite—are filled with raspberry syrup.

• *Turn left and walk along Kraanlei, passing the **House of Alijn** (with a tourable interior—see "Sights in Ghent," later). Continue along the pleasant canal, curving right with the road. You arrive at a square called Sint-Veerleplein, dominated by the imposing...*

## ⓬ Castle of the Counts (Gravensteen)

Built in 1180 by Philip of Alsace, this rough-stone fortress was designed not to protect the people of Ghent, but to intimidate the city's independence-minded citizens. It was modeled on the Krak des Chevaliers in Syria, which Phillip visited during the Second Crusade. At the time, it was outside the city walls. Today, you can tour the castle (see details under "Sights in Ghent," later).

This castle was inhabited only briefly; the counts of Flanders moved to what would later become the (more comfortable) pal-

ace of Holy Roman Emperor Charles V. In 1540, Charles V (who was born in Ghent but ruled from Spain) demanded a huge tribute. When the citizens refused, he came here personally to crush the rebellion. The leaders of Ghent had to pay the money, then beg forgiveness, on their knees, with nooses around their necks. Today, you'll see many allusions to the noose around town, in par-

**GHENT**

ticular the very popular beer called **'t Stropke**—"The Noose." The people of Ghent are often called "noose bearers" *(Stroppedragers)*.

Also on the square is the fancy, sculpture-adorned entrance to the **Old Fish Market** (Oude Vismijn), home of the TI and a sprawling brasserie with waterfront seating. Study the facade: That's Neptune on top; below him are Ghent's two rivers: the Scheldt (male) and the Lys (female). It's said that Ghent is the child of these two rivers. Notice how this fish market sits directly across the river from the meat market we saw earlier.

• *If you'd like to end this walk early, you could catch tram #1 to the train station from right in front of the Castle of the Counts (direction: Flanders Expo).*

*Otherwise, to continue to a particularly pleasant square, exit Sint-Veerleplein down Kleine Vismarkt street. Cross the bridge to one final stop.*

## ⓭ Groentenmarkt Square

As you cross the bridge to the Groentenmarkt ("Vegetable Market"), look for the long, medieval **Butchers Hall** (Groot Vleeshuis) to the right (closed Mon). The hall looks like it's seen better days, but it's worth a peek inside to see its impressive wooden vault (built entirely without nails, and clearly employing shipbuilders' expertise). For hygienic reasons, until the 19th century, this was the only place in town allowed to sell meat.  You'll see local cured ham hanging from the rafters. The shop inside sells specialty products from East Flanders.

Outside, the lean-to shacks once sold offal and sausages, giving the adjacent square its name: Pensmarkt ("Sausage market"). For a snack stop on the square, look for Belgian-fries purveyor **Frituur Filip.** Across the square from the Butchers Hall is a good traditional bakery (Himschoot); next to that, a café sells delicious takeaway waffles, and to the right of that is the **Tierenteyn Verlent mustard shop** (at #3, closed Sun). Made in the cellar, then pumped into a barrel in the back of the shop, the mustard is some of the horseradish-hottest you'll ever sample. They use no preservatives, so you'll need to refrigerate it—or use it for today's picnic.

• *Head to the far end of the Butchers Hall, then the building beyond it. The bridge here affords another good view of Ghent's canals. Near this bridge, various companies sell* **cruises** *along the canals of Ghent (see "Tours in Ghent," earlier). Or you can backtrack (turn right along the river) to the* **Castle of the Counts** *(with a handy tram #1 stop) or the*

*House of Alijn. Korenmarkt, where we started our tour, is just a block and a half away. In fact, most of what's worth seeing in Ghent is within a few steps of here. Enjoy.*

## Sights in Ghent

Most of Ghent's sights, including its top sight—the cathedral—cluster either in the historic city center (easily accessible on foot) or south of the core, near the train station.

### ST. BAVO'S CATHEDRAL AND GHENT ALTARPIECE

The main church of Ghent, St. Bavo's Cathedral (Sint-Baafska-thedraal) houses the greatest art treasure in the city (and perhaps the country—maybe tied with the *Manneken-Pis*): the exquisite Van Eyck *Adoration of the Mystic Lamb* altarpiece, widely known as the Ghent Altarpiece. Besides this great work of art, the church is also home to a soaring Gothic nave, an elaborately carved pulpit, an altar painting by Rubens depicting the town's patron saint (and the church's namesake), and more. A visit to the cathedral and altarpiece is worth ▲▲.

The fuss that the people of Ghent make over Van Eyck's altarpiece can feel out of proportion. But when you see it in person—meticulously restored and lovingly presented all by itself in a darkened chapel—you realize it's truly a world-class masterpiece. This is where modern oil painting was born. It's where invaders—from kings to conquerors to Nazis—have come to steal this potent symbol of civilization. It's where art pilgrims journey to admire the sensuous detail and provocative symbolism of a work that signals a medieval world awakening to the new age of the Renaissance.

**Cost and Hours:** Free to enter church; €12.50 to see original Ghent Altarpiece, choir, and Rubens painting; €16 to add augmented reality (AR) crypt visit; church open daily 8:30-17:30; altarpiece viewable Mon-Sat 10:00-17:00, Sun from 13:00; Sint-Baafsplein, +32 9 225 1626, www.sintbaafskathedraal.be.

**Buying Tickets and Crowd-Beating Tips:** Once inside the church, you can buy tickets and enter the paid area in the left transept (just left of the altar). The altarpiece zone can be unpleasantly crowded with long lines on weekends (Fri-Sun) and any day in summer (July-Aug). Try to visit on a weekday; if you must come at a busy time, prebook your ticket online for no extra charge.

**Crypt Visit:** While I was skeptical about the AR headset, I appreciated its additional context and information—it truly helps set the stage for seeing the amazing altarpiece. But you can have a completely satisfying altarpiece experience without the AR show.

To figure out if you want to add the crypt, read my "Augmented Reality in the Crypt" description (stop #7 on the tour below). There are two options (same price): The "40 Minute" version (includes 20-minute AR show) is enough for the casual visitor; the "60 Minute" version doubles the amount of content (some is interesting, but about half is pointless trivia).

**Length of This Tour:** A quick spin through the church interior takes about 20 minutes; the altarpiece deserves at least 30 minutes (longer if you opt for the AR show in the crypt).

## ➌ SELF-GUIDED TOUR
### The Church

• *Begin by standing in the square in front of the cathedral's main entrance.*

➊ **Exterior View:** Take in the cathedral's sheer bulk, with its jowl-stretching view up the 292-foot tower. The church was erected from about 1350 until 1559 on the site of earlier structures dating back to 942. It's named for St. Bavo (*Baaf* in Flemish), a Ghent-area nobleman who gave up his materialistic existence to help the poor and establish a monastery here. (The massive St. Bavo Church—or Grote Kerk—in Haarlem, in the Netherlands, is named for the same saint.)

• *Step inside and look down the...*

➋ **Nave:** Appreciate the sheer volume of this structure, with its spacious 100-foot-high ceiling, Gothic arches, and stained glass. Notice three telltale materials: red brick (the nave walls), yellow stone (the pillars, also the exterior tower), and—for the valuable area around the altar—the gray stone of the choir. As in the Church of St. Nicholas, all the interior decorations and stained glass date from the 19th century (following the iconoclasm of the 16th century, when much of the church's Gothic ornamentation was destroyed).

PATER
DAMIAAN

• *Head for the right aisle and follow it up to the front of the church. On your way, pause at the second chapel and look for a statue of...*

➌ **Pater Damiaan:** Father Damien (1840-1889) was a Flemish missionary who went to Hawaii to care for lepers, but after 16 years died of leprosy himself. Canonized in 2009, he's a rare

# St. Bavo's Cathedral

30 Meters
30 Yards

**ANNEX**

**WC**

**CRYPT**
(LOWER LEVEL)

**CHOIR**

**TICKET OFFICE**

**ALTAR**

**ENTRANCE TO ALTARPIECE AREA**

**N A V E**

**BOOK SHOP**

1 View of Exterior & Entrance
2 Nave
3 Statue of Pater Damiaan
4 Rococo Pulpit
5 Statue of St. Bavo
6 Ghent Altarpiece Ticket Desk & Entrance
7 Augmented Reality in the Crypt
8 RUBENS – St. Bavo Entering the Monastery of Ghent
9 VAN EYCK – Adoration of the Mystic Lamb
10 Replica of Van Eyck Altarpiece

saint with a connection to the US, and an important figure both to Belgians and to Hawaiians.

• *Take a few steps into the nave to admire the remarkable...*

❹ **Rococo Pulpit:** This elaborately carved pulpit was made in the 1740s from white stone and carved wood, with golden highlights. The scene represents the tree of life and the tree of knowledge. The Carrara marble statues just beneath the pulpit drive home a Counter-Reformation message: The woman with the sun on her bosom (representing the power of her faith) wakes up the winged old man on the left (representing time). It's time to wake up to the Catholic faith. The smug frat-boy angels at the bases of the staircases offer a lesson in appropriate worship. The angel on the left watches the pulpit intently, and the one on the right points up to the pulpit while glancing scoldingly to the back of the church: Hey, you in the back row—pay attention! Up above, notice the two hard-working cupids struggling to raise the cross. Finally, on the very top, notice the golden serpent. Follow its winding body to find the pudgy, winged baby (a sure sign of Rococo) prying the apple of sin from the snake's mouth.

• *Now walk up the middle of the nave as far as you can. In the distance, above the main altar, find the white statue backed by a golden sunburst.*

❺ **Statue of St. Bavo:** The beloved local saint is on his way to heaven. This seventh-century saint was once a wealthy and rambunctious young soldier but became a born-again Christian after the death of his wife. Bavo rejected his life of materialism and became a hermit-monk, living for a time in a hollow tree. He is also the patron saint of Haarlem, in the Netherlands.

## The Altarpiece Area

It's been free to visit everything you've seen until this point. The famous Ghent Altarpiece is treated as a separate sight within the church. When you pay to see the altarpiece, you also gain access to areas around the choir (behind the altar)—including a closer look at that statue of St. Bavo and a fine Rubens altar painting.

Find the ❻ **ticket desk and entrance** in the left transept and buy your altarpiece ticket, then proceed into the next zone of the church. On your right, stairs lead down to the crypt; if you're skipping the crypt, continue to stop #8.

### ❼ Augmented Reality in the Crypt

After descending into the crypt, you'll be given an augmented reality (AR) headset and quick instructions on how to use it. The headset lets you see the real world, while superimposing additional information on top of it (rather than replacing it entirely, as in virtual reality). You'll get used to it, but move slowly at first and watch your step.

The headset provides running commentary as it directs you to various points where illustrations and characters appear on the vaults and altars to tell you the story of the Ghent Altarpiece. You'll "meet" several of the big names behind this masterpiece, and learn about how this famous work has been stolen and returned, again and again.

Without the AR headset, the crypt is skippable: Romanesque foundations, tombs of bishops, and faint traces of 15th-century

GHENT

paintings that were whitewashed over by Calvinists, then redis-covered in the 1930s. One worthwhile sight down here, almost ig-nored by the commentary, are the clothed 19th-century replicas of Van Eyck's famous nude Adam and Eve paintings from the Ghent Altarpiece. It wasn't Adam and Eve's nakedness that was offen-sive—it was the unflinching realism of Adam's hairy legs, Eve's bulging stomach, and their spindly legs. They were just too differ-ent from the idealized nudes of the classical world.

• *Whether or not you toured the crypt, once you're inside the altarpiece paid zone, make your way up (by stairs or elevator) to floor 2. (Good WCs are on level -1.) You'll enter a small chapel. Before proceeding ahead, look right to notice...*

### ❽ Peter Paul Rubens: *St. Bavo Entering the Monastery of Ghent*

This work depicts the moment the bad-boy-turned-saint started on his righteous course. Bavo, in the red cloak, kneels before the abbot

to become a monk (Rubens portrayed himself as Bavo). The lower grouping shows Bavo's estate manager distribut-ing his master's belongings to the poor. He's watched, on the left, by Bavo's daughter and her servant. Rubens modeled them after his two wives—his older first wife (in the giant hat) and his much younger, more voluptuous second wife, Hélène Fourment, in the red dress. (The Flemish like to say, with a wink, "An old billy goat loves a young leaf.") For more about Rubens, see the sidebar on page 248.

Notice the complex composition. Above, Bavo and the bishop form a diagonal line along the staircase. Below, the women and poor people form another diagonal line, perfectly parallel. Keep this dynamic Baroque canvas (1624), pregnant with motion, in mind—it's quite the contrast with the very static composition of the medieval altarpiece we're about to see.

• *Proceed out of the chapel and into the ambulatory (the area that rings the outside of the choir). Turn left and head to the back of the church. There, in a big chapel, gorgeously lit and displayed in a giant glass case, is the...*

### ❾ Ghent Altarpiece: Van Eyck's *Adoration of the Mystic Lamb*

The highlight of the church (and of all Ghent, for art lovers) is Jan and Hubert van Eyck's *Adoration of the Mystic Lamb* (known as the Ghent Altarpiece, and as *"Lam Gods"* in Dutch). It's been called

**GHENT**

the most influential painting in art history, as it was the first masterpiece done in the new medium of oil, and the first to portray the unidealized realism of the everyday world.

Hubert van Eyck (c. 1385-1426) began the painting, but after his death, his better-known younger brother Jan (c. 1390-1441) picked up the brush and completed his vision. Finished in 1432, this altarpiece represents a monumental stride in Northern European art from medieval stiffness to Renaissance humanism. The first work signed by Jan van Eyck, it's also considered one of the first works of the Flemish Primitives, characterized by a precise dedication to detail (if imperfect mastery of perspective).

The work is monumental: 15 feet wide and 11 feet tall, composed of a dozen separate panels, depicting hundreds of figures, and weighing more than a ton. It challenges visitors with its complex symbolism, multitude of rich details, and sheer scale, but it rewards those willing to invest the time to take it all in. And thanks to a recently completed restoration on the lower panels, the colors glow. Notice the nose smudges on the glass case—from art lovers who just couldn't resist getting closer...closer...closer...to examine the details.

**Upper Panels:** The original panels will likely be absent through around 2026—undergoing a similar restoration at the Fine Arts Museum. But replica panels should be displayed in their place. Either way, here's what you'll see:

God—in a rich red robe and three-tiered crown—presides over the scene, raising his hand in a solemn blessing. He's flanked by Mary in her traditional blue and John the Baptist in a green robe over his ascetic camel-hair shirt. Though holy, these figures are obviously modeled on flesh-and-blood people with individualized traits, such as God's jug ears, John's scraggly hair, and Mary's parted lips as she reads along from her book. Ogle the incredible richness of the jewels they wear. The hem of God's robe has an inscription written in pearls, one of the numerous quotes woven into the altarpiece (for instance, "King of Kings" and "Behold the Lamb of God").

Serenading God from either side is a heavenly choir. Unlike earlier altarpieces, these musical angels don't play harps, but rather a 15th-century organ. They have no wings or halos, and each face is unique. Hymnals of the time indicated which face a singer should make when singing a particular note; today's experts can guess which notes the angels are singing from their expressions.

## Ghent Altarpiece

ADAM · ANGELIC CHOIR · MARY · GOD · JOHN THE BAPTIST · ANGELIC CHOIR · EVE

KNIGHTS & JUDGES — JUST JUDGES — SELF-PORTRAITS

ADORATION OF THE LAMB — POPES — LAMB OF CHRIST — MARTYRS — PROPHETS — ANGELS — 12 APOSTLES

PILGRIMS, HERMITS & ST. CHRISTOPHER — ST. CHRISTOPHER

The outermost panels, depicting Adam and Eve, are probably the first Renaissance-era nudes painted north of the Alps. Though Eve still has the big belly and high waistline typical of medieval Eves, Adam steps boldly forward. His toes break the plane of his niche, a revolutionary example of (still not quite perfect) Italian-inspired perspective. You can actually see each hair on Adam's legs. (And notice how Adam really does look a good bit like his creator, who, after all, made Adam in his own image...there's a definite family resemblance.)

**Lower Panels and the Adoration:** The main scene, play-ing out across five separate panels, depicts the adoration of the Lamb—that is, Jesus, the sacrificial victim who saved the world from sin. The symbolic ungulate poses proudly atop an altar in the middle of a green field. It's the end of days (as described in Revela-tion 14:1), and everyone has traveled to the New Jerusalem (the towers in the background) to worship the Lamb of God. Angels kneel around the altar; popes, cardinals, confessors, and abbots wave palm branches (upper left); a legion of female martyrs gathers (upper right); Old Testament prophets read from their books (lower left); the 12 apostles and Church fathers assemble (lower right); and assorted saints, pagan writers, and Jewish prophets put in an appearance before their savior.

The adoration party spills over into the side panels, as still more worshippers arrive. To the right are groups of pilgrims and hermits, led by the giant St. Christopher (in red). To the left are figures on horseback—knights and judges. Focus in on the bottom-left panel, called the *Just Judges*. It likely has self-portraits of Hubert and Jan van Eyck (the third and fourth figures in), but the painting you see is a copy—the original panel was stolen in 1934 (see the sidebar).

Throughout the lower Adoration panels, notice the diversity of the people assembled, wearing all different styles of clothing and headwear—from Asia, India, and the rest of the known world at the time.

Now return to the main panel of the Lamb. A dove (the Holy Spirit) hovers overhead, from which lasers of light stream out over the pristine, shadowless landscape. In the foreground, the Fountain of Life spews water into a jeweled trough.

The Lamb of Christ at the center of the work had special meaning here in Ghent, whose wool trade put it on the map. It's too bad that the animal itself—which scholars suspect was later retouched by a lesser artist—isn't particularly well-depicted. He looks more like a fully grown sheep...and is that an extra ear I see?

**Exterior Panels:** Historically, the wings of the hinged altarpiece were typically folded shut, revealing the simpler paintings on the outside panels (the dazzling altarpiece interior was opened for viewing only for feast days and worship). You can see these recently restored panels now by circling around the back side. The top panels depict the Annunciation, when an angel (on one panel) came to Mary (on the other) to tell her she would bear God's child. The angel's announcement—"Hail Mary, full of grace"—is written in Latin across the panel. Mary replies, "I am the servant of the Lord." Notice that Mary's words are upside-down—they're intended for God above. Through the windows

## Coveted, Looted, Stolen, Lost

It's a miracle the Ghent Altarpiece has survived for six centuries. It's been the victim of a half-dozen art thefts—perhaps the most stolen painting in existence—and the focus of several international scandals.

In 1566, Protestant iconoclasts stormed St. Bavo's, hell-bent on burning the altarpiece as a symbol of Catholic idolatry. Fortunately, the priests had hidden it safely away at the top of the cathedral tower. In 1794, Napoleon carried off the altarpiece's four central paintings as war trophies and displayed them in the Louvre (1794-1815). In 1821, the king of Prussia smuggled several panels to Germany. Those works were so prized by the world community that the Treaty of Versailles (which ended World War I) specifically ordered Germany to return the panels.

In 1934, someone broke into St. Bavo's and stole the *Just Judges* panel. The thief, possibly a Flemish currency banker, said in his last words that only he knew where the lost panel was.

In World War II, the Ghent Altarpiece got caught up in the battle between Hitler's gang of art looters and the Allies' Monuments Men, a team of art preservationists. Hitler coveted the work as a symbol of the supremacy of Teutonic art. The altar was on its way to safe storage at the Vatican when it had to be hastily squirreled away in the French Pyrenees. The Nazis discovered it and spirited it away to Neuschwanstein Castle in Bavaria, then stored it in an Austrian salt mine. At war's end, the Monuments Men tracked it down and returned it to its rightful home: St. Bavo's.

In 2008, some 20 Ghent police officers tore up 225 square feet of a parking garage looking for the missing *Just Judges* panel, following a tip from an amateur sleuth. As late as 2015, another tip drew public attention but was deemed not credible by the authorities.

Today we can enjoy the Ghent Altarpiece in all its restored glory...except for that one pesky piece, the lower left *Just Judges* panel. Nearly a century after it was stolen, the panel has yet to turn up. What you see here is a top-notch copy, and the theft remains Belgium's greatest unsolved art mystery.

of Mary's chamber, we get a glimpse of medieval Ghent. Below, kneeling in the lower panels, are the donors who commissioned the work—the mayor of Ghent and his wife. Accompanying them are two St. Johns—the Baptist and the Evangelist.

**A Final Look:** Before leaving, take a moment to review the entire altarpiece and consider what it all means. Scholars mull over the various symbols, the inscriptions, and the cast of saints. The keystone is clearly the venerated lamb at the center of the work. The animal is positioned on a vertical line that descends from God to dove to lamb to the fountain. So—in symbolic terms—God sent the Holy Spirit to Christ on earth who gave his life to bring the faithful the waters of eternal life. John the Baptist is prominently featured on the altarpiece because it was he who proclaimed the arrival of God on earth: *"Ecce Agnus...Behold the Lamb of God who takes away the sins of the world."* (At the time the altarpiece was built, the church was dedicated not to St. Bavo but to John the Baptist.)

But forget the theology and simply bask in the astonishing level of detail. The countryside scenes are decorated with dozens of different identifiable species of plants and flowers. The feathered wings of the angels around the lamb can be matched to a variety of actual birds (peacocks, pigeons, swallows). And in the jeweled amulet around the neck of the singing angel (in the scene next to Adam), you can see a faint reflection of the window that decorated the chapel where this altarpiece originally stood. All these lush details—faces, robes, jewels, plants, human flesh—reinforced a theological message that was new to Europe: The hand of God could be found in the beauty of everyday things.

*• From here, you'll exit the chapel to the left and continue circling around the ambulatory to the main nave of the church. In the second chapel on your left, you should see a* ❿ *Replica of the Van Eyck Altarpiece. This is handy in case the real altarpiece room is crowded. (And you'll often hear tour guides here, explaining the work, since they aren't allowed to do that in the main room.)*

*Finally, consider heading into the choir area to stand in front of the altar and get a closer look at the statue of St. Bavo that we saw from a distance earlier.*

*Now go in peace, feeling fortunate you've laid eyes on the Ghent Altarpiece...just in case it gets stolen once again.*

## OTHER SIGHTS IN THE HISTORIC CENTER

Besides the cathedral, there are several worthwhile sights in this area. Note that the **Church of St. Nicholas** and the **belfry** are covered earlier, in my Ghent City Walk.

### House of Alijn (Huis van Alijn)

This small museum re-creates scenes from Belgian daily life through the last few centuries. All in all, it's a mildly intriguing collection of bric-a-brac, from dishes, toys, cribs, and kitchen appliances, to a statue of a woman wiping a baby's bum.

**Cost and Hours:** €9; Mon-Tue and Thu-Fri 9:00-17:00, Sat-Sun 10:00-18:00, closed Wed; Kraanlei 65, +32 9 235 3800, www.huisvanalijn.be.

**Visiting the Museum:** The rooms guide you through a calendar year, showcasing customs, holidays, and rites-of-passage—some universal and some specific to Belgium. You'll see rooms devoted to birth, showing Belgian christening dresses and

the "pink box" of childcare products the government distributes to new mothers. One room features teenage memorabilia—cringe at the 1970s and 1980s fashions. The room on getting older explains how Belgians mourn after the death of a loved one.

You'll see 19th-century antiques like wooden toy soldiers and 20th-century antiques like rotary telephones and Atari consoles. There are few labels or descriptions, but the objects (and their time periods) speak for themselves. The tranquil courtyard of what used to be an almshouse (a refuge for poor elderly women) hosts a little café.

### ▲Castle of the Counts (Gravensteen)

Though it dates from 1180, this fortress has morphed over the centuries, and much of it is rebuilt and restored. While impres-

sive from the outside, it's mostly bare inside. Still, it's a fun opportunity to get a feel for the medieval world as you twist through towers and ramble over ramparts.

**Cost and Hours:** €12, includes audioguide, daily 10:00-18:00, +32 9 225 9306, Sint-Veerleplein, www.gravensteengent.be.

**Visiting the Castle:** Take advantage of the included audioguide, which attempts to inject a little levity into this very dry sight (available in English, it's narrated by well-known Belgian comedian Wouter Deprez).

Gravensteen has all the parts of a typical castle: courtyard and keep, throne room, chapel, 18-foot-deep dungeon, and ramparts. There are displays of authentic swords and suits of armor, along with a reconstructed guillotine that was last used in 1861. For fans of torture museums, this one has real instruments of "persuasion" (see sidebar), including an exhibit showing how waterboarding was

GHENT

# Castle of the Counts: A Torturer's Toolbox

In the Middle Ages, torture was used to extract confessions from heretics and criminals, and to punish the convicted prior to execution. Torturers had a huge toolkit with which to practice their art.

One device was the rack, designed to pull the victim's limbs apart. A prisoner's arms and legs were tied to opposite ends of the machine. Then the torturer turned the crank, expanding the rack and leaving the victim with dislocated joints, or even limbless.

Another nasty tool was a finger screw—a set of bars and screws that tightened to crush fingers and toes. Since finger screws were small and portable, they were a favorite of traveling medieval interrogators.

The iron maiden was a spike-filled cabinet, just tall enough to fit a standing human. It had small holes through which torturers inserted sharp objects to stab prisoners, sometimes killing them. A variant was the torture chair, entirely covered in spikes. Victims' wrists were tied to the arms of the chair, and weights were attached to their legs and feet. Sitting in the chair usually resulted in death from blood loss.

For public executions, prisoners would be stretched over a wheel, and the executioner would break their bones with an iron hammer, leaving them to die from shock and dehydration. For less serious crimes, prisoners received the gift of one swift and deadly blow to the neck.

Then there was waterboarding. In medieval times jailers poured water—and often bodily fluids—down prisoners' throats. To avoid drowning, "suspects" might drink the liquid, which resulted in a sort of intoxication and often death. The modern variation—practiced by the Japanese during World War II, the French in Algeria, and the CIA at Guantanamo Bay—could be described as "slow-motion drowning." Interrogators covered prisoners' faces with cloth or another thin material, then  poured water over their nose and mouth, triggering the gag reflex and a sensation of drowning.

Today, although 146 members of the United Nations have ratified an international convention outlawing torture, it remains rampant worldwide. Carl Jung's observation is still relevant: "The healthy man does not torture others—generally it is the tortured who turn into torturers."

practiced by the Inquisition centuries before the US resorted to it after 9/11. If you climb to the top of one of the towers (lots of claustrophobic stairs), you'll get good views—and the feeling that you're the ruler of your own castle.

### ▲Ghent Design Museum (Design Museum Gent)

This collection celebrating the Belgian knack for design is closed through late 2024 for an extensive renovation and expansion.

When open, it's enjoyable for everyone, but worth ▲▲▲ for those interested in 17th- to 21st-century decorative arts: furniture, glass, ceramics, and jewelry. Check the website for updates (Jan Breydelstraat 5, +32 9 267 9999, www. designmuseumgent.be).

## MUSEUMS NEAR THE TRAIN STATION

Several museums are closer to the train station than to the historical center, which makes them ideal to visit on your way in or out of Ghent. The Fine Arts Museum and the Stedelijk Contemporary Art Museum are located at Citadelpark, while the Ghent City Museum is a bit farther north of the station.

### ▲Fine Arts Museum (Museum voor Schone Kunsten)

This museum offers a good, representative look at Northern European art. It's one of the most user-friendly collections of Low Countries art you'll find in Belgium, with lesser-known yet fun works by artists such as Bosch, Rubens, Van Dyck, and Magritte—making it worth ▲▲ for art lovers. Note that the upper panels from the Ghent Altarpiece are being restored here until 2026; keep an eye out for the possibility of watching restorers at work.

**Cost and Hours:** €12, includes audioguide, Tue-Fri 9:30-17:30, Sat-Sun 10:00-18:00, closed Mon, in Citadelpark along Fernand Scribedreef street, +32 9 323 6700, www.mskgent.be.

**Getting to the Citadelpark Museums:** To reach Citadelpark and its museums from the train station (about a 10-minute walk), exit straight ahead to the modern sculpture in the middle of the plaza. Turn right and walk up the tree- and bike-lined Koningin Astridlaan about five minutes, then cross the road and enter Citadelpark. Walk straight ahead, then curl around the left side of the big, modern building at the center of the park; as you round the far side, the Neoclassical entrance to the Fine Arts Museum is across the small street, and the Stedelijk Contemporary Art Museum (with a large *S.M.A.K.* sign over the entrance) is on your right.

GHENT

**Visiting the Museum:** You'll enter into a large central hall used mainly for temporary exhibits. To the right (in numbered rooms) are older works, and to the left (in lettered rooms) are 19th- and 20th-century works and temporary exhibits. To take a counterclockwise, loosely chronological spin though the collection, turn right from the entrance, and watch for the pieces I've highlighted here. Several works are well-described by posted English plaques, and the included audioguide provides even more insight.

**Room 1:** In **Rogier Van der Weyden**'s *The Virgin of the Carnation* (1480), the Baby Jesus makes a benediction gesture with his little hand. This small painting was designed as a focal point for personal meditation.

**Room 2:** A jarring work by **Hieronymus Bosch,** *Christ Carrying the Cross* (c. 1510-1516) features a severe-looking Jesus sur-

rounded by grotesque faces. Typical of the Middle Ages, Bosch believed that evil was ugly—and all but three faces on this canvas (forming a diagonal, from lower left to upper right) are hideous. The serene woman to the left of Christ is Veronica, who has just wiped his face. In the upper right, with an ashen complexion, is the stoic good thief, flanked by a doctor and a taunting monk. Meanwhile, in the lower right, the orange-tinged unrepentant thief sneers back at his hecklers.

Nearby, Bosch's c. 1485-1495 portrait of **St. Jerome**—who was his personal patron saint ("Hieronymus")—shows the holy hermit having discarded his clothes. Just above his legs, notice the owl (representing evil) sinisterly eyeing a titmouse (good).

**Room 5:** In here you'll find **Peter Paul Rubens'** altar painting (c. 1635) depicting St. Francis of Assisi receiving the stigmata—the wounds of the crucified Christ—from a six-winged angel, whose own hands and feet are fastened to a cross. Francis' brother Leo stares in amazement from below. From here, enter Room 7, then turn right to find the next room.

**Room 6:** This room features **Pieter Brueghel the Younger**'s 1616 copy of his more famous father's much-loved *Peasant Wedding in a Barn*. The elder painter trained his kids to carry on the family business—and younger

Brueghel became a talented painter in his own right. In his *Village Lawyer* (1621), displayed to the right, we see the attorney behind a desk piled with papers, as peasants bring items to barter for his services. Go up the stairs in this room, enter Room 13, then turn right into the circular room.

**Room 14:** Rubens' student **Anthony van Dyck** depicts the mythological story of *Jupiter and Antiope* (c. 1620)—a horned-and-horny god about to inseminate a sleeping woman. This problematic theme is thoughtfully handled by the posted description, which notes that it can either be taken as dated and old-fashioned, or as "a reminder that misogyny is still alive and well."

From here, you can continue to explore this wing of older paintings. When you're ready for a fresh perspective, head back to the main entry hall, and this time, turn left into the modern (lettered) wing.

**Room B:** You'll find works by homegrown Belgian modernist **René Magritte**. His clever *Perspective II*—part of a larger series—wryly replaces the four subjects on Edouard Manet's famous *Balcony* painting with coffins. Nearby are similar surrealist works by **Paul Delvaux**. A Belgian artist who studied, worked, and taught in Brussels, Delvaux became famous for his surrealistic paintings of nude women, often wandering through weirdly lit landscapes. They cast long shadows, wandering bare breasted among classical ruins. Also in this room, look for works by **Frits Van der Berghe** (*The Singing Statue,* 1928), whose style is reminiscent of Max Ernst's Expressionism.

**Other Modern Works:** The museum takes the next few rooms to introduce you to some lesser-known Belgian representatives of various modern styles. **Room C** features Belgian abstract artists Jules Schmalzigaug, Georges Vantongerloo, Pierre-Louis Flouquet, and Jozef Peeters. **Room D** displays works from Sélection, which was the name both of a gallery and a magazine that celebrated Belgian representatives of the avant-garde styles of the early decades of the 20th century. Survey the works by Gustave De Smet, Frits Van der Berghe (again), Constant Permeke, and others—and judge for yourself whether they succeeded.

**Room H** features Expressionism and re-establishes the international context: Find the *Portrait of Physician Ludwig Adler* by Viennese Secessionist painter Oskar Kokoschka. The artist uses dynamic, expressionistic brushstrokes to capture the personality, rather than a precise reproduction, of his subject. See also the works by Kokoschka's contemporaries, Ernst Ludwig Kirchner and Erich Heckel, who went in their own directions but kept the same general aesthetic.

And there's much more to see, including Belgium's answer to the Impressionists and Post-Impressionists (**Room P** has a substantial display of the pointillist works of Théo van Rysselberghe). Just explore and enjoy the opportunity to get to know some great Belgian artists who are largely unknown outside of their homeland.

### Stedelijk Contemporary Art Museum (Stedelijk Museum voor Actuele Kunst, a.k.a. SMAK)

This art gallery is constantly changing both the "permanent" collection and many temporary exhibits. Worth a visit only for art lovers, it's conveniently located just across the street from the Fine Arts Museum.

**Cost and Hours:** €12 (or more during special exhibits), Tue-Fri 9:30-17:30, Sat-Sun 10:00-18:00, closed Mon, +32 9 323 6001, www.smak.be. For directions on how to reach the museum, see "Getting to the Citadelpark Museums," earlier.

### ▲Ghent City Museum (Stadsmuseum Gent, a.k.a. STAM)

This cutting-edge museum, housed in a beautiful 14th-century Gothic abbey complex called Bijloke, explains the history of Ghent with all the bells and whistles you'd expect in this fashion-forward city. The permanent exhibit traces the city's history in high-tech treatments mixed with historic artifacts. Everything is explained in English.

**Cost and Hours:** €10; Mon-Tue and Thu-Fri 9:00-17:00, Sat-Sun 10:00-18:00, closed Wed, last entry one hour before closing; Godshuizenlaan 2, +32 9 267 1400, www.stamgent.be.

**Getting There:** From the train station, it's a 15- to 20-minute walk: Exit straight ahead, then angle left up the busy, tram-tracks-lined Koning Albertlaan. After the bridge, turn right on Godshuizenlaan. Or, from the station, you could ride tram #4 to the Veergrep stop, backtrack a long block to the first busy road, and turn right.

**Visiting the Museum:** Begin in the modern annex, where you'll buy your ticket on the ground floor, then head upstairs to the first floor. In the Ghent Today room, you can walk across a giant aerial photograph of the modern city sprawl and (in the middle) examine an elevated model of the old center. Then cross over to the old abbey complex, where you'll slowly circle the courtyard for a clockwise, chronological loop that traces the story of Ghent.

Besides viewing the excellent exhibits, you can peer down into the abbey church, nuns' dormitory, and refectory. Mixed between the six rooms of the main collection are some fascinating themed detours; for example, you'll learn about the theft of the still-missing *Just Judges* panel of the Ghent Altarpiece, housed in St. Bavo's Cathedral. Your visit ends with a walk through the old church building.

## OUTER GHENT

### Museum Dr. Guislain

Just west of the town center, this museum—set in Belgium's first mental hospital—traces the history of medical achievements in psychiatry. You'll see displays of instruments, research milestones, and art from the time mental illness was considered demonic possession up until contemporary treatments.

**Cost and Hours:** €10; Tue-Fri 9:00-17:00, Sat-Sun 13:00-17:00, closed Mon, last entry one hour before closing; Jozeph Guislainstraat 43, +32 9 398 6950, www.museumdrguislain.be.

**Getting There:** Take tram #1 (direction: Wondelgem/Evergem) to the Guislainstraat stop. Look for the Dr. Guislain Psychiatric Center (with decorative 19th-century brickwork), follow the cloister to the right, and then follow signs to the museum.

### Groot Begijnhof

Begijnhofs were homes for communities of lay women: places to live, pray, and serve society without taking religious vows. Unlike most Flemish cities with just one begijnhof, Ghent has three. Groot Begijnhof is the largest—and its Flemish Gothic Revival architecture differs greatly from the begijnhof in Bruges (described in the "Sights & Experiences in Bruges" chapter).

**Cost and Hours:** Free, daily 6:00-23:00, main office at Groot Begijnhof 67, +32 9 228 2308, www.grootbegijnhof.be.

**Getting There:** From Korenmarkt take bus #18 (direction: Merendree), get off at the Schoolstraat stop, turn right on Schoolstraat, and look for the arched gateway at the end of the next side street.

# Sleeping in Ghent

A convention town, Ghent is busiest in spring (April-June) and fall (Sept-mid-Dec); things are quieter (and prices lower) in early July (before the Ghent Festivities) and August, and even more so in the winter. These listings are near the town center, a 30-minute walk or a 15-minute tram ride from the train station; see "Arrival in Ghent," earlier, for details.

In addition to the places listed here, the TI's website (www.visitgent.be) lists dozens of options for B&Bs, which may offer a better value than a big hotel. For some travelers, Airbnb-type rentals can be another good alternative.

**$$$$ Pillows Grand Boutique Hotel Reylof** is the city's splurge, with 156 plush rooms and an elegant lobby. It's on a workaday street, a short walk west of the town center (air-con, elevator, Hoogstraat 36, +32 9 235 4070, www.pillowshotels.com/ghent, ghent@pillowshotels.com).

**$$$ Hotel Harmony** is a classy, four-star, family-run boutique hotel with 40 contemporary chic rooms ideally located on the embankment in the town center (air-con, elevator, heated outdoor pool in summer, Kraanlei 37, +32 9 324 2680, www.hotel-harmony. be, info@hotel-harmony.be).

**$$$ Monasterium PoortAckere,** a monastery until 1998, is now a no-frills hotel with rooms that still evoke the aura of monks, seminarians, and visiting clergy. The 104 rooms—spread across several buildings—are all different; some are fresh and modern, while others feel barely updated since the last monks checked out. Breakfast, served in the refectory, costs extra (air-con and elevator for some rooms, limited pay parking, Oude Houtlei 56, +32 9 269 2210, www.monasterium.be, info@monasterium.be).

**$$ Chambreplus** rents four rooms with modern design. The garden suite, which costs a little more, includes a private hot tub and fireplace. While the rooms are comfy, they're run as an afterthought to the ground-floor travel agency—you'll be largely on your own after checking in (no breakfast, two-night minimum for weekends, air-con, Hoogpoort 31, +32 9 226 3181, www. chambreplus.be; Kris, Indira, and Jeroen).

**$$ Erasmus Hotel,** capably run by Peter, has 12 well-maintained rooms around a creaky wooden staircase in a classic 400-year-old building a short walk from the embankment. A cluttered hallway gives access to a museum-like breakfast room and a delightful Renaissance garden. Staying here feels like visiting a charming time warp (no elevator, Poel 25, +32 9 224 2195, www. erasmushotel.be, info@erasmushotel.be).

**$$ Ibis Gent Centrum St-Baafs Kathedraal** offers affordable, cookie-cutter, chain-hotel comfort in 120 rooms right next to the cathedral (breakfast extra, elevator, Limburgstraat 2, +32 9 233 0000, www.ibishotel.com, h0961@accor.com).

**¢ De Draecke,** Ghent's very institutional hostel with a helpful staff, has 119 beds (including some in private rooms) in a charming residential zone a short walk from the castle (Sint-Widostraat 11, +32 9 233 7050, www.jeugdherbergen.be, gent@vjh.be).

# Eating in Ghent

My Ghent dining recommendations are within a 10- to 15-minute walk of the three spires downtown (Belfry, St. Bavo's, and St. Nicholas). For the nicer dinner places, reservations are always wise.

## FAST, AFFORDABLE, CENTRAL LUNCHES

If you're day-tripping (or just busy sightseeing and want a quick bite), these are good choices.

**$ Alice,** a tea room tucked on a side street near St. Michael's

Bridge, serves simple lunches, soups, and sandwiches in a delightful candy-box interior or in the garden (Tue-Sat 10:00-17:00, closed Sun-Mon, Onderbergen 6, +32 9 277 9235).

**$ Souplounge** is basic, but cheap and good. They offer four daily soups, along with salads. Eat inside or at the outdoor tables overlooking one of Ghent's most scenic stretches of canal (Tue-Sun 10:00-19:00, closed Mon, Zuivelbrugstraat 6, +32 9 223 6203).

**$ Tasty World** serves up decent veggie burgers with various toppings, plus a wide range of fresh fruit juices and salads (Mon-Sat 11:00-21:00, closed Sun, Hoogpoort 1, +32 9 225 7407).

**$$ Balls & Glory,** a small Belgian chain that got its start in Ghent, specializes in gigantic meatballs—four flavors per day are noted on the chalkboard menu. Get yours to go or pay a few euros more to eat in their hip dining room at shared stainless-steel tables or out on the sidewalk (Mon-Sat 11:30-21:00, closed Sun, Jakobijnenstraat 6, +32 486 678 776).

**$ Frituur Filip,** a fry shack attached to the Meat Hall on the Pensmarkt, serves *real* Belgian *frites* cooked twice in ox fat. Try them with Filip's homemade *stoofvleessaus*—the sauce skimmed off his Flemish stew (Thu-Tue 11:30-21:00, closed Wed).

**$ Frituur Tartaar,** facing the belfry, is another central standby that locals swear by for *frieten* and other deep-fried Belgian munchies (Wed-Thu 11:30-14:00 & 17:00-22:00, Fri-Sun 11:30-22:00, closed Mon-Tue, Emile Braunplein 12).

**Dessert:** At the popular **Damass** ice cream shop, you can hang out and people-watch or get a cone and stroll (at the north end of Korenmarkt, #2C, closed Tue).

**Grocery Stores:** You'll find a well-supplied **Albert Heijn** below the former post office on Korenmarkt (Mon-Sat until 20:00, Sun 9:00-11:45, Korenmarkt 16).

## ACROSS THE RIVER, IN PATERSHOL

This former sailors' quarter—a very short walk across the river from the historical center—is one of Ghent's most inviting neighborhoods for dining. Stroll the streets and simply drop in on any place that looks good. Peek into courtyards, many of which hide restaurant and café tables. It's hard to go wrong in Patershol, but here are some particularly well-regarded favorites:

**$$$ De Acht Zaligheden** ("The Eight Beatitudes") prides itself on its regional and seasonal dishes with an always-innovative presentation. Their fixed-price dinners are a good value (Wed-Sun 12:00-14:00 & 18:00-22:00, closed Mon-Tue, Oudburg 4, +32 9 224 3197).

**$$$ Mémé Gusta,** a few steps from the Castle of the Counts, has ramshackle-chic decor, a welcoming and easygoing vibe, and a tempting menu of Belgian classics. The owners were the winners of

GHENT

# Ghent Hotels & Restaurants

ZILVERHOF

Lieve Canal

ST-MAGRIETSTR.

LANGE STEENESTRAAT

PRINSENHOF

Langesteen-straat

VROUWE.

PLOTERS.

ZEUG.

PATERSHOL

GEWAD

ABRAHAMSTRAAT

**7**

HARING

GELDMUNT

BALLEN

CORD.

HOUSE OF ALIJN

**2**

CASTLE OF THE COUNTS

KRAANLEI

**17**

JAN BREYDELSTR.

Gravensteen #1 (to stn.)

Sint-Veerleplein

Leie River

LANGE.

To Museum Dr. Guislain

BURGSTRAAT

**27**

**16**

OLD FISH MARKET

**1**

**24**

Burgstraat #1

**28**

BUTCHERS HALL

**12**

Groenten-markt

**10**

**4**

BROUWERSSTR.

DESIGN MUSEUM (CLOSED UNTIL 2024)

DRABSTR.

**15**

HOOG.

RAMEN

**5**

POEL

CANAL CRUISES

**14**

BAKERY, WAFFLE & MUSTARD SHOPS

**1**

KORENLEI

GRASLEI

DONKERSTEEG

ST-MICHAELSTR.

OUDE HOUTLEI

FORMER POST OFFICE

Korenmarkt

ST. NICHOLAS

**25**

ST. MICHAEL'S

ST. MICHAEL'S BRIDGE

CATALONIE.

MASON'S GUILD HOUSE

**8**

**20**

Korenmarkt #1 (from stn.)

Korenmarkt #1 (to stn.)

ST-NIKLAASSTR.

**3**

SCHUURKEN-STR.

**11**

ZWARTEZUSTERSSTR.

JAKOBIJN.

VOLDERSTR.

ONDERBERGEN

AJUINLEI

Leie River

KORTE MEER

VELDSTRAAT

To Citadel Park Museums, Ghent City Museum, Train Station &

**31**

200 Meters

200 Yards

GHENT

## Accommodations

1. Pillows Grand Boutique Hotel Reylof
2. Hotel Harmony
3. Monastarium PoortAckere
4. Chambreplus
5. Erasmus Hotel
6. Ibis Gent Centrum St-Baafs Kathedraal
7. De Draecke Hostel

## Eateries & Nightlife

8. Alice
9. Souplounge
10. Tasty World
11. Balls & Glory
12. Frituur Filip
13. Frituur Tartaar
14. Damass Ice Cream
15. De Acht Zaligheden
16. Mémé Gusta
17. Het Moment
18. Valentijn
19. Oudburg St. Eateries
20. Pakhuis
21. Jus
22. To Walpoortstraat Eateries & Shops
23. De Dulle Griet
24. 't Dreupelkot

## Shopping & Services

25. Grocery
26. Serpentstraat
27. Burgstraat
28. Jan Breydelstraat
29. Antiek-Depot
30. Launderette
31. Bike Rental (2)

GHENT

a reality TV show *(My Popup Restaurant)*, giving the place a certain celebrity cachet among Belgians (Tue and Thu-Sat 12:00-14:00 & 18:00-22:00, Wed 18:00-22:00, closed Sun-Mon, Burgstraat 19, +32 9 398 23 93).

**$ Het Moment,** across the street from Mémé Gusta, is a trendy, classy coffee shop with a few outdoor tables and a refined drawing-room interior; they serve quiches and soups for a light lunch (closed Thu, Burgstraat 20, +32 476 42 14 57).

**$$$$ Valentijn,** in the heart of Patershol, has a romantic, dressy interior and a no-fuss menu of classics. On Saturday, they serve only a four-course fixed-price dinner (Mon-Wed and Fri-Sat from 18:30, closed Thu, Sun open for lunch only, reservations recommended, Rodekoningstraat 1, +32 9 225 0429, www. restaurantvalentijn.be).

**Oudburg Street:** This street is worth a stroll, at lunch or dinner, to survey a wide range of options. Every other address seems to be a sushi restaurant, but you'll also find Indian, Portuguese, Turkish (Ankara at #44 is good), Naples-style pizza, vegetarian, traditional Belgian (Aba-Jour, at #20), even a tiki bar. A few of the places on the right side of the street have seating along the canal. De Acht Zaligheden and Valentijn, both recommended above, are also at the start of this street.

## SOUTH OF THE CATHEDRAL

The areas described above are cute, cobbled, fairytale Ghent—and on a short visit, it makes sense to focus your time there. But if you'd like to get into a more workaday part of town—with some interesting, contemporary-feeling eateries—head south from St. Bavo's.

**$$$ Pakhuis** is a gorgeously restored, late-19th-century warehouse now filled with a classy, lively brasserie and bar. In this airy, two-story, glassed-in birdhouse of a restaurant, they serve up good traditional Belgian food with an emphasis on locally sourced and organic ingredients. It's tucked down a nondescript brick alley a few steps off the river, but worth a slight detour (good lunch deals, fixed-price dinners available, reserve ahead, Mon-Sat 12:00-23:00, closed Sun, Schuurkenstraat 4, +32 9 223 5555, www.pakhuis.be).

**$$$ Jus** feels upscale but not pretentious, with elevated, modern Belgian dishes in a sophisticated interior or outside on a pedestrian shopping zone a couple of blocks south of the cathedral. Reservations are smart (fixed-price meals available; Tue-Fri 12:00-13:30 & 18:00-20:30, Sat open for dinner only, closed Sun-Mon; Mageleinstraat 43, +31 9 286 37 63, http://jusgent.be).

**Walpoortstraat and De Krook:** About a 10-minute walk south of the cathedral, you leave the touristy core of Ghent behind and reach lively, local Walpoortstraat, with a fun variety of design shops and eateries. A block over is the city's super-modern, recently opened library building, called **De Krook**—a striking, multilevel structure with a bike garage underneath and a lovely canalfront embankment on three sides. It's fun to simply wander over here (for the most interesting route, see the walking directions under "Shopping in Ghent," below), then browse for lunch. On Lammerstraat, which connects Walpoortstraat to De Krook, you'll find **$$ Aywa,** with good, takeaway Lebanese dishes (closed Sun-Mon, at #12), and—across the street—**$$ Soep Plus,** with a variety of healthy, flavorful soups and salads; their outdoor seating, in back, is on the plaza facing De Krook (closed Sat-Sun, at #33).

## GHENT'S BAR SCENE

Two touristy bars in the center are worth considering if you want to sample a wide range of Belgian favorites: beer or gin.

**De Dulle Griet** ("Mad Maggie," named after the large red cannon nearby) on Vrijdagmarkt serves up 500 types of beer in a cozy, sprawling bar with beer glasses hanging from the ceiling. There's also ample seating out on the square (Tue-Sat 12:00-24:00, Sun until 19:30, Mon from 16:30, Vrijdagmarkt 50, +32 9 244 2455).

**'t Dreupelkot,** guarded by Blackie the white dog, is a cozy little bar along the river offering more than 200 types of Dutch and Flemish gin, or *jenever* (daily from 15:00 until late, Groentenmarkt 12, +32 476 750 067).

# Shopping in Ghent

Ghent has an enjoyable real-world feel that makes it a fun place to browse—not for souvenirs, but for interesting, design-oriented items. While not as urbane as Brussels or as cutting-edge as Antwerp, Ghent is creative, yet still accessible. Here are some interesting places to browse:

### Serpentstraat

This little pedestrian street, buried deep between the cathedral and Vrijdagmarkt square (described in my Ghent City Walk), has a fun, funky collection of creative shops. The street kicks off with a pair of clothing boutiques (Wild Muse on the right, Nathalie Engels on the left). Woven along the rest of the street are interesting design stores, a funky record shop, boutiques for hip kids, creative greeting card purveyors, and other intriguing shops.

### Streets near the Castle of the Counts

The busy, tram-lined **Burgstraat,** just across the bridge from the castle, is an enjoyable place to window-shop at several furniture and home-decor shops and art galleries. The side street **Jan Brey-**

delstraat has an eclectic array of clothing, linens, jewelry, design, and chocolate shops.

## Walpoortstraat and Nearby

Walpoortstraat and the adjoining Sint-Pietersnieuwstraat, about a 10-minute stroll southeast of the cathedral, have some of Ghent's most creative and interesting shops.

**Shopping Your Way from the Belfry to Walpoortstraat:** There are several ways to reach Walpoortstraat from the center, but this route, which strings together mostly pedestrianized shopping streets, is especially pleasant. Beginning at the elongated square at the belfry, the middle of Ghent's three big towers, head south along the pedestrianized Mageleinstraat, with restaurants (including the recommended Jus, at #43), tearooms, upscale shoe stores, and mid-range international clothing shops. After two short blocks, you'll pop out at a fine little square ringed by interesting old buildings. Continue straight ahead down Kalandestraat to the handsome Kalandeberg square—with a gurgling fountain, outdoor seating, and a pair of inviting café/bakeries with sidewalk tables. Angle left at the bottom of the square to continue down Koestraat, which takes you to busier Kortedagsteeg. Here the shops and clientele gradually morph from mainstream middle-aged to creative hipster. As you cross the bridge, look left to see the bold new library building, De Krook. You're now on Walpoortstraat, and the transformation is complete.

**Shops Around Walpoortstraat:** The blocks in which Walpoortstraat becomes Sint-Pietersnieuwstraat are fun and picturesque. Wedged between enticing cafés and restaurants are clothing boutiques, vintage and secondhand stores, and some cool design depots (including **Axeswar Design Trendshop** at #12 and **Piet Moodshop** at the top of the street, Sint-Pietersnieuwstraat 94). Closer to the canal, at **Yuzu,** chocolatier Nicolas Vanaise decorates pralines with shiny metallic finishes and infuses them with creative flavors—including Asian elements (closed Sun-Mon, Walpoortstraat 11A).

## Antiques near Vrijdagmarkt

**Antiek-Depot** is a sprawling antique mall made for browsing. It sits along a postcard-perfect gabled street just north of Vrijdagmarkt square (closed Tue, Baudelostraat 15).

# Ghent Connections

**From Ghent by Train to: Brussels** (3/hour, 35 minutes), **Brussels Airport** (1/hour direct, 1 hour), **Bruges** (4/hour, 30 minutes), **Antwerp** (3/hour, 1 hour), **Ypres/Ieper** (hourly, 1 hour), **Paris** (2/hour, 2.5 hours, change at Brussels Midi/Zuid/South to Thalys train),

**Amsterdam** (hourly, 2.5 hours, transfer in Antwerp; cheaper on slightly slower IC/InterCity trains than on the pricey Thalys trains), **Delft** (2/hour, 2.5 hours, transfer in Antwerp and Rotterdam or Roosendaal). For train information, see www.belgiantrain.be; see also the "Transportation" section of the Practicalities chapter.

# BELGIUM: PAST & PRESENT

Belgium as a nation is less than 200 years old, but its history stretches back to Europe's roots. Located where France, Germany, and the Netherlands meet, it's a unique mix of all three.

## ROMANS AND INVASIONS (AD 1-1300)

Julius Caesar invades (57 BC), conquering the Belgae people who gave the region its name. After Rome's fall (c. 400), the Low Countries shatter into a patchwork of local dukedoms ravaged by invaders, from Franks to Vikings. By AD 1000, several self-governing cities begin to emerge, well located for trade along rivers that flow into the North Sea.

### Sights

- Bruges: Original fort (ruins at Crowne Plaza Hotel), Basilica of the Holy Blood
- Brussels: St. Michael's Cathedral, model in City Museum, Tour d'Angle (tower) from city wall
- Ghent: Castle of the Counts

## BOOMING TRADE TOWNS (1300-1500)

Bruges, the midway port between the North Sea and Mediterranean trade routes, becomes Europe's richest and most cosmopolitan city. English-grown wool is woven into cloth in Flanders factories, then shipped abroad by German merchants, all financed by Italian bankers.

As Bruges' harbor silts up, trade shifts to industrious Ghent

# Belgium Almanac

**Official Name:** Royaume de Belgique/Koninkrijk België, or simply Belgique in French and België in Dutch

**Size:** With only 12,000 square miles, it's slightly smaller than the state of Maryland, and one of the smallest countries in Europe. About 11.5 million Belgians are packed into their little country—58 percent are Flemish, 31 percent are Walloon, and 11 percent are "mixed or other."

**Geography:** Belgium's flat coastal plains in the northwest and central rolling hills make it easy to invade (just ask Napoleon or Hitler). There are some rugged hills and ridges in the south-east Ardennes Forest. The climate is temperate.

**Latitude and Longitude:** 50°N and 4°E. The latitude is similar to Calgary, Canada.

**Biggest Cities:** Antwerp has a half-million inhabitants, Ghent has 250,000, and little Bruges has almost 120,000. Brussels has 170,000 people in the city proper, but 1.2 million in the capital region.

**Economy:** With few natural resources, Belgium imports most of its raw materials and exports a large volume of manufactured goods, making its economy unusually dependent on world markets. It can be a sweet business—Belgium is one of the world's top exporters of chocolate. It's prosperous, with a Gross Domestic Product of nearly $557 billion and a GDP per capita of about $48,000. As the "crossroads" of Europe, Brussels is the headquarters of NATO and the de facto capital of the European Union.

**Government:** Belgium is a parliamentary democracy, and its official head of state is King Philippe. Voting is compulsory. An average of 90 percent of registered voters participate in general elections (compared with 55 percent in the US).

**Flag:** Belgium's flag is composed of three vertical bands of black, yellow, and red.

**The Average Belgian:** The average Belgian is 41 years old and will live to be 81. He or she is also likely to be divorced—Belgium has the highest divorce rate in Europe, with 70 for every 100 marriages. Beer is the national beverage: On average, Belgians drink 20 gallons a year, just behind the Dutch and just ahead of the Brits.

and to the bustling port city of Antwerp, which then becomes northern Europe's greatest trading city. Meanwhile, the smaller town of Brussels sells waffles and beer to passing travelers along the Germany-Bruges highway.

Politically, the Low Countries are united through marriage with the cultured, French-speaking dukes of Burgundy. Duke Philip the Good (c. 1450) rules an empire stretching from Amsterdam to Switzerland, and his cultured court is a center of art (Van Eyck, Memling, and Van der Weyden), literature, ideas, and pageantry.

But Belgium's medieval golden age was threatened by events of the wider world.

### Sights

- Bruges: Bell tower, Gothic Room in the City Hall, and Church of Our Lady; Flemish Primitive art in Groeninge and Sint-Janshospitaal museums; luxury goods and trade artifacts in Gruuthuse Museum
- Brussels: Grand Place, medieval street Rue des Bouchers, Notre-Dame du Sablon Church, Royal Museums of Fine Arts of Belgium
- Antwerp: Riverfront and Old Town
- Ghent: Cathedral and bell tower, Van Eyck *Adoration* altarpiece at St. Bavo's Cathedral

## PROTESTANTS VS. CATHOLICS AND SPANISH RULERS (1500s)

Belgium's economy stagnates after Columbus' discoveries shift trade to a global market. A much-celebrated royal marriage between the houses of Burgundy and Habsburg (1477) brings Burgundian Belgium under the rule of the Habsburgs in distant Austria and Spain.

Meanwhile, Protestantism spreads through the Low Countries. In 1566, angry Protestants rise up, vandalizing Catholic churches ("iconoclasm"). Belgium—ruled by the ultra-Catholic Habsburgs—becomes the main battleground, as Spanish troops arrive to brutally punish the heretic Protestants. The thriving city of Antwerp falls to Spanish troops (1585), causing that city's best and brightest to flee to the Netherlands.

Ultimately, while the Netherlands wins independence from Spain, Belgium remains under the Catholic Habsburgs, ruled from their regional capital, Brussels.

## Sights

- Antwerp and Ghent: Church cathedral interiors stripped bare by Protestant iconoclasts and later redecorated in Baroque style
- Brussels: Tapestry designs at Textilux Center

## ELEGANT DECLINE (1600-1800)

Belgium languishes under foreign rule while the world moves on. The Netherlands enjoys a golden age of self-rule and global sea trade, and France and England rise to superpower status. The Belgians survive as bankers, small manufacturers, and lacemakers—but on a small scale fitting their geographical size. Antwerp rebounds to become a flourishing cultural center of publishing houses and the flamboyant art of Peter Paul Rubens.

Whenever wars between nearby neighbors break out, tiny Belgium gets caught in the cross fire. Louis XIV of France bombs Brussels (1695) to punish the rest of Europe (his foes in the Nine Years' War). Later, Napoleon invades Belgium and topples the monarchy, ending nearly two centuries of Habsburg rule. When the rest of Europe rallies against Napoleon, where do they send their troops? To Belgium, of course, where they finally defeat Napoleon at Waterloo. Belgium—now little more than a pawn in the game of larger powers—hits rock bottom.

## Sights

- Bruges: Lace Center
- Brussels: Fashion and Lace Museum, Grand Place guildhalls, *Manneken-Pis*
- Near Brussels: Mémorial 1815 (museum) at Waterloo
- Antwerp: Rubens House, Rockox House, Museum Plantin-Moretus, Paleis op de Meir (Napoleon's palace)

## A TINY NATION BECOMES AN EMPIRE (1800s)

Europe's nobles install a king to rule all the Low Countries. Belgians resist this Dutch-controlled government and, in August 1830, take to the streets of Brussels to battle Dutch soldiers. They win their independence and choose their own constitutional monarch, King Leopold I (the great-great-great-grandfather of today's king).

Under Leopold I, Belgium rapidly becomes Europe's leader in Industrial Revolution technology. Soon coal from Belgian mines

# Typical Church Architecture

History comes to life when you visit a centuries-old church. Even if you wouldn't know your apse from a hole in the ground, learning a few simple terms will enrich your experience. Note that not every church has every feature, and a "cathedral" isn't a type of church architecture, but rather a designation for a church that's a governing center for a local bishop.

**Aisles:** Long, generally low-ceilinged arcades that flank the nave

**Altar:** Raised area with a ceremonial table (often adorned with candles or a crucifix), where the priest prepares and serves the bread and wine for Communion

**Apse:** Space behind the altar, sometimes bordered with small chapels

**Barrel Vault:** Continuous round-arched ceiling that resembles an extended upside-down U

**Choir:** Intimate space reserved for clergy and choir, located within the nave near the high altar and often screened off

**Cloister:** Covered hallways bordering a square or rectangular open-air courtyard, traditionally where monks and nuns got fresh air

**Facade:** Exterior of the church's main (west) entrance, usually highly decorated

**Groin Vault:** Arched ceiling formed where two equal barrel vaults meet at right angles

**Narthex:** Area (portico or foyer) between the main entry and the nave

**Nave:** Long central section of the church (running west to east, from the entrance to the altar) where the congregation sits or stands during the service

**Transept:** One of the two parts forming the "arms" of the cross in a traditional cross-shaped floor plan; runs north-south, perpendicularly crossing the east-west nave

**West Portal:** Main entry to the church (on the west end, opposite the main altar)

is fueling Ghent facto-
ries to make cloth, which
is shipped on Belgium's
state-of-the-art rail system.

Under King Leopold
II, tiny Belgium becomes
a global empire. Leopold
claims Africa's Congo—a
region 80 times bigger than Belgium—as his own private colony.
The Belgians brutally exploit the Congo's rubber and ivory resources to finance massive building projects. Brussels becomes a world-
class capital of broad boulevards and monumental buildings with
columns and domes, all frosted with delicate Art Nouveau.

## Sights

- Brussels: Upper Town buildings, Parc du Cinquantenaire;
  Galeries Royales St. Hubert, BELvue Museum
- Antwerp: Central Station
- Bruges and Brussels: Choco-Story: The Chocolate Museum

## WORLD WARS, EUROPEAN UNION
## (1900-2000)

In 1914, prosperous Belgium is suddenly transformed into a horrif-
ic battle-scape, as Germany dukes it out with England and France

in World War I. Some of
the worst fighting takes
place at Flanders Fields
near Ypres (Ieper).

As Belgium recovers
in the 1920s, a new phe-
nomenon appears—news-
paper comics—and Hergé
thrills Europeans with his
tales of the adventurous
young reporter, Tintin.

When World War II breaks out, Nazi Germany easily con-
quers Belgium, imposing five long years of brutal occupation. Late
in the war, Belgium is the site of Germany's last-gasp offensive, the
Battle of the Bulge.

After the war, Brussels becomes the center of the budding
movement toward European unity. It pioneers the Common Market (1957), the BeNeLux economic union (1960), and is a stalwart
of NATO. In 1992, Belgium—along with 11 other countries—becomes a founding member of the European Union.

# The Battle for Belgium: Flanders vs. Wallonia

Although little, peace-loving Belgium seems like a warm and cozy place, its society is split right down the middle by a surprisingly contentious linguistic divide: the Dutch-speaking people of Flanders (in the north) versus the French speakers of Wallonia (in the south). To travelers, it almost seems as if Flanders and Wallonia are different countries. Each region has its own "national" tourist office, which effectively ignores the other half of the country. One prime minister said that Belgians are united only by the king, a love of beer, and the national soccer team.

From its earliest days, "Belgium" was less a country than a patchwork of dukedoms joined awkwardly together not by language, but by foreign rulers. For centuries, the two language groups coexisted side-by-side as they were successively dominated by Burgundian, Habsburg, Spanish, French, and Dutch overlords.

That changed in 1830, when the modern nation-state of Belgium was born, forcing the two regions together. It was Belgium's French-speaking aristocracy and industrialists that had led the drive for independence from the Netherlands. They said, "Belgium will be French, or it will not be." And so it was: Linguistic and cultural oppression ruled the day, as the Dutch language spoken in Flanders was suppressed. Education at prestigious universities, for example, was only in French. These days, the tables have turned—Flanders today has the healthier, wealthier economy and more inhabitants than Wallonia.

Language issues still dominate Belgium's politics. Some Flemish feel they'd have been better off had Belgium remained part of the Netherlands, which would have respected their native tongue. That's why most Flemish people are not particularly nationalistic about their language—rather than being blinded by Flemish pride, they readily acknowledge that what they speak is a dialect of Dutch.

Whereas a generation ago, virtually every Belgian spoke both Dutch and French, nowadays when Flemish students choose a "second" language to study, many choose English. Meanwhile, in a strange role reversal, Francophones are choosing to learn Dutch, which they realize will open up employment options. On my last visit to Brussels, I saw a sign in a shop window saying, "Bilingual staff wanted."

The Belgian government has taken steps to involve everyone. In 1970, Belgium began decentralizing itself, over time becoming a federal state with three semiautonomous regions: Flanders, Wallonia, and the bilingual city-state of Brussels. But the 21st century has seen the rise of Flemish nationalist parties. As with Catalunya in Spain and Scotland in the United Kingdom, no one knows where a push for independence might lead.

## Sights

- Near Bruges: Flanders Fields (near Ypres)
- Bruges: René Magritte paintings in Groeninge Museum
- Brussels: Atomium, European Parliament quarter, Magritte Museum, Belgian Comic Strip Center
- Antwerp: Sint-Andries fashion district, ModeMuseum, "Little Island" area, 't Zuid district
- Ghent: Design Museum

## BELGIUM TODAY

Brussels is the de facto capital of the European Union—a kind of "Washington, DC" for this "United States of Europe."

But, ironically, Belgium itself struggles to unite its own diverse population. Since 1970, it's been a nation officially divided into three semi-autonomous regions: Dutch-speaking Flanders, French-speaking Wallonia, and bilingual Brussels (for more on this divide, see the sidebar). It also strives to bring African immigrants (including from its former colony of Congo) into the diverse mix.

The Belgian political landscape is splintered into several different parties, divided largely along language lines. Fortunately, Belgium has a popular (if symbolic) ruler—King Philippe and his charming family. In 2016, a terrorist attack in Brussels shocked the nation; since then, security has been tighter, but the country also seems more unified.

Belgium has seen many centuries of turbulence, but that hasn't stopped it from becoming a forward-thinking nation with a long and rich cultural heritage. It welcomes you to come and make your own history.

# PRACTICALITIES

This chapter covers the practical skills of European travel: how to get tourist information, pay for things, sightsee efficiently, find good-value accommodations, eat affordably but well, use technology wisely, and get between destinations smoothly. For more information on these topics, see RickSteves.com/travel-tips.

## Travel Tips

**Travel Advisories:** Before traveling, check updated health and safety conditions, including restrictions for your destination, on the travel pages of the US State Department (www.travel.state. gov) and Centers for Disease Control and Prevention (www.cdc. gov/travel). The US embassy website for Belgium is another good source of information.

**Covid Vaccine/Test Requirements:** It's possible you'll need to present proof of vaccination against the coronavirus and/or a negative Covid-19 test result to board a plane to Europe or back to the US. Carefully check requirements for each country you'll visit well before you depart, and again a few days before your trip. See the websites listed above for current requirements.

**ETIAS Registration:** The European Union may soon require US and Canadian citizens to register online with the European Travel Information and Authorization System (ETIAS) before entering Belgium and other Schengen Zone countries (quick and easy process). For the latest, check www.etiasvisa.com.

**Tourist Information:** National tourist offices **in the US** can be a wealth of information. Before your trip, request or download any specific information you may want, such as city maps and schedules of upcoming festivals.

For Brussels and French-speaking Wallonia, go to www.visitbelgium.com; for Dutch-speaking Flanders, check out www.visitflanders.com. At either website, you can access hotel and city guides, brochures for ABC lovers (antiques, beer, and chocolates), maps, and information about WWI and WWII battlefields.

In **Belgium,** a good first stop is generally the tourist information office (abbreviated **TI** in this book). TIs are in business to help you spend money in their town—which can color their advice—but I still swing by to pick up a city map, and get info on public transit, walking tours, special events, and nightlife. Some TIs have information on the entire country or at least the region, so you can pick up maps and other info for destinations you'll be visiting later in your trip. Note that Belgian TIs are state-run, so they're not as tainted by a drive for profits.

**Emergency and Medical Help:** For any emergency service—ambulance, police, or fire—call **112** from a mobile phone or landline (operators typically speak English). If you get sick, do as the Belgians do and go to a pharmacist for advice. Or ask at your hotel for help—they'll know the nearest medical and emergency services.

**Theft or Loss:** To replace a passport, you'll need to go in person to the US Consulate and Embassy (see next). If your credit and debit cards disappear, cancel and replace them (see "Damage Control for Lost Cards," on page 328). File a police report, either on the spot or within a day or two; you'll need it to submit an insurance claim for lost or stolen items, and it can help with replacing your passport or credit and debit cards. For more information, see RickSteves.com/help.

**US Embassy and Consulate:** Brussels—dial +32 2 811 4300, after-hours emergency +32 2 811 4000 (Boulevard du Régent 27, https://be.usembassy.gov.

**Canadian Embassy:** Brussels—dial + 32 2 741 0611 (Avenue des Arts 58, www.ambassade-canada.be).

**Time Zones:** Belgium, like most of continental Europe, is generally six/nine hours ahead of the East/West Coasts of the US. The exceptions are the beginning and end of Daylight Saving Time: Europe "springs forward" the last Sunday in March (two weeks after most of North America) and "falls back" the last Sunday in October (one week before North America). For a handy time converter, use the world clock app on your phone or download one (see www.timeanddate.com).

**Business Hours:** Most stores throughout Belgium are open from about 9:00 or 10:00 until 18:00-20:00 on weekdays, but close earlier on Saturday and may or may not open on Sunday. Popular destinations are even more crowded on weekends. Many museums and sights are closed on Monday.

**Watt's Up?** Europe's electrical system is 220 volts, instead of North America's 110 volts. Most electronics (laptops, phones, cameras) and appliances (newer hair dryers, CPAP machines) convert automatically, so you won't need a converter, but you will need an adapter plug with two round prongs, sold inexpensively at travel stores in the US.

**Rip up this book!** Turn chapters into mini guidebooks: Break the book's spine and use a utility knife to slice apart chapters, keeping gummy edges intact. Reinforce the chapter spines with clear wide tape; use a heavy-duty stapler; or make or buy a cheap cover (see the Travel Store at RickSteves.com), swapping out chapters as you travel.

**Discounts:** Discounts for sights are generally not listed in this book. However, seniors (age 65 and over), youths under 18, and students and teachers with proper identification cards (obtain from www.isic.org) can get discounts at many sights—always ask. Some discounts are available only to European citizens.

**Online Translation Tips:** Google's Chrome browser instantly translates websites; Translate.google.com and DeepL.com are also handy. The Google Translate app converts spoken English into most European languages (and vice versa) and can also translate text it "reads" with your phone's camera.

**Going Green:** There's plenty you can do to reduce your environmental footprint when traveling. When practical, take a train instead of a flight within Europe, and use public transportation within cities. In hotels, use the "Do Not Disturb" sign to avoid daily linen and towel changes (or hang up your towels to signal you'll reuse them). Bring a reusable shopping tote and refillable water bottle (Europe's tap water is safe to drink). Skip printed brochures, maps, or other materials that you don't plan to keep—get your info online instead. To find out how Rick Steves' Europe is offsetting carbon emissions with a self-imposed carbon tax, go to RickSteves.com/about-us/climate-smart.

# Money

Here's my basic strategy for using money wisely in Europe. I pack the following and keep it all safe in my money belt.

**Credit Card:** You'll use your credit card for purchases both big (hotels, advance tickets) and small (little shops, food stands). Many European businesses have gone cashless, making a card your only payment option. A "tap-to-pay" or "contactless" card is the most widely accepted and simplest to use.

**Debit Card:** Use this at ATMs to withdraw a small amount of local cash. Wait until you arrive to get euros (European airports have plenty of ATMs); if you buy euros before your trip, you'll pay bad stateside exchange rates. While most transactions are by card these days, cash can help you out of a jam if your card randomly doesn't work, and can be useful to pay for things like tips and local guides.

**Backup Card:** Some travelers carry a third card (debit or credit; ideally from a different bank) in case one gets lost or simply doesn't work.

**Stash of Cash:** I carry $100-200 in US dollars as a cash back-up, which comes in handy in an emergency (for example, if your debit card gets eaten by the machine).

## BEFORE YOU GO

**Know your cards.** For credit cards, Visa and MasterCard are universal while American Express and Discover are less common. US debit cards with a Visa or MasterCard logo will work in any European ATM.

**Go "contactless."** Get comfortable using contactless pay options. Check to see if you already have—or can get—a tap-to-pay version of your credit card (look on the card for the tap-to-pay symbol—four curvy lines), and consider setting up your smartphone for contactless payment (see next section for details). Both options are widely used in Europe and are more secure than a physical credit card: Instead of recording your credit card number, a one-time encrypted "token" enables the purchase and expires shortly afterward.

**Know your PIN.** Make sure you know the numeric, four-digit PIN for each of your cards, both debit and credit. Request it if you don't have one, as it may be required for some purchases. Allow time to receive the information by mail—it's not always possible to obtain your PIN online or by phone.

**Report your travel dates.** Let your bank know that you'll be using your debit and credit cards in Europe, and when and where you're headed.

**Adjust your ATM withdrawal limit.** Find out how much you can withdraw daily and ask for a higher daily limit if you want to

## Exchange Rate

### 1 euro (€) = about $1.10

To convert prices in euros to dollars, add about 10 percent: €20=about $22, €50=about $55. Like the dollar, one euro is broken into 100 cents. Coins range from €0.01 to €2, and bills from €5 to €200 (bills over €50 are rarely used).

Check www.oanda.com for the latest exchange rates.

get more cash at once. Note that European ATMs will withdraw funds only from checking accounts, not savings accounts.

**Find out about fees.** For any purchase or withdrawal made with a card, you may be charged a currency conversion fee (1-3 percent) and/or a Visa or MasterCard international transaction fee (less than 1 percent). If you're getting a bad deal, consider getting a new card. Reputable no-fee cards include those from Capital One, as well as Charles Schwab debit cards. Most credit unions and some airline loyalty cards have low or no international transaction fees.

## IN EUROPE
### Using Credit Cards and Payment Apps

**Tap-to-Pay** or **Contactless Cards:** These cards have the usual chip and/or magnetic stripe, but with the addition of a contactless symbol. Simply tap your card against a contactless reader to complete a transaction (your pin may be required). This is by far the easiest way to pay and has become the standard in much of Europe. Some small businesses (such as market stalls or food stands) accept *only* tap cards, and sometimes don't accept cash.

**Payment Apps:** Just like at home, you can pay with your smartphone or smartwatch by linking a credit card to an app such as Apple Pay or Google Pay. To pay, hold your phone near a contactless reader; you may need to verify the transaction with a face scan, fingerprint scan, or passcode. If you've arrived in Europe without a tap-to-pay card, you can easily set up your phone to work in this way.

**Other Card Types: Chip-and-PIN** cards have a visible chip embedded in them; rather than swiping, you insert the card into the payment machine, then enter your PIN on a keypad. **Swipe-and-sign** credit cards—with a swipeable magnetic stripe, and a receipt you have to sign—are increasingly rare.

**Will My US Card Work?** Usually, yes. On rare occasions, at self-service payment machines (such as transit-ticket kiosks, tollbooths, or fuel pumps), some US cards may not work. Usually a tap-to-pay card does the trick in these situations. Just in case, carry cash as a backup and look for a cashier who can process your payment if your card is rejected. Drivers should be prepared to move on to the next gas station if necessary. (In some countries, gas stations sell prepaid gas cards, which you can purchase with any US card.) When approaching a toll plaza or ferry ticket line, use the "cash" lane.

## Using Cash

**Cash Machines:** European cash machines work just like they do at home—except they spit out local currency instead of dollars, calculated at the day's standard bank-to-bank rate. In most places, ATMs are easy to locate—in Belgium ask for a *geldautomaat* (Dutch) or a *distributeur* (French). When possible, withdraw cash from a bank-run ATM located just outside that bank.

If your debit card doesn't work, try a lower amount—your request may have exceeded your withdrawal limit or the ATM's limit. If you still have a problem, try a different ATM or come back later.

Avoid "independent" ATMs, such as Travelex, Euronet, Moneybox, Your Cash, Cardpoint, and Cashzone. These have high fees, can be less secure, and may try to trick users with "dynamic currency conversion" (see next).

**Dynamic Currency Conversion:** When withdrawing cash at an ATM or paying with a credit card, you'll often be asked whether you want the transaction processed in dollars or in the local currency. Always refuse the conversion and *choose the local currency.* While DCC offers the illusion of convenience, it comes with a poor exchange rate, and you'll wind up losing money.

**Exchanging Cash:** Minimize exchanging money in Europe; it's expensive (you'll generally lose 5 to 10 percent). In a pinch you can find exchange desks at major train stations or airports. Banks generally do not exchange money unless you have an account with them.

## Security Tips

Pickpockets target tourists. Keep your cash, credit cards, and passport secure in your money belt, and carry only a day's spending money in your front pocket or wallet.

Before inserting your card into an ATM, inspect the front. If anything looks crooked, loose, or damaged, it could be a sign of a card-skimming device. When entering your PIN, carefully block other people's view of the keypad.

Avoid using a debit card for purchases. Because a debit card pulls funds directly from your bank account, potential charges incurred by a thief will stay on your account while your bank investigates.

To access your accounts online while traveling, be sure to use a secure connection (see the "Tips on Internet Security" sidebar, later).

## Damage Control for Lost Cards

If you lose your credit or debit card, report the loss immediately to the respective global customer-assistance centers. With a mobile phone, call these 24-hour US numbers: Visa (+1 303 967 1096), MasterCard (+1 636 722 7111), and American Express (+1 336 393 1111). From a landline, you can call these US numbers collect by going through a local operator.

You'll need to provide the primary cardholder's identification-verification details (such as birth date, mother's maiden name, or Social Security number). You can generally receive a temporary card within two or three business days in Europe (see RickSteves.com/help for more).

If you report your loss within two days, you typically won't be responsible for unauthorized transactions on your account, although many banks charge a liability fee.

## TIPPING

Tipping in Belgium isn't as automatic and generous as it is in the US. For special service, tips are appreciated, but not expected. As in the US, the proper amount depends on your resources, tipping philosophy, and the circumstances, but some general guidelines apply.

**Restaurants:** Belgian restaurants include a service charge, although it's common to round up the bill. If paying with a credit card, be prepared to tip separately with cash or coins; credit card receipts don't often have a tip line. For more details on tipping in restaurants, see page 340.

**Taxis:** For a typical ride, round up your fare a bit (for instance, if the fare is €4.50, pay €5). If the cabbie hauls your bags and zips you to the airport to help you catch your flight, you might want to toss in a little more.

**Services:** In general, if someone in the tourism or service industry does a super job for you, a small tip of a euro or two is appropriate...but not required. If you're not sure whether (or how much) to tip, ask a local for advice.

## GETTING A VAT REFUND

Wrapped into the purchase price of your Belgian souvenirs is a Value-Added Tax (VAT) of about 21 percent. You're entitled to get most of that tax back if you purchase more than €50 worth of goods at a store that participates in the VAT-refund scheme. Typically, you must ring up the minimum at a single retailer—you can't add up your purchases from various shops to reach the required amount. (If the store ships the goods to your US home, VAT is not assessed on your purchase.)

Getting your refund is straightforward...and worthwhile if you spend a significant amount.

**At the Merchant:** Have the merchant completely fill out the refund document (they'll ask for your passport; a photo of your passport usually works). Keep track of the paperwork and your original sales receipt. Note that you're not supposed to use your purchased goods before you leave Europe.

**At the Border or Airport:** Process your VAT document at your last stop in the European Union (such as at the airport) with the customs agent who deals with VAT refunds (allow plenty of extra time to deal with this process). At some airports, you'll have to go to a customs office to get your documents stamped and then to a separate VAT refund service (such as Global Blue or Planet) to process the refund. At other airports, a single VAT desk handles the whole thing. (Note that refund services typically extract a 4 percent fee, but you're paying for the convenience of receiving your money in cash immediately or as a credit to your card.) Otherwise, you'll need to mail the stamped refund documents to the address given by the merchant.

## CUSTOMS FOR AMERICAN SHOPPERS

You can take home $800 worth of items per person duty-free, once every 31 days. Many processed and packaged foods are allowed, including cheeses, dried herbs, jams, baked goods, candy, chocolate, oil, vinegar, condiments, and honey. Fresh fruits and vegetables and most meats are not allowed, with exceptions for some canned items. As for alcohol, you can bring in one liter duty-free (it can be packed securely in your checked luggage, along with any other liquid-containing items).

To bring alcohol (or liquid-packed foods) in your carry-on bag on your flight home, buy it at a duty-free shop at the airport. You'll increase your odds of getting it onto a connecting flight if it's packaged in a "STEB"—a secure, tamper-evident bag. But stay away from liquids in opaque, ceramic, or metallic containers, which usually cannot be successfully screened (STEB or no STEB).

For details on allowable goods, customs rules, and duty rates, visit http://help.cbp.gov.

# Sightseeing

Sightseeing can be hard work. Use these tips to make your visits to Belgium's finest sights meaningful, fun, efficient, and painless.

## MAPS AND NAVIGATION TOOLS

A good map is essential for efficient navigation while sightseeing. The maps in this book are concise and simple, designed to help you locate recommended destinations, sights, hotels, and restaurants. In Europe, simple maps are generally free at TIs and hotels.

You can also use a mapping app on your mobile device, which provides turn-by-turn directions for walking, driving, and taking public transit. Google Maps, Apple Maps, and CityMaps2Go allow you to download maps for offline use; ideally, download the areas you'll need before your trip. For certain features, you'll need to be online—either using Wi-Fi or an international data plan.

## PLAN AHEAD

Set up an itinerary that allows you to fit in all your must-see sights. For a one-stop look at opening hours, see this book's "At a Glance" sidebars for Bruges, Brussels, Antwerp, and Ghent. Since the Covid-19 pandemic, hours for museums and sights have been unstable. Both before and during your trip, confirm the latest opening days and times with the TI or on a museum or sight's official website (listed throughout this book).

Don't put off visiting a must-see sight—you never know when a place will close unexpectedly for a holiday, strike, or restoration. Many museums are closed or have reduced hours at least a few days a year, especially on holidays such as Christmas, New Year's, and Labor Day (May 1). A list of holidays is in the appendix; check for possible closures during your trip. In summer, some sights may stay open late. Off-season hours may be shorter.

Going at the right time helps avoid crowds. This book offers tips on the best times to see specific sights. Try visiting popular sights very early or very late. Evening visits (when possible) are usually more peaceful, with fewer crowds. Late morning is usually the worst time to visit a popular sight.

If you plan to hire a local guide, reserve ahead by email. Popular guides can get booked up.

Study up. To get the most out of the self-guided tours and sight descriptions in this book, read them before you visit. The Groeninge Museum is much more entertaining if you've boned up on your Flemish Primitives the night before.

## RESERVATIONS AND ADVANCE TICKETS

Many popular sights in Europe come with long lines—not to get in, but to buy a ticket. Visitors who buy tickets online in advance (or who have a museum pass covering these key sights) can skip the line and waltz right in. Advance tickets are generally timed-entry, meaning you're guaranteed admission on a certain date and time.

For some sights, buying ahead is required (tickets aren't sold at the sight and it's the only way to get in). At other sights, buying ahead is recommended to skip the line and save time. And for many sights, advance tickets are available but unnecessary: At these uncrowded sights you can simply arrive, buy a ticket, and go in.

Don't confuse the reservation options: available, recommended, and required. Use my advice in this book as a guide. Note any must-see sights that sell out long in advance and be prepared to buy tickets early. If you do your research, you'll know the smart strategy.

Given how precious your vacation time is, I'd book in advance both where it's required (as soon as your dates are firm) and where it will save time in a long line (in some cases, you can do this even on the day you plan to visit).

You'll generally be emailed an eticket with a QR or bar code that you'll store on your phone to scan at the entrance (if you prefer, you can print it out). At the sight, look for the ticket-holders line rather than the ticket-buying line; you may still have to wait in a security line.

**Sightseeing Passes:** Some cities offer sightseeing passes that offer free or discounted admission to several sights. Do the math to determine if a sightseeing pass makes sense for your visit. Even with a sightseeing pass, you'll often still need to make reservations for the most popular sights.

## AT SIGHTS

Here's what you can typically expect:

**Entering:** You may not be allowed to enter if you arrive too close to closing time. And guards start ushering people out well before the actual closing time, so don't save the best for last.

Many sights have a security check. Allow extra time for these lines. Some sights require you to check day packs and coats. (If you'd rather not check your day pack, try carrying it tucked under your arm like a purse as you enter.)

**Photography:** If the museum's photo policy isn't clearly posted, ask a guard. Generally, taking photos without a flash or tripod is allowed. Some sights ban selfie sticks; others ban photos altogether.

**Audioguides and Apps:** Some sights offer audioguides with excellent recorded descriptions in English. In some cases, you'll rent a device to carry around (if you bring your own plug-in earbuds, you'll enjoy better sound). Increasingly, museums and sights instead offer an app you can download with their audioguide (often free; check websites from home and consider downloading in advance as not all sights offer free Wi-Fi).

**Temporary Exhibits:** Museums may show special exhibits in addition to their permanent collection. Some exhibits are included in the entry price, while others come at an extra cost (which you may have to pay even if you don't want to see the exhibit).

**Expect Changes:** Artwork can be on tour, on loan, out sick, or shifted at the whim of the curator. Pick up a floor plan as you enter and ask museum staff if you can't find a particular item.

**Services:** Important sights usually have a reasonably priced on-site café or cafeteria (handy and air-conditioned places to rejuvenate during a long visit). The WCs at sights are free and generally clean.

**Before Leaving:** At the gift shop, scan the postcard rack or thumb through a guidebook to be sure you haven't overlooked something that you'd like to see. Every sight or museum offers more than what is covered in this book. Use the information I provide as an introduction—not the final word.

## Sleeping

Extensive and opinionated listings of good-value rooms are a major feature of this book's Sleeping sections. Rather than list accommodations scattered throughout a town, I choose hotels in my favorite neighborhoods that are convenient to your sightseeing.

My recommendations run the gamut, from dorm beds to luxurious rooms with all the comforts. I like places that are clean, central, relatively quiet at night, reasonably priced, friendly, small enough to have a hands-on owner or manager, and run with a respect for Belgian traditions. I'm more impressed by a handy location and fun-loving philosophy than oversized TVs and a fancy gym. Most of my recommendations fall short of perfection. But if I can find a place with most of these features, it's a keeper.

Book your accommodations as soon as your itinerary is set, especially if you want to stay at one of my top listings or if you'll

## Sleep Code

Hotels in this book are categorized according to the average price of a standard double room with breakfast in high season.

| | |
|---|---|
| **$$$$** | **Splurge:** Most rooms over €170 |
| **$$$** | **Pricier:** €130-170 |
| **$$** | **Moderate:** €90-130 |
| **$** | **Budget:** €50-90 |
| **¢** | **Backpacker:** Under €50 |
| **RS%** | Rick Steves discount |

Unless otherwise noted, credit cards are accepted, hotel staff speak basic English, and free Wi-Fi is available. Comparison-shop by checking prices at several hotels (on each hotel's own website, on a booking site, or by email). For the best deal, *book directly with the hotel.* Ask for a discount if paying in cash; if the listing includes **RS%**, request a Rick Steves discount.

be traveling during busy times. See the appendix for a list of major holidays and festivals in Belgium.

Some people make reservations a few days ahead as they travel. This approach fosters spontaneity, and booking sites make it easy to find available rooms, but—especially during busy times—you run the risk of settling for lesser-value accommodations.

## RATES AND DEALS

I've categorized my recommended accommodations based on price, indicated with a dollar-sign rating (see sidebar). Room prices can fluctuate significantly with demand and amenities (size, views, room class, and so on), but relative price categories remain constant. Cities in Belgium all charge a hotel tax; it's calculated differently everywhere, but assume you'll pay a few extra euros per person, per night.

**Booking Direct:** Once your dates are set, compare prices at several hotels. You can do this by checking hotel websites and booking sites such as Hotels.com or Booking.com. After you've zeroed in on your choice, book directly with the hotel itself. This increases the chances that the hotelier will be able to accommodate special needs or requests (such as shifting your reservation). And when you book on the hotel's website, by email, or by phone, the owner avoids the commission paid to booking sites, giving them wiggle room to offer you a discount, a nicer room, or a free breakfast (if it's not already included).

**Getting a Discount:** Some hotels extend a discount to those who pay cash or stay longer than three nights. And some accommodations offer a special discount for Rick Steves readers, indi-

# Using Online Services to Your Advantage

From booking services to user reviews, online businesses play a greater role in travelers' planning than ever before. Take advantage of their pluses—and be wise to their downsides.

## Booking Sites

Booking websites such as Booking.com and Hotels.com offer one-stop shopping for hotels. While convenient for travelers, they're both a blessing and a curse for small, independent, family-run hotels. Without a presence on these sites, these hotels become almost invisible. But to be listed, a hotel must pay a sizable commission...and promise that its own website won't undercut the price on the booking-service site.

Here's the work-around: Use the big sites to research what's out there, then book directly with the hotel by email or phone, in which case hotel owners are free to give you whatever price they like. Ask for a room without the commission mark-up (or ask for a free breakfast, if not included, or a free upgrade). If you do book online, be sure to use the hotel's own website. The price will likely be the same as on a booking site, but your money goes to the hotel, not agency commissions.

As a savvy consumer, remember: When you book with an online service, you're adding a middleman who takes a cut. To support small, family-run hotels whose world is more difficult than ever, book direct.

## Short-Term Rental Sites

Rental juggernaut Airbnb (along with other short-term rental sites) allows travelers to rent rooms and apartments, often providing more value, space, and amenities than a cookie-cutter hotel. Airbnb fans appreciate feeling part of a real neighborhood and getting into a daily routine as "temporary Europeans." Some places are run by thoughtful hosts, allowing you to get to know a local and keep your money in the community; but beware: others are impersonally managed by large, absentee agencies.

cated in this guidebook with the abbreviation **"RS%."** Discounts vary: Ask for details when you reserve. Generally, to qualify for this discount, you must book direct (not through a booking site), mention this book when you reserve, show this book upon arrival, and sometimes pay cash or stay a certain number of nights. In some cases, you may need to enter a discount code (which I've provided in the listing) in the booking form on the hotel's website. Rick Steves discounts apply to readers with either printed or digital books. Understandably, discounts do not apply to promotional rates.

Critics of Airbnb see it as a threat to "traditional Europe." Landlords can make more money renting to short-stay travelers, driving rents up—and local residents out. Traditional businesses are replaced by ones that cater to tourists. And the character and charm that made those neighborhoods desirable to tourists in the first place goes too. Some cities have cracked down, requiring owners to obtain a license and to occupy rental properties part of the year (and staging disruptive "inspections" that inconvenience guests).

As a lover of Europe, I share the worry of those who see residents nudged aside by tourists. But as an advocate for travelers, I appreciate the value Airbnb can provide in offering the chance to stay in a local building or neighborhood with potentially fewer tourists.

## User Reviews

User-generated review sites and apps such as Yelp and TripAdvisor can give you a consensus of opinions about everything from hotels and restaurants to sights and nightlife. If you scan reviews of a restaurant or hotel and see several complaints about noise or a rotten location, you've gained insight that can help in your decision-making.

As a guidebook writer, my sense is that there is a big difference between the uncurated information on a review site and the vetted listings in a guidebook. A user review is based on the limited experience of one person, who stayed at just one hotel in a given city and ate at a few restaurants there. A guidebook is the work of a trained researcher who forms a well-developed basis for comparison by visiting many restaurants and hotels year after year.

Both types of information have their place, and in many ways, they're complementary. If something is well reviewed in a guidebook and also gets good online reviews, it's likely a winner.

## TYPES OF ACCOMMODATIONS

### Hotels

In this book, the price for a double room ranges from $65 (very simple, toilet and shower down the hall) to $250 (maximum plumbing and more), with most clustering at about $130. You'll pay more at Brussels hotels and less at Bruges B&Bs. A hearty breakfast with cereal, meats, local cheeses, fresh bread, yogurt, juice, and coffee or tea is generally included, though you often can opt out for a cheaper room rate.

Some hotels can add an extra bed (for a small charge) to turn a double into a triple; some offer larger rooms for four or more people (I call these "family rooms" in the listings). If there's space for an extra cot, they'll cram it in for you. In general, a triple room is cheaper than the cost of a double and a single. Three or four people can economize by requesting one big room.

**Arrival and Check-In:** Hotels and B&Bs are sometimes located on the higher floors of a multipurpose building with a secured door. In that case, look for your hotel's name on the buttons by the main entrance. When you ring the bell, you'll be buzzed in.

Hotel elevators are common, though small, and some older buildings still lack them. You may have to climb a flight of stairs to reach the elevator (if so, you can ask the front desk for help carrying your bags up).

Most European countries require hotels to collect your name, nationality, and passport number. At check-in, the receptionist might ask for your passport and may keep it for several hours. If you're not comfortable leaving your passport at the desk, bring a copy to give them instead.

If you're arriving early in the morning, your room probably won't be ready. Check your bag safely at the hotel and dive right in to sightseeing.

**In Your Room:** Most hotel rooms have a TV and free Wi-Fi, which can vary in strength and quality. Simpler places rarely have a room phone.

**Checking Out:** While it's customary to pay for your room upon departure, it can be a good idea to settle your bill the day before, when you're not in a hurry and while the manager's there.

**Hotelier Help:** Hoteliers can be a good source of advice. Most know their city well, and can assist you with everything from public transit and airport connections to finding a good restaurant, the nearest launderette, or a late-night pharmacy.

**Hotel Hassles:** Even at the best places, mechanical breakdowns occur: Sinks leak, hot water turns cold, toilets may gurgle or smell, the Wi-Fi goes out, or the air-conditioning dies when you need it most. Report your concerns clearly and calmly at the front desk.

If you find that night noise is a problem (if, for instance, your room is over a nightclub or facing a busy street), ask for a quieter room in the back or on an upper floor. To guard against theft in your room, keep valuables out of sight. Some rooms come with a safe, and other hotels have safes at the front desk. I've never bothered using one, and in a lifetime of travel, I've never had anything stolen from my room.

For more complicated problems, don't expect instant results. Above all, keep a positive attitude. Remember, you're on vacation.

If your hotel is a disappointment, spend more time out enjoying the place you came to see.

## Bed-and-Breakfasts

B&Bs offer double the cultural intimacy and—often—nicer rooms for a good deal less than most hotel rooms. Hosts usually speak English and are interesting conversationalists.

Belgium has a variety of cozy, funky, affordable B&Bs well run by gregarious entrepreneurs and typically located up a flight or two of steep, narrow stairs. Local TIs have lists of B&Bs, and there's always Booking.com, but you'll save money by booking directly with the B&B itself.

## Short-Term Rentals

A short-term rental—whether an apartment, a house, or a room in a private residence—is a popular alternative, especially if you plan to settle in one location for several nights. For stays longer than a few days, you can usually find a rental that's comparable to—and cheaper than—a hotel room with similar amenities. Plus, you'll get a behind-the-scenes peek into how locals live.

Many places require a minimum stay and have strict cancellation policies. And you're generally on your own: There's no reception desk, breakfast, or daily cleaning service.

**Finding Accommodations:** Websites such as Airbnb, FlipKey, Booking.com, and VRBO let you browse a wide range of properties. Alternatively, rental agencies such as InterhomeUSA. com and RentaVilla.com can provide a more personalized service (their curated listings are also more expensive).

Before you commit, be clear on the location. I like to virtually "explore" the neighborhood using Google Street View. Also consider the proximity to public transportation and how well connected the property is with the rest of the city. Ask about amenities (elevator, air-conditioning, laundry, Wi-Fi, parking, etc.). Reviews from previous guests can help identify trouble spots.

Think about the kind of experience you want: Just a key and an affordable bed...or a chance to get to know a local? Some hosts offer self check-in and minimal contact; others enjoy interacting with you. Read the description and reviews to help shape your decision.

**Confirming and Paying:** Many places require payment in full before your trip, usually through the listing site. Be wary of owners who want to take your transaction offline; this gives you no recourse if things go awry. Never agree to wire money (a key indicator of a fraudulent transaction).

**Apartments or Houses:** If you're staying in one place for several nights, it's worth considering an apartment or rental house. Apartment or house rentals can be especially cost-effective for

## Making Hotel Reservations

Reserve your rooms as soon as you've pinned down your travel dates. For busy national holidays, it's wise to reserve far in advance (see the appendix).

**Requesting a Reservation:** For family-run hotels, it's generally best to book your room directly by email or phone. For business-class and chain hotels, or if you'd rather book online, reserve directly through the hotel's official website (not a booking website). Almost all of my recommended hotels take reservations in English. Here's what the hotelier wants to know:

- Type(s) of room(s) you want and number of guests
- Number of nights you'll stay
- Arrival and departure dates, written European-style as day/month/year (18/06/25 or 18 June 2025)
- Special requests (en suite bathroom, cheapest room, twin beds vs. double bed, quiet room)
- Applicable discounts (such as a Rick Steves discount, cash discount, or promotional rate)

**Confirming a Reservation:** Most places will request a credit-card number to hold your room. If the hotel's website doesn't have a secure form where you can enter the number directly, share this info by phone.

**Canceling a Reservation:** If you must cancel, it's courteous—and smart—to do so with as much notice as possible, especially for

groups and families. European apartments, like hotel rooms, tend to be small by US standards. But they often come with laundry facilities and small, equipped kitchens, making it easier and cheaper to dine in.

**Rooms in Private Homes:** Renting a room in someone's home is a good option for those traveling alone, as you're more likely to find true single rooms—with just one single bed, and a price to match. These can range from air-mattress-in-living-room basic to plush-B&B-suite posh. While you can't expect your host to also be your tour guide—or even to provide you with much info—some are interested in getting to know the travelers who pass through their home.

**Other Options:** Swapping homes with a local works for people with an appealing place to offer (don't assume where you live is not interesting to Europeans). Good places to start are HomeExchange.com and LoveHomeSwap.com. To sleep for free, Couchsurfing.com is a vagabond's alternative to Airbnb. It lists millions of outgoing members who host fellow "surfers" in their homes.

| From: | rick@ricksteves.com |
|---|---|
| Sent: | Today |
| To: | info@hotelcentral.com |
| Subject: | Reservation request for 19-22 July |

Dear Hotel Central,

I would like to stay at your hotel. Please let me know if you have a room available and the price for:
• 2 people
• Double bed and en suite bathroom in a quiet room
• Arriving 19 July, departing 22 July (3 nights)

Thank you!
Rick Steves

smaller family-run places. Cancellation policies can be strict; read the fine print before you book. Many discount deals require pre-payment and can be expensive to change or cancel.

**Reconfirming a Reservation:** Always call or email to reconfirm your room reservation a few days in advance. For B&Bs or very small hotels, I call again on my arrival day to tell my host what time to expect me (especially important if arriving late—after 17:00).

**Phoning:** For tips on calling hotels overseas, see page 349.

## Hostels

A hostel provides cheap beds in dorms where you sleep alongside strangers for about $30 per night. Travelers of any age are welcome if they don't mind dorm-style accommodations and meeting other travelers. Most hostels offer kitchen facilities, guest computers, Wi-Fi, and a self-service laundry. Hostels almost always provide bedding, but the towel's up to you (though you can usually rent one). Family and private rooms are often available.

**Independent hostels** tend to be easygoing, colorful, and informal (no membership required; www.hostelworld.com). You may pay slightly less by booking directly with the hostel. **Official hostels** are part of Hostelling International (HI) and share an online booking site (www.hihostels.com). HI hostels typically require that you be a member or else pay a bit more per night.

**PRACTICALITIES**

# Eating

Belgians are among the world's leading carnivores and beer consumers. Belgium is where France meets northern Europe, and you'll find a good mix of both Germanic and French influences here. The Flemish were ruled by the dukes of Burgundy and absorbed some of the fancy French cuisine and etiquette of their overlords. (The neighboring Dutch, on the other hand, were ruled by the Spanish for 80 years and picked up nothing.) And yet, once Belgian, always Belgian: They cook with beer rather than wine.

## RESTAURANT PRICING

I've categorized my recommended eateries based on the average price of a typical main course, indicated with a dollar-sign rating (see sidebar). Obviously, expensive specialties, fine wine, appetizers, and dessert can significantly increase your final bill.

The categories also indicate the personality of a place: **Budget** eateries include street food, takeaway, order-at-the-counter shops, basic cafeterias, and bakeries selling sandwiches. **Moderate** eateries are nice (but not fancy) sit-down restaurants, ideal for a pleasant meal with good-quality food. Most of my listings fall in this category—great for a taste of the local cuisine at a reasonable price.

**Pricier** eateries are a notch up, with more attention paid to the setting, presentation, and (often inventive) cuisine. **Splurge** eateries are dress-up-for-a-special-occasion-swanky—typically with an elegant setting, polished service, and pricey and refined cuisine.

## DINING TIPS

For listings in this guidebook, I look for restaurants that are convenient to your hotel and sightseeing. When restaurant-hunting, choose a spot filled with locals, not the place with the big neon signs boasting, "We Speak English and Accept Credit Cards." Venturing even a block or two off the main drag leads to higher-quality food for a better price.

Belgians eat lunch when we do, but they eat dinner later. If you dine earlier than 19:30 at a restaurant, you'll eat alone (or with other tourists). For cheaper alternatives, consider eating at one of Belgium's affordable chain restaurants, a fry shop, or a bar, café, or brasserie (all described next).

Note that there's no free tap water in Belgium. While a glass of water comes with a smile in the Netherlands, France, and Germany, that's not the case in Belgium, where you'll either pay for water, enjoy the beer, or go thirsty.

**Tipping:** At Belgian restaurants that have waitstaff, tax and service are included, although it's common to round up the bill

## Restaurant Price Code

Eateries in this book are categorized according to the average cost of a typical main course. Drinks, desserts, and splurge items can raise the price considerably.

| | |
|---|---|
| **$$$$** | **Splurge:** Most main courses over €20 |
| **$$$** | **Pricier:** €15-20 |
| **$$** | **Moderate:** €10-15 |
| **$** | **Budget:** Under €10 |

In Belgium, a *frites* stand or other takeout spot is **$**; a basic café or sit-down eatery is **$$**; a casual but more upscale restaurant is **$$$**; and a swanky splurge is **$$$$**.

after a good meal (usually 5-10 percent; so, for an €18.50 meal, pay €20). If you order your food at a counter, don't tip.

## Chain Restaurants

While excellent restaurants abound in Belgium, several local chains offer affordable, quick, and predictably good meals. Keep an eye out for these convenient choices.

**Exki** tries hard to be healthy in a country famous for its deep-fried foods and beer-based sauces. Their prepared meals (soups, salads, wraps) emphasize fresh produce, and while the food can be hit-or-miss, it's a handy break from heavy Belgian fare.

**Le Pain Quotidien** ("The Daily Bread") began as an artisanal bakery in Brussels...before its relentless march toward world domination. Although it now has 200 locations in more than a dozen countries, it's still considered a local shop among Belgians. It's a reliable fallback for fresh breads, pastries, and sandwiches.

**Balls & Glory** is a small, fun Flemish chain offering tasty, hand-crafted, softball-sized meatballs. Each day their rotating menu highlights different flavors of meatball.

## Cafés, Bars, and Brasseries

For a more casual meal, or drinks only, try a bar, café, or brasserie. If you go to one of these places, in general, you can seat yourself, but avoid tables with a sign saying *"reservé"* or *"voorbehouden."* Unlike cafés in Italy or France, the cost of a drink or meal in Belgium is the same at the bar, at a table, or outside on the terrace. If all you want is a drink, you can wait for the server to come around or order directly from the bar. You generally pay for drinks as you go (especially if you're sitting outside), unless you specify you want to open a tab. If you're also ordering food, you pay for everything—drinks and your meal—at the end, as you would at a restaurant.

## Fast Food Fry Shops

Just like every village in England has its "chippy" (for fish-and-chips), and every German burg has its *Wurst* stand (for sausages), every Belgian town has a favored *frituur* (fry shop) or *frietkot* (fry shack). While the pinnacle is the fried potato, there's a wider variety of deep-fried treats than you might expect, such as sausages and meatballs (described later, under "Belgian Cuisine").

Belgian-style fries *(frieten)* taste so good because they're deep-fried twice—once to cook them and once to brown them. Traditionally, fries are generously topped with sauces *(sausen)*. These can be mayo, tartar sauce, curry ketchup, *currysaus* (without the ketchup), or another flavored sauce (see list below). Ketchup is sometimes available. You'll generally pay extra (typically less than €1) for any sauce—including mayo.

*Américaine:* Mayo with herbs and a dash of Tabasco

*Joppiesaus:* Sweet yellow curry and onion sauce

*Pickles:* Mayo with pickle relish

*Provencaalse:* Sweet-and-sour tomato flavor

*Samuraisaus/samoeraisaus:* Mayo with spicy chili flavor and a hint of tomato

*Stoofvlees:* Rich Belgian beef stew made with beer; there's also a mayo-based sauce infused with *stoofvlees* flavor

## BELGIAN CUISINE

Although this book's coverage focuses on the Flemish part of the country, people speak French first in Brussels—so both languages are given here (Dutch/French); if I've listed only one word, it's used nationwide. While the French influence is evident everywhere, it's ratcheted up around Brussels.

## Meat Appetizers and Snacks

These can be served at a *frituur* or *frietkot* (described above) or sometimes at bars or restaurants as appetizers. Many of these meat dishes are fried.

*Ballekes in tomatensaus:* Meatball dish with tomato sauce

**Bicky Burger:** Mystery-meat patty (a combination of pork, chicken, and horse meat) sold at snack stands nationwide; typically deep-fried and topped with a sweet ketchup, a brown spicy sauce, and a secret, yellow "Bicky Dressing" (made with mayonnaise, mustard, cabbage, onion, and other vegetables)

*Bitterballen (petites croquettes):* Meat croquettes, battered in breadcrumbs and deep-fried; typically served as bar snacks, along with a drink made with bitters

***Boulet, Balleke, Frikadel,*** or ***Gehaktbal*** *(boulette):* Various terms for meatballs, which can be fried, boiled, or grilled. Some meatballs are filled with a surprise; for example, *vogelnestje*—see below

***Frikandel*** *(fricandelle):* Minced-meat sausage, usually deep-fried; the basic Belgian wiener

***Frikandel speciaal:*** *Frikandel* served with mayo, ketchup, and chopped onions (sometimes called a ***curryworst***—not to be confused with a German *Currywurst*)

***Kippenworst:*** Chicken sausage; anything that starts with *kip* or includes *de poulet* indicates it's made with chicken

***Viandel:*** Variation of *Frikandel*—skinny, deep-fried, often with a crunchy, herbed crust

***Vleeskroketten:*** Similar to *Bitterballen* but bigger

***Vogelnestje*** ("bird's nest"): Meatball stuffed with a hard-boiled egg

## Traditional Dishes

Here are some classic Belgian dishes that may appear on menus. If you see the term *à la flamande,* that means it's cooked "in the Flemish style" (for instance, made with beer or smothered in a sauce of butter, chopped parsley, and crumbled hard-boiled egg).

***Biersoep/soupe à la bière:*** Beer soup

***Filet américain:*** Similar to steak tartare, this raw beef dish is named for the American meat grinder it was widely made with after World War II

***(Gentse) Waterzooi:*** Creamy stew made with chicken, eel, or fish; originated in Ghent

***Konijn met pruimen/lapin à la flamande:*** Marinated rabbit braised in onions and prunes

***Luikse ballekes/boulets à la liégeoise:*** Meatballs made in Liège sauce (a dark syrup from apples, pears, and dates)

***Luikse salade/salade liégeoise:*** A warm salad of green beans, potatoes, tomatoes, and bacon

***Stoofvlees/carbonnade:*** Rich beef stew flavored with onions, beer, and mustard; similar to French *bœuf bourguignon* but often sweetened with brown sugar or gingerbread

***Vol-au-vent:*** A rich and creamy chicken stew made with meatballs and lots of butter, typically used as the filling for a puff pastry sandwich

## Seafood

Belgium is known for its **mussels** *(mosselen/moules).* They can be served plain *(natuur/nature),* with white wine *(witte wijn/vin blanc),* with shallots or onions *(marinière),* in a mushroom cream sauce *(à la* *crème)*, or in a tomato sauce *(provençale)*. You get a big-enough-for-two bucket and a pile of fries. Go local by using one empty shell to tweeze out the rest of the *mosselen*. From about mid-July through April, you'll get the big Dutch mussels (most are from the coastal Zeeland area). Locals take a break from mussels in May and June, when only the puny Danish kind are available.

Here are some other popular seafood dishes:

**Caricoles/escargots *(de mer)*:** Sea snails. Very local, seasonal, and hard to find—usually sold hot by street vendors

**Grnaalkroket/croquettes de crevettes:** Minced North Sea shrimp and Béchamel stuffed in a breaded, deep-fried roll

**Noordzee garnalen/crevettes grises:** Little gray shrimp caught off the North Sea coast

**Paling in het groen/anguilles au vert:** Eel in green herb sauce; this classic dish isn't always available, as good-quality eel is in short supply

**Tomaat garnaal/tomattes crevettes:** North Sea shrimp served inside a carved-out tomato

## Vegetables and Side Dishes

**Asperges:** White asparagus, available only in spring, and usually served in cream sauce

**Rode kool/chou rouge à la flamande:** Red cabbage with onions and prunes

**Spruitjes/choux de Bruxelles:** Brussels sprouts (in cream sauce)

**Stoemp:** Mashed potatoes and vegetables

**Witloof/chicoree** or **chicon:** Bitter, coarse endive—the classic Belgian vegetable—served both raw and cooked

## Snacks

Popular snacks include fries (*Frieten;* described earlier) and cheese. While the French might use wine or alcohol to rub the rind of their cheese to infuse it with flavor, the Belgians use (surprise, surprise) beer. There are 350 types of Belgian cheeses. From Flanders, look for Vieux Brugge ("Old Bruges") and Chimay (named for the beer they use on it); from Wallonia, Remoudou and Djotte de Nivelles are good. Here are some other popular snacks:

**Croque monsieur:** Grilled ham-and-cheese sandwich

**Pistolet:** Puffy, round bread-roll sandwich

**Tartine de fromage blanc:** Open-face cream-cheese sandwich, often enjoyed with a *lambic* beer (described later) and found mostly in traditional Brussels bars

## Desserts and Sweets

Belgium is famous for chocolate. The two basic types of Belgian chocolates are **pralines** (what we generally think of as "chocolates"—a hard chocolate shell with a filling) and **truffles** (a softer, crumblier shell with filling). For more on chocolates, see page 51. A *dame blanche* is a chocolate sundae.

Another Belgian specialty is waffles. You'll see little windows, shops, and trucks selling *wafels/gaufres;* either plain (for Belgians and purists) or topped with fruit, jam, chocolate sauce, ice cream, or whipped cream (for tourists). Belgians recognize two general types of waffles. The common takeout version, sold around the clock, is the dense, sugar-crusted, and very sweet **Liège-style waffle** *(Luikse/liégois),* usually served warm. **Brussels-style waffles** *(Brusselse)* are lighter and fluffier, dusted with powdered sugar and sometimes topped with marmalade. Though Americans think of "Belgian" waf-

fles as a breakfast food, Belgians generally have them (or pancakes, *pannenkoeken*) as a late-afternoon snack. Brussels-style waffles are less widely available to go, though you may find them at teahouses or cafés in the afternoon (from about 14:00 until 18:00).

Another popular sweet is *speculoos,* spicy gingerbread biscuits served with coffee. For the Belgian answer to peanut butter or Nutella, look for *speculoos* spread—thick, creamy, and with the flavor of gingerbread cookies. (Trader Joe's sells this in the US with a "Cookie Butter" label.) *Speculoos* is also a delicious ice cream flavor—worth trying.

## BEVERAGES
### Belgian Beers

Belgium has hundreds of varieties and brands of beer, more than any other country—the locals take their beers as seriously as the French do their wines. Even small café menus include six to eight varieties; specialty bars stock hundreds. Connoisseurs and novices alike can be confused by the many choices, and casual drinkers probably won't like every kind offered, since some varieties don't even taste like beer. Belgian beer is generally yeastier, sweeter, less bitter, and higher in alcohol content than beers in other countries. You must be 16 years old to legally enjoy a good Belgian beer (18 to drink wine and hard liquor).

To bring out their flavor, different beers are served cold, cool, or at room temperature, and each has its own distinctive glass. Whether wide-mouthed, tall, or fluted, with or without a stem, tulip-shaped or straight, the glass is meant to highlight a particular beer's qualities. The choice of glass is so important that if, for some reason, a pub doesn't have the proper glass for a particular beer, they will ask the customer if a different glass will be acceptable—or if they'd like to change their beer order.

To get a basic draft beer in Flanders (Bruges, Antwerp, or Ghent), ask for *een pintje* (ayn pinch-ya; a pint); in Brussels, where French prevails, request *une bière* (oon bee-yair).

But don't insist on beer from the tap. The only way to offer so many excellent beers and keep them fresh is to serve them bottled. In fact, because many specialty beers ferment in the bottle, some of the most famous brews come *only* in bottles. Increasingly, though, bars are adding a few high-end brands to their draft menus.

Belgians pair beer with food, much as the French pair wine. In general, lighter-colored beers (blonde or *Tripel*) go well with chicken or pork; darker beers pair nicely with beef; and wheat beers complement seafood.

### Specialty Beers

Specialty beers can be much more alcoholic than what you're used to back home, and tourists often find themselves overwhelmed by a single pint of Belgian brew. Bottles (and often menus) list the alcohol percentage of each type of beer. For comparison, most mass-market American beers are 4-6 percent alcohol by volume (ABV), while a heavy Belgian ale can run 7-9 percent—and a few powerful beers can be 10-12 percent, or even higher.

Monk-run Trappist breweries have given the beer world the terms *Enkel, Dubbel,* and *Tripel* (single, double, triple). While originally these indicated the amount of malt used to gain a higher alcohol content (described later), these days they have more to do with the style of beer: *Enkel* is a very light (nearly "lite") blonde ale; *Dubbel* is a dark, sweet beer; and *Tripel* is a very strong, golden-colored pale ale. The less commonly used term *Quadrupel* is a gimmick to emphasize a beer's alcohol content—usually more than 10 percent.

Some beer producers have returned to their medieval roots, flavoring their beer with a secret mix of spices called *gruit*. This can result in some surprising bouquets that charm and puzzle beer aficionados.

### Beers by Type

Here's a breakdown of types of beer, with some common brand names. This list is just a start, and you'll find many beers that don't fall into these neat categories.

**Ales** (Blonde/Red/Amber/Brown): Easily recognized by their color. Try a blonde or golden ale (Leffe Blonde, Duvel), a rare and bitter sour red (Rodenbach), an amber (Palm, De Koninck), or a brown (Leffe Bruin). *Saison* beers are "seasonal" (summer-brewed), lightly alcoholic pale ales.

**Lagers** *(Pils)*: Light, sparkling, Budweiser-type beers. Popular brands include Jupiler, Stella Artois, and Maes.

*Lambics:* Wild-yeast beers. *Lambics*—popular in Brussels—get their start in open vats, where they're exposed to naturally occurring wild yeasts in the air. Some brand names include Cantillon, Lindemans, and Mort-Subite ("Sudden Death").

*Lambics* are often blended with fruits to counter their sour flavor. Fruit *lambics* include cherry *(kriek)*, raspberry *(frambozen)*, peach *(pêche)*, or blackcurrant *(cassis)*. People who don't usually enjoy beer tend to like these tart but sweet varieties, similar to a dry pink champagne. *Gueuze*—a dry, sour, double-fermented *lambic* nicknamed "Brussels champagne"—is more of an acquired taste.

**White** (*Witte* or *Witbier*): Milky-yellow summertime beers made from wheat. White beer, similar to a Hefeweizen, is often flavored with spices such as orange peel or coriander.

**Trappist and Abbey Beers:** Heavily fermented, malty, monk-brewed beers. For centuries, between their vespers and matins, Trappist monks have been brewing beer. Three typical ones are *Tripel*, with a blonde color, served cold with a frothy head; *Dubbel*, dark, sweet, and served cool; and *Enkel*, made especially by the monks for the monks, and considered a fair trade for a life of celibacy. These styles originated at the Westmalle monastery; other official Belgian Trappist monasteries are Rochefort, Chimay, Orval, Achel, and Westvleteren (the last one's brews are often voted the "best in the world" and are hard to find). "Abbey beers" *(abdijbier)* emulate the Trappist style, but are produced at other monasteries or by commercial brewers; St. Bernardus is one popular abbey beer. Try the Trappist Chimay Blauw/Bleu—extremely smooth, milkshake-like, and complex.

**Strong Beers:** The potent brands include Duvel ("devil," because of its high octane, camouflaged by a pale color), Verboten Vrucht ("forbidden fruit," with Adam and Eve on the label), and the not-for-the-fainthearted brands of Judas, Satan, and Lucifer. Gouden Carolus is good, and Delerium Tremens speaks for itself.

**Mass-Produced Beers:** Connoisseurs say you should avoid the mass-produced labels (Leffe, Stella, and Hoegaarden—all owned by AB InBev, which owns Budweiser in America) when you can enjoy a Belgian craft beer (such as Westmalle or Chimay) instead.

## Other Alcoholic Drinks

Belgians drink a lot of fine **wine**, but it's almost all imported. In general, Flanders prefers Bordeaux wines (which used to be delivered to the busy Flemish ports of Bruges and Antwerp), while

## What Language Barrier?

People speak Dutch in Bruges, Ghent, and Antwerp—but with a Flemish accent. You will meet some French-only speakers in Brussels, but it's generally a minor issue: You'll find almost no language barrier in Belgium, as all well-educated folks, nearly all young people, and almost everyone in the tourist trade also speak English. Regardless, it's polite to use some Dutch or French pleasantries (see the survival phrases in the appendix).

inland Wallonia prefers Burgundy wines (which were delivered overland).

The distilled grain alcohol *jenever* (yah-NAY-ver) is spiced with juniper berries and often called "continental gin" or "Dutch gin" in English. (English traders eventually created a similar drink and called it simply gin.) *Jonge jenever* (young) is sharp and served chilled; *oude jenever* (old) is mellow and more commonly poured at room temperature (the terms refer to whether they use the older or newer distilling technique). I prefer *oude jenever*, which is smooth and soft, with a more mature flavor—like a good whisky. *Jenever* can be sipped, or it can be chugged with a *pils* chaser (this combination is called a *kopstoot*—headbutt; or you can sink the shot of *jenever* into the beer to create a *duikboot*—submarine).

### Nonalcoholic Drinks

Belgian restaurants typically charge for tap **water** or refuse to serve it. Since you're paying anyway, you might as well spring a bit more for mineral water, still or sparkling (Spa brand is popular). Many cafés/bars have a juicer for making fresh-squeezed **orange juice.**

Belgians love their **coffee,** enjoying many of the same drinks (espresso, cappuccino) served in American or Italian coffee shops. Coffee usually comes with a small *speculoos* spice cookie. A *koffie verkeerd* (fer-KEERT, "coffee wrong") is an espresso with a lot of steamed milk—the closest thing to a latte.

## Staying Connected

One of the most common questions I hear from travelers is, "How can I stay connected in Europe?" The short answer? More easily and affordably than you might think.

The simplest solution is to bring your own device—phone, tablet, or laptop—and use it much as you would at home, following the money-saving tips, such as getting an international plan or connecting to free Wi-Fi whenever possible. Another option is to buy a European SIM card for your mobile phone. Or you can use

## Tips on Internet Security

Make sure that your device is running the latest versions of its operating system, security software, and apps. Next, ensure that your device and key programs (like email) are password-protected. On the road, use only secure, password-protected Wi-Fi. Ask the hotel or café staff for the specific name of their network, and make sure you log on to that exact one.

If you must access your financial info online, use a banking app rather than accessing your account on a browser, and use a cellular connection, not Wi-Fi. Never log on to personal finance sites on a public computer. If you're very concerned, consider subscribing to a VPN (virtual private network).

European landlines and computers to connect. More details are at RickSteves.com/phoning.

## USING YOUR PHONE IN EUROPE

Here are some budget tips and options.

**Sign up for an international plan.** To stay connected at a lower cost, sign up for an international service plan through your carrier. Most providers offer a simple bundle that includes calling, messaging, and data. Your normal plan may already include international coverage (for example, T-Mobile's covers data and text, but not voice calls).

Before your trip, research your provider's international rates. Activate the plan a day or two before you leave, then remember to cancel it when your trip's over.

**Use free Wi-Fi whenever possible.** Unless you have an unlimited-data plan, save most of your online tasks for Wi-Fi. Most accommodations in Europe offer free Wi-Fi. Many cafés (including Starbucks and McDonald's) offer hotspots for customers; ask for the password when you buy something. You may also find Wi-Fi at TIs, city squares, major museums, public-transit hubs, airports, and aboard trains and buses.

**Minimize the use of your cellular network.** The best way to make sure you're not accidentally burning through data is to put your device in "airplane" mode (which also disables phone calls and texts) and connect to Wi-Fi networks as needed. When you need to get online but can't find Wi-Fi, simply turn on your cellular network (or turn off airplane mode) just long enough for the task at hand.

Even with an international data plan, wait until you're on Wi-Fi to Skype or FaceTime, download apps, stream videos, or do other megabyte-greedy tasks. Using a navigation app such as

**PRACTICALITIES**

# How to Dial

Here's how to dial from anywhere in the US or Europe, using the phone number of one of my recommended Bruges hotels as an example (050 615 852). If a number starts with 0, drop it when dialing internationally (except when calling Italy).

## From a US Mobile Phone
Phone numbers in this book are presented exactly as you would dial them from a US mobile phone. For international access, press and hold 0 (zero) to get a + sign, then dial the country code (32 for Belgium) and phone number.

▸ To call the Bruges hotel from any location, dial +32 50 615 852.

## From a US Landline
Replace + with 011 (US/Canada access code), then dial the country code (32 for Belgium) and phone number.

▸ To call the Bruges hotel from your home landline, dial 011 32 50 615 852.

## From a European Landline
Replace + with 00 (Europe access code), then dial the country code (32 for Belgium, 1 for the US) and phone number.

▸ To call the Bruges hotel from a French landline, dial 00 32 50 615 852.

▸ To call my US office from a Belgian landline, dial 00 1 425 771 8303.

## From One Belgian Phone to Another
To place a domestic call (from a Belgian landline or mobile), drop +32 and dial the phone number (including the initial 0).

▸ To call the Bruges hotel from Brussels, dial 050 615 852.

## More Dialing Tips
**Local Numbers:** European phone numbers and area codes can vary in length and spacing, even within the same country. Mobile phones use separate prefixes (for instance, in Belgium, mobile prefixes have four digits and begin with 04).

**Toll and Toll-Free Calls:** It's generally not possible to dial European toll or toll-free numbers from a US mobile or landline (although you can sometimes get through using Skype). Look for a direct-dial number instead.

**Calling the US from a US Mobile Phone, While Abroad:** Dial +1, area code, and number.

**More Phoning Help:** See HowToCallAbroad.com.

Google Maps over a cellular network can require lots of data, so download maps when you're on Wi-Fi, then use the app offline.

Limit automatic updates. By default, your device constantly checks for a data connection and updates app content. Check your device's settings menu for ways to turn this off, and change your email settings from "auto-retrieve" to "manual" (or from "push" to "fetch").

**Use Wi-Fi calling and messaging apps.** Skype, WhatsApp,

FaceTime, and Google Meet are great for making free or low-cost calls or sending texts over Wi-Fi worldwide. Just log on to a Wi-Fi network, then connect with friends, family members, or local contacts who use the same service.

**Buy a European SIM card.** If you anticipate making a lot of local calls, need a local phone number, or your provider's international data rates are expensive, consider buying a SIM card in Europe to replace the one in your (unlocked) US phone or tablet. SIM cards are sold at department-store electronics counters, some newsstands (you may need to show your passport), and vending machines. If you need help setting it up, buy one at a mobile-phone shop. There are generally no roaming charges when using a European SIM card in other EU countries, but confirm when you buy.

## WITHOUT A MOBILE PHONE

It's less convenient but possible to travel in Europe without a mobile device. You can make calls from your hotel and check email or get online using public computers.

Most **hotels** charge a fee for placing calls. You can use a prepaid international phone card (usually available at newsstands, tobacco shops, and train stations) to call out from your hotel.

Some hotels have **public computers** in their lobbies for guests to use; otherwise, you may find them at public libraries (ask your hotelier or the TI for the nearest location). On a European keyboard, use the "Alt Gr" key to the right of the space bar to insert the extra symbol that appears on some keys. If you can't locate a special character (such as @), simply copy and paste it from a web page.

## MAIL

You can mail one package per day to yourself worth up to $200 duty-free from Europe to the US (mark it "personal purchases"). If you're sending a gift to someone, mark it "unsolicited gift." For details, visit www.cbp.gov, select "Travel," and search for "Know Before You Go." The Belgian postal service works fine, but for quick transatlantic delivery (in either direction), consider services such as DHL (DHL.com).

# Transportation

Figuring out how to get around in Europe is one of your biggest trip decisions. **Cars** work well for two or more traveling together (especially families with small kids), those packing heavy, and those delving into the countryside. **Trains** and **buses** are best for solo travelers, blitz tourists, city-to-city travelers, and those who want to leave the driving to others. Short-hop **flights** within Europe can creatively connect the dots. Be aware of the potential downside of

**PRACTICALITIES**

each option: A car is an expensive headache in any major city; with trains and buses you're at the mercy of a timetable; flying entails a trek to and from a usually distant airport and leaves a larger carbon footprint.

Because of the short distances and excellent public transportation systems in Belgium, I recommend connecting Antwerp, Ghent, Bruges, and Brussels by train. Frequent trains connect each of these cities faster and easier than you could by driving. But for other destinations, a car could be a good alternative. Arrange to pick up your car in the last big city you'll visit, then use it to lace together small towns and explore the countryside. For more detailed information on transportation throughout Europe, see RickSteves.com/transportation.

## TRAINS

The easiest way to reach nearly any Belgian destination is by train. Connections are fast and frequent. Because Belgium is bilingual, the rail system has a complicated identity; it's NMBS in Dutch but SNCB in French (luckily, it has a good English website—www.belgiantrain.be). InterCity (IC) trains are speedy for connecting big cities, and the high-speed Thalys is the fastest (the speed comes at a price; see "High-Speed International Trains," later). InterRegio (IR) trains connect smaller towns and make more stops along the way. Throughout Belgium, smoking is prohibited in trains and train stations.

### Schedules

To get train schedules in advance, consult the Belgian rail site: www.belgiantrain.be (+32 25 282 828). The German Rail (Deutsche Bahn) website is also useful and has comprehensive schedules for almost anywhere in Europe (www.bahn.com).

At train stations, check the TV screens listing upcoming departures. The direction of the train is identified by its final station. If you can't find your train, or are unclear on departure details, visit an information booth or enlist the help of any official-looking employee.

### Tickets

**Buying Tickets:** It's easy to buy etickets for Belgian trains. You can download the **SNCB app** and buy tickets as you go (using your US credit card; etickets appear in the app immediately after purchasing). Or you can purchase tickets **online** at www.belgiantrain.be (you'll be emailed a PDF that you can print or download to your phone). **Ticket machines** and **ticket windows** at Belgian train stations also take US credit cards.

**Ticket Deals:** If you're not traveling with a rail pass, consider

Belgian Train Lines

North Sea

NETHERLANDS
Eindhoven
Amsterdam

Zeebrugge
Ostend
Bruges
Antwerp

Flanders
Ghent
Hasselt

Ypres
Leuven
Maastricht

Kortrijk
Brussels
Aachen

To London

Lille
Tournai

BELGIUM
Liège

GERMANY

Mons
Charleroi
Namur

Charleroi
Wallonia

Bastogne

FRANCE
LUX.
To Koblenz

100 Kilometers

50 Miles

To Paris
Luxembourg City

the country's money-saving deals. Those under age 26 can get a
Youth Multi ticket (a.k.a. Go Pass 10; €55 for 10 rides anywhere
in Belgium, shareable). A similar Standard Multi deal is available
for anyone 26 or over for €87 (cheaper in the app). Both youths and
seniors (age 65+) can get a same-day round-trip ticket to anywhere
in Belgium for about €7 (but the senior version is not valid before
9:00 on weekdays). Up to four kids under 12 travel free with each
paying passenger 12 or older. There are also weekend discounts for
round-trips (50 percent off, valid Fri after 19:00). For more information, visit www.belgiantrain.be.

**Bike Fees:** If you're traveling with a bike, you'll pay extra to
bring it on the train (€4 for a one-way trip).

## High-Speed International Trains

Fast **Thalys** trains connect Brussels with Amsterdam, Cologne, and
Paris (www.thalys.com). The **Eurostar** train zips between London
and Brussels in two hours—faster and easier than flying (www.
eurostar.com). French **TGV** trains link Brussels with Charles
de Gaulle Airport, outside Paris, in under two hours (www.tgv-
europe.com).

When traveling to Dutch cities (such as Amsterdam or Rotterdam), you have two options: **Thalys** trains are faster and more
expensive (potentially double or even triple the cost); **IC** (InterCity)
trains are a better value unless you're in a huge rush. For example,
a standard ticket from Antwerp to Amsterdam might take almost

# Rail Pass or Point-to-Point Tickets?

Will you be better off buying a rail pass or point-to-point tickets? It pays to know your options and choose what's best for your itinerary.

## Rail Passes

A Eurail Benelux Pass lets you travel by train in Belgium, the Netherlands, and Luxembourg for three to eight days (consecutively or not) within a one-month period. All three countries are also covered (along with most of Europe) by the classic Eurail Global Pass.

Discounted rates are offered for seniors (age 60 and up) and youths (ages 12-27). Up to two kids (ages 4-11) can travel free with each adult-rate pass (but not with senior rates). All passes offer a choice of first or second class for all ages.

While most rail passes are delivered electronically, it's smart to get your pass sorted before leaving home. For more on rail passes, including current prices and purchasing, visit RickSteves.com/rail.

## Point-to-Point Tickets

If you're taking just a couple of train rides, buying individual point-to-point tickets may save you money over a pass. Use this map to add up approximate pay-as-you-go fares for your itinerary, and compare that to the price of a rail pass plus reservations. Keep in mind that significant discounts on point-to-point tickets may be available with advance purchase.

*Map shows approximate costs, in US dollars, for one-way, second-class tickets on faster trains.*

two hours and cost €20 on an IC train; on Thalys, you can shave off about 30 minutes, but the ticket can cost up to €75 (depending on the route). If you have a rail pass, Thalys requires expensive seat reservations, while IC trains don't require them—see "Reservations for Rail Pass Holders," later. Before you book, pay close attention to your options for train types—and the cost implications.

While Thalys, Eurostar, and TGV trains are expensive, they do offer significant price discounts, with restrictions, on tickets reserved in advance (most three months ahead, Eurostar available six months ahead). Each company sells tickets online or through US agents such as RickSteves.com/rail. In Europe, you can buy tickets at any major train station in any country or at any travel agency that handles train tickets (expect a booking fee). Note that Eurostar tickets between Brussels and London can qualify you for a discounted regional train connection in Belgium. For more on these trains, see page 219.

## Rail Passes

All rail passes that cover Belgium also cover the Netherlands and Luxembourg. Collectively, they're called "Benelux," and count as one country as far as rail passes are concerned. Most visits to Belgium don't cover enough miles to justify a rail pass, but if your itinerary extends beyond this relatively small region, a multicountry rail pass could make sense.

For more detailed advice on figuring out the smartest rail pass options for your train trip, visit RickSteves.com/rail.

**Reservations for Rail Pass Holders:** For the most part, you can hop on nearly any Belgian train with just your rail pass. But the fast Thalys trains that run between Brussels and Amsterdam, Cologne/Dortmund, and Paris do require paid reservations and a rail pass that covers both ends of the trip. On Brussels–Amsterdam and Brussels–Cologne/Dortmund trains, you can avoid this extra cost simply by choosing a regular non-Thalys train, which doesn't require seat reservations. The Brussels–Paris direct route, however, is served only by Thalys trains and is not covered by the Benelux rail pass—reserve as far ahead as possible for that stretch.

## BUSES

While you'll mostly use trains to travel in this region, you can also consider buses. There's no unified national bus company for Belgium—various destinations are served by different companies. Flanders is served largely by De Lijn (www.delijn.be), while French-speaking areas have TEC (www.infotec.be). Flanders has one set price for city bus tickets—€2.50 for one hour. If you plan to use city buses and trams in Bruges, Ghent, and Antwerp, consider getting a 10-ride ticket for €17—it's good all over Flanders. Eurolines and Flixbus buses connect Belgium to other European cities (www.eurolines.de, www.flixbus.com).

## TAXIS AND RIDE-BOOKING SERVICES

Most European taxis are reliable and cheap. In many cities, two people can travel short distances by cab for little more than the cost of bus or subway tickets. If you like ride-booking services such as Uber, their apps usually work in Europe just like they do in the US: Request a car on your mobile phone (connected to Wi-Fi or data), and the fare is automatically charged to your credit card.

## RENTING A CAR

It's cheaper to arrange most car rentals from the US, so research and compare rates before you go. Most of the major US rental agencies (including Avis, Budget, Enterprise, Hertz, and Thrifty) have offices throughout Europe. Also consider the two major Europe-based agencies, Europcar and Sixt. Consolidators such as Auto Europe (AutoEurope.com—or the sometimes cheaper AutoEurope.eu) compare rates at several companies to get you the best deal.

Wherever you book, always read the fine print. Check for add-on charges—such as one-way drop-off fees, airport surcharges, or mandatory insurance policies—that aren't included in the "total price."

### Rental Costs and Considerations

If you book well in advance, expect to pay roughly $350-500 for a one-week rental for a basic compact car. Allow extra for supplemental insurance, fuel, tolls, and parking.

**Manual vs. Automatic:** Almost all rental cars in Europe are manual by default—and cars with a stick shift are generally cheaper. If you need an automatic, reserve one specifically. When selecting a car, don't be tempted by a larger model, as it won't be as maneuverable on narrow, winding roads or when squeezing into tight parking lots.

**Age Restrictions:** Some rental companies impose minimum and maximum age limits. Young drivers (25 and under) and seniors (69 and up) should check the rental policies and rules section of car rental websites.

**Choosing Pickup/Drop-off Locations:** Always check the hours of the locations you choose: Many rental offices close from midday Saturday until Monday morning and, in smaller towns, at lunchtime. When selecting an office, confirm the location on a map. A downtown site might seem more convenient than the airport but could actually be in the suburbs or buried deep in big-city streets. Pedestrianized and one-way streets can make navigation tricky when returning a car at a big-city office or urban train station. Wherever you select, get precise details on the location and allow ample time to find it.

**Crossing Borders in a Rental Car:** Be aware that international trips—say, picking up in Brussels and dropping off in Amsterdam—can be expensive if the rental company assesses a drop-off fee for crossing a border.

Always tell your car-rental company exactly which countries you'll be entering. Some companies levy extra insurance fees for trips taken in certain countries with certain cars (such as BMWs, Mercedes, and convertibles). Double-check with your rental agent that you have all the documentation you need before you drive off.

**Picking Up Your Car:** Before driving off in your rental car, check it thoroughly and make sure any damage is noted on your rental agreement. Rental agencies in Europe tend to charge for even minor damage, so be sure to mark everything. Find out how your car's gearshift, lights, turn signals, wipers, radio, and fuel cap function, and know what kind of fuel the car takes (diesel is common in Europe). When you return the car, make sure the agent verifies its condition with you.

## Car Insurance Options

When you rent a car in Europe, the price typically includes liability insurance, which covers harm to other cars or motorists—but not the rental car itself. To limit your financial risk in case of damage to the rental, choose one of these options: Buy a Collision Damage Waiver (CDW; also called "loss damage waiver" or LDW by some firms) with a low or zero deductible from the car-rental company (roughly 30-40 percent extra), get coverage through your credit card (free, but more complicated), or get collision insurance as part of a larger travel-insurance policy.

Basic **CDW** costs $15–30 a day and typically comes with a $1,000-2,000 deductible, reducing but not eliminating your financial responsibility. When you reserve or pick up the car, you'll be offered the chance to "buy down" the deductible to zero (for an additional $10–30/day; this is sometimes called "super CDW" or "zero-deductible coverage").

If you opt for **credit-card coverage,** you must decline all coverage offered by the car-rental company—which means they can place a hold on your card to cover the deductible. In case of damage, it can be time-consuming to resolve the charges. Before relying on this option, quiz your card company about how it works.

If you're already purchasing a **travel-insurance policy** for your trip, adding collision coverage can be an economical option. For example, Travel Guard (TravelGuard.com) sells affordable renter's collision insurance as an add-on to its other policies; it's valid everywhere in Europe except the Republic of Ireland, and some Italian car-rental companies refuse to honor it, as it doesn't cover you in case of theft.

For more on car-rental insurance, see RickSteves.com/cdw.

## Navigation Options

If you'll be navigating using your phone or a GPS unit from home, remember to bring a car charger and device mount.

**Your Mobile Phone:** The mapping app on your phone works fine for navigating Europe's roads. To save on data, most apps allow you to download maps for offline use (do this before you need them, when you have a strong Wi-Fi signal). Some apps—including Google Maps—also have offline route directions, but you'll need mobile data access for current traffic. For more on using a mapping app without burning through data, see "Using Your Phone in Europe," earlier.

**GPS Devices:** If you want a dedicated GPS unit, consider renting one with your car (about $20/day, or sometimes included—ask). These units offer real-time turn-by-turn directions and traffic without the data requirements of an app. The unit may come loaded only with maps for its home country; if you need additional maps, ask. Make sure you know how to use the device—and that the language is set to English—before you drive off.

**Paper Maps and Atlases:** Even when navigating primarily with a mobile app or GPS, I always have a paper map, ideally a big, detailed regional road map. It's invaluable for getting the big picture, understanding alternate routes, and filling in if my phone runs out of juice. The free maps you get from your car-rental company usually don't have enough detail. It's smart to buy a better map before you go, or pick one up at a local gas station, bookshop, newsstand, or tourist shop.

## DRIVING

**Road Rules:** Traffic cameras are everywhere in Belgium; speeding tickets for even a few kilometers over the limit are common. Kids under age 12 (or less than about 5 feet tall) must ride in an appropriate child-safety seat. Seat belts are mandatory for all, and two beers under those belts are enough to land you in jail. Be aware of typical European road rules; for example, many countries require headlights to be turned on at all times, and nearly all forbid hand-held mobile-phone use. In Europe, you're not allowed to turn right on a red light unless a sign or signal specifically authorizes it, and on expressways it's illegal to pass drivers on the right. Ask your car-rental company about these rules, or check the "International Travel" section of the US State Department website (www.travel.state.gov, search for your country in the "Learn About Your Destination" box, then click on "Travel and Transportation").

**Fuel:** Gas (*benzine* in Dutch, *essence* in French) is expensive—about $6 per gallon. Diesel (*diesel* or *dieselolie* in Dutch, *gazole* in French) is about the same—$6 per gallon—but diesel cars get better mileage, so try to rent a diesel to save money. Be sure you know what type of fuel your car takes before you fill up. Some pumps are color-coded: Unleaded pumps are green and labeled "E," while diesel pumps (often yellow or black) are labeled "B". Gas is most expensive on freeways and cheapest at big supermarkets. Some of the filling stations in Belgium are unmanned, and your US credit cards should work at self-service gas pumps if you have a chip and a PIN code. If not, look for stations with an attendant or be sure to carry sufficient cash in euros.

**Parking:** Finding a parking place can be a headache in larger cities. Ask your hotelier for ideas, and pay to park at well-patrolled lots (blue *P* signs direct you to parking lots). Parking structures usually require that you take a ticket with you and pay at a machine on your way back to the car. These machines accept euro coins (and sometimes bills); US credit cards should work.

## FLIGHTS

To compare flights, begin with an online travel search engine: Kayak is the top site for flights to and within Europe, easy-to-use Google Flights has price alerts, and Skyscanner includes many inexpensive flights within Europe. To avoid unpleasant surprises, before you book be sure to read the small print about refunds, changes, and the costs for "extras" such as reserving a seat, checking a bag, or printing a boarding pass.

**Flights to Europe:** Start looking for international flights at least four to six months before your trip, especially for peak-season travel. Depending on your itinerary, it can be efficient and no more expensive to fly into one city and out of another. If your flight requires a connection in Europe, see my hints on navigating Europe's top hub airports at RickSteves.com/hub-airports.

**Flying Within Europe:** Flying between European cities is surprisingly affordable. Before buying a long-distance train or bus ticket, check the cost of a flight on one of Europe's airlines, whether a major carrier or a no-frills outfit like EasyJet or Ryanair, along with Brussels Airlines (www.brusselsairlines.com). Be aware that flying with a discount airline can have drawbacks, such as minimal customer service, time-consuming treks to secondary airports, and a larger carbon footprint than a train or bus.

**Flying to the US and Canada:** Because security is extra tight for flights to the US, be sure to give yourself plenty of time at the airport (see www.tsa.gov for the latest rules).

# Resources from Rick Steves

## Begin Your Trip at RickSteves.com

My mobile-friendly **website** is *the* place to explore Europe in preparation for your trip. You'll find thousands of fun articles, videos, and radio interviews; a wealth of money-saving tips for planning your dream trip; travel news dispatches; a video library of travel talks; my travel blog; our latest guidebook updates (RickSteves.com/update); and the free Rick Steves Audio Europe app. You can also follow me on Facebook, Instagram, and Twitter.

Our **Travel Forum** is a well-groomed collection of message boards where our travel-savvy community answers questions and shares their personal travel experiences—and our well-traveled staff chimes in when they can be helpful (RickSteves.com/forums).

Our **online Travel Store** offers bags and accessories that I've designed to help you travel smarter and lighter. These include my popular carry-on bags (which I live out of four months a year), money belts, totes, toiletries kits, adapters, guidebooks, and planning maps (RickSteves.com/shop).

Our website can also help you find the perfect **rail pass** for your itinerary and your budget, with easy, one-stop shopping for rail passes, seat reservations, and point-to-point tickets (RickSteves.com/rail).

## Rick Steves' Tours, Guidebooks, TV Shows, and More

**Small Group Tours:** Want to travel with greater efficiency and less stress? We offer more than 40 itineraries reaching the best destinations in this book...and beyond. Each year about 30,000 travelers join us on about 1,000 Rick Steves bus tours. You'll enjoy great guides and a fun bunch of travel partners (with small groups of 24 to 28 travelers). You'll find European adventures to fit every vacation length. For all the details, and to get our tour catalog, visit RickSteves.com or call us at +1 425 608 4217.

**Books:** This book is just one of many books in my series on European travel, which includes country and city guidebooks, Snapshots (excerpted chapters from my bigger guides), Pocket Guides (full-color little books on big cities), "Best Of" guidebooks (condensed, full-color country guides), and my budget-travel skills handbook, *Rick Steves Europe Through the Back Door*. A complete list of my titles—including phrase books, cruising guides, and travelogues on European art, history, and culture—appears near the end of this book.

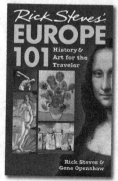

PRACTICALITIES

**TV Shows and Travel Talks:** My public television series, *Rick Steves' Europe,* covers Europe from top to bottom with over 100 half-hour episodes—and we're working on new shows every year (watch full episodes at my website for free). My free online video library, Rick Steves Classroom Europe, offers a searchable database of short video clips on European history, culture, and geography (Classroom.RickSteves.com). And to raise your travel I.Q., check out the video versions of our popular classes (covering most European countries as well as travel skills, packing smart, cruising, tech for travelers, European art, and travel as a political act—RickSteves.com/travel-talks).

**Audio Tours on My Free App:** I've produced dozens of free, self-guided audio tours of the top sights in Europe. For those tours and other audio content, get my free **Rick Steves Audio Europe app,** an extensive online library organized by destination. For more on my app, see page 22.

**Radio:** My weekly public radio show, *Travel with Rick Steves,* features interviews with travel experts from around the world. It airs on 400 public radio stations across the US. An archive of programs is available at RickSteves.com/radio.

**Podcasts:** You can enjoy my travel content on several free podcasts. The podcast version of my radio show brings you a weekly, hour-long travel conversation. My other podcasts include a weekly selection of video clips from my public television show, my audio tours of Europe's top sights, and live recordings of my travel classes (RickSteves.com/watch-read-listen/audio/podcasts).

# APPENDIX

## Holidays and Festivals

This list includes selected festivals in major cities, plus national holidays observed throughout Belgium. Many sights and banks close on national holidays—keep this in mind when planning your itinerary. Before planning a trip around a festival, verify the dates with the festival website, the Belgian national tourist office (www. visitbelgium.com), or my "Upcoming Holidays and Festivals in Belgium" web page at Ricksteves.com/europe/belgium/festivals.

| | |
|---|---|
| **Jan 1** | New Year's Day |
| **Feb/March** | Carnival (Mardi Gras) |
| **March/April** | Easter Weekend (Good Friday-Easter Monday): April 7-10, 2023; March 29-April 1, 2024 |
| **May 1** | Labor Day |
| **May** | Ascension and Procession of the Holy Blood, Bruges: May 18, 2023; May 9, 2024 |
| **Mid-May** | Zinneke Parade, Brussels (even years only; procession with music, dance, and floats, www. zinneke.org) |

| | |
|---|---|
| **May/June** | Pentecost and Whit Monday: May 28-29, 2023; May 19-20, 2024 |
| **June** | Brussels Film Festival (www.brff.be) |
| **Late June/ early July** | Ommegang Pageant, Brussels (historic costumed parade to Grand Place, www.ommegang.be) |
| **Mid-late July** | Ghent Festivities (free concerts, fireworks, street performers, market, www.gentsefeesten.be) |
| **July 21** | Belgian Independence Day (parades, fireworks) |
| **Aug** | Brussels Summer Festival (concerts, street performers, www.bsf.be) |
| **Aug** | Musica Antiqua Festival, Bruges (medieval music, www.mafestival.be) |
| **Aug 15** | Assumption Day (procession in Bruges) |
| **Mid-Aug** | Carpet of Flowers, Brussels (celebrated even years only, www.flowercarpet.be) |
| **Mid-Oct** | Ghent Film Festival (www.filmfestival.be) |
| **Nov 1** | All Saints' Day |
| **Nov 11** | Armistice Day |
| **Dec** | "Winter Wonders" Christmas Market, Brussels (www.plaisirsdhiver.be) |
| **Dec 6** | St. Nicholas Day (Sinterklaas; processions and presents for children) |
| **Dec 25** | Christmas |

# Books and Films

To learn more about Belgium past and present, check out a few of these books or films.

## Nonfiction

*The Guns of August* (Barbara Tuchman, 2004). This Pulitzer Prize-winning chronicle follows the outbreak of World War I and events along the Western Front, including Belgium.

*In Flanders Fields: The 1917 Campaign* (Leon Wolff, 1958). In a classic account of the Flanders battle at Passchendaele, Wolff details how Allied forces captured a few thousand yards at the cost of tens of thousands of lives.

*King Leopold's Ghost* (Adam Hochschild, 1999). This best-seller provides a clear-eyed examination of Belgium's exploitation of its Congo colony.

*A Tall Man in a Low Land: Some Time Among the Belgians* (Harry

Pearson, 1999). Pearson offers a wry look at contemporary Belgium through the eyes of an outsider.

*The Wisdom of the Beguines: The Forgotten Story of a Medieval Women's Movement* (Laura Swan, 2016). Swan explores *beguinages*, communities of like-minded women who aided their towns' poor and vulnerable.

## Fiction

*The Abyss* (Marguerite Yourcenar, 1968). One of Belgium's greatest novelists tells the story of an atheist in Renaissance Bruges.

*The Adventures of Tintin* series (Hergé, 1929-1976). These classic comics feature the irrepressible boy reporter and his dog.

*The House of Niccolò* series (Dorothy Dunnett, 1999). This three-volume series traces an audacious apprentice who rises to lead a mercantile empire in 15th-century Flanders.

*The Lady and the Unicorn* (Tracy Chevalier, 2003). Uncover the creation story of the famous *Lady and the Unicorn* tapestries, which were woven by a master craftsman in Brussels.

*Pallieter* (Felix Timmermans, 1916). A Flemish classic, this "ode to life" details a young man's journey recovering from a life-threatening disease.

*Resistance* (Anita Shreve, 1995). In Nazi-occupied Belgium, the wife of a resistance fighter shelters an American bomber pilot.

*The Square of Revenge* (Pieter Aspe, 2013). Bruges' medieval architecture conceals a bizarre mystery for Inspector Van In to solve.

## Films

*The Adventures of Tintin* (2011). Steven Spielberg's adaptation of the beloved Belgian comic book hero follows Tintin on a treasure hunt for a sunken ship.

*The Battle of the Bulge* (1965). This historical drama starring Henry Fonda recounts the surprise Nazi attack on the Western Front in 1944.

*Get Out Your Handkerchiefs* (1978). Shot in the Ardennes, this wacky romantic comedy starring Gérard Depardieu won the Academy Award for Best Foreign Language Film.

*If It's Tuesday, This Must Be Belgium* (1969). A comedic group of travelers from the US races through seven countries in 18 days on a bus tour.

*In Bruges* (2008). This dark comedy was filmed...in Bruges.

*The Monuments Men* (2014). In this action-drama, a WWII platoon goes on a mission to rescue Nazi-stolen art treasures—including Bruges' Michelangelo piece *Madonna and Child* and the Ghent Altarpiece.

# Conversions and Climate

## Numbers and Stumblers

- Europeans write a few of their numbers differently than we do. 1 = 1, 4 = 4, 7 = 7.
- In Europe, dates appear as day/month/year, so Christmas 2025 is 25/12/25.
- Commas are decimal points and decimals are commas. A dollar and a half is $1,50, one thousand is 1.000, and there are 5.280 feet in a mile.
- When counting with fingers, start with your thumb. If you hold up your first finger to request one item, you'll probably get two.
- What Americans call the second floor of a building is the first floor in Europe.
- On escalators and moving sidewalks, Europeans keep the left "lane" open for passing. Keep to the right.

## Metric Conversions

A **kilogram** equals 1,000 grams (about 2.2 pounds). One hundred **grams** (a common unit at markets) is about a quarter-pound. One **liter** is about a quart, or almost four to a gallon.

A **kilometer** is six-tenths of a mile. To convert kilometers to miles, cut the kilometers in half and add back 10 percent of the original (120 km: 60 + 12 = 72 miles). One **meter** is 39 inches—just over a yard.

| | |
|---|---|
| 1 foot = 0.3 meter | 1 square yard = 0.8 square meter |
| 1 yard = 0.9 meter | 1 square mile = 2.6 square kilometers |
| 1 mile = 1.6 kilometers | 1 ounce = 28 grams |
| 1 centimeter = 0.4 inch | 1 quart = 0.95 liter |
| 1 meter = 39.4 inches | 1 kilogram = 2.2 pounds |
| 1 kilometer = 0.62 mile | 32°F = 0°C |

## Clothing Sizes

When shopping for clothing, use these US-to-European comparisons as general guidelines (but note that no conversion is perfect).

**Women:** For pants and dresses, add 32 in Belgium (US 10 = Belgian 42). For blouses and sweaters, add 8 for most of Europe (US 32 = European 40). For shoes, add 30-31 (US 7 = European 37/38).

**Men:** For shirts, multiply by 2 and add about 8 (US 15 = European 38). For jackets and suits, add 10. For shoes, add 32-34.

**Children:** Clothing is sized by height—in centimeters (2.5 cm = 1 inch), so a US size 8 roughly equates to 132-140. For shoes up to size 13, add 16-18, and for sizes 1 and up, add 30-32.

## Fahrenheit and Celsius Conversion

Europe takes its temperature using the Celsius scale, while we opt for Fahrenheit. For a rough conversion from Celsius to Fahrenheit, double the number and add 30. For weather, remember that 28°C is 82°F—perfect. For health, 37°C is just right. At a launderette, 30°C is cold, 40°C is warm (usually the default setting), 60°C is hot, and 95°C is boiling. Your air-conditioner should be set at about 20°C.

## Belgium's Climate

First line, average daily high; second line, average daily low; third line, average days without rain. For more detailed weather statistics for destinations in this book (as well as the rest of the world), check Wunderground.com.

| J | F | M | A | M | J | J | A | S | O | N | D |
|---|---|---|---|---|---|---|---|---|---|---|---|
| 41° | 44° | 51° | 58° | 65° | 71° | 73° | 72° | 69° | 60° | 48° | 42° |
| 30° | 32° | 34° | 40° | 45° | 53° | 55° | 55° | 52° | 45° | 38° | 32° |
| 9 | 11 | 14 | 12 | 15 | 15 | 13 | 12 | 15 | 13 | 10 | 11 |

# Packing Checklist

Whether you're traveling for five days or five weeks, you won't need more than this. Pack light to enjoy the sweet freedom of true mobility.

## Clothing

- ☐ 5 shirts: long- & short-sleeve
- ☐ 2 pairs pants (or skirts/capris)
- ☐ 1 pair shorts
- ☐ 5 pairs underwear & socks
- ☐ 1 pair walking shoes
- ☐ Sweater or warm layer
- ☐ Rainproof jacket with hood
- ☐ Tie, scarf, belt, and/or hat
- ☐ Swimsuit
- ☐ Sleepwear/loungewear

## Money

- ☐ Debit card(s)
- ☐ Credit card(s)
- ☐ Hard cash (US $100-200)
- ☐ Money belt

## Documents

- ☐ Passport
- ☐ Other required ID: Vaccine card/Covid test, entry visa, etc.
- ☐ Driver's license, student ID, hostel card, etc.
- ☐ Tickets & confirmations: flights, hotels, trains, rail pass, car rental, sight entries
- ☐ Photocopies of important documents
- ☐ Insurance details
- ☐ Guidebooks & maps

## Electronics

- ☐ Mobile phone
- ☐ Camera & related gear
- ☐ Tablet/ebook reader/laptop
- ☐ Headphones/earbuds
- ☐ Chargers & batteries
- ☐ Phone car charger & mount (or GPS device)
- ☐ Plug adapters

## Toiletries

- ☐ Basics: soap, shampoo, toothbrush, toothpaste, floss, deodorant, sunscreen, brush/comb, etc.
- ☐ Medicines & vitamins
- ☐ First-aid kit
- ☐ Glasses/contacts/sunglasses
- ☐ Face masks & hand sanitizer
- ☐ Sewing kit
- ☐ Packet of tissues (for WC)
- ☐ Earplugs

## Miscellaneous

- ☐ Daypack
- ☐ Sealable plastic baggies
- ☐ Laundry supplies: soap, laundry bag, clothesline, spot remover
- ☐ Small umbrella
- ☐ Travel alarm/watch
- ☐ Notepad & pen
- ☐ Journal

## Optional Extras

- ☐ Second pair of shoes (flip-flops, sandals, tennis shoes, boots)
- ☐ Travel hairdryer
- ☐ Picnic supplies
- ☐ Disinfecting wipes
- ☐ Water bottle
- ☐ Fold-up tote bag
- ☐ Small flashlight
- ☐ Mini binoculars
- ☐ Small towel or washcloth
- ☐ Inflatable pillow/neck rest
- ☐ Tiny lock
- ☐ Address list (to mail postcards)
- ☐ Extra passport photos

# Dutch Survival Phrases

Northern Belgium speaks Dutch, but for cultural and historical reasons, the language is often called Flemish. Most Belgian people speak English, but if you learn the pleasantries and key phrases, you'll connect better with the locals. To pronounce the guttural Dutch "g" (indicated in phonetics by *h*), make a clear-your-throat sound, similar to the "ch" in the Scottish word "loch."

| | | |
|---|---|---|
| **Hello. / Goodbye.** | Hallo. / Tot ziens. | **hah**-loh / toht zeens |
| **Good day.** | Dag. | da*h* |
| **Good morning.** | Goedemorgen. | **hoo**-deh-mor-*h*ehn |
| **Good afternoon.** | Goedemiddag. | **hoo**-deh-mid-da*h* |
| **Good evening.** | Goedenavond. | **hoo**-dehn-ah-fohnd |
| **Do you speak English?** | Spreekt u Engels? | shpraykt oo **eng**-ehls |
| **Yes. / No.** | Ja. / Nee. | yah / nay |
| **I (don't) understand.** | Ik begrijp (het niet). | ik beh-*h*ripe (heht neet) |
| **Please. (can also mean "You're welcome")** | Alstublieft. | **ahl**-stoo-bleeft |
| **Thank you.** | Dank u wel. | dahnk oo vehl |
| **I'm sorry.** | Het spijt me. | heht spite meh |
| **Excuse me.** | Pardon. | **par**-dohn |
| **No problem.** | Geen probleem. | *h*ayn **proh**-blaym |
| **Good.** | Goede. | **hoo**-deh |
| **one / two / three** | een / twee / drie | ayn / t'vay / dree |
| **What does it cost?** | Wat kost het? | vaht kohst heht |
| **Is it free?** | Is het vrij? | is heht fry |
| **Can you please help me?** | Kunt u alstublieft helpen? | koont oo **ahl**-stoo-bleeft **hehl**-pehn |
| **Where can I buy / find...?** | Waar kan ik kopen / vinden...? | var kahn ik **koh**-pehn / **fin**-dehn |
| **I'd like / We'd like...** | Ik wil graag / Wij willen graag... | ik vil *h*ra*h* / vy **vil**-lehn *h*ra*h* |
| **...a room.** | ...een kamer. | ayn **kah**-mer |
| **...a train / bus ticket to ____.** | ...een trein / bus kaartje naar ____. | ayn trayn / boos **kart**-yeh nar ____ |
| **...to rent a bike.** | ...een fiets huren. | ayn feets **hoo**-rehn |
| **Where is...?** | Waar is...? | var is |
| **...the train / bus station** | ...het trein / bus station | heht trayn / boos **staht**-see-ohn |
| **...the tourist info office** | ...de VVV | deh fay fay fay |
| **...the toilet** | ...het toilet | heht **twah**-leht |
| **men / women** | mannen / vrouwen | **mah**-nehn / **frow**-ehn |
| **left / right** | links / rechts | links / re*h*ts |
| **straight ahead** | rechtdoor | **reht**-dor |
| **What time does it open / close?** | Hoe laat gaat het open / dicht? | hoo laht *h*aht heht **oh**-pehn / di*h*t |
| **now / soon / later** | nu / straks / later | noo / strahks / **lah**-ter |
| **today / tomorrow** | vandaag / morgen | **fahn**-da*h* / **mor**-*h*ehn |

# In a Dutch Restaurant

The all-purpose Dutch word *alstublieft* (**ahl**-stoo-bleeft) means "please," but it can also mean "here you are" (when the server hands you something), "thanks" (when taking payment from you), or "you're welcome" (when handing you change).

| | |
|---|---|
| **I'd like / We'd like...** | Ik will graag / Wij willen graag... <br> ik vil *h*rah / vy **vil**-lehn *h*rah |
| **...a table for one / two.** | ...een tafel voor een / twee. <br> ayn **tah**-fehl for ayn / t'vay |
| **...to reserve a table.** | ...een tafel reserveren.    ayn **tah**-fehl **ray**-zehr-feh-rehn |
| **...the menu (in English).** | ...het menu (in het Engels). <br> heht meh-**noo** (in heht **eng**-ehls) |
| **Is this table free?** | Is deze tafel vrij?    is **day**-zeh **tah**-fehl fry |
| **to go** | om mee te nemen    ohm may teh **nay**-mehn |
| **with / without** | met / zonder   meht / **zohn**-der |
| **and / or** | en / of   ehn / of |
| **special of the day** | dagschotel   **dah**s-hoh-tehl |
| **specialty of the house** | huisspecialiteit    **hows**-shpeh-shah-lee-tite |
| **breakfast / lunch / dinner** | ontbijt / middagmaal / avondmaal <br> **ohnt**-bite / **mid**-dah-mahl / **ah**-fohnd-mahl |
| **appetizers** | hapjes   **hahp**-yehs |
| **main courses** | hoofdgerechten   **hohfd**-*h*eh-re*h*-tehn |
| **side dishes** | bijg erechten   **bye**-heh-reh-tehn |
| **bread / cheese** | brood / kaas   brohd / kahs |
| **sandwich** | sandwich   **sand**-vich |
| **soup / salad** | soep / sla   soop / slah |
| **meat / chicken / fish** | vlees / kip / vis   flays / kip / fis |
| **fruit / vegetables** | vrucht / groenten   fru*h*t / *h*roon-tehn |
| **dessert / pastries** | gebak   *h*eh-**bahk** |
| **mineral water / tap water** | mineraalwater / kraanwater <br> min-eh-rahl-**vah**-ter / **krahn**-vah-ter |
| **milk** | melk   mehlk |
| **(orange) juice** | (sinaasappel) sap    **see**-nahs-ah-pehl (sahp) |
| **coffee / tea** | koffie / thee   **koh**-fee / tay |
| **wine / beer** | wijn / bier   vine / beer |
| **red / white** | rode / witte   **roh**-deh / **vit**-teh |
| **glass / bottle** | glas / fles   *h*lahs / flehs |
| **Cheers!** | Proost!   prohst |
| **More. / Another.** | Meer. / Nog een.    mayr / no*h* ayn |
| **The same.** | Het zelfde.   heht **zehlf**-deh |
| **The bill, please.** | De rekening, alstublieft. <br> deh **ray**-keh-neeng **ahl**-stoo-bleeft |
| **Is service included?** | Is bediening inbegrepen? <br> is beh-**dee**-neeng in-beh-*h*ray-pehn |
| **tip** | fooi   foy |
| **Tasty.** | Lekker.   **leh**-ker |

# French Survival Phrases

When using the phonetics, try to nasalize the <u>n</u> sound.

| | | |
|---|---|---|
| **Good day.** | Bonjour. | bohn-zhoor |
| **Mrs. / Mr.** | Madame / Monsieur | mah-dahm / muhs-yuh |
| **Do you speak English?** | Parlez-vous anglais? | par-lay-voo ahn-glay |
| **Yes. / No.** | Oui. / Non. | wee / nohn |
| **I understand.** | Je comprends. | zhuh kohn-prahn |
| **I don't understand.** | Je ne comprends pas. | zhuh nuh kohn-prahn pah |
| **Please.** | S'il vous plaît. | see voo play |
| **Thank you.** | Merci. | mehr-see |
| **I'm sorry.** | Désolé. | day-zoh-lay |
| **Excuse me.** | Pardon. | par-dohn |
| **No problem.** | Pas de problème. | pah duh proh-blehm |
| **It's good.** | C'est bon. | say bohn |
| **Goodbye.** | Au revoir. | oh ruh-vwahr |
| **one / two / three** | un / deux / trois | uhn / duh / trwah |
| **four / five / six** | quatre / cinq / six | kah-truh / sank / sees |
| **seven / eight** | sept / huit | seht / weet |
| **nine / ten** | neuf / dix | nuhf / dees |
| **How much is it?** | C'est combien? | say kohn-bee-an |
| **Write it?** | Ecrivez? | ay-kree-vay |
| **Is it free?** | C'est gratuit? | say grah-twee |
| **Included?** | Inclus? | an-klew |
| **Where can I buy / find...?** | Où puis-je acheter / trouver...? | oo pwee-zhuh ah-shuh-tay / troo-vay |
| **I'd like / We'd like...** | Je voudrais / Nous voudrions... | zhuh voo-dray / noo voo-dree-ohn |
| **...a room.** | ...une chambre. | ewn shahn-bruh |
| **...a ticket to ___.** | ...un billet pour ___. | uhn bee-yay poor ___ |
| **Is it possible?** | C'est possible? | say poh-see-bluh |
| **Where is...?** | Où est...? | oo ay |
| **...the train station** | ...la gare | lah gar |
| **...the bus station** | ...la gare routière | lah gar root-yehr |
| **...tourist information** | ...l'office du tourisme | loh-fees dew too-reez-muh |
| **Where are the toilets?** | Où sont les toilettes? | oo sohn lay twah-leht |
| **men / women** | hommes / dames | ohm / dahm |
| **left / right** | à gauche / à droite | ah gohsh / ah drwaht |
| **straight** | tout droit | too drwah |
| **pull / push** | tirez / poussez | tee-ray / poo-say |
| **When does this open / close?** | Ça ouvre / ferme à quelle heure? | sah oo-vruh / fehrm ah kehl ur |
| **At what time?** | À quelle heure? | ah kehl ur |
| **Just a moment.** | Un moment. | uhn moh-mahn |
| **now / soon / later** | maintenant / bientôt / plus tard | man-tuh-nahn / bee-an-toh / plew tar |
| **today / tomorrow** | aujourd'hui / demain | oh-zhoor-dwee / duh-man |

# In a French Restaurant

| | |
|---|---|
| **I'd like / We'd like...** | Je voudrais / Nous voudrions... <br> zhuh voo-dray / noo voo-dree-ohn |
| **...to reserve...** | ...réserver...    ray-zehr-vay |
| **...a table for one / two.** | ...une table pour un / deux. <br> ewn tah-bluh poor uhn / duh |
| **Is this seat free?** | C'est libre?    say lee-bruh |
| **The menu (in English), please.** | La carte (en anglais), s'il vous plaît. <br> lah kart (ahn ahn-glay) see voo play |
| **service (not) included** | service (non) compris <br> sehr-vees (nohn) kohn-pree |
| **to go** | à emporter    ah ahn-por-tay |
| **with / without** | avec / sans    ah-vehk / sahn |
| **and / or** | et / ou    ay / oo |
| **breakfast / lunch / dinner** | petit déjeuner / déjeuner / dîner <br> puh-tee day-zhuh-nay / day-zhuh-nay / dee-nay |
| **special of the day** | plat du jour    plah dew zhoor |
| **specialty of the house** | spécialité de la maison <br> spay-see-ah-lee-tay duh lah may-zohn |
| **appetizers** | hors d'œuvre    or duh-vruh |
| **first course (soup, salad)** | entrée    ahn-tray |
| **main course (meat, fish)** | plat principal    plah pran-see-pahl |
| **bread / cheese** | pain / fromage    pan / froh-mahzh |
| **sandwich / soup** | sandwich / soupe    sahnd-weech / soop |
| **salad** | salade    sah-lahd |
| **meat / chicken** | viande / poulet    vee-ahnd / poo-lay |
| **fish / seafood** | poisson / fruits de mer <br> pwah-sohn / frwee duh mehr |
| **fruit / vegetables** | fruit / légumes    frwee / lay-gewm |
| **dessert** | dessert    day-sehr |
| **mineral water** | eau minérale    oh mee-nay-rahl |
| **tap water** | l'eau du robinet    loh dew roh-bee-nay |
| **(orange) juice** | jus (d'orange)    zhew (doh-rahnzh) |
| **coffee / tea / milk** | café / thé / lait    kah-fay / tay / lay |
| **wine / beer** | vin / bière    van / bee-ehr |
| **red / white** | rouge / blanc    roozh / blahn |
| **glass / bottle** | verre / bouteille    vehr / boo-tay |
| **Cheers!** | Santé!    sahn-tay |
| **More. / Another.** | Plus. / Un autre.    plew / uhn oh-truh |
| **The same.** | La même chose.    lah mehm shohz |
| **The bill, please.** | L'addition, s'il vous plaît. <br> lah-dee-see-ohn see voo play |
| **Do you accept credit cards?** | Vous prenez les cartes?    voo pruh-nay lay kart |
| **tip** | pourboire    poor-bwahr |
| **Delicious!** | Délicieux!    day-lees-yuh |

For more user-friendly French phrases, check out *Rick Steves' French Phrase Book* or *Rick Steves' French, Italian & German Phrase Book*.

# INDEX

INDEX

# MAP INDEX

## Explore Europe

At ricksteves.com you can browse through thousands of articles, videos, photos and radio interviews, plus find a wealth of money-saving travel tips for planning your dream trip. And with our mobile-friendly website, you can easily access all this great travel information anywhere you go.

## TV Shows

Preview the places you'll visit by watching entire half-hour episodes of *Rick Steves' Europe* (choose from all 100 shows) on-demand, for free.

*your travel dreams into affordable reality*

## Radio Interviews

Enjoy ready access to Rick's vast library of radio interviews covering travel tips and cultural insights that relate specifically to your Europe travel plans.

## Travel Forums

Learn, ask, share! Our online community of savvy travelers is a great resource for first-time travelers to Europe, as well as seasoned pros.

## Travel News

Subscribe to our free Travel News e-newsletter, and get monthly updates from Rick on what's happening in Europe.

## Classroom Europe®

Check out our free resource for educators with 500 short video clips from the *Rick Steves' Europe* TV show.

## Rick's Free Travel App

*Gear up for your next adventure at ricksteves.com*

## Light Luggage

Pack light and right with Rick Steves' affordable, custom-designed rolling carry-on bags, backpacks, day packs and shoulder bags.

## Accessories

From packing cubes to moneybelts and beyond, Rick has personally selected the travel goodies that will help your trip go smoother.

## Save time and energy

This guidebook is your independent-travel toolkit. But for all it delivers, it's still up to you to devote the time and energy it takes to manage the preparation and logistics that are essential for a happy trip. If that's a hassle, there's a solution.

## Rick Steves Tours

A Rick Steves tour takes you to Europe's most interesting places with great guides and small groups. We follow Rick's favorite itineraries, ride in comfy buses, stay in family-run hotels, and bring you intimately close to the Europe you've traveled so far to see. Most importantly, we take away the logistical headaches so you can focus on the fun.

## Join the fun

This year we'll take thousands of free-spirited travelers—nearly half of them repeat customers—along with us on 50 different itineraries, from Athens to Istanbul. Is a Rick Steves tour the right fit for your travel dreams?

Find out at ricksteves.com, where you can also check seat availability and sign up. Europe is best experienced with happy travel partners. We hope you can join us.

**See our itineraries at ricksteves.com**

## BEST OF GUIDES

*Full-color guides in an easy-to-scan format. Focused on top sights and experiences in the most popular European destinations*

Best of England
Best of Europe
Best of France
Best of Germany
Best of Ireland
Best of Italy
Best of Scotland
Best of Spain

## COMPREHENSIVE GUIDES

*City, country, and regional guides printed on Bible-thin paper. Packed with detailed coverage for a multi-week trip exploring iconic sights and venturing off the beaten path*

Amsterdam & the Netherlands
Barcelona
Belgium: Bruges, Brussels,
  Antwerp & Ghent
Berlin
Budapest
Croatia & Slovenia
Eastern Europe
England
Florence & Tuscany
France
Germany
Great Britain
Greece: Athens & the Peloponnese
Iceland
Ireland
Istanbul
Italy
London
Paris
Portugal
Prague & the Czech Republic
Provence & the French Riviera
Rome
Scandinavia
Scotland
Sicily
Spain
Switzerland
Venice
Vienna, Salzburg & Tirol

HE BEST OF ROME

e, Italy's capital, is studded with
an remnants and floodlit-fountain
es. From the Vatican to the Colos-
, with crazy traffic in between, Rome
derful, huge, and exhausting. The
, the heat, and the weighty history

of the Eternal City where Caesars walked
can make tourists wilt. Recharge by taking siestas, gelato breaks, and after-dark
walks, strolling from one atmospheric
square to another in the refreshing evening air.

*l Pantheon—which
t dome until the
y 2,000 years old
r over 1,500).*

*Athens in the Vat-
ies the humanistic
.*

*adiators fought
other, entertaining*

Rick Steves books are available from your favorite bookseller.
Many guides are available as ebooks.

### Complete your library with...

# Credits

## RESEARCHERS

For help with this edition, Rick and Gene relied on...

### Cameron Hewitt

Cameron Hewitt was born in Denver, grew up in Central Ohio, and moved to Seattle in 2000 to work for Rick Steves' Europe. Since then, he has spent about 100 days each year in Europe—researching and writing guidebooks, blogging, tour guiding, and making travel TV (described in his memoir, *The Temporary European*). Cameron married his high school sweetheart, Shawna, and enjoys taking pictures, trying new restaurants, and planning his next trip.

### Carrie Shepherd

After a childhood spent traipsing around New England, Carrie spent a college semester in London, which spurred her to explore and travel as much as her budget and employers allow. She's spent her career writing and editing arts and entertainment content, and now works as a guidebook editor and researcher for Rick Steves' Europe.

## ACKNOWLEDGMENTS

Thank you to Risa Laib for her 25-plus years of dedication to the Rick Steves guidebook series.

# PHOTO CREDITS

Avalon Travel
Hachette Book Group
1700 Fourth Street
Berkeley, CA 94710

Printed in Canada by Friesens.
Fourth Edition. First printing April 2023.

ISBN 978-1-64171-378-8

For the latest on Rick's talks, guidebooks, tours, public television series, and public radio show, contact Rick Steves' Europe, 130 Fourth Avenue North, Edmonds, WA 98020, +1 425 771 8303, RickSteves.com, rick@ricksteves.com.

**Rick Steves' Europe**
**Managing Editor:** Jennifer Madison Davis
**Assistant Managing Editor:** Cathy Lu
**Editors:** Glenn Eriksen, Julie Fanselow, Suzanne Kotz, Rosie Leutzinger, Teresa Nemeth, Jessica Shaw, Carrie Shepherd
**Researchers:** Cameron Hewitt, Carrie Shepherd
**Graphic Content Director:** Sandra Hundacker
**Maps & Graphics:** Orin Dubrow, David C. Hoerlein, Lauren Mills, Mary Rostad, Amanda Sharpe

**Avalon Travel**
**Senior Editor & Series Manager:** Madhu Prasher
**Associate Managing Editors:** Jamie Andrade, Sierra Machado
**Copy Editor:** Kelly Lydick
**Proofreader:** Jennifer Malnick
**Indexer:** Stephen Callahan
**Production & Typesetting:** Lisi Baldwin, Jane Musser
**Cover Design:** Kimberly Glyder Design
**Maps & Graphics:** Kat Bennett

# COLOR MAPS

*Belgium • Brussels • Bruges*

Jardin Botanique

"PETIT RING"

Botanique/
Kruidtuin

## SIGHTS

1. To AfricaMuseum
2. To Atomium & Mini-Europe
3. Belgian Comic Strip Center
4. BELvue Museum
5. Bourse (Stock Exchange)
6. Brewery Museum
7. Choco-Story: The Chocolate Museum
8. Church of St. Nicolas
9. City Museum
10. European Parliament, Parlamentarium & House of European History
11. Fashion & Lace Museum
12. Galeries Royales St. Hubert
13. GardeRobe MannekenPis
14. Grand Place
15. Magritte Museum
16. Manneken-Pis Statue
17. Musical Instruments Museum
18. Notre-Dame du Sablon Church

19. Palace of Justice
20. To Park of the Cinquantenaire
21. Place du Grand Sablon
22. Place du Petit Sablon
23. Place Poelaert (View) & Elevator to Marolles
24. To Royal Belgian Institute of Natural Sciences
25. Royal Museums of Fine Arts
26. Royal Palace
27. Rue des Bouchers
28. St. Michael's Cathedral
29. Tour d'Angle (Tower)
30. Town Hall

### Transportation

31. Central/Centraal Train Station
32. To Midi/Zuid Train Station
33. To Nord/Noord Train Station
34. City Bus Tour Departure Point

BOULEVARD PACHECO

RUE ROYALE

RUE DE ASSOCIATION

R. DU CONGRÈS

RUE DE LIGNE

RUE DE LA CROIX DE FER

RUE DE LOUVAIN

LONIES

PALAIS DE LA NATION

RUE DE LA LOI

PALAIS DE LA NATION

RUE ROYALE

Parc/
Park

PARC

Parc de Bruxelles

PLACE DES PALAIS

RUE LAMBERMONT

US EMBASSY

RUE ZINNER

Arts-Loi/
Kunst-Wet

RUE DE LA LOI

RUE GUIMARD

RUE J. DE LALAING

RUE DE LA LOI

Square Frère-Orban

RUE JOSEPH II

RUE DE SPA

RUE DE LA LOI

BOULEVARD "PETIT RING"

AVENUE DES ARTS

RUE DU COMMERCE

RUE DE L'INDUSTRIE

RUE BELLIARD

RUE DE LA SCIENCE

RUE D'ARLON

JSÉE LVUE

PALAIS DU ROI

RUE DUCALE

RUE BREDERODE

RUE DE LA PÉPINIÈRE

Trône/
Troon

RUE DU

RUE MARIE DE BOURGOGNE

MONTOYER

RUE DE TRÈVES

LUXEMBOURG TRAIN STATION

Square de Meeûs

Place du Luxembourg

LEOPOLD QUARTER

EUROPEAN PARLIAMENT

BOULEVARD DE WATERLOO

AVE. MARNIX

RUE D'EGMONT

RUE DU CHAMP DE MARS

Porte de Namur/
Naamse Poort

STASSART

CH. D'IXELLES

RUE D'EDIMBOURG

RUE DE NAPLES

RUE D'ALSACE-LORRAINE

RUE DU TRÔNE

RUE CAROLY

RUE DE PARNASSE

RUE D'IDALIE

R. VAUTIER

MATONGE

DE WAVRE

RUE MAJ.R DUBREUCQ

26

10

20

24

N

# Bruges

R-30

Canal

To Ostende

KLAVERSTR.

ST. GILES

N. GISTEL STR.

L. RAMSTR.

HOEDENMAKERS STR.

WEST-GISTELSTR.

EZELSTRAAT

JAN BONINSTR.

ST.-JORISTRAAT

ST.-CLARA

MIRAELSTR.

AUGUSTIJNENREI

GOUDEN-HAND STR.

GOUDEN-HANDREI

POTTERIEREI

RAAMSTR.

ROZENDAL

GROENESTR.

OUDE ZAK

POTTENMAKERS

POITEVINSTR.

Woensdag-markt

GENTHOF

SPIEGELREI

SPINOLAREI

ST. WALBURG

BEENHOUWERSSTRAAT

Stadspark Sebrechts

ST. JAMES

ST.-JAKOBSSTR.

GEENWEINSTR.

ST. PALM STR.

OLD STOCK EXCHANGE

TOLL-HOUSE

ACAD

Jan van Eyckplein

BURGHERS' LODGE

CHOCO-STORY

FRIET MUSEUM 17

CITY THEATER

VLAMINGSTRAAT

ST.-JANSSTR.

St. Jansplein

WAPEN

BOOM STR.

RIDDER STR.

To Ostende

Eiermarkt 10

City Tour Bruges B

HISTORIUM & i

CROWNE PLAZA 13

Muntplein

GELDMUNTSTR.

ST. AMAND

BRUGES BEER EXP. 7

20

Markt 22

BELL TOWER

WOLLESTR.

Burg 3

REN. HALL 25

CITY HALL 12

Vismarkt 15

MOERSTRAAT

KUIPERSTR.

HELMSTR.

ZILVERSTRAAT

STEENSTRAAT

BREIDEL

BASILICA OF HOLY BLOOD 5

24

Huide-vetters-plein

WULFHAGESTRAAT

NOORDZANDSTR.

Stevinplein

OUDE BERG

H.-GEEST

NIEUWSTR.

BOURGOGNE BREWERY

DIJVER B

EEKHOUT

ARENTSHUIS MUSEUM

2

ARENTSHUIS MUSEUM 18

't Zand 28

t'Zand (Underground) B P

SMEDENSTR.

VRIJDAGMARKT

ZUIDZANDSTR.

K. VULDERSTR.

ST. SALVATOR

CHURCH OF OUR LADY 11

GROENINGE MUSEUM

GRUUTHUSE MUSEUM

19

CHOCOLATE ROW

CHOCO. KAST.-STR.

HAUWERSTR.

MAGDALENASTRAAT

HENDRIK CONSCIENCELAAN

i

CONCERT HALL

KONING ALBERTLAAN

WESTMEERS

OOSTMEERS

SINT-JANSHOSPITAAL MEMLING COLLECTION

26

OLD ST. JOHN

NIEWE GENTWEG

ALMS-HOUSE

OUDE GENTWEG

WIJN.-KATELIJNESTR.

NOORDSTR.

ARSENAALSTR.

WERKHUIZ

VISSPANSTR.

De Halve Maan Brewery

Walplein 14

Zonnekemeers 10

BEGIJNHOF 4

23

PROF. D. SEBRECHTSSTR.

Minnewater

Minne-water

KATELIJNE

BARGEWEG

BUS STN.

TRAIN STATION

B Stationsplein

Stationsplein

BUITEN BEGIJNVEST

Katelijn-vest

BUITEN KATELIJNEVEST

R-30

To Ostende via Freeway

K. ALBERT LAAN

GUIDO GEZELLELAAN

HOEFIJZERLAAN

Z. STEENSTR.

PAALSTR.

ZWINSTR.

HAUWERSTR.

## SIGHTS

1. Adornes Domein
2. Arentshuis Museum
3. Basilica of the Holy Blood
4. Begijnhof
5. Bell Tower
6. Bourgogne des Flandres Brewery
7. Bruges Beer Experience
8. Burg Square
9. Choco-Story: The Chocolate Museum
10. Chocolate Shops (6)
11. Church of Our Lady
12. City Hall
13. Crowne Plaza Hotel (Ruins)
14. De Halve Maan Brewery
15. Fish Market
16. Folklore Museum
17. Friet Museum
18. Groeninge Museum
19. Gruuthuse Museum
20. Historium
21. Lace Center
22. Markt Square
23. Minnewater
24. Postcard Canal View
25. Renaissance Hall
26. Sint-Janshospitaal Memling Collection
27. St. Janshuys Windmill
28. 't Zand Square

# Let's Keep on Travelin'

Your trip doesn't need to end.

Follow Rick on social media!